Hard Fighting

This book is dedicated to the Volunteer and the volunteer ethos which, when married to commitment and reinforced by good training and leadership, can produce results that cannot be bettered.

Any descendant of
Padre Skinner is
a friend of mine!

Jhahän Hunb

Hard Fighting

A History of the Sherwood Rangers Yeomanry 1900–1946

Jonathan Hunt

Pen & Sword
MILITARY

First published in Great Britain in 2016 by
Pen & Sword Military
an imprint of
Pen & Sword Books Ltd
47 Church Street
Barnsley
South Yorkshire
S70 2AS

ISBN 978 1 84884 891 7

A CIP catalogue record for this book is available from the British Library

Typeset in Ehrhardt by
Mac Style Ltd, Bridlington, East Yorkshire
Printed and bound in the UK by CPI Group (UK) Ltd,
Croydon, CRO 4YY

Pen & Sword Books Ltd incorporates the imprints of Pen & Sword
Archaeology, Atlas, Aviation, Battleground, Discovery, Family History,
History, Maritime, Military, Naval, Politics, Railways, Select, Transport,
True Crime, and Fiction, Frontline Books, Leo Cooper, Praetorian Press,
Seaforth Publishing and Wharncliffe.

For a complete list of Pen & Sword titles please contact
PEN & SWORD BOOKS LIMITED
47 Church Street, Barnsley, South Yorkshire, S70 2AS, England
E-mail: enquiries@pen-and-sword.co.uk
Website: www.pen-and-sword.co.uk

Contents

*Italics in **bold** indicate the involvement of the Sherwood Rangers*

Acknowledgements		ix
Maps		xi
Photographs and Illustrations		xii
Foreword		xv
Preamble		xviii

Part I: The Boer War, 1899–1902   1

Chapter 1	Casus Belli	3
Chapter 2	Learning Curve *Modder River – Magersfontein – Colenso*	6
Chapter 3	**Mounted Irregulars**	9
Chapter 4	**Balance Shifts** *Spion Kop – Relief of Kimberley – Paardeburg – Monte Cristo –* *Relief of Ladysmith – Fall of Bloemfontein*	15
Chapter 5	**Baptism of Fire** ***Action at Boshof***	20
Chapter 6	**Advance on Pretoria** *Relief of Mafeking – Action at Lindley – Fall of Johannesburg –* *Fall of Pretoria – Action at Heilbron – Action at Rhenoster River*	26
Chapter 7	**Pursuit of Steyn and de Wet** *Brandwater Basin – Action at Krugersdorp –Action at Oliphants* *Nek – Action at Vaalbank – Action at Tygerfontein – Action at* *Buffelshoek – Action at Syferbult – Second Action at Oliphants* *Nek*	36
Chapter 8	**Guerrilla Warfare**	44
Chapter 9	**Lichtenburg** ***Defence of Lichtenburg***	50
Chapter 10	**Second Squadron** ***Action at Zeerust – South Africa 1900–2***	57

Part II: Haldane and the Territorial Force, 1900–14   61

Chapter 11   Khaki   63

Part III: The Great War, 1914–19   69

Chapter 12   Mobilization   71

Chapter 13   Gallipoli   75
                  Gallipoli – Landing at Suvla Bay – Action at Salt Lake –
                  Action at Ismail Ogu Tepe – Battle at Scimitar Hill – Egypt –
                  Gallipoli 1915

Chapter 14   Macedonia   84
                  Macedonia – Action at Kosturino – Action at Doiran – Action at
                  Gola Ridge – Action in the Struma Valley – Defence of the River
                  Struma – Action at Kopaci – Macedonia 1916–17

Chapter 15   Palestine – Redeployment   93
                  Egypt 1915–16

Chapter 16   Palestine – Gaza   98
                  Third Battle of Gaza – Charge at Ras Ghannam – Beersheba
                  – Action at Bir Abu Khuff – Action at Wadi Kohle – Action at
                  Khuweilfe – Sheria

Chapter 17   Palestine – Advance on Jerusalem   105
                  Action at El Mughar/Junction Station – Battle of Nabi
                  Samweil – Nabi Samweil – Bietunye – Biet ur el Foqa – Biet ur el
                  Tahata – El Jib – Action at Kh. Kebabe – Action at Suffa – Action
                  at Mosque Sheik ab ed Din

Chapter 18   Palestine – Reorganization and Repositioning   116
                  The Defence of Jerusalem and Jaffa – The Capture of Jericho – Tel
                  Saur – Raid on Amman

Chapter 19   Palestine – Second Raid into Trans Jordan   121
                  Action at Umm esh Shert track – Action at Es Salt – Shunet
                  Imrin – Jis en Damiye Crossing – Umm esh Shert Crossing – Action
                  at El Huweij – Withdrawal from Es Salt – The Damiye Track

Chapter 20   Palestine – The Affair of Abu Tulul   130
                  Abu Tulul – Defence of the El Ghoraniye Bridgehead – Action at
                  Wadi er Rame

Chapter 21   Palestine – Final Campaign   136
                  Advance across Plain of Sharon – Nazareth – El'Affule – Beisan
                  – Jenin – Megiddo – Capture of Haifa – Charge on the Guns at
                  the Karmelheim – Damascus – Beirut – Homs – Aleppo – Palestine
                  1917–18

Part IV: Inter War Years, 1919–39   147

Chapter 22   A Peace Fit for Heroes   149

Part V: The Second World War, 1939-42 – The Beginning   151

Chapter 23   Unhorsed   153
                 Mobilization and Deployment – Action at Jaffa (Tel Aviv) –
                 Haifa – Cyprus – Sidi Barrani – Bardia – Tobruk – Benghazi

Chapter 24   Abyssinia, Tobruk, Benghazi and Crete   161
                 Abyssinia – Gondar – Amba Giogis – Action at Debarech – Ras
                 Ayalu – Wolchefit – Cyrenaica – El Agheila – Siege of Tobruk
                 – Defence of Benghazi – El Adem – El Gubi – Crete – Defence
                 of Suda Bay – Defence of Maleme – Khelevis – St John's Hill –
                 Withdrawal to Sphakia – Aegean – Turkey

Chapter 25   Armoured Training   169
                 Palestine – Karkur – Egypt – Cairo – Sollum –
                 Gazala – Tobruk – El Alamein – Matruh

Part VI: The End of the Beginning, 1942–43   173

Chapter 26   Battle of Alam el Halfa   175
                 Alam el Halfa

Chapter 27   Battle of El Alamein   179
                 Western Desert – El Alamein – Action at Miteiriya Ridge –
                 Action at Kidney 'Ridge' – Action at Rahman Track – Action at
                 Tel el Aqqaqir Feature – Action at Galal Station

Chapter 28   Advance on Tripoli   189
                 Cyrenaica – Action at El Agheila – Advance on Tripoli – Marble
                 Arch – Sirte – Misurata – Bu Ngem Road – Action at Wadi Zem
                 Zem – Tripoli

Chapter 29   Battle of Tebaga Gap   197
                 Mareth Line – Wadi Zigzaou –Matmata Hills – Djebel Tebaga –
                 Action at Roman Wall – Tebaga Gap – Action at Point 201 –
                 Action at Wadi Hernel – Action at Point 209 – Action at Wadi
                 Mataba – Action at Chebket en Nouiges

Chapter 30   'From a Scent to a View ...'   211
                 Action at Wadi Akarit – Roumana Gap – Enfidaville – Action at
                 Takrouna – Tunis – North Africa 1940–43

Chapter 31   Return Home   215

Part VII: The Beginning of the End, 1944   217

Chapter 32   **D Day**   219
                 Normandy Landings – le Hamel – la Rivière – Meuvaines –
                 Asnelles sur Mer – Arromanches – Ryes – Buhot – Sommervieu

Chapter 33   **Battle for Normandy**   243
                 Bayeux – Villers Bocage – Action at Point 103 – St Pierre –
                 Cristot – le Parc de le Boislonde – Odon – Battle of Fontenay
                 le Pesnel – St Nicholas Farm – Defence of Rauray – Chouain
                 – Action at Hottot – Caumont – Action at Bricquessard – Action
                 at Cahagnes – Action at Jurques – Action at la Binge – Action
                 at Ondefontaine – Mont Pinçon – Conde sur Noireau – Action at
                 Noireau Crossing – Action at Berjou – Chambois

Chapter 34   **Pursuit into Belgium**   262
                 Seine 1944 – Flesselles – Action at Doullens – Ghent – Brussels –
                 Herschot

Chapter 35   **Battle for Gheel**   266
                 Albert Canal – Beringen – Battle for Gheel

Chapter 36   **MARKET GARDEN Salient**   274
                 Grave – Nijmegen –Dekkenswald – Groesbeek – Reichswald
                 Forest –First British in German Border Crossing – Beek – Wyler

Chapter 37   **Battle of Geilenkirchen**   276
                 Duren – Paulenburg – Schinnen – Crossing R. Wurm –
                 Breach of Seigfried Line – Action at Prummen – Fall of
                 Geilenkirchen – Action at Wurm – Action at Beek – Apweiler

Part VIII: The End, 1944–45   287

Chapter 38   **Operation BLACKCOCK**   289
                 Schinveld –Schinnen – Roer – Action at Vintelen – Action at
                 Kievelburg– Action at Honten –Action at Breberen – Action at
                 Laffelde – Action at Selstan – Action at Hiensburg

Chapter 39   **Operations VERITABLE and LEEK**   294
                 Nijmegen- Reichwald Forest – Rhineland – Battle for Cleve –
                 Battle for Goch – River Niers – Battle for Weeze – Action at
                 Hussenoff – Actions at Issum

Chapter 40   **Final Advance**   298
                 Rhine – Rees – Issleburg – Dinxperloo – River Ijssel – Rurlo –
                 Lochem – Enschede – Henglo — Cloppenburgh –
                 Bremen – North West Europe 1944-45

Author's Comment   305
Battle Honours   311
Bibliography   312
Index   314

Acknowledgements

I consulted many books, publications and other documents while compiling this history of the Sherwood Rangers Yeomanry during the period covered by the book. While some are of minor or peripheral importance, they are nevertheless important. We knew little about the Boer War and in the case of the First World War our knowledge was confined to that gleaned from Hugh Tallents' excellent record. In the case of the Second World War there are now approaching thirty, mostly autobiographical, published accounts, so we already knew a great deal.

The missing link in all cases, however, was the context in which the Regiment served its country over those years. I found that the basic facts had been recorded and became clear, once they were found, but the significance of the Regiment's contribution in either tactical or strategic terms was seldom clear. That, surely, is the element which is the most important weight in the scales of history on which posterity will judge the Regiment.

Much fresh information has been found in scrapbooks of newspaper cuttings which, whilst revealing really significant information, did not reveal the identity of the newspaper itself. I apologise if I have, as a result, quoted a newspaper either without identifying it, or misidentifying it, since often an intelligent assumption is possible. I have often quoted other peoples' words as they not only add authenticity but also a valuable and interesting insight into the person. Since, on many occasions, this is a member of the Regiment, what he wrote and how he expressed himself, like a photograph, forms part of our history. In that connection I would add that, whenever the words used are not my own, they are shown as quoted matter.

An extract from *A Song of Sherwood* by Alfred Noyes is used with acknowledgements to The Society of Authors as Literary Representative of the Estate of Alfred Noyes. I chose this extract because I found words from this poem had been quoted in at least two books by Sherwood Rangers who served in action. Also they named their tanks after Robin Hood and his Merry Men (and Maid Marion). However above all the poem is about a call to arms, which is the very foundation of the citizen's response to a threat to his country, and the essence of this history.

The poem *Aristocrats* is by Captain Keith Douglas, who was killed serving with the Regiment.

My appreciation to Chris Woodward, Steve Cox and their team who, as volunteers, look after the Sherwood Rangers' archives and who have been the source of much of the local information and all the photographs I have used. The Regiment is so lucky to have their commitment.

I also express my gratitude to my fellow Trustees, and Major Nick Cornish TD our Honorary Treasurer, who have looked after the business side of this project. Much useful information was gleaned from battlefield tours to NW Europe by the Sherwood Rangers OCA since 1994, especially in the form of detailed research by Captain M. A. Elliott and contributions by Major John Semken CB MC, Captain David Render, Captain Stuart Hills MC, Jean Pierre Benamou OBE and many others. The late, great, Corporal Ken Ewing did much of the organisation in the early days and then worked with Captain Elliott. These tours still take place and ensure that the achievements of wartime Sherwood Rangers are known to subsequent generations.

I have made a point of using every gallantry and service citation which I have identified to help tell the story. Sometimes I have indicated them as citations and at others blended them into the narrative. I am grateful to those who wrote the citations – one assumes they were all members of the Regiment. The citations have been used to assist this account since they provide a rare, corroborated, contemporaneous account of low-level fighting, perhaps embellished to a degree (sometimes without regard to the author's personal safety) but essentially authentic. What is special about them is that it is the accumulation of many such actions, the vast majority of which are never recorded, which win battles, and few other sources like them, in terms of being contemporaneous accounts, can be found elsewhere. Finally they name, forever, brave young men whose identity as members of the Regiment may otherwise have been lost to history.

I would like to thank the following: Henry Wilson and Richard Doherty, my editor, both of Pen and Sword, who between them have acted with astonishing forbearance, in aiding the creation of both my books, Tim Webster for the excellent maps, and the rest of the Pen and Sword team; my wife Sue Hunt, Colonel Geoffrey Norton TD, Captain David Render and Captain Michael Elliott who have all proof-read *Hard Fighting* and left it better than they found it, especially David who features in it; Don Scott, my neighbour, who produced, amongst other things, the war diaries of 82 Assault Squadron Royal Engineers which first made me realise that all was not as it should have been on Gold Jig Green.

Jonathan Hunt

December 2015

Maps

1. South Africa   2
2. Action at Boshof   22
3. Methuen's Area of Operations   24
4. Aegean Sea   74
5. Gallipoli   76
6. Greek Macedonia   82
7. Palestine   92
8. Third Battle of Gaza   96
9. Battles of Junction Station and Nabi Samweil   102
10. Second Raid on Trans Jordan; The Affair of Abu Tulul   122
11. Megiddo and Haifa   134
12. Ethiopia   161
13. North Africa   162
14. Battles of Alam el Halfa and El Alamein   174
15. The Advance and Battle of Tebaga Gap   198
16. North West Europe   218
17. Gold Beach   231
18. Battle for Normandy   244
19. Battle of Geilenkirchen   278

Photographs and Illustrations

List of Photographs

1. Officers of the Sherwood Rangers (L) and the larger Yorkshire Dragoons at Serlby Park on 5 May 1899 following the inspection by the C-in-C, Field Marshal Viscount Wolseley. Lords Galway and Scarbrough are seated centre (L and R).
2. The C-in-C taking the salute at Serlby.
3. 27 January 1900 on the eve of deployment to South Africa. L to R: Col J. Thorpe (CO SRY 1880–82), Lt A. C. (Job) Williams (KIA), Capt M. S. Dawson (OC SRY Service Sqn to June 1900 and OC 2nd Service Sqn to Jan 1902), Lt H. O. (Hop) Peacock, Lt Col Lord Galway (serving CO SRY 1882–1903), Lt R. T. O. (Bertie) Sheriffe (OC SRY Service Sqn June–Sep 1900), Major A. E. Whitaker (CO SRY 1910–14), Lt H. Thorpe, (CO SRY 1915–17 and 19/20 and son of Col Thorpe) and Lt Col H. Denison (CO SRY 1903–10).
4. Lt H. H. (Bertie) Wilson DSO, OC SRY Service Sqn Sep 1900–May 1901.
5. Lt Gen Lord Methuen, Commander 1st Division. (*History of 3 IY*, Birkin)
6. The shell that was said to have killed Major General le Comte de Villebois-Mareuil at Boshof on 5 April 1900 (By kind permission of Captain Mick Holtby)
7. Lt Col G. J. Younghusband CB commanded 3rd Imperial Yeomanry 1899–1900. (*History of 3 IY*, Birkin)
8. The Sherwood Rangers Yeomanry and their ladies at Serlby Park, Bawtry, at their Camp and Field Day in 1903. Lord Galway's last camp as CO, this was attended by Lord Roberts and Lord Chesham, the inspecting officer; all three are seen seated.
9. The Sherwood Rangers marching past at Camp between the Boer War and First World War. Note the new prominence given to the rifle, demonstrating the tactical emphasis on the cavalry being able to fight both mounted and dismounted and the priority given to rifle shooting.
10. The Sherwood Rangers parading in Retford Market Square at Easter 1915 just prior to embarking for Egypt.
11. Gallipoli, October 1915. Lala Baba from Nebrunsi Point.
12. Gallipoli, October 1915 (L to R) Maj H. Tallents DSO, CO of SRY 1928–34, Maj H. Thorpe DSO, CO SRY 1915–17 and 1919–20, Lt R. E. Brassey, Lt E. Davies.
13. Struma Valley, Greek Macedonia 1916. SRY Patrol. Note the man in the tree. The country in the Struma Valley was very close which led to many surprise contacts with the enemy. (Percy Laws, SRY archives)
14. River Struma 1916 from an SRY Observation Post. (Percy Laws, SRY archives)

15. On 23 June 1917 the HMT *Cestrian* was torpedoed off Skyros whilst transporting the Regiment from Greece to Egypt. All the men were saved but the horses and baggage were lost. (Percy Laws, SRY archives)
16. Wells were the 'vital ground' of the advance from Gaza to Jerusalem. Troops fought from well to well but, even so, they and their horses sometimes went days, rather than hours, without watering.
17. April 1918. 5 Mounted Brigade (including the Regiment) resting at midday during the march from Gaza to Jerusalem prior to the Second Raid into TransJordan.
18. Elements of 14 (Imperial Service) Cavalry Brigade on parade in 1918, prior to Allenby's final advance.
19. Lt Col Francis Vernon Willey CMG CBE MVO TD, later 2nd Baron Barnby, (CO 1920–28) and dog, which has clearly mastered the 'laidback yeoman' look.
20. The senior ranks of the Regiment at a post-First World War Camp. The very heroes for whom the land was to be made fit?
21. The Sherwood Rangers Yeomanry in 1937 marching past at Brocklesby Park, Lincolnshire, ancestral home of the Earls of Yarborough.
22. Lt Col the 5th Earl of Yarborough MC (commanded 1937–40) and on his left Lt Col the Marquis of Titchfield, later 7th Duke of Portland KG (commanded 1934–37).
23. In Palestine there was good shooting to be had. Second left Lt P. J. D. McCraith MC and CO SRY 1953–57 and, extreme right, Donny Player.
24. (L) Col E. O. (Flash) Kellett DSO MP commanded the Sherwood Rangers Yeomanry 1940–43, KIA on 22 March 1943, and Lt Col J. D. (Donny) Player who took over from him on 6 March 1943 and was KIA on 24 April 1943.
25. Lt Gen Bernard Montgomery (Monty), commander of Eighth Army, revered by the Sherwood Rangers in the desert for giving them deliverance. He is wearing his multi-badged bush hat, clearly bearing the Regiment's cap badge. The hat is now displayed in the Australian War Memorial (Museum) in Canberra, complete with SRY badge, albeit in need of a polish. (Imperial War Museum)
26. 1941. Tobruk had a substantial network of tunnels providing protection from the daily air raids. However, Flash Kellett believed that using the tunnels during air raids would damage the Regiment's offensive culture, and instead ordered that, when under attack, the Regiment should return fire.
27. Lt Col Michael (Mike) Laycock MC TD took command of the Sherwood Rangers on the beach on 6 June 1944 and was KIA on 11 June 1944 in St Pierre.
28. Lt Col S. D. (Stanley) Christopherson DSO MC and Bar TD commanded the Sherwood Rangers Yeomanry 1944–46. He was A Squadron Leader in the Desert and early on in NW Europe, when the Regiment won 14 Battle Honours, and he commanded in NW Europe when the regiment won 16 Battle Honours.
29. March 1943 at Tebaga Gap. L to R: Tprs Ken Ewing, John Stephenson, Jigger Lea, Paddy Ryan and their 75mm Sherman.
30. Padre Leslie Skinner, revered regimental padre in NW Europe. (SRY archives)

31. Sherwood Rangers' tanks entering Tripoli on 26 January 1943 after the fight for Libya, which had included Wadi Zem Zem, where they suffered their heaviest losses thus far in the war.

32. This encapsulates the logistical challenge created by modern warfare: trucks are almost more important than tanks and certainly outnumber them many times over, putting unbearable pressure on inadequate road systems to deliver the capacity that enables the armour to advance and fight.

33. Investiture London 1944: (L to R) Cpl Derek Lenton MM, MQMS John Scott MM, Sgt Erny Thwaites MM, SSM Henry Hutchinson MM, KIA April 1945, Sgt Guy Sanders MM, KIA at Berjou August 1944, Sgt George Dring MM and Bar and Cpl James Loades MM.

34. Asnelles-sur-Mer taken at noon on D Day showing a troop of the Regiment's amphibians advancing to contact, southwards, apparently without infantry support having just broken out of the beachhead.

35. (L to R) Maj Gen D. A. H. Graham, GOC 50th (Northumbrian) Division, Lt Gen Sir Brian Horrocks, Commander XXX Corps, Maj Gen Ivor Thomas, GOC 43rd (Wessex) Division.

36. (L to R) Capt Jack Holman MC and Captain Jimmy McWilliam.

37. The first DD tank of the Sherwood Rangers to enter Bayeux at 10.50 on 7 June 1944. The non-amphibious tanks of A Squadron had already taken the town at first light, the first major town liberated by the Allies.

38. Sgt George Dring and his crew on *Akilla* in Normandy: (L to R): Sgt Dring, Tprs Hodkin, Denton, Bennet and Cpl Gold.

39. Gheel 11 September 1944. The 17-pounder Firefly Shermans of Cpl Burnett (KIA the next day) and Sgt Stan Nesling DCM advancing through the main square in Gheel with the 75mm Sherman of Stuart Hills MC in support. Note that, despite being in action, all three commanders have their heads out.

40. (L to R) Capt John Gauntley MC and Capt Neville Fearn DSO.

41. Geilenkirchen November 1944. The Regiment in rain and mud supporting 84th US Division breaching the Siegfried Line.

42. Issum, 6 March 1945. The Regiment had linked up with Ninth US Army in the town two days earlier and was advancing east out of Issum supporting 71 Brigade. During the day the Regiment won two MCs.

43. At an investiture 30 November 1944. L to R: Maj John Semken MC, Lt Col Stanley Christopherson DSO MC and Bar, facing centre Maj

List of Illustrations

Lord Methuen's force in action: Imperial Yeomanry defeating the Boer
attack on the British convoy near Zwartzkopjesfontein   27

'A Gallant Defence': How the garrison at Lichtenburg held out against the
Boers under de la Rey   52

A diagram of a DD Sherman with its flotation screen raised   224

Foreword

by Antony Beevor

One of the greatest excitements of my later childhood was to be allowed to put on the full dress uniform of the Sherwood Rangers. The green tunic had hussar frogging of gold braid and was surmounted by a busby with osprey plume. Hugh Tallents, who fought with the regiment in the First World War and commanded it soon afterwards, was the kindest of uncles. He told me and my cousin John how he had commanded a detachment of the regiment during the visit of King Alfonso XIII of Spain to Welbeck. Officers and Yeomen with drawn sabres had stood guard by the air intakes to the underground ballroom to make sure that Iberian anarchists could not drop a bomb down onto the guests below.

Hugh Tallents, who also wrote the regimental history of the Sherwood Rangers in the First World War, was the most modest of men. He did not talk much about his experiences, but I remember him explaining how the yeomanry regiments in Palestine charged Turkish machineguns with their sabre squadrons in waves, just far enough apart to force the enemy gunners to keep changing the range on their sights. I cannot be sure, but I suspect that my own determination to join the cavalry came from this time. I was so pleased to discover later that my own regiment the 11th Hussars and the Sherwood Rangers had liked and respected each other in the desert and in Normandy, as the books of Stanley Christopherson and Myles Hildyard indicate.

The twin qualities of cavalry spirit and professionalism, which envious regiments might attempt to regard as mutually exclusive, lay at the heart of the Sherwood Rangers and their hugely impressive performance in both world wars. Whether in the hunting field or from just living in the country, officers and yeomen alike seem to have acquired that vital instinct for terrain. It served them well in the Boer War; at the Dardanelles and in Palestine during the First World War; a quarter of a century later in the Western Desert and Libya, and then finally in the fighting from Normandy to Germany.

Their other great advantage was that the regiment never seemed to suffer from a martinet as commanding officer, who made everyone's life hell. There were strong characters, such as Colonel Flash Kellett in the desert, but no control-minded obsessives. In any case, that would not have been the yeomanry way. With so many family friends at all levels, relations between ranks were fairly informal.

The priority was to get the job done, and done well, and having as much fun as possible in the circumstances.

Raised for home defence in 1794, the Sherwood Rangers did not serve abroad until the Boer War, and only then as a company of mounted infantry in the Imperial Yeomanry, an invention which horrified Field Marshal Wolseley. But since the Boers outfought the regular regiments of the British Army with ease, new mobile tactics were urgently needed if the British Empire was not to be humiliated in the eyes of the world. The yeomanry, by caring so well for their horses in the terrible conditions, soon outshone their regular counterparts, and by their dash and initiative also proved superior in the field.

In the First World War, the Sherwood Rangers began by defending the Norfolk coast against the possibility of German landings, but in the spring of 1915, as part of the 2nd Mounted Division, they shipped to Egypt for the widening war against the Ottoman Empire. By the time they landed at Alexandria, the decision had been taken to attack the Dardanelles. The leisurely landings at Gallipoli were soon in trouble. The furious Turkish counter-attacks prevented the Allied forces from seizing the high ground.

In August, with every effort to break out thwarted, the yeomanry regiments were sent in as infantry. My uncle's account of their experiences, true to the uncomplaining attitude of his generation, never revealed fully the horrors they endured from thirst, dust, flies and sickness. The regiment was withdrawn to Egypt in November. Almost all its casualties had been from disease. Reduced to a composite squadron in strength, it took part in the 1916 Macedonian campaign, a belated attempt to prop up Serbia. But in 1917 the regiment's redeployment in Egypt was in preparation for General Allenby's Palestine campaign. This was to be the crowning glory for British yeomanry regiments, with the Sherwood Rangers foremost among them, as Jonathan Hunt's account shows.

The Second World War saw the regiment not just maintain its fine reputation, but enhance it quite astonishingly. The start back in Palestine as a mounted regiment on internal security duties was hardly propitious. But once the regiment was mechanized as an armoured unit in the desert, that combination of cavalry dash, dry humour and professionalism drew the admiration of all. One of the great works of wartime literature, *From Alamein to Zem-Zem*, was penned by the poet Keith Douglas, a troop leader in A squadron.

For D-Day, the regiment was one of those selected to swim their Sherman tanks into the beach, a truly terrifying experience in such rough conditions. After liberating Bayeux on the morning of 7 June, the regiment advanced south only to come up against the formidable Panzer Lehr Division. Casualties were high, but that was certainly not due to a lack of professionalism. The sabre squadrons did not restrict their firing, as some regular regiments did, in an attempt to lessen the arduous and uncomfortable task of reloading the tank with main armament and machine-gun ammunition. They knew that laziness cost lives.

Word of the regiment's excellence soon spread. Every infantry battalion in 50th Division longed to have the Sherwood Rangers as their armoured support. So did the Americans later. The Sherwood Rangers joined the American 82nd Airborne division near Nijmegen during Operation MARKET GARDEN and became the first British troops on German soil. And during that waterlogged autumn, won praise again in their support for the American 84th Infantry Division in the battle for Geilenkirchen.

During the final advance in April 1945, the Sherwood Rangers captured the German headquarters in Bremen with its garrison commander, thus ensuring the fall of this important port. Finally, on the night of 5 May, the ceasefire order came. Every weapon was loosed off into the sky and every bottle opened. As Jonathan Hunt observes, the Sherwood Rangers had fought and advanced for 3,000 miles, winning thirty battle honours. It is a truly impressive story.

Antony Beevor

Preamble

A Song of Sherwood
by Alfred Noyes

Robin Hood is here again: all his merry thieves
Hear a ghostly bugle-note shivering through the leaves,
Calling as he used to call, faint and far away,
In Sherwood, in Sherwood, about the break of day ...

Where the deer are gliding down the shadowy glen
All across the glades of fern he calls his merry men —
Doublets of the Lincoln green glancing through the May
In Sherwood, in Sherwood, about the break of day ...

Calls them and they answer: from aisles of oak and ash
Rings the Follow! Follow! and the boughs begin to crash,
The ferns begin to flutter and the flowers begin to fly,
And through the crimson dawning the robber band goes by.

On 5 May 1899 inter-regimental manoeuvres took place across parts of southern Yorkshire between the Sherwood Rangers Yeomanry, a volunteer hussar regiment raised in Nottinghamshire in 1794, and their neighbouring yeomanry regiment, the Queen's Own Yorkshire Dragoons, raised in West Yorkshire in the same year. 'The Rangers', as they were known to the Dragoons, were commanded by George Edmund Milnes Monckton-Arundell, 7th Viscount Galway of Serlby. 'The Dragons', as they were known to the Rangers, were commanded by Galway's good friend and neighbour, Alfred Frederick George Beresford Lumley, 10th Earl of Scarbrough, of Sandbeck, West Riding. The manoeuvres ended in a final parade and inspection in the park at Serlby in north Nottinghamshire.

The inspecting officer was none other than Field Marshal Garnet Viscount Wolseley KCB GCMG, the Commander-in-Chief. His inspection took place after the field exercise had reached its dénouement, an inconclusive fight for Serlby, in front of a crowd estimated at 6,000 which, to quote the local newspaper 'completed three sides of a gigantic square the fourth being open to the sleeping woodlands'.

The report continued:

> Within this expansive area the Brigade manoeuvred – the Yorkshire Dragoons in uniforms of dark blue with white facings, the Nottinghamshire Rangers in their well-known colours of green and gold, both regiments magnificently mounted upon horses of bay or brown or black ... marching slowly or trotting freely according to order and in harmony with the changing music ... their swords and accoutrements dancing in the sunlight.

This event harked back to a bygone age, and was merely the last in an oft-repeated series of similar events marking the culmination of the two aristocratic regiments' periods of annual training stretching back a century.

After the parade the Commander-in-Chief issued this order:

> The Commander-in-Chief has much pleasure in expressing his satisfaction with the field and parade movements executed today by the Nottinghamshire and Yorkshire Dragoons. The drill and turn out reflect credit on Colonel Viscount Galway and Colonel the Earl of Scarbrough the officers, non-commissioned officers and yeomen of both regiments.

Before the order had been published, Viscount Wolseley had informed Lord Galway that the Sherwood Rangers were a 'smart and well-ordered regiment who could ride their horses with credit, march and go through their evolutions with considerable distinction'. This was in fact a fair reflection of their worth, since the quality of both men and horses was high and the men were much more committed to their soldiering than their exotic and dated appearance suggested.

These remarks, however, may not have reflected the Commander-in-Chief's real views, for he was on the record as a critic of the English upper class and its approach to soldiering, that 'vulgar, snobbish and ignorant class which still infused the army with the redcoat spirit a decade after it had changed its uniform to khaki'. Given that he had just inspected two regiments who would have regarded 'infused with the redcoat spirit' as understatement so far as they were concerned, it has to be acknowledged that he must have been on his very best behaviour that day.

The Commander-in-Chief, on whom Gilbert based his 'modern major general', owed his elevated position to an outstanding career during campaigns in Africa, against the Ashanti and Zulu, and in Egypt. This was one of his minor duties, it was an honour for the two regiments that he had come to inspect them despite having weightier matters on his mind than a couple of obsolescent home defence cavalry regiments.

On the day before Sir Alfred Milner, the High Commissioner for South Africa and Lieutenant Governor of the Cape, based in Cape Town, had informed the British Government, that the Boers, led by Paul Kruger, President of the South

African Republic (Transvaal), were arming. Lord Wolseley would therefore also have been aware of the delicate negotiations due to take place in Bloemfontein, Orange Free State, South Africa, at the end of the month, between Milner and Kruger, which would, if they did not go well, lead to war. Sir Alfred Milner had no intention that they would go well for Kruger, and knew that Kruger would not accept the terms he had in mind for him.

Had Wolseley known of Milner's intentions he might not have been all that concerned since he was privately of the view that 'what was needed to correct the attitudes of the upper classes' just mentioned 'was a war which would be the making of the British Army'. It would certainly not have crossed the Commander-in-Chief's mind for one moment, as he sat astride his charger watching the 'evolutions' of the yeomanry surrounded by the 'sleeping woodlands' of Serlby on that idyllic spring day, that his highly-trained professional standing army would, in seven short months, be rocked to its core by an enemy which it outnumbered by several times and which included no professional soldiers.

Further, it is debateable who would have been the more appalled, the gallant Commander-in-Chief had he known he would shortly call out both regiments for service overseas in the circumstances just described, or the two gallant yeomanry units had they known they would shortly be wearing khaki.

Part I

The Boer War

1899–1902

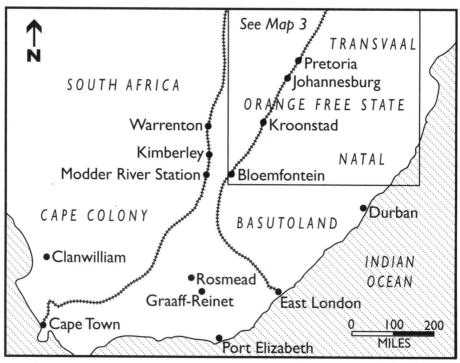

Map 1: South Africa.

Chapter 1

Casus Belli

May–October 1899

The friction in South Africa was between the British provinces of Cape Colony and Natal in the south, and the republics of Transvaal and Orange Free State to the north, which were virtually independent of Britain and the homelands of Afrikaners of Dutch descent, known as Boers. The best summary of the *casus belli* for the coming war is found in each side's ultimatum.

Kruger, the legendary and dour President of the South African Republic (Transvaal), got his ultimatum in first, delivering it on 9 October 1899, on behalf of both the Transvaal and Orange Free State, some twelve weeks after his meeting in Bloemfontein with Milner. It accused Great Britain of breaching treaties by interfering in the internal affairs of the Transvaal and the Free State and by massing troops, and demanded that both activities be reversed within forty-eight hours, or the Government of the South African Republic would, with great regret, be compelled to regard the action as a formal declaration of war.

The British ultimatum had also been drafted and was to have been issued on 11 October, but was destined never to be so. Britain demanded of the Government of the Transvaal:

1. The concession of full equality to the *Uitlanders*.
2. That the status of Britain, as the paramount power in South Africa, be accepted by the Boers.
3. An end to police persecution by the Boers, of Cape Coloureds, Indians, Africans from the colonies and other British coloured subjects.

The *Uitlanders* were the disenfranchised, predominantly white, settlers, mostly British, but from all over the Empire as well, who had been attracted to the Transvaal by good employment prospects in the gold mines. Gold in industrial quantities had been discovered there within the previous quarter of a century. By this stage the *Uitlanders* were in a significant majority over the Boers, and favoured unification with the British-controlled Cape Province, Rhodesia and Natal. Suffice it to say this first concession demanded by Britain was irreconcilable with the Boers' philosophy, which was the birth of apartheid, based on the principle of denying citizenship to anyone not a Boer. None knew that better than Sir Alfred Milner.

By international standards the British Army was not large with an establishment of 340,000, but a strength of 316,000, including all regulars and reservists, whereas other European countries counted their armies in millions. This is explained partly by the fact that the Royal Navy took the main responsibility for our home defence. Any force to fight in South Africa would have to be drawn mainly from two army corps and a cavalry division, about 85,000 men in total when other increments were added. Although limited numerically, they were the cream of the standing army, all fully professional, highly trained and well equipped.

The War Office was known to be split by factions – as ever between cavalry and infantry, but at that time, for a change, mainly between 'Africans' and 'Indians'. The former were led by Wolseley and General Sir Redvers Buller, whose service had mostly taken place in Africa. The 'Indians' were led by Field Marshal Lord Roberts, whose service had been in India. In addition the Secretary of State for War, the Marquis of Lansdowne, had served politically in India and therefore was not unbiased. It follows that Wolseley and he did not get on. The War Office now needed answers to two questions: how many troops were needed, specifically in Natal, the northern tip of which, around Ladysmith, was flanked by the two Boer republics, to deter an invasion, and how likely was that a possibility? Secondly: how many troops would be needed to invade and defeat the Boer republics should that become necessary? (See Map 3 p.34).

The answer came from Major General Sir John Ardagh, Director of the Intelligence Department at the War Office. The Orange Free State and Transvaal could together muster a civilian army of 54,000, which, with internal security provided for, would leave them with an offensive force of 34,000, well equipped with Mauser rifles and artillery. At the time of this assessment only 5,000 British troops guarded the Cape and Natal and therefore the Boers' strength posed a major threat to British possessions in South Africa until the British garrison could be reinforced. Ardagh's further assessment was that the Boers were not a serious military adversary, lacking in both the ability to lead or re-supply large formed bodies of men in the field, and that they had a dread of British cavalry, as did most British generals, and would give up after one good fight. He went on to advise, on that basis, that the only cross-border offensive tactics the Boers would employ, or could carry off successfully, would be raiding parties of 2,000 to 3,000 men.

This part of the assessment was right as it applied to the capability of the Boers to invade and hold Cape Colony or Natal in a pre-emptive attack, as some in Britain believed they might try to do, but a serious underestimate of capability if applied to the Boers' ability to defend themselves and fight for their homeland and way of life. Accordingly, how big should be the British response to the threat in order to put the Boers back in their box? Wolseley was quite clear:

1. Call out onto Salisbury Plain I Corps, commanded by Buller, which would lead any major deployment. It consisted of 35,000 men and was half the total force available, the aim being to 'terrify Kruger from long range'.

2. Buy the corps transport for South Africa, namely 11,000 mules costing £500,000, to show intent.
3. As a hedge against Kruger failing to be swayed, send a first contingent of 10,000 to South Africa immediately to secure the defence of British interests there from being overwhelmed by a surprise attack.

The decision taken was to send the 10,000 troops Wolseley had advocated.

Preparations were immediately put in hand to assemble and despatch 10,000 seasoned troops who were to be firm in Natal by mid-October and, with the 5,000 already in South Africa, would represent a force of 15,000 under the newly-appointed commander in Natal, Major General Penn Symons, chosen by Lansdowne in July, and so naturally an India man. He was a known firebrand with no experience of Africa. As it turned out, the troops were just about in position as Kruger issued his ultimatum. To command overall in South Africa Lansdowne chose Lieutenant General Sir George White VC.

However, shortly after the despatch of the 10,000, but before Kruger's declaration, the Cabinet decided to despatch I Corps, commanded by Buller, to South Africa in response to the most up-to-date intelligence that Kruger was making final preparations for war, and had not been deterred by news of the initial deployment. Fully mobilized, including reservists, I Corps would number 47,000. With the 15,000 already on the ground by the time it got there, that would make a total force of 62,000, nearly double the Boer combat strength of 34,000. The advanced guard of I Corps, including its commander, Buller, also now appointed in overall command in South Africa, sailed on 14 October; the main body was to start landing in South Africa in mid-November, and be complete by early-December.

With war now declared, and the Free State in the war, a key advantage was that the corps would be able to invade on a centre line out of the Cape into the enemy territory of the Orange Free State leading straight to the capitals of the two states, Bloemfontein and Pretoria. This was a much less hilly and more open line of advance, rather than through Natal and the mountainous country covering the approaches to the Transvaal that would have been the only option had the Transvaal been the sole opponent. There was, unfortunately, a fly in the ointment, a rather large one as it turned out. Before Buller was appointed formally, he had given strong advice to Lansdowne that, because of the risk the Boers' capability represented, the initial force of 10,000 headed for northern Natal should not be deployed north of the Tugela river. Buller's analysis was that the area north of the Tugela, forming a wedge between Transvaal and the Free State, and including the town of Ladysmith, was not the Boers' soft underbelly but a trap for the British. This turned out to be the most correct assessment by anyone. Unfortunately, before the wise head of General White, who was also against such a deployment, arrived in South Africa, Symons, in response to the mobilization of the Transvaal and the Free State, had not only pushed a brigade north of the Tugela but, unwisely, split it between Ladysmith and Dundee, farther north still. Buller was unaware of this.

Chapter 2

Learning Curve

October–December 1899

In October the Boers also got their 'retaliation' in first. On the 11th they attacked out of the Orange Free State into Cape Province and out of the Transvaal into Natal. By the time Buller landed at Cape Town at the end of October, they had virtually all the British forces in South Africa surrounded and besieged in the three key British border towns, Ladysmith in Natal and Mafeking and Kimberley in the Cape. Worse, in Natal, Symons, the commander on the ground, had been killed in almost the first action, and the besieged troops, a formidable force on paper, had suffered several defeats and heavy losses. These included an entire cavalry regiment on one occasion and an infantry battalion on another being outmanoeuvred, captured and taken prisoner by the Boers while trying, unsuccessfully, to fight their way out. Finally, there was a real fear that the Afrikaners of Dutch descent, a substantial majority in the Cape and hostile to the British, might rise up and side with the Boers. In short the situation was threatening to explode.

The arrival of Buller and I Corps in November seemed to stabilize matters. Nevertheless, because of the ill-advised deployment north of the Tugela, Buller could no longer stick to his original plan to take his whole force along the favourable line of advance out of the Cape into the Free State and thus bring about a quick conclusion. Instead, he had to deploy the lion's share, under his own command, to Natal to relieve Ladysmith, which was where the greatest problem seemed to be. He then directed the balance, consisting of an augmented 1st Division, under command of Lieutenant General Lord Methuen, concurrently to relieve Mafeking and Kimberley.

That should have been an end to the crisis – but it wasn't. Methuen, with responsibility for defending Cape Colony, and in the process, for relieving Mafeking and Kimberley, had marched north-east from Cape Town on a centre line which would eventually lead him to both Kimberley and Mafeking. Thus he had to cross the Modder river where the Boers lay in wait and inflicted a tactical defeat on him on 28 November. Further, at the beginning of what became known as Black Week, he suffered another tactical defeat at Magersfontein on 11 December. It is worth noting that, although the Boers were commanded by General Piet Cronje, these setbacks were caused by the tactical flair of one General Jacobus Herculaas

('Koos') de la Rey, his second in command, who came from a small town called Lichtenburg, of which more later.

De la Rey believed that the Boer tactic of defending from the top of *kopjes* (the colloquial name for the small hills abounding in what was typically an open rolling terrain) exposed them to artillery fire and reduced the effect of their own fire because they were shooting into the ground. He, therefore, entrenched his force at ground level, enabling his rifle fire to sweep parallel to the ground through successive ranks of Methuen's infantry, who helped him a lot by advancing upright at the walk from the front rather than prone at the crawl from the side. Unsurprisingly, given this astute approach to soldiering, de la Rey became one of the most effective Boer commanders.

If that was not enough, again in Black Week, Buller suffered a major and deeply humiliating defeat, including significant casualties at Colenso in Natal trying to cross the Tugela on 15 December, and a number of minor ones later in attempting unsuccessfully to relieve Ladysmith. In each of the three besieged towns starvation and disease were becoming another major embarrassment.

The British had brought a mix of forces which, despite superior numbers, professionalism, equipment and training, failed to make their numerical superiority tell. This was because, in accordance with conventional wisdom, they were predominantly infantry, and so lacked mobility, and, compared to the Boers, who functioned as light cavalry and used 'home advantage' to live off the land, were heavily dependent on logistical support. This tied them to the roads and railways along the valley bottoms and kept them on the defensive, protecting their lines of re-supply. Further, unless mounted, they could not deploy into the country and take offensive action.

The infantry may have discarded their red tunics in favour of khaki uniforms, which aided concealment, but they had not changed their tactics, which still too often involved total exposure, advancing on their feet in tightly-drawn ranks and files in open country, which meant they were mown down in swathes by the hail of fire from modern magazine-fed rifles and machine guns. Wolseley had got the war he had wished for.

To this point conventional wisdom had been that these modern weapons had rendered cavalry obsolete in favour of infantry. The lesson of Black Week was the opposite: it was the pedestrian infantry who were more vulnerable because of their inability to evade the fire, whereas troops mounted on horses in open country could more easily outrun and evade the slow traversing static machine gun and rifle. The answer was to mount the infantry on horses and also make use of the flexibility of cavalry. This is the moment to consider the distinction between cavalry equipped with sabres as well as rifles, and mounted infantry. If a unit was dependent for its success on its ability to optimize the performance of its horses in action, to be successful it had to master the skills of cavalry, which involved a high standard of horse-mastership, the art of optimizing the performance of horses. If the horses were merely a means of conveyance to a point where the riders dismounted and fought on foot, leaving the horses with handlers, they were mounted infantry. In this new world, however, even cavalry, since they were equipped with rifles, must rediscover the ability to fight on foot as infantry. This was a reversion to the original role of dragoons or, even further back, to Henry V's campaign which ended at Agincourt when his entire army marched on horseback to provide manoeuvre but then fought mostly on foot.

The question raised by this poor performance in the field by the cream of the British Army against what looked like a bunch of almost comically shaggy countrymen on even shaggier ponies, but who were in fact competent light cavalry, went far beyond the tactical situation on the ground in South Africa. Unless restored quickly, decisively and competently it would raise questions about Great Britain's ability to maintain dominion over its Empire, and could trigger a chain reaction, not just in the rest of Africa but elsewhere as well. The news of these setbacks brought several separate decisions by the Government.

Starting from the top, Field Marshal Lord Roberts VC, the leading 'Indian' and Wolseley's contemporary and rival, would be appointed to overall command in South Africa in place of Buller, who would in turn replace White, who, as commander in Natal, was blamed most of all for the reverses there. Roberts took with him, as his Chief of Staff, General Lord Kitchener, the hero of Omdurman and saviour of Khartoum, the 'coming man'. Next, the decision was taken to mobilize and send, post-haste, II Corps, including the cavalry division, altogether 45,000 men.

In addition, there was a mobilization of volunteers from the Empire. This exceeded expectations. The reverses had triggered strong patriotic emotions of support for the British cause from amongst the, mostly white, Dominions They also felt common cause with the *Uitlanders* with whom they had much in common. This would manifest itself over time in over 35,000 reinforcements, many of them arriving as mounted troops. The Sherwood Rangers would meet some in their transit camp, Maitland Camp, in South Africa, and would report being impressed with the number of countries from which these volunteers had come.

Finally, so far as the UK was concerned, there was the decision to mobilize British volunteer units. Over the period covered by the first two years of the war 227,500 officers and men would embark for South Africa from all parts of the Empire.

Chapter 3

Mounted Irregulars

December 1899–January 1900

On 29 November and 16 December respectively two urgent cypher telegrams, particularly relevant to the yeomanry, were sent by Buller to the War Office. In the first he wrote 'I shall mount infantry and let them ride in trousers as the Boers do'. In the second he went further:

Would it be possible for you to raise eight thousand irregulars in England. They should be equipped as mounted infantry, be able to shoot as well as possible and ride decently. I would amalgamate them with colonials.

On 18 December Lord Galway received the following from J. Davidson at the War Office:

Dear Lord Galway
Lord Wolseley desires me to acknowledge your letter of yesterday and to say he hopes we will employ a force of yeomanry as mounted rifles. They must of course be good shots.

In the light of that letter what happened next is interesting. George Wyndham, the junior minister in the War Office, acted immediately on Buller's request. He proposed raising 20,000 mounted infantry, mainly in South Africa, and that 7,000 volunteers should be sent to augment existing mounted infantry units. His key decision in this connection, however, was to mobilize the yeomanry. 'The yeomanry were still too largely a theatrical reminiscence of the cavalry that fought in the Crimea and the Peninsula, but the material was excellent – better than the men recruited for the regular army.' It was also stated that 'they have an existing machinery and depots for ease of enlistment'. He recommended to Lansdowne that the chain of command be by-passed altogether, which appears to conflict with Davidson's letter. He clearly did not trust the general staff to do it if asked. Instead, he decided to be guided by some friends of his as 'they are men of affairs, and as masters of foxhounds, they are in touch with the young riding farmers and horse-masters of this country'. Lord Galway was one of the foxhunting friends. In all thirty-six peers and twenty-seven MPs took part in the war and about half the yeomanry were deemed middle class. That is an unremarkable figure, given the pedigree of the yeomanry, and probably reflects normality. Thus was born the

Imperial Yeomanry. The regular Army had almost no control over its creation; a committee of existing foxhunting yeomen or their supporters organized it, two of them offered to help fund it, and it also received a sum of £50,000 from Wernher-Beit, the Johannesburg gold-mining company.

The plan was that, rather than mobilize entire yeomanry regiments, each would raise a service squadron of 120 men, between 25 and 50 per cent of the parent yeomanry, which would be called a company and given a number. Each such sub-unit would then form part of a new regiment to be called an Imperial Yeomanry regiment, made up of four companies, which would be also given a distinguishing number. Yorkshire and Nottinghamshire were designated to raise one such regiment. Wolseley was furious when he heard about the idea for the Imperial Yeomanry, saying that to go 'into the highways and byways' and pick up civilians 'quite regardless of whether they have learned the rudiments of discipline' was a 'dangerous experiment' and that 'the yeomanry would be very little use in the field'. It appears, given Wolseley's reaction, that Wyndham was right that the idea would not have been pursued actively if it had been entrusted to the chain of command.

The War Office authorized the raising of volunteers for South Africa but, even before this was formally published locally, notices signed by yeomanry colonels were posted in conspicuous places throughout Yorkshire and Nottinghamshire on Christmas Eve 1899 to seek enlistments. No doubt something similar occurred elsewhere. The following is the text of the notice.

IMPERIAL YEOMANRY

1. *In accordance with a communication issued by the War Office, offers of service to form a Nottinghamshire contingent of the Imperial Yeomanry are invited from the Sherwood Rangers and South Notts. Hussars and also from Nottinghamshire Volunteers and Civilians who may possess the necessary qualifications, as given below, and who will be specially enrolled for the purpose.*
2. *The term of enlistment for officers and men will be for the duration of the war.*
3. *Men will be provided by Government with arms, ammunition, equipment and regimental transport.*
4. *Men will be provided with the necessary equipment and clothing complete free of all expense to them, with the exception of certain small necessaries, which they will be required to provide for themselves, and which will be notified later.*
5. *Horses must comply with the following conditions: Six years old and upwards, height 14–2 to 15–2 hands; bays, browns, and chestnuts preferred. No greys taken. The general description of horse required are stout, active cobs, with good legs and feet.*
6. *Men are invited to show up horses of their own which comply with the above conditions, and if accepted they will be valued by a committee of officers*

appointed for the purpose, the owner will have the option of at once selling his horse to the committee, when it will become the property of the county contingent, or he can keep the horse as his own property, receiving the value put upon the horse by the committee at the end of the campaign in the event of loss.

7. The committee of officers will, if possible, purchase a sufficient number of horses to mount all men otherwise qualified who are unable to comply with the above paragraph (6), but preference will be given to men who comply with it, provided they are equally well qualified.

8. The pay will be at cavalry rates. Gratuities and allowances will be those in Special Army Order of May 10th 1899

QUALIFICATIONS

All candidates must be from 20 to 35 years of age, and of good character, and must pass the usual medical examination. Volunteers and civilians must satisfy the undersigned that they are good riders and shots.

Applications for enrolment should be addressed without delay, to

The ADJUTANT, Headquarters Sherwood Rangers, Retford: or to
The ADJUTANT, South Notts. Hussars, Park Row, Nottingham

Colonel Rolleston, Commanding the South Notts. Hussars, has applied to the War Office for the command of the Nottinghamshire Force
GALWAY
Colonel, Sherwood Rangers.
L. ROLLESTON
Colonel, South Notts. Hussars.
BOLTON
Colonel, Yorkshire Hussars.
SCARBROUGH
Colonel, Yorkshire Dragoons.

Nottingham, 23 December, 1899

The Imperial Yeomanry caught the national imagination. Offers to serve poured in. In the case of the Sherwood Rangers the vast majority were from existing young serving members who, being unburdened of the many responsibilities of livelihood and family that prevented those who were older, were free to go, and competition for the limited places was intense. Lord Galway, as the commanding officer, led the selection process and received letters begging to serve from throughout the regiment and beyond. Not all were successful.

The Sherwood Rangers formed 10 Company of the 3rd Regiment of Imperial Yeomanry, the Yorkshire Hussars 9 Company, the Queen's Own Yorkshire Dragoons 11 Company, and the South Notts Hussars 12 Company. Troopers were equipped with the Lee-Enfield rifle and officers with a revolver; none carried sabres. The raising of the regiment was led by the Earl of Scarbrough, the second, but eldest surviving, son of the 9th Earl, who had died in 1884. He was born in 1857 at Tickhill Castle, which made him 43 at the time. After Eton he had been commissioned into the 7th Hussars, serving with them between 1876 and 1883. He joined the Yorkshire Dragoons thereafter. After his service in the Boer War, he continued to serve in the newly-formed Territorial Force, forerunner of the Territorial Army, being finally appointed Director General of the Territorial Force between 1917 and 1921. He was promoted honorary major general in 1921. This record of service, covering both the Boer War and the Great War, confirms him as the outstanding Territorial of his generation. Outside of his TF career he was Lord Lieutenant of West Yorkshire between 1892 and 1904, was appointed CB (1904), KCB (1911), GBE (1921) and became a Knight of the Garter (1929).

Command of the regiment, however, went to Lieutenant Colonel George John Younghusband. Lord Scarbrough wrote to Lord Galway:

> I think I have secured the best CO that our army can provide for 3rd Battalion Imperial Yeomanry.
>
> I am satisfied I was right in standing aside tho' I must own to a depression of spirits at the present moment.

There is no doubt he too would have made an excellent commanding officer, but Younghusband was to prove a fine choice. A regular officer commissioned into the Army in 1878, he transferred into the Guides, the Indian Regiment with the best fighting record, with whom he gained extensive experience of active service. Following the Boer War he was promoted to major general and knighted after a distinguished career. Lord Scarbrough agreed to serve as his second in command. Although Galway was not considered for service due to age, both he and Lady Galway played a critical role, with others in a similar position, in running the regiment's home headquarters. This involved supporting the regiment more closely than could the official chain of re-supply, overstretched by the size of the mobilization of the regular Army which was given priority.

The funding for the SRY company came from two sources, the government, at the rate of £35 per man to equip the man, and at £40 per horse to buy the horse, and was expended by Lord Galway. He equipped 143 men and bought fifty-four horses. It is not clear from where the remainder of the horses came but, if not from the government, they must have been privately owned by Sherwood Rangers. The second source was a reversion to the time-honoured method of paying to raise volunteers by private subscription, as had been used to raise the regiment in 1794. The county raised about £4,000 for the SRY and the SNH companies, which was spent by both regiments on twenty-three Adler field-glasses, a Maxim machine gun each, waterproofs, folding beds and life insurance of £100 per man. Lord Galway himself bought forty-five saddles, 110 binoculars and eighty cardigans. In short, something like a third to a half of the total cost of mobilizing and supporting the Sherwood Rangers Yeomanry service company was provided privately.

Another initiative, triggered by mobilization, was that Lord Galway contacted Lord Brownlow to suggest the raising of a Lincolnshire service squadron for South Africa. Lord Brownlow, of Belton House, Grantham, was Lord-Lieutenant of Lincolnshire and, therefore, the appropriate channel through which to pursue such an initiative. The reason for the contact was that the Sherwood Rangers was a four- rather than six-troop regiment, and Lincolnshire had no yeomanry regiment of its own, but many keen volunteers. This would have been a way of resolving that problem. Brownlow was also a former under-secretary of state for war, in which capacity he had wrestled with the problem of the viability of small yeomanry regiments.

The Sherwood Rangers' squadron mobilized formally at Yeomanry Headquarters, Retford. Captain M. S. Dawson of Compton Castle, Bath, was selected to command the squadron; he had joined the Rangers in 1892. The troop leaders were Lieutenants H. O. (Hop) Peacock (1894), R. T. O. (Bertie) Sheriffe (1897) of Quorn Lodge, Melton Mowbray, Herbert (Bertie) H. Wilson (1897) of Melbourne, Derbyshire, and Arthur C. (Job) Williams. Job Williams was from Horndean, Hampshire, and was recruited by Lord Galway. Two other long-time regimental officers had also volunteered and were mobilized, but did not serve in the company. They were Captain Thomas R. Starkey of Norwood Park, Southwell (1886–1896) and Captain J. F. (Joe) Laycock of Wiseton Hall (1890). Starkey's war service is not known but something of Laycock's is. He had met Major General John French, who was commanding the Cavalry Division, following an exercise in which Laycock, using the stars, had successfully led his squadron across Salisbury Plain at night. French was impressed and promised him a role on his staff in the event of war. When this one began Laycock sent French a telegram reminding him of his promise and was invited to accompany him as a supplementary staff officer. They had arrived in Cape Town on 11 October 1899.

Lord Galway received a letter from HQ Imperial Yeomanry expressing concern that none of the officers had regular service and stating 'some names … will be submitted to you', but no changes were made.

Finally, after just five weeks (including Christmas and the New Year holidays), the Company of 121 all ranks was given a tremendous farewell. There was a public dinner on 25 January in the Victoria Hall in Nottingham for all those volunteering, mostly Sherwood Rangers and South Notts Hussars. The dinner had been arranged by the leading families of the county, headed by the Duke of Portland as Lord-Lieutenant. On 27 January there was a dismounted parade of the Sherwood Rangers' contingent in their newly-issued khaki uniforms in Retford Market Square, watched by a large crowd of well-wishers. Each man wore a sprig of gorse in bloom in his broad-brimmed bush hat, the regiment's colours of green and gold, presented at the moment of departure by Lord Galway's daughter, the

Honourable Violet Monkton. Each service squadron had a similar parade, the Yorkshire Hussars and Yorkshire Dragoons in Sheffield, and South Notts Hussars in Nottingham, all of which also drew large crowds.

They left by train for Liverpool and sailed next day, 28 January 1900, on the SS *Winifredian*, the second ship to sail but the first to arrive in South Africa. The mobilization just described was the first deployment of yeomanry overseas in which 3rd Imperial Yeomanry found themselves in the vanguard and is therefore a significant event in Sherwood Rangers' history.

Unexpectedly, the yeomanry mobilization triggered nationally a wider patriotic response which helped create almost universal active public support for the prosecution of the war, and acted as a counterbalance to the bad news of Black Week.

Chapter 4

Balance Shifts

January–March 1900

Despite the problems arising from Black Week, a positive factor was the underlying reality that, whilst victory seemed a long way off, the Boers had, in fact, already lost the war. As predicted, despite all their successes, they were unable to capitalize by advancing on Durban and Cape Town. However, the Boers were not done with yet. On 24 and 25 January 1900 Buller tried again to break through to Ladysmith. If Colenso had been an attempt to outflank the Boers from the left, this attack (immortalized in football grounds by the plagiarizing of its name 'Spion Kop') was the right-flanking attempt to take the hill of that name. Again the result was a British tactical defeat with heavy losses. However, Buller gained something from it. He finally grasped that if the Boers were to be defeated in a conventional attack, the British infantry would have to take every opportunity to advance, not on their feet necessarily, but by using dead ground to provide concealment. In addition their progress must be achieved by a combination of covering fire and movement, a process to become known as 'pepper potting'.

Lord Roberts and II Corps, with a strength of 45,000, landed at Cape Town and was firm by early February, whilst the Sherwood Rangers and their fellow volunteers were still at sea. On 11 February Roberts was ready. His force was a leviathan led by Major General John French's cavalry division and followed by 7th, 6th, and 9th Infantry Divisions; the battle-scarred 1st was left in reserve, virtually in disgrace, under Methuen, to cover Roberts' lines of communication. II Corps crossed into the Orange Free State and were already some 600 miles up-country on a line north-east of Cape Town, the centre line Buller had wanted to take with his own corps and that Methuen had taken.

It was the start of an advance along the axis of the western railway line to Kimberley – then across country to Bloemfontein, capital of the Orange Free State – along the midland railway line into the Transvaal, then to Johannesburg and finally to Transvaal's capital, Pretoria, and an inevitable strategic victory. However, he was not unopposed and was not without problems.

Roberts' opposition was provided by Cronje, who, as mentioned, had been in command on the western front from the beginning, whose 'battle honours' included Modder river and Magersfontein. Unfortunately for Roberts, Cronje was still supported by de le Rey and by General Christiaan de Wet. De Wet was already considered one of the best and most resolute of the Boer leaders, which he was to confirm repeatedly in the years ahead, and became regarded as the best guerrilla commander. He, as well as de le Rey, was destined to feature significantly in this account.

Roberts' main problem was that of re-supply. It was not so much the lack of it, nor even the distances, but the significant volume, coupled with the lack of an adequate road system on which to carry it once the railway (itself narrow-gauge) had to be exchanged for wagons and oxen.

Almost immediately he ordered the cavalry division under French to divert from the line of march, by-pass all opposition and relieve Kimberley which was thought close to surrender. This was duly achieved on 16 February, not without the loss of unsustainable numbers of horses.

Due to climate and disease this country was hostile to the wellbeing of horses. African Horse Sickness which, in its severest form, was untreatable and fatal, was the key cause. The attrition started immediately after landing and never ceased and was contained only by a constant supply of remounts. During the next two years approximately 250,000 horses would be imported for war service. Few would survive. Men also suffered from the lack of drinkable water and food, which forever seemed to contain a high percentage of sand. In addition, the hostile conditions also led to ill health and death amongst the men, typhoid being one of the main killers.

Shortly after the relief of Kimberley, as expected, Roberts came up against Cronje's defensive positions on the Modder at Magersfontein, part of a force of 10,000 Boers in the vicinity of Kimberley. What became the Battle of Paardeberg was joined. Roberts prevailed, and secured the surrender of Cronje and his commando of 4,000. However, his command suffered heavy casualties by the same tactics as each side had applied when Methuen had met Cronje. The victory, the first of the war for the British, was finally secured on 27 February over de Wet who had, nevertheless, fought well; the road to Bloemfontein was open.

Better still, Buller's I Corps, now 30,000 strong, secured Monte Cristo, the key to turning the Boers' extreme left flank, and the road to Ladysmith was at last open. He duly broke the siege – also on 27 February. Buller was then able to take the offensive against the 25,000 Boers in the vicinity of Ladysmith, and start to carry out the plan he had come to execute three months earlier.

At this stage 3rd Imperial Yeomanry disembarked from the relative comfort of the *Winifredian* at Cape Town on 20 February 1900, the first Yeomanry regiment to arrive. From the ship they moved five miles to Maitland Camp, the horses almost unrideable with excitement after their confinement. This was the transit camp for all disembarking troops. Whilst the regiment had built up their personal skills during the month-long voyage, more work-up training was needed, followed by careful assessment, before they could be passed fit for operations and cleared to move over 600 miles up-country to the war zone. This commenced with mounted drills, followed by a riding test for all ranks during which Colonel Younghusband was able to see his regiment in training for the first time.

Dawson reported to Lord Galway:

> Our CO, however, does not mean to let the grass grow under our horses' feet and is giving us regular long days: for instance today we had reveille at 5 a.m. and with the exception of 15 minutes for breakfast and about half an hour for lunch I have been on the trot all day till about 06.30 p.m.... The 'Subs' are all playing up well & we had the distinction of having the best section (Sheriff's) when the GOC had his parade on Thursday.

Further, General Brabazon, who had overall command of the Yeomanry, had told Younghusband that 'this was the best riding Irregular Cavalry I have ever seen, which include Colonies and Cape Mounted Men'. Younghusband expressed himself 'delighted with the capability, equipment and general excellence of the whole regiment' and observed that 'all, including the general public had commented that the horses were the best that had yet entered South Africa'.

Third Imperial Yeomanry was the first yeomanry unit to complete initial training, which took just under two weeks. They heard that Cronje had been captured with over 4,000 men and wondered if they would see action. There followed four days of musketry practice on the ranges at Stellenbosch. Although they would entrain to do so, there was an initial march to the railhead during which another vital part of their induction to operational soldiering was demonstrated, the importance of stowage of personal kit and the consequences of poor stowage. The evidence of their progress was described as the contents of a hardware store strewn along the road from Maitland Camp to the railhead.

At Stellenbosch, as a result of a chance meeting, the Sherwood Rangers entertained both Cecil Rhodes and Rudyard Kipling, and members were entertained in turn by Rhodes at his house. It also seems that Peacock 'almost sold' Rhodes a horse 'too good for this job'. With a good pass for shooting under their belts, their next destination was the massive remount depot at Paarl, where they were brought up to strength in horses.

At last they were operational, and began to learn of their role and the formations and regiments with which they would work. Third Imperial Yeomanry would form one of three (initially) regiments in 1 Yeomanry Brigade under command of Brigadier General Lord Chesham, Charles William Compton Cavendish, 3rd Baron Chesham, a descendant of the 4th Duke of Devonshire, who held the ancient Royal Office of Master of the Buckhounds. He was 49, and, although he had served in both the 10th Hussars and Coldstream Guards, owed his appointment to command the brigade to a highly-regarded period of service as a volunteer in the Buckinghamshire Yeomanry, which he had trained to a very high standard whilst commanding. This had led to his being given command of 10th Imperial Yeomanry, and then almost immediate promotion to command the brigade.

The other two Imperial Yeomanry regiments in the brigade were 5th, commanded by Lieutenant Colonel Meyrick, consisting of two companies from Northumberland, and one from each of Shropshire and Worcestershire, and 10th, under Lieutenant Colonel Eric Smith in succession to Lord Chesham, with two companies from Buckinghamshire and one from each of Berkshire and Oxfordshire. Both regiments had arrived in South Africa within a week of 3rd Imperial Yeomanry and were joined by a fourth regiment, 15th, which arrived at the end of March, and so would have been a month or so behind the other regiments in reaching the war zone. It was commanded by Lieutenant Colonel L. Sandwith, and mirrored 10th Imperial Yeomanry with two companies from Buckinghamshire and one from each of Berkshire and Oxfordshire.

The brigade was to join Roberts whose corps was in the area of Bloemfontein, capital of the Orange Free State, which had fallen unopposed on 13 March. However, the advance had duly exposed Roberts' weakness in relation to logistics, in which he took little interest. As a result he was incapable of advancing to Pretoria without an extended period to re-equip. This meant bringing sufficient re-supply of everything from boots to horses up the single railway line from Cape Town on the coast and then by ox-cart across country. In particular 1 Imperial Yeomanry Brigade was to come under command of 1st Division, which may have been in disgrace, but was, nevertheless, the senior infantry division in the Army's order of battle, having served under Wellington in the peninsula during the Napoleonic Wars, gaining a fine fighting record.

Its commander, Lord Methuen, had been demoted by Roberts, from force commander in the Cape, by virtue of Roberts taking that command on his arrival in theatre. In addition, because of Methuen's defeat at Magersfontein, his only command now was 1st Division, from which Roberts had removed almost all its formations and units, re-allocating them to other divisions; one brigade refused to serve under Methuen. Methuen kept only two infantry brigades and, as mentioned, was charged with protecting the lines of communication. It did not help Methuen that he was an 'African', and the nominee of Wolseley, whilst Roberts was an 'Indian'. No matter, it was probably the low point of his career. Indeed, Hop Peacock was to write in April, 'I am sorry we are under Lord Methuen as he has, I am afraid, lost all dash.' However he was to play a pivotal role over the following year, so far as the Sherwood Rangers were concerned, and so some background is needed. Paul Sanford Methuen was the eldest son of 2nd Baron Methuen of Wiltshire who had died in 1891. He was born in 1846 and so was 54. Commissioned into the Scots Guards, he had seen both extensive active service in Africa including, significantly, a period in the mid 1880s commanding a corps of mounted rifles called Methuen's Horse, as well as some key desk jobs, such as deputy adjutant-general in South Africa. More important to the Sherwood Rangers would have been the fact that he had started his soldiering in the Wiltshire Yeomanry. He was therefore one of those rarities, a senior regular formation commander who understood the volunteer ethos and how best to harness it.

These, then, were the formations with which 1 Imperial Yeomanry Brigade would serve, and protection of the lines of communication was the role they would be asked to perform, when they arrived. However, there was hope of something more heroic, because the division was also on standby to form a flying column to relieve Mafeking, still under siege and 100 miles to the north, when Roberts had sufficient resources for the task.

On 13 March 3rd Imperial Yeomanry received orders to march the sixteen miles to Wellington and entrain for Kimberley 600 miles up country: 'The road was two inches deep in dust, it being the end of the dry season, and with a gentle wind behind us the dust hung with us.' At Wellington they became part of Roberts' re-supply problem since they had to face a delay as the regiment was fitted into the railway's load schedule, causing them to be split into individual companies and inserted as room permitted, which took a number of days.

The Sherwood Rangers moved on 17 March, after the Yorkshire Hussars. Peacock wrote:

> five officers per carriage, eight men per carriage. All horses in open trucks, packed very close. We run along under 15 miles per hour round hills up and down rises. No tunnels. The line is well guarded, sentries on every bridge. We had the most interesting time ... as we passed Belmont Gras Pan and Modder River ... Belmont was a hopeless looking spot to take; a large plain over a mile across and a kopje at the far side with crowds of Boers in it in trenches ... Modder too was a terrible sight. One could still see dead horses and pits cut for shooting from.

The whole regiment had arrived at Kimberley by 26 March, the first unit in the brigade to arrive and the first Imperial Yeomanry regiment to commence operations.

Chapter 5

Baptism of Fire

March–April 1900

First Division was based on Boshof, fifty miles north-east of Kimberley, in the Free State near the frontier with the Cape. Third Imperial Yeomanry found on arrival that, following the fall of Bloemfontein, Roberts regarded the Boers as defeated and had reconfigured his force for the pursuit. Accordingly, 1st Division's role had been altered from protection of the lines of re-supply to clearing the country along the Vaal river to the west of Roberts' centre line. The task was to outflank the Boers and drive towards the besieged Mafeking. As squadrons arrived they found they were badly needed; the division had very few of the mobile troops necessary for the new task and so they were occupied immediately with patrolling or escort duties in the general area of Boshof. They also carried out search operations of homesteads looking for weapons, and reconnaissance and information-gathering for the main force – classic cavalry tasks – on either side of the border. The country was alive with unrest, and Boer commandos were known to be in the area, intent on preventing Roberts from achieving his objectives by attacking his supply lines.

Companies immediately found themselves in action. The Yorkshire Hussars and Sherwood Rangers were on a joint patrol between 22 March and 4 April without incident but the Yorkshire Dragoons, on patrol between 24 March and 3 April across the border, were in action three times, killing two enemy. The South Notts Hussars, arriving last, were first required between 29 March and 1 April to escort seventy-two ox wagons from Carters Ridge to Boshof, and were also engaged in a minor skirmish with a group of Boers without loss on either side.

Hop Peacock gave an insight into Roberts' problems with re-supply:

> Horses and transport are the great scarcity out here, as one can't move without both.... The ox is a useful hardworking beast, but a very slow mover and can't do many miles per day. They have to be grazed in the daytime, so they only move in the evening and the very early morning. But it is a marvellous sight to see 30 oxen in-spanned to a wagon. They all know their places and out of all the thousands here the black boys know their own lots, and where each ox has to go.

On 5 April the stakes were raised when Methuen received intelligence that a commando, led by one Major General George Henri Anne-Marie Victor le Comte de Villebois-Mareuil, to accord him his full name, was nearby; the informant was in fact Villebois-Mareuil's native assistant. Methuen ordered Chesham to intercept and attack Villebois-Mareuil immediately. Chesham deployed with the SRY and SNH companies of 3rd Imperial Yeomanry. Third Imperial Yeomanry was commanded by the Earl of Scarbrough during this action, Younghusband being indisposed with eczema. In addition, there were two companies of 10th Imperial Yeomanry, a squadron of Kimberley Light Horse and a battery of 4th Royal Field Artillery (RFA), about 750 men in all. These were all the uncommitted mobile troops available to the division at that time.

Major General le Comte de Villebois was an interesting man. A French nationalist who had been a professional infantry officer in the French Army, he had fought with distinction in the Franco-Prussian War. In the early 1880s he was promoted to colonel and appointed the youngest commanding officer in the French Army. When France planned to invade Madagascar in the late 1880s he transferred to the French Foreign Legion. He saw the Boer War as a chance to avenge the French humiliation by the British known as the 'Fashoda Incident', which occurred in the Sudan in 1898, when the French tried to drive the British from Egypt but were instead comprehensively outmanoeuvred diplomatically by their opponents. He is quoted as saying:

> But she [England] … gave us a Hundred Years' War, and for a hundred years she has robbed the farmers from the Cape. Since then she has violated every peace treaty. Her hatred being even fiercer against the Boer, for there is French blood flowing through their veins.

He had recently been promoted major general and commander of all foreign volunteers fighting for the Boers and, through them, was intent on grinding his anti-British axe. Captain Dawson (OC SRY) tells the story of this action which started on a Sunday with the regiment at leisure in Boshof:

> At about 11 a.m., while our horses were out grazing & and we were all expecting a quiet time we got an order to saddle up immediately in light marching order & take a day's rations; it was noon before we were ready & we [SRY] were then detailed to escort the guns: a battery of which were to go with all the mounted troops here – the guns were late in starting & the others got a considerable start of us but the gunner in command took it fairly easy & we walked & trotted in a S. direction for about 8 miles & then watered our horses – we then went another mile & a half or so and found the others.

Scarbrough added:

> We found them [the Boers] holding a kopje as usual & the mounted troops were ordered to encircle it. The Rangers were told off to escort the guns & the S Notts. were told to work round the left flank of the kopje & cut off the

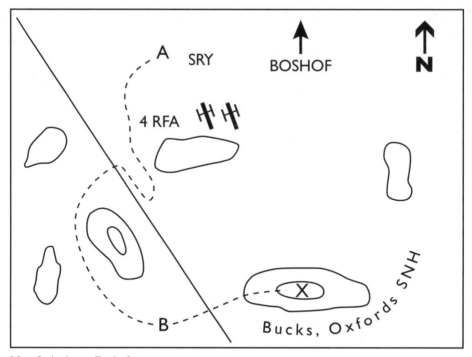

Map 2: Action at Boshof.

enemy's retreat, [which] we succeeded in doing, coming into action at about 700 yards and keeping up a sniping fire for about two hours while the centre and right worked up under cover to assault the hill.

Dawson continued:

We got under cover with the guns at A [see map of the action above] & the gunner went forward to look for a position & I dismounted my men – in about 10 minutes time he returned & I remounted & just then Chesham came up told me to leave the guns & advance in support of a squadron going between the two kopjes I have marked towards B. So we started off in extended files at a canter down the valley ... the Boers began to pot at us & I found 3 & 4 sections bearing away to the right – after going another couple of hundred yards I found Chesham was directing them to go under cover of the right hand kopje & so turned half right & took shelter – so far there was little harm done only three horses hit, all able to go – we dismounted & were then told by a Lt in the KMC ... to take 50 men to the Boer position which had to be stormed.... I sent off Peacock with the remainder of his No. 1 section and Williams with his complete No. 3 they started off along the dotted line dismounted at B where the KMC had a Maxim & then advanced up the slope of the kopje

Peacock took up the narrative:

> We opened out and started towards the kopje and then dismounted and
> marched on and lay down, with the help of a maxim gun on our left which
> covered our advance, we managed to gain the foot of the kopje and get under
> cover of the rocks. Little by little, and rock by rock we wormed our way along,
> waiting for five minutes to collect ourselves and take a ping at any man we saw
> moving. They kept it dropping amongst us, and just before we got halfway
> up and were nearing the wire fence Christian got one through the right thigh
> (only the flesh fortunately, so he is doing well), what I did not like was the
> standing still cutting the wire fence! But we kept going on and turned a bit
> left towards the point of the kopje. When we got about 100 yards from the
> top we fixed bayonets and with a yell charged up to within 30 yards of 'em,
> and they fairly did rattle around us, but fortunately they went high. Then up
> went their white flags, three of them along the ridge. Then came the sad time
> as poor Lt Williams rushed out with Sgt Turner, and the brutes shot them
> both, killing Williams and hitting Turner through the arm. I seized Francis'
> rifle and shot the brute stone dead, but too late to save our pal.

Dawson continued:

> The guns then opened for the first time (Lord Scarbrough commented 'why
> they did not do so before goodness only knows') & a shell landed almost
> among our men but killed Villebois the Boer general – two more shells were
> sent on the kopje and the Boers began to bolt like rats towards the northern
> end & a small kopje there – they were met by more of the yeomen & then
> threw down their arms.

Peacock concluded:

> They then put down their arms and gave up 62 prisoners, seven killed and
> six wounded. Mostly French. We fortunately killed their general.... On him
> we found a minute plan of Boshof, showing the camps and pickets [a picket
> – or picquet – is a small body of troops deployed to provide early warning
> against, or to forestall, an attack] and the whole plan for a night attack on the
> day we came in, so we just forestalled them. We captured their horses and a
> load of dynamite.... I was given charge of the prisoners to start with, and was
> relieved by the Berks.
>
> Our casualties were Lieutenant Williams (Sherwood Rangers), Lieutenant
> Boyle and Sgt Patrick Campbell, both of 10 Imperial Yeomanry killed and
> about 17 wounded.
>
> Lieutenant Boyle of the Buckinghamshire Yeomanry was accorded the
> dubious distinction of being the first yeomanry officer killed in the war.
> This was unfortunate, given he had donated no fewer than thirty horses to

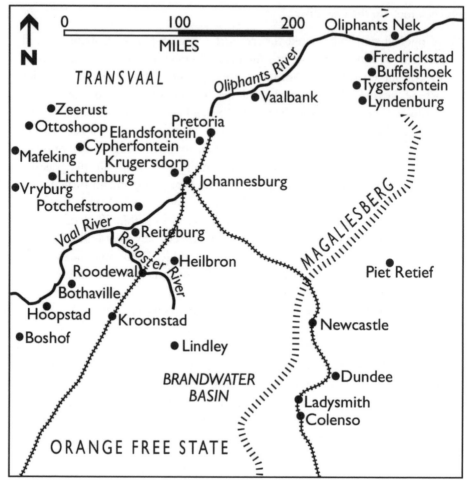

Map 3: Methuen's Area of Operations.

his company. For his gallantry Sergeant G. Turner was recommended for a commission in place of Williams.

Younghusband wrote to Lord Galway from Boshof on 6 April:

As you will have seen from the papers the Sherwood Rangers are covering themselves with glory. The storming of the kopje by Peacock and Williams was very fine & I have especially reported on their gallantry. Very sad poor Williams being killed but he died without pain or sorrow & flushed with the joy of victory.... By lucky coincidence the little action was of considerable value to us for a celebrated general like Villebois is not sent loose with 5 superior officers and a cart of dynamite without some big scheme being on hand. As far as we can make out they were shaping for the Modder bridge and after blowing that up to turn westwards to raise the whole country against us.... The Sherwoods have been doing famously all through, the sections well looked after & well commanded & Dawson commanding the company with great success.

Roberts signalled to Methuen:

Accept my hearty congratulations on your successful performance of yesterday. I am delighted to hear that the Imperial Yeomanry had a chance and that all your troops did so well. The result is most satisfactory.

A Reuters' report dated 9 April observed:

All troops with Lord Methuen are very efficient. The condition of the horses greatly superior to what I have seen elsewhere. The Yeomanry are most careful to save their horses by dismounting upon every opportunity, frequently leading them when marching at a walk. The Yeomanry have set examples to the Regular cavalry in quickly noticing and following the excellent methods of horse management employed by the colonial mounted troops. The yeomanry experiment promises to yield most excellent results. The men are very good and exceedingly well led.

Finally, Peacock wrote to Galway on 10 April:

This last week has been a sad time. That fight was horrible – & poor Job's death has quite unnerved me. I feel miserable – Poor boy he was so plucky & cheery the whole time and we were close together [when he was killed].

I never meet a soul now who does not hate Africa & long to be home again – but I'm afraid we have very much more before us than people think....

Peacock's health deteriorated from this moment. The cause was rheumatism and he was invalided back down the line before the end of April and eventually home to the UK. His war was not over, however, since he became involved with purchasing horses in the United States for service in South Africa and later returned there, but not with the Sherwood Rangers.

This was the first general engagement by a yeomanry unit, and therefore by volunteers, for well over a century. It was almost unique in terms of the war from this point onwards because the British rarely again caught, fought, defeated, captured and forced the surrender of a Boer commando; they always managed to slip away at the last.

Chapter 6

Advance on Pretoria

May–July 1900

On 5 May Roberts completed his ponderous re-supply and was able to recommence his advance on Pretoria. On 6 May, before the Sherwood Rangers left Boshof, Dawson reported to Galway:

I have sent down to hospital altogether 33 men – 14 on their way home invalided. We came in 5 weeks ago 110 strong, yesterday we were 60 all told not counting those on detached duties. If we stay here much longer we will have only horses left. That is what I least expected.... I have 50 spare horses....

Not for long though.

First Division lost out on the task of relieving Mafeking which was given instead to Mahon and his South African irregular Imperial Light Horse, supported by some token British infantry. Mafeking was duly relieved on 17 May. After a ten-day halt at Kroonstad, the advance recommenced, Johannesburg falling to Roberts unopposed on 31 May. On 5 June he was in Pretoria, capital of the Transvaal, which again fell unopposed, thus ending the conventional phase of the war.

The conventional wisdom was that with the fall of Pretoria the war was over, which many took as the cue to return home. Major Joe Laycock was among them, with the consent of French under whom he had seen some action, initially at the siege of Ladysmith. He then took a part in the Battle of Elandslaagte, distinguishing himself by removing the breech-blocks of two Boer guns and bringing them back to the British lines. French was then sent to command a force being assembled on the Orange river to relieve Mafeking and Kimberley and Laycock went with him. He was used by French as a liaison officer to enable French to maintain contact with a number of other commanders, but particularly Lord Roberts, following the latter's arrival in theatre. Roberts was initially based in Cape Town before moving up-country to take command on the ground. This role was said to have involved Laycock in some hair-raising escapades as he sought to evade the Boers on his journeys, which were invariably on horseback. He was awarded a DSO.

The fall of Pretoria might have ended the war but Roberts' corps was too ponderous to lay a glove on the Boer armies who had faded away before him and,

LORD METHUEN'S FORCE IN ACTION: IMPERIAL YEOMANRY DEFEATING THE BOER ATTACK ON THE BRITISH CONVOY NEAR ZWARTKOPJESFONTEIN. (From a sketch by a Correspondent with Lord Methuen's Force.)

because Roberts was incapable of refusing them the choice, opted to slip away into the veldt.

First Division's role during this period was centred on Boshof which they used as their patrol base till mid-May before commencing an advance along the Vaal river on Roberts' left flank and to his rear, via Hoopstad (14 May), Bothaville (24 May), Kroonstad and Potchefstroom (30 May). Third Imperial Yeomanry had continued its patrolling role. Many groups of Boers were also operating in the same area, and skirmishes resulted. The attrition on men and horses from ill health continued; for example, as mentioned, Scarbrough continued in command of 3rd Imperial Yeomanry for much of the period whilst Younghusband was indisposed.

The routine was broken when, on 29 May, Methuen was ordered to march to Lindley, where 13th Imperial Yeomanry was besieged and under severe attack by a much larger Boer force. The 13th was no ordinary unit, being known as the 'Millionaires' Own' because those serving in its companies were particularly wealthy. The correct titles of the companies were: the Duke of Cambridge's Own Imperial Yeomanry, Dublin Hunt and the remaining two were called Belfast. They boasted within their ranks a high number of not just wealthy individuals, but individuals from many of Ireland's titled families. The regiment was commanded by a regular officer, Lieutenant Colonel Basil Spragge.

They were still in the process of travelling up country to join 9th Division under Colvile with the object of adding much needed mobility to an infantry division.

Colvile had sent them a signal to join his division at Lindley. With the imminent fall of Pretoria, the Boer capital, which occurred on 5 June, Lindley had become the new capital and the area was swarming with Boers. However, 9th Division moved from Lindley only hours before 13th Imperial Yeomanry trekked in on 27 May, by which time Lindley had inevitably reverted to Boer control. Thirteenth Imperial Yeomanry attempted to hold the town, but was driven out and took up positions in a row of kopjes. Spragge sent a messenger to Colvile seeking his help. Colvile decided not to change his plans since he was under orders which conflicted with sending elements of his division to assist Spragge. As a result, Roberts gave Methuen the task of relieving Spragge, but this was two days after Colvile had declined, and when 1st Division was two days' march away. This meant a delay totalling four long days before 13th Imperial Yeomanry could be relieved.

Methuen was now showing signs that he was recovering from the humiliation of his earlier setbacks, and demonstrating his excellent command skills. He deployed 1 Yeomanry Brigade to relive 13th Imperial Yeomanry. They reached Lindley on 1 June. It became clear that 13th Imperial Yeomanry had been defeated and had surrendered the night before, despite having fought well. They had taken heavy casualties, including some with very high profiles; the remainder had been taken prisoner by the Boer commando, which had withdrawn from Lindley with their prisoners.

Methuen ordered Chesham's brigade to pursue the commando and Younghusband, now back in command, provided an account of 3rd Imperial Yeomanry's part in the subsequent action. His plan was to overhaul the Boer column carrying the prisoners, using part of 3rd Imperial Yeomanry, leaving the remainder to picket his centre line so as to avoid being cut off:

> With reference to the part taken by the Regiment under my command in action near Lindley on June 1st 1900, I have the honour to report as follows:
>
> 2. At about 1030 a.m. the Brigade was lying about nine miles west of the Lindley-Kroonstad road. Here I received orders from Brigadier General Lord Chesham to follow 10th Yeomanry Regiment in a sweep N and NE round a line of heights between us and Lindley, which scouts had found held by the enemy. At the same time I was to sweep a bit wider than 10th Regiment, and cut the Lindley-Heilbron road. Starting off as directed, we kept sweeping round N to NE on a wider radius of the same sweep which 10th Regiment made on a smaller radius. At 1115 we first came in touch with the enemy holding a kraal on a summit of a hill on our inner flank. I sent a troop [YD] to try the place, and this was driven back, but immediately after a few shells from the Field Battery and Pom-poms drove out the enemy. I immediately pushed in a troop [YD] and occupied it.
>
> 3. At about 12 noon with three squadrons I hit the Lindley-Heilbron road, my fourth squadron [YH] being a mile or so north, protecting our outer flank and working small parties of Boers out of the farms and kopjes.

On the Lindley-Heilbron road we intercepted one of the enemy's ambulances, and took the three doctors on with us as medical assistants.

At the same point we were checked by a very accurate shellfire of two of the enemy's guns, as well as fairly hot fire from riflemen. Captain Dawson, one of the squadron leaders [SRY], was here wounded and several ... men and horses hit. Our fire, both machine guns and rifles at ranges ranging between 500 and 2000 yards, however, shortly drove off the enemy's horsemen and guns, and we continued our advance.

At about 1230 I first caught sight of the enemy's convoy streaming away eastwards, and decided that we should be carrying out the spirit of our instructions by pushing further round and, if possible, intercepting the convoy. At the same time we hoped to cut off two guns and possibly rescue the prisoners.

4. Accordingly, we pressed steadily on, occasionally checked, during one of which Captain Starkey [YD] was wounded and here and there having to leave troops to temporarily protect our flanks, until about 1345 we arrived at an almost precipitous cliff down which there seemed to be no possible means of advance, while further detour would take us very wide of the convoy. From this summit we had a complete and commanding view of the convoy which was passing away eastwards and south-east at great pace. I at once decided to scramble down the cliff as best we could and to cut the convoy at a point which would leave 16 carts and two guns at the rear. After a severe scramble we got to the bottom of the cliff, the operation being covered by the fire of a troop. The descent was a tedious operation, and by the time three troops got down it became apparent that if we were to do anything it must be done at once.

5. These three troops were under Captain Rolleston [SNH] and Lieutenants Sheriffe and H. H. Wilson [both SRY], and I wish to bring to the attention of the Brigadier General the very gallant manner in which these three officers now carried out their instructions. Forming line entire at very wide intervals under cover of a *spruit* bank they charged swiftly up the grassy slope, burst through the convoy at the pre-arranged gap, drove a strong party of Boers out of a kopje just across the road and occupied it. The point where we cut the convoy, it turned out just behind the prisoners of 13th Yeomanry Brigade [sic], and one of them slipped off the cart and came and told us. But they were very strongly guarded and the few men I had with me were incapable of further offensive operations.

The position we now held, though weakly, was an exceedingly commanding one. We had cut off 16 carts and the two guns which were now trekking back towards Lindley and we were practically outside the enemy's line of retreat.

7. Before making our final dash, I had sent an urgent message explaining the situation and pressing for reinforcements, but this message unfortunately missed my own following squadron and arrived at the Brigadier General at a moment when I believe from the wide extended nature of the operations it was impossible for him to send me reinforcements.

8. Our position, though commanding, now became the object of the very close attention of the enemy to our left front. Several hundred rifles poured a heavy fire into us at 500 yards range whilst to our front and right smaller parties galled us considerably.

    Our men, though few, however, fired steadily and accurately and the enemy, beyond wounding one or two men and several horses, made no impression on us.

9. At 1400. I received an order from the Brigade Major Imperial Yeomanry, timed at 1345 p.m., to retire to Lindley.

10. This for my small force had become a very difficult operation, and I would respectfully submit that the conduct of the officers and men who eventually safely executed it is worthy of the highest praise. Pursuing old Afridi tactics, we got off our first kopje by leaving three crack shots, smart men and well horsed, to keep up a tremendous fusillade, whilst the rest of us got to our horses and threaded off as best we could to another position in the rear. The fire was now very heavy from all sides, the Boers having even marked our ranges with cleft sticks and bits of paper and plying it hot on anyone passing there. About this time Captain Rolleston, who had behaved with the greatest gallantry throughout, was severely wounded and several of his men and horses knocked over.

11. The retirement was however conducted with the greatest steadiness by Lieutenant Knowles (who succeeded Captain Rolleston) and H. H. Wilson, each of these officers seizing kopjes to the right and left of the road in succession and covering each other's retirement with admirable coolness. How trying to young troops and young officers the operation was, may be judged from the fact that on several occasions small parties of Boers were well in rear of each party, firing into men and horses at close range.

    To add to the trouble many of the Boers had put on Yeomanry uniforms taken from 13th Regiment and thus took us frequently at great disadvantage.

    Thus steadily retiring, the enemy was gradually beaten off and we marched into Lindley only 25 strong but unmolested. I regret, however, greatly, to say that whilst we had been so hotly engaged by the enemy, with great skill and wonderful knowledge of the country, they had spirited away southward and south-eastward the wagons and guns which we had cut off.

12. I hope I shall be in order in bringing to the notice of the Brigadier General the admirable conduct of all ranks throughout the day, and especially so of the two troops of the South Notts Hussars (No. 12 Squadron) and one troop of the Sherwood Rangers (No. 10 Squadron). No veteran troops could have done better than these.

13. I should like also to bring to his notice the good work done throughout the day by my 2nd in C. Major the Earl of Scarbrough, as well as the extremely gallant behaviour throughout of Captain and Adjutant H. B. Pierce. This very smart and zealous officer was in the forefront of the fighting throughout the day, and he behaved with conspicuous coolness and courage from first to last.

14. Under a separate cover, with the consent of the Brigadier General, I propose bringing to his notice the names of the NCOs and men who distinguished themselves. Our casualties included the three Squadron Commanders – Captain Rolleston, Dawson, and Starkey [on secondment to YD from SNH] – and 23 killed, wounded and missing of our ranks (all men taken prisoner were all wounded or unhorsed). We lost from all causes 44 horses (later found to be 74) including officers' chargers.

The three wounded squadron leaders were replaced next day by Lieutenants Sheriffe (SRY), Simpson (YD), and Birkin (SNH), respectively. Note the change from 'company', the term for an infantry sub-unit to 'squadron', the term for a cavalry sub-unit and likewise 'troop' rather than 'section'. It is clear that, irrespective of how they were described, they were being used in a mobile role much more typical of cavalry than of mounted infantry. On the morning following the action, the Sherwood Rangers and South Notts Hussars were paraded in front of Lord Methuen, who complimented and thanked them for their gallant services.

The following from Captain Dawson's account of the action is notable for amplifications on Younghusband's report and addressed an ambiguity in that report by confirming that he went into the final phases of the action with two SRY troops commanded by Sheriffe and Wilson and one SNH troop commanded by Rolleston. It will be seen later that, according to Sheriffe, there were two troops from each squadron, bringing out the point that both SRY and SNH were under strength; throughout this campaign 3rd Imperial Yeomanry, in common with most other units, seldom went into action at better than 50 per cent of establishment. This may explain why Younghusband was unclear how many troops from each squadron were with him. Finally the parts of his report covering other than operational matters described graphically the problems with obtaining the resources the regiment needed to survive:

I think you will be pleased at the way in which 3rd IY and more particularly 10th Squadron [SRY] behaved on the 1st inst., and daresay some particulars will appear in the papers, but like all such successes we have had to pay for it & the SR share of it is 1 killed 8 wounded and 1 missing, the latter being my SM [Sergeant Major], Cottle [captured but released ten months later]: I am myself laid on the shelf for the time by a shot which went right through my knee cap from the front sideways without however breaking anything or touching the joint.…

[On being wounded I realized] I had no bones broken I got helped up on my horse & went on a short way but found I could not stand the trotting so I had to come on slowly, and a quarter of a mile further on we were fired on by a gun.… I followed on but could not manage to get any further so came into the town [Lindley] which was then occupied by our men: went to the nearest hospital.

I was very sorry to hear of the loss of Tomlinson: he was one of our very best men & a most efficient NCO. I hear his horse was shot during the retirement & he started to run & would not stop when called on, so they shot him – I hope & believe it was a painless death as he was shot right through the chest probably through the heart. Two of our men were not brought in till the next day, but the Boers had looked after them & made them comfortable. Starkey was shot through the toe of his boot, the bullet cutting two of his toes & lodging in the ball of his big toe – it was got out on the spot & I think he'll not be long getting right: I am sharing a room at the hotel here with him in a bed!!! The first I have seen since the *Winifredian*, quite a strange experience, & we are just in clover, though there is no sugar in the town: it has been occupied 8 times in the last month & the landlord a Scotch Boer doesn't half like it.

Rolleston is also here; his shot struck him behind the left shoulder blade, travelled along his back & broke his right arm: they feared it was serious at first, but the Dr now says he is likely to do well.

Our draft has never arrived & our fellows are ragged to a degree & I can't get money to pay them, I may be able to get something done here but without an SM pay sheets are awkward things: for the present Turner is acting SM. Your telegrams about the Boshof skirmish never reached us, nor have we got the tobacco etc. Lady Galway so kindly sent, perhaps we never shall as the last account we had of the draft was that the IYs at Maitland were trying to collar them, officer & men – Please remember me to Lady Galway who is I hope well.

This reflects badly on the chaotic personnel management and re-supply capabilities of a professional army.

Lieutenant Bertie Sheriffe assumed command of the Sherwood Rangers in place of Captain Dawson. In his first report home to Galway on 2 July he described the action at Lindley.

I have been in command since the time Dawson got shot. Our Rangers behaved splendidly all through that long day. At the finish our forces with Colonel Younghusband consisted of 2 troops Sherwoods and 2 troops South Notts. & we were fighting from 11.a.m. to 5 p.m. None of us had drunk anything all day. Lord Methuen came round my lines on Sunday following & complimented the squadron on the good day's work which was satisfactory.

Turner has now got his commission.

All in good health but I can muster only 38 on parade and only 10 horses left of those we brought out.

With the whole division concentrated in Lindley the town was secure, even though the hills around were alive with Boers. At this point, further reinforcements, 3,000 led by Douglas, brought the division up to a strength of 11,000.

The surrender of 13th Imperial Yeomanry was seized on by those opposed to the concept of use of volunteers, but *The Times* produced a more balanced summary:

Thus through the astonishing gallantry of one regiment [no more than 100 strong when in contact] were the captive 13th nearly rescued from the midst of 3,500 Boers under de Wet ... [who] a few days afterwards, in conversation with a British officer, confessed that he had never had such a *mauvais quart d'heure* during the campaign, and his staff confessed that his casualties had been heavy. The misfortune of one Yeomanry Regiment on one day was therefore gallantly balanced by the intrepid bravery of another yeomanry regiment on the next.

A letter to *The Times* compared Colvile's response to Spragge's request for help with Methuen's, the one being to do nothing even though only eighteen miles distant, whereas the other:

started in half an hour ... and marched 44 miles in 25 hours.... On these facts I offer no judgement, but in common with others who this disaster has touched, I submit the case for an enquiry has been made out....

There was indeed a court of enquiry, which sat on 25 September 1900, but into Spragge's actions, not Colvile's. This exonerated Spragge and found the capture of the 13th to have been a 'chance of war'. However, that was not an end to the matter since Colvile was eventually sacked by Roberts, in part due to this incident, so, for those most aggrieved by it, justice was done.

Between 4 and 6 June General Christiaan de Wet executed a series of daring raids on Roberts' re-supply columns and supply dumps. The least significant was the destruction of Colvile's re-supply echelon, leaving the division cut off without rations at Heilbron. On 5 June, Methuen, having received orders to do so, marched once again to Colvile's assistance. After several skirmishes, the two formations linked up on 7 June, much to the relief of 9th Division, which had been without rations for two days. It was 1st Division's yeomanry, Sherwood Rangers and South Notts Hussars, who were providing the forward screen at the time, and who made the breakthrough that brought Colvile relief.

De Wet's raids had inflicted far greater damage than the destruction of a divisional supply column. His main objective was a massive supply dump at Roodewal railway station, holding ammunition of all calibres for all weapon types. The contents of the dump had been delayed there pending repair of the bridge over the Rhenoster river. The raid resulted in the capture of as much re-supply as de Wet could carry and the destruction of the remainder.

First Division was ordered to intercept de Wet. Advancing through Kroonstad, they came up with the Boer general, commanding a large formation, on 11 June at the Rhenoster river. It was a significant action for 3rd Imperial Yeomanry. Birkin wrote:

> This was the beginning of a general action. The mounted troops were sent out skirmishing on either flank, the guns opened fire from the centre upon the strong position held by the Boers, while Chesham advanced with 5th and 10th Regiments to the left flank in order to silence the Boer 15-pounder. After the engagement had been some time in progress, Younghusband was ordered with 3rd Regiment to cross to the right flank to the support of Spens and his force; there he immediately saw the possibility of turning the Boer left flank and galloped to the position and engaged them. At this point 10th (SRY) and 11th (QOYD) squadrons were for some time very heavily and accurately shelled, but on keeping up a persistent fire they succeeded eventually in driving the enemy back onto their own guns.... The guns of the division accurately shelled the whole of the Boer position, thus contributing largely to their ultimate disorderly retirement.

Younghusband added:

> the Yeomen even under this severe ordeal were by no means dismayed & continued to hold the position gained tenaciously and ply such of the enemy as were still in range with rifle fire.

He then withdrew to the railway line because the regiment was too weak to push on across the open against 'such large mounted bodies of the enemy'.

Dawson sent his last report to Galway on 18 July:

> We were practically besieged in Lindley for four weeks.
>   The draft you sent out turned up in Lindley slightly before we left having been unable to join the Regt.... The Regt was only about 180 strong and wandering about with Methuen in an aimless sort of way in the triangle between Kroonstad, Heilbron and Lindley.

Or, as Methuen would have put it, the division spent the remainder of June patrolling that section of Roberts' lines of re-supply through the Orange Free State. Within the Yeomanry Brigade the opportunity was taken for Chesham to be given leave of absence, while Lord Scarbrough was called back to the UK on urgent business. Third Imperial Yeomanry, on coming upon one of the largest stud farms in the country during this phase, took the opportunity to bring itself up to strength in horses.

When Dawson had been invalided home to England, he wrote again to Galway about what he had seen whilst returning to Cape Town at this time:

> The amount of stores of all sorts delayed at McKinley's must be seen to be believed, thousands of pounds have been spent which will do absolutely no good to those for whom they were intended. I suppose the difficulties of transit account for this but I can't help thinking there's also some considerable want of management.

Chapter 7

Pursuit of Steyn and de Wet

July–August 1900

Roberts' next vital objective, following the formal surrender of the Boers, was to capture Steyn and de Wet, who had refused to stop fighting. Steyn was President of the Orange Free State and its outstanding leader. Christiaan de Wet was fast achieving folk hero status, as again and again he appeared to swoop down on the British, inflict real damage and disappear. In fact, he wasn't the dashing character that his actions implied; his secrets were the old staples of careful planning and preparation, which he applied probably better than any other commander on either side. As to his personal qualities, he was described as 'blunt, charmless and brutal'.

Roberts diverted virtually all the troops under his direct command to the task, indicating the priority he gave it. Hamilton, Roberts' favourite commander, had broken his collar-bone during the final advance on Pretoria, so he gave the job of bringing Steyn and de Wet to book to Major General Sir Archibald Hunter, Buller's Chief of Staff, who had excelled during the siege of Ladysmith. In July Roberts sent Hunter in pursuit of Steyn and de Wet and their 8,000 Boer supporters who had holed up in the Brandwater Basin, backed up against the border with Basutoland. This neighbouring territory was a no-go area to the Boers.

In addition to his own column numbering 2,000, Hunter had under command 8th, 12th, 20th and 21st Divisions, all minus detachments guarding centre lines and lines of supply. A third of the enemy slipped through his net before it could be closed, but Hunter pressed on. The rest surrendered at the end of July, at which point Hunter discovered, to his annoyance, that Steyn and de Wet had led the group that had earlier slipped through his lines. The capture and surrender of such a large body of Boers in the Brandwater Basin turned out to be a pyrrhic victory. Those who surrendered, although greatest in number, were least committed to the fight; the 2,000 who had evaded Hunter with Steyn and de Wet were committed to fighting on.

Methuen's column, still smaller than a full division, but including Chesham's brigade as its key element, had not been involved with Hunter. It continued on its old tasks defending the lines of communication to Pretoria and the rear areas within the Orange Free State. However, following the escape of Steyn and de Wet, there was a change of role to that of an offensive column. It was, as a result, re-deployed by train north of the Vaal into the Transvaal, west of Johannesburg, to the area of Krugersdorp, and quickly refitted with new uniforms, horses and supplies.

As soon as Methuen's column was ready to move, it recommenced operations. Immediately it came into contact with, and engaged, a strong Boer body but not that led by Steyn and de Wet, who were resting up for two weeks at Reitzburg. Having made contact with the Boer commando, Methuen pressed it hard on a daily basis along a line northward towards the Magaliesberg Mountains and Oliphants Nek, the only pass through the Magaliesbergs. The commando was brought to action at Oliphants Nek on 22 July. It was part of a plan, the other half of which was that Baden Powell and his column would be lying in ambush on the far side of the nek, when Methuen drove the Boer commando through.

Younghusband reported on the action:

2. At about 0800 a.m. I received an order from one of Lord Methuen's Staff Officers to move the regiment up alongside the pom-poms, a few hundred yards in front.

   As we arrived abreast of the enemy he opened with his guns & I took my regiment into the scrub to the left front of the battery and dismounted.

3. To our front & 500 yards distant, a spur from the main range to the left ran into the valley, and on this we noticed a small party of horsemen, five or six belonging to our forces. Just as we dismounted, a hot fire was opened on this party & it retired, leaving a horse on top of the ridge.

4. Considering the occupation of this point very necessary, I at once sent forward a squadron with instructions to dismount & retake the position. This duty was promptly effected by Lieutenant Wombwell with the Yorkshire Hussar Squadron, his dispositions being admirably made.

5. The squadron, during the operation & subsequent retention of the spur, came under a very hot & accurate fire from a party of above 20 of the enemy, who held a commanding position from 800 to 1,000 yards distant, & Lieutenant R. B. Wilson was dangerously wounded & two men (one belonging to 10th Reg.) were severely wounded.

An assault by infantry took place on the position that was inflicting such damage on the Yorkshire Hussars as Birkin recalled:

It was on this occasion that the Yeomanry first had the opportunity of witnessing a regular infantry advance. Absolutely cool and determined, as if the affair was the most ordinary thing in the world, the men of the 'Fighting 5th' advanced in open order – an unfaltering line of valour – and drove the Boers helter-skelter into the trees beyond.

Younghusband continued:

6. At about 11 a.m. the action of 5th Fusiliers, who had now taken the main range to our left, relieving the pressure on Lieutenant Wombwell's squadron, & I ordered him to rejoin the regiment & advance with the rest of the force.

7. At about 12 noon, as we were standing extended 400 yards to the left of the guns, we received orders from Lord Chesham to support 10th regiment, which was to make a dash at the Nek up to 2½ miles distant.

8. Moving down to the low ground & scrub to our front at a trot, we moved as fast as possible through very rough country towards the pass. On emerging from this we noticed 10th Regiment dismounted at the edge of the scrub to our right. To our front lay a perfectly open and level stretch of about a mile to a low kopje lying between us and the Nek.

   I sent one troop [SRY] rapidly forward to turn this by the left, another [SNH] to turn it by the right, and when these were well under way, one to cover my advance towards it.

   Finding the kopje unoccupied, we pushed rapidly across the open ground and seized it. Another mile of perfectly open country now lay between us and the Nek. After carefully scanning the crest with glasses, I pushed the three troops, as previously arranged, forward, & drawing no fire, moved quickly forward & seized the pass on both sides of the road.

9. On arriving, we could see no sign of the enemy, but in the woody country below & about 3 miles distant, we saw General Baden Powell's mounted troops.

Clearly, Baden Powell had failed to get his stops in place in time. The Boers were away and free.

Steyn and de Wet now broke cover and trekked north for the Vaal with a force numbering 2,500. On 28 July 3rd and 10th Imperial Yeomanries, but particularly the Sherwood Rangers and South Notts Hussars, found themselves in a running battle at Vaalbank with a large force of Boers, whom they never identified, but were almost certainly Steyn and de Wet's men. They put the Boers under huge pressure, and would have inflicted a heavy defeat had there not been women and children amongst them. This made the yeomanry hold back. This was a tactic the enemy used shamelessly on a number of occasions. Although the Boers escaped as a result, at least their well-prepared and deliciously hot meal, no doubt prepared by the women, did not. Captured intact, it was consumed with genuine delight. A stomach full of a hot fresh meal was a rare prize, almost above victory in this war of attrition.

Steyn and de Wet crossed into the Transvaal on 6 August and Hunter's pursuit recommenced. This time the columns deployed included Methuen's 1st Division, representing a significant moment of rehabilitation of the division as a first-ranking formation. It had developed a considerable reputation in protecting Roberts' rear areas and lines of re-supply, and had in the process earned some complimentary nicknames such as the 'Mobile Marvels' and the 'Mudcrushers', because of their ability to cover large distances, and 'The Salvation Army' and 'Beechams', soldiers' humour for 'relieving' so many towns and garrisons.

At this stage it consisted of 9 Infantry Brigade and Chesham's 1 Imperial Yeomanry Brigade with four yeomanry regiments. Methuen's handling of his yeomanry, which was of a very high standard, was key to his success, and the yeomanry were lucky to have him. His understanding of how to command volunteers had been crucial, enabling him to support and train them and give them confidence. He never patronized them, and used them to the full, but obviously understood the limit of their capability. Nor was he a remote commander. Birkin wrote, 'Lord Methuen working like a trooper (literally) to try and get a wagon over the spruit'; not bad for a man of 55. Finally, 3rd Imperial Yeomanry was clearly one of the most effective regiments in the brigade, judged by the number of times it was given the lead.

The other two columns involved in this phase were commanded by Kitchener and Smith-Dorrien, the three columns, totalling 12,000 men, being under Kitchener's overall control.

De Wet and Steyn were making towards Oliphants Nek, which was about to become significant once more. A fourth column of 8,000, under Major General Sir Ian Hamilton, who had recovered from his broken collar bone, had been ordered to block the pass. This was to be a key operation involving the best commanders in the British Army, and its best formations, other than those under Buller. Roberts described its importance:

> I shall be greatly disappointed if de Wet and Steyn manage to escape. Hunter's successes in the Brandwater Basin and the flight of de Wet and Steyn over the Vaal practically closes the war so far as the Orange River Colony is concerned. The new operation ... is an intensely interesting and exciting operation, rendered more so by the great size of the country and the extraordinary mobility of the Boers, who manage to slip away in the most marvellous manner.

Methuen was best placed to intercept the Boers because he was already north of the Vaal. However, he was moved by Kitchener from a perfect blocking position covering the main crossing point, which, in fact, de Wet used shortly afterwards, to another farther downstream. Kitchener then also mis-deployed the other columns so that they were out of position, leaving Methuen's command as the only one remotely in contact with de Wet, but pursuing him instead of being in his path. They caught him at Tygersfontein on 7 August in the hills along the Vaal. Methuen moved out at first light, 3rd Imperial Yeomanry not only leading but also providing both flank screens, and reinforced by a composite squadron, making five in all. The Yorkshire Hussars were protecting the left flank which they achieved by moving onto and holding a line of heights which commanded in enfilade a complete view of all the ground relevant to this action out to eight or ten miles. The regiment came into contact with de Wet at 0700. He was holding a line of kopjes on their right flank and opened fire. Younghusband reported:

> I opened Maxim fire at 1,900 yards on the kopje and sent word to Lieut Simpson [SNH] to outflank & gradually shift the enemy from his position. This duty, under cover of guns & Maxim fire was admirably executed by Lieut Doxat [later to earn a VC] & a portion of … the Yorkshire Dragoons. Lieut Doxat's movements were indeed so smart that we could see some fifty of the enemy hustled off the first kopje being unexpectedly taken in flank & rear. After a few shells had been planted on it the next kopje was then easily captured….
>
> The further advance of the column was now open but after proceeding about a mile the advance squadron under Lieut Birkin [SNH] was brought to a standstill by enemy positions facing and flanking at from 2,000 to 400 yards. At the same time the right-flank squadron was checked by a hot fire from a rocky ridge to the right flank. Lieut Birkin made two attempts to push on and again a third attempt supported by a squadron of 5th Imperial Yeomanry but on each occasion found the ground so open and the enemy's position so unsuitable for a mounted or dismounted attack, that he wisely refrained from persisting.

At 1020, as Birkin's attacks were being resisted, the Yorkshire Hussars reported a body of 200 horsemen about four or five miles distant moving at a great pace north-north-east. Later they reported that nineteen more men issued from the hills and headed in the same direction. The Yorkshire Hussars were certain these were the only enemy that withdrew before nightfall. It became clear later that this was Steyn and de Wet and their close protection. At 1100 Methuen ordered elements of his infantry to attack the rocky ridge to the right which was key to the position. Chesham ordered Younghusband to detach the Sherwood Rangers and Yorkshire Dragoons to support the infantry in the dismounted role. It soon became apparent that this combined infantry and yeomanry attack was having the desired effect and an attack by the regiment to capture the rocky kopje, which had stopped them three times, was feasible. Younghusband ordered forward two squadrons of SNH led by Lieutenant Birkin, and the composite squadron, to capture the feature, supported by covering machine-gun fire. Birkin made a right-handed mounted sweep, then dismounted and attacked successfully the twenty or thirty enemy who still held on. But with Steyn and de Wet gone, Methuen would have to start all over again the next day.

Methuen next made contact with Steyn and de Wet on 8 August, having received reports of their location and detached Chesham with the 3rd, 5th, and 10th Imperial Yeomanries under command; as a fully-mounted formation, they could move much faster than his main column. Chesham trekked north-north-east, 3rd Imperial Yeomanry leading, and, by noon on 9 August, and undetected, was within three miles of de Wet's rearguard astride the pass at Buffelshoek where the main party had laagered after Tygersfontein, but had marched from that location earlier to get ahead. Following their midday halt, the regiment prepared to attack this much larger force as quickly as possible, whilst the factor of surprise was with them. Third Imperial Yeomanry was still leading.

Major Gascoigne [YH], the regimental second-in-command, recorded:

> we trotted some three miles towards the enemy. A range stretched all along their left flank, and it was obvious that possession of this was of the utmost importance. So we kept to the left so as to head them off.
>
> The first kopje we came to was taken by a rush, one troop of the Yorkshire Dragoons under Sergt Fox almost galloping onto the enemy.
>
> We dismounted under fire & drove them off.
>
> Colonel Younghusband at once ordered all the dismounted men of the two squadrons we had with us ... Yorkshire Hussars and South Notts. Hussars, the other squadrons were away on other duties, to double on as fast as possible to the next kopje half a mile further on.

Younghusband reported:

> I at once dashed in at the enemy's front with ... the two sqns having dismounted under a friendly wave of ground 30 yards from the enemy, [and we were] over into them before they could blow their noses. Such a scene of confusion you never saw, some looking this way some that, some running, some standing bewildered & all wondering what the deuce was happening. We gave them a rare peppering as you may imagine and accounted for a good many.

Unfortunately, Younghusband was wounded in the leg whilst crossing the open ground.

> I was too badly hit to go on myself but the Sherwoods and [Dragoons] coming up, I sent on Major Gascoigne [who took command] to push home the success. I believe we captured 6 wagons and a lot of ammunition, 900 sheep & odds and ends of prisoners.

There was no time to lose if the kopje on the enemy's left flank, which formed the vital ground in relation to this position, was to be secured and Gascoigne reacted quickly to ensure this was achieved. With the Boers denied a position from which to delay and defend and with the Sherwood Rangers and Yorkshire Dragoons arriving, having been released from their attachments at Tygersfontein, the action turned into a race for each of a line of five more kopjes, all of which were taken by the regiment, leaving Steyn and de Wet's rearguard in full retreat. Chesham and Methuen joined the action at 1600. The Boers' screen had been broken and, although exhaustion prevented pursuit, accurate artillery fire was brought to bear on the retreating enemy column. The brigade laagered at 1700.

The pursuit continued and, on 12 August, a final push was made to catch de Wet. Methuen left his infantry at Frederikstad and continued with his yeomanry, who were lightly equipped. De Wet took a more westerly route which enabled Methuen to cut him off at Syferbult where the Boers were engaged again and forced to abandon a captured field gun. However, this was all in vain since Steyn and de Wet once again managed 'to slip away in the most marvellous manner' as Lord Roberts had put it.

Birkin wrote:

Every endeavour was made to cut off de Wet and surround him at Oliphants Nek where Hamilton was thought to be in position to bar his progress. This march was the most trying that had been undertaken throughout the guerrilla campaign, the column only halting one hour in forty-eight. Men were dropping from saddles from sheer inability to keep awake. It was so disheartening to find on arrival at the Nek that Ian Hamilton had failed and that de Wet and his convoy had passed through a few hours before.

The Times of 31 August reported:

Every column in the District which knew of Lord Methuen's pursuit was loud in its praise of him. And it is not too much to say that nothing could have exceeded his zeal and generalship. He was untiring in his efforts. Shortness of food and forced marches both by night and by day were counted as nothing. No movement of de Wet's was left unchecked, and to Lord Methuen alone belongs the credit of having got the Boer army, a force far exceeding his own, into a corner from which, save through the mistake of others, there was no escape.

Lord Methuen speaks very highly of the behaviour of the Yeomanry, whose courage and determination have given them a place amongst the best and bravest. In all Lord Methuen marched 84 miles in three days, besides fighting on 12th, and having already marched and fought on 7th, 9th and 10th; in all 160 miles and four fights in eight days....

It should be emphasized that in every action so far described in this account the yeomanry were outnumbered by a factor of two or three.

The reason Hamilton was not covering the Nek was that he had simply failed to cover enough ground. He had achieved but thirty miles in the same period as Methuen covered eighty-four miles and de Wet forty-five. Birkin's anger at what was considered to be Hamilton's failure to carry out his clear orders was widely shared all the way up the chain of command to Kitchener. Only Roberts did not blame him, which was seen as favouritism. It has since been said that de Wet did not pass though Olifants Nek, he used a crossing said to be fit only for baboons, and so Hamilton should be absolved, but that explanation can only have referred to Seyn, de Wet and their rearguard which they had handled so well against Methuen. His main party and wagon train, which also contained his womenfolk, had, according to Birkin, crossed through the Nek. So had Hamilton obeyed his orders and been there to prevent them from doing so, that may well have been sufficient to discourage those who now trekked again on the back of his escape, from doing so.

Younghusband's wound ended his command of the regiment. He wrote:

> in vacating command of the Regiment, I wish to offer to all ranks my heartiest thanks for the support and assistance I have received from all ranks. The record of the Regiment during the Boer War is one which the oldest Corps might be proud of, and none will look back on it with greater pride and affection towards 3rd Imperial Yeomanry and all who compose it than myself.

He was rightly appointed CB for his tour of command. Major R. F. T. Gascoigne, Yorkshire Hussars, was confirmed in command of the regiment, taking over a strength of 191 compared to 500 when 3rd Imperial Yeomanry landed in South Africa.

Methuen's column was withdrawn to recuperate and refit, their greatest problem being a shortage of horses. They were ordered to Mafeking which they reached on 28 August, staying there in a tented camp, a luxury unknown for many weeks, till 8 September when they marched out, operational once more.

Before they did so Captain Bertie Sheriffe, commanding the Sherwood Rangers, wrote a report to Lord Galway, dated 7 September:

> We came here 9 days ago after our endeavour to catch de Wet which unfortunately we didn't. Not Methuen's or our fault, some *terrible* blunder, troops withdrawn from Oliphants Nek unknown to us & de Wet got through & so escaped after all our hard work of 10 days, little sleep or food fought him 5 times in 8 days and our gallant Colonel wounded … such a nice letter from him yesterday thanking *all men* and officers for their work….
>
> Before we got here [I] had 17 men walking, had to shoot most of the horses, now we have got practically remounted on Frescan ponies, very good sorts, but very soft and no condition & I fear I can only raise 40 men on parade.

Chapter 8

Guerrilla Warfare

September–December 1900

T he war was at a crossroads. The conventional phase was over with the enemy's capitals and commercial and industrial heartlands captured. However, the lamentable and repeated failure to capture Steyn and de Wet gave the Boers such self-confidence and resolve that many, who had given up and gone home, saddled up and trekked again. So, instead of the guerrilla campaign forming a mere short-lived footnote, it became one of its most notable and memorable features, prolonging the war for almost two more years.

The *Official History* describes this phase:

> The Boers operated from no base and towards no objective, [their] victories lay in escapes, and in the length of time during which [they] could remain untrapped. Who could never be said to advance or retire, but merely to move, now this way now that, [their] tactics rendered unfathomable, either by utter lack or rapid change of purpose.

What made this remarkable was that it was achieved with no, or only very basic, access to any formal structured process of re-supply. In its way, it was a heroic campaign, fought by people as hard as nails, for whom, literally, no sacrifice was too great. The British retaliated by subdividing divisions into columns, which hunted the elusive commandos, gradually refining tactics by occupying the towns the Boers liked to use as temporary refuges. They built blockhouses along the railways to entrap commandos in smaller areas of country, thus making it easier to catch them. They burned homesteads and, most controversially, removed those who re-supplied the Boers from their homesteads into camps which were administered so negligently that disease took hold and casualties and global opprobrium resulted.

The other effect of this new phase was that the strategy and purpose of the high command on both sides and what was happening on the ground began to separate with grand design on the one hand and improvisation on the other. British high-level strategy developed into securing peace as quickly as possible by negotiation, made difficult by inability to agree what terms to offer. So far as the Boers were concerned, that part of their national leadership which the British tried to negotiate with was not in contact with their commandos, so they neither knew where their generals were, nor had sustainable means of communication with them.

On 8 September, Methuen's column, once again operational, started to trek. It was destined to continue virtually nonstop till 16 December, as Birkin describes:

> Very little impedimenta were allowed, even blankets being forbidden, and the consequent result to the men was one of harrowing discomfort. When it is considered that the column was marching at a level of 4,000 feet above the sea, it will be apparent that the situation was by no means an enviable one. To lie week after week on the hard frosty unsympathetic ground, as the men of Lord Methuen's column had done, with scanty food – and sometimes none at all – is a challenge to which any man might show the white feather, and it is to be feared that many people at home did not realize to the full the hardships that were being endured for them.

Methuen endured the same privations as his men. He realized that the weight carried by horses was the critical factor if he was to close with the Boer commandos and, such was the respect in which he was held, his yeomanry endured the resultant privations. Their task was to harry and bring to book the elusive commando led by General Christiaan de Wet, and therefore the area of their operations was west and north-west of Johannesburg, and north of a line Mafeking-Johannesburg, mostly in West Transvaal.

On 26 September Captain Sheriffe resigned the command of the Sherwood Rangers squadron. His health had not held up. Lieutenant Wilson, the only one of the original five officers who deployed from the UK still with the squadron, was appointed to command in his place. In his first report to Lord Galway, Wilson wrote:

> There are a good many Boers on commando in the Lichtenburg district. De la Rey & Lessamer are the principle agitators, and are showing a good deal of fight.
>
> I am still acting Adjutant … so Turner is the only officer with the Sherwoods at present.

On 19 October 5th Imperial Yeomanry supported by 3rd Imperial Yeomanry were ambushed when trying to cut off the enemy's retreat. Fifth Imperial Yeomanry suffered heavy losses, including seventy horses, when advancing at the gallop through a cornfield which had been interlaced with barbed wire. A quick riposte by the division's infantry and artillery restored the position. Little then happened so far as 3rd Imperial Yeomanry was concerned from 20 October onwards, the division being inactive at Otto's Hoop. The reason for the sudden lack of activity is that their enemy had gone to ground at Cypherfontein in the Zwartruggen Hills nearby. There a meeting took place, starting on 20 October, between Botha, President of the Free State, and Steyn, who at that point succeeded Kruger as President of the Transvaal. It was also attended by de la Rey. De Wet was to attend, but did not arrive before it had to break up prematurely. The conference was held to discuss future plans. Only two decisions were taken, the first to fight on, and the second an embryonic plan to stop the farm-burning by carrying the fight into Natal and the Cape, and thus away from the ground where their own farms were positioned.

Field Marshal Lord Roberts handed over command to General Lord Kitchener in November and, having declared the war as 'practically over', a mere eighteen months early as it turned out, returned to England to succeed Wolseley as Commander-in-Chief in January 1901.

Chesham, who had been invalided home, wrote:

> No men can have done better than the men of the First Brigade, and I shall always feel the greatest pride and pleasure at having had the very happy and honourable association with the good men of the various Counties who have formed the Brigade.

He had in turn served them well.

On 26 November the division was at Lichtenburg, a charming small town about fifty miles south-east of Mafeking, and 150 miles due west of Johannesburg, which, it should be remembered, was home to de la Ray. The occupation denied the local commandos, led by de la Ray from using the town. The division stayed, with only minor excursions, till 19 December. Third Imperial Yeomanry was actually based at de la Rey's farm on the Mafeking road, about two miles north of the town. However, fighting continued elsewhere.

On 13 December Wilson reported to Galway from de la Rey's farm:

> This is a very nice place and we are in one of the best farmhouses in the country. It belongs to General de la Rey who is fighting round here.
>
> We had one or two days fighting before coming here. The last day we caste in with a small column, under Colonel Money. The Boers made quite a lively attack on our convoy.... The regiment is very much split up now, as one squadron, Yorkshire Dragoons is down near Vryburg, and the South Notts at Otto's Hoop, and the remainder here.

A Loose End

One loose end is the manner of Villebois's death. Legend has it he was killed by the first shell fired by the gunner battery, which is validated by this correspondence:

Loues Farm
Mafeking

Nov. 15th [1900]
Lord Galway

Sir

In a batch of papers which have been sent up to the outpost mess from camp I find a piece of news published in *Nottingham Daily Guardian* about the shell which was found on the coppice after the Boshof fight.... After the Boers had been disarmed & a guard put over them the rest of the Sherwoods were told off to search the kopje for wounded. In doing so I came across the shell it being the first shell we had seen & heard explode. I thought I would take it as a curio.... We had it in No.1. tent for a considerable time after that when it disappeared. The next I can learn about it is that it has arrived at Greatford with Lieutenant Peacock. It seems Lieutenant Peacock had occasion to go into our tent & took a fancy to it. He asked about it & finally the men gave it to him, I being in hospital at the time.

Believe me to be

Yours Respectfully
J. .... Nist?
817 Sherwood Rangers
10th 3rd IY, S.A.

The following piece of news, which appeared in the papers in the autumn of 1900, then triggered the correspondence which follows:

The shell which killed Colonel Villebois de Mareuil, near Boshof, is on view for ten days at 42, South Audley Street, W. It has been mounted as a trophy on an ebony base and is to be presented to Lord Galway and the officers of the Sherwood Rangers contingent of Imperial Yeomanry to commemorate their first engagement.

WAR OFFICE   10/10/1900

My dear Galway
The enclosed announcement – for which I am sure you are not responsible – strikes me as being in bad taste. A suitable commemorative of the first engagement of your gallant corps will be regarded by everyone as appropriate but I don't think it should commemorate the death of Villebois or be, so to speak, decorated with his scalp.

May I suggest that in any further public references the personal matter should be kept in the background?

This is friendly & unofficial.

Yours sincerely,
Lansdowne

My dear Lansdowne, Oct.23.1900
Your letter is the first I had seen or heard of the paragraph on the shell. The para. reads very like the concoction of the reporter and the tradesman with a view to advertising the latter's shop and getting people to go to it. Of course, as you will know in these days of sensational paragraphs and sensational headings, it is impossible for me in any way to control what may appear in

the press. I do not even know who is having the shell mounted as a trophy for the Regiment.

As for this Villebois Mareuil, there was a very strong feeling all over the county, which has in no way died out, of repugnation at Lord Methuen having put a monument up to him. ...

Remaining yours very truly

Galway

My dear Galway, 24/10
Thanks for your letter.

Please see yesty's *Daily Express* for a picture, and description of the trophy.

Even if we are to agree with you that too much honour was done to Villebois de Mareuil after his death it surely would not follow that in order to correct a fault on one side, it was desirable to commit one on the other.

Yours inf

L

To Lord Galway
My Lord, October 24th
The shell we are mounting for your Lordship in now complete. May we ask the favour of keeping it a few days on view at our establishment, there being so much interest attached to it?

Should you require it at once, it shall be forwarded.

Thanking you in anticipation.

I am My Lord
Yours Obliged Servant
pro *J Machmichael*

My dear Lansdowne, October 25. 1900
I don't take in the *Express* but will try and see it.... It could have been a mistake for me to send another paragraph hunting after the first through the papers, as it could only have called greater attention to it, and I think you will agree in this....

Besides which what could I have written on the matter. I could not say the shell did not kill Villebois Mareuil, as it is stated it did so, & I know no more. I certainly could not say I was sorry one of our shells had killed an enemy of the Queen & country. It is what shells are meant to do, and the only regret is that the percentage that did was not greater! ...

Remaining
Yours sincerely
Galway

However, did the shell explode and kill Villebois? The marriage, for the first time, of the following accounts of the action offers a different explanation:

> Then up went their white flags, three of them along the ridge [wrote Peacock].
> … Williams rushed out with Sgt Turner, and the brutes shot them both, killing Williams dead and hitting Turner through the arm. I seized Francis' rifle and shot the brute [note the singular] stone dead,… .

An Internet account of Villebois's death states: 'During his last minutes he shot two or three with his pistol, stood up during the battle to encourage his men, and was shot in the back.'

This implies that Villebois shot Williams and Turner whilst flying a flag of surrender and Peacock shot Villebois in response. Was the story of the shell a diversion from one in which it could be said that Peacock shot Villebois whilst Villebois was flying a flag of surrender which, if true, could have had serious consequences for all concerned?

The shell exists to this day and is on display at the Sherwood Rangers' museum at Thoresby. At the very least it is a relic of the first general engagement by volunteers in modern times. Volunteers contributed decisively to the winning for Britain of most of her wars of the twentieth century, so the shell represents a significant moment in history.

Chapter 9

Lichtenburg

December 1900–March 1901

On 19 December Methuen's column became mobile once more, but retained responsibility for garrisoning Lichtenburg and its environs. Methuen left a garrison consisting of 1st Battalion Northumberland Fusiliers, with about 400, from 1st Division's 9 Brigade; 100 Paget's Horse under Major Paget; twenty Kimberley Light Horse under Colonel Peakham; two guns of the New Zealand Battery of Artillery and, last but not least, the Sherwood Rangers; about 600 all ranks. The Sherwood Rangers' strength was two officers, Captain Wilson and Lieutenant Turner and about forty NCOs and yeomen. The Northumberlands, known as 'Fighting Fifth' (they had been the 5th Regiment of Foot), were commanded by Lieutenant Colonel C. G. C. Money CB who was also garrison commander. He had commanded the battalion at Omdurman in 1898 where he earned his CB.

The Sherwood Rangers' initial task was to garrison de la Rey's Farm. On 1 January, having spent an uninterrupted Christmas there, enhanced by the receipt from home of the Christmas convoy of plum pudding and beer, they were relieved by the squadron of Paget's Horse. They re-deployed into Lichtenburg itself which was described as 'well favoured with trees and intersected with hedges of fig and quince.... The town stands on a slight eminence, and is surrounded on three sides by higher ground separated by a small river which runs through the valley beneath'. The new billet was in houses on the east side of the church square, with the officers in the parsonage.

Captain Wilson reported to Lord Galway:

> I have put all the men in houses so that they do not suffer from the rains which are very heavy just now.
>
> Our work is much lighter now that we have come into the town, because the infantry do all the night work and we only have to find the day pickets.
>
> Col Money of the Northumberland Fusiliers is our commandant and he seems a very able man. He has surrounded the town with trenches and earthworks and we have six months' provisions. I don't think the Boers will attack it, although there are plenty of them about here.

The role of the mounted troops was to maintain pickets on the high ground surrounding the town. They were also occasionally ordered to send out patrols.

On 5 January the Sherwood Rangers captured eight Boers in the small village of Manana. On 17 January they were deployed at a canter with Paget's Horse under command, when it was reported that the mail cart had been captured. During the attempt to locate and recover the cart they were counter-attacked by a large commando, and some thirty men of Paget's horse were slow to withdraw and were captured, including Paget himself, who was only there as a volunteer. All the captives were soon released, save for Major Paget. The reason this patrol went badly was that Paget miscalculated his horses' endurance, pursuing the enemy till his horses did not have the stamina to withdraw fast enough when the enemy turned and sought to cut them off.

Garrison life, with the exception of these skirmishes, was tedious, the monotony being broken by inter-unit sport, particularly cricket, football and, for the officers, polo. Unknown to Colonel Money and his 'sporting' garrison, on 2 March a force of 2,000 to 3,000 Boers had assembled under the command of de la Rey, Smuts, du Toit, and Vermaas. Dr C. J. Moller, a Boer, gives a revealing insight into the Boers' mindset and also of their resolve and cohesion.

> We are lying one and a half hours from Lichtenburg. It is already settled we move from here tonight, I expect it will be to a few miles of the place, I am confident of success – We dare not fail. Our faith and determination prevent failure, it forebodes success. Why are we not fighting a more worthy enemy?
>
> The damnable lies told about us by England are too terrible to be left unpunished.
>
> To excuse their burning of homesteads and taking of innocent women and children captives, we are accused of laying waste farms and homesteads etc., thus leaving families destitute – was a more confounded lie ever told?
>
> 3rd March: ... At one o'clock we came to within a few thousand yards of Lichtenburg, drew the horses into line and lay down in front of them till 2.30 [am]. Then, leaving our horses, we made a general advance on to Lichtenburg. No one knew what was awaiting him, we knew the English were ahead, but where and when we should stumble against the enemy, no one knew, we marched through a rank grass as high as mealies.
>
> Scarcely out of this than we stumbled against barbed wire. We knew that these were the first defences of the enemy and we had passed them – Momentarily I expected to hear the 1st Challenge of the enemy's sentinels – For a few minutes it did not come, on we went, you could only hear the cracking of dried sticks under our feet – Beyond this everything was silent.
>
> We must now be right up to the fort, for the call 'Halt, who goes there' rang out clear in the midnight air. No answer from us, but we moved forward another few paces. Suddenly a rifle shot rang out, we fell down flat and lay still; most bullets went overhead.
>
> Then General Smuts gave the order to lie still while he inspects the other positions. – In the meantime some burghers gave way – It was at this stage,

Fighting Fifth, Paget's Horse, and Sherwoods in redoubt.

Paget's Horse firing from the redoubt on the Boer reinforcements.

Men retiring from advance trenches.

Men retiring from advance trenches.

"A GALLANT DEFENCE": HOW THE GARRISON AT LICHTENBURG HELD OUT AGAINST THE BOERS UNDER DELAREY. (From a sketch by a Corporal of Paget's Horse.)

when we were right on the English entrenchments that two of our men were shot dead, and some others wounded.

Others seeing some burghers give way, mistook the movement for a general retreat and began moving back also.

Commandant du Toit had entered the town as far as the church, but retired also on seeing the others.

We found that had he stayed till daylight, either all his men would have had to surrender, or been killed, for he was right in the midst of the English entrenchments and forts.

By sunrise our whole division had withdrawn again; on our part it would have been useless storming any of the forts for we were without any cover.

Having reached our horses again, a report was received that Commandant Vermaas with 300 men was still in the town. It was so confirmed by the heavy firing which we heard. There was no chance to send any men to him, as the outside forts were still held by the enemy.

Captain Wilson takes up the narrative

The circumference of this place is between 4 & 5 miles so you can understand that it was an impossibility to keep them out on all sides at once. The Boers advanced soon after 3 a.m. in the dark & the first thing I heard was the sound of firing in the town itself & bullets striking about my windows. They had managed to get a good many of their men into the town beforehand & these were firing from the houses all over the town. We [SRY] got into the inner defences as soon as possible & the infantry pickets stuck to their trenches on the edge of the town. They were fired at not only from the front but from behind as well, & as most of their trenches had no back cover, a good many were killed. On the N. side their attack was repulsed, some Boers being killed within 10 yds of the trenches, but in the S. side they got in & were soon all over the town. There are so many trees here & hedges, that it was impossible to clear them out.

In some cases they had galloped straight through the wire at the trenches.

The following account of the action is based on the version in Birkin's book, written after the war, by which time he was a colonel and a past commanding officer of 3rd Imperial Yeomanry.

Elements of the Sherwood Rangers under Lieutenant Turner were despatched, about ten in all, to reinforce the infantry picket on the Manana Road, on the eastern side of the town, and were soon hard at work with their rifles. The east side having been checked, Turner was ordered to reinforce other pickets more to the south. As he approached the first he was met by a heavy fire but succeeded in reaching a farmhouse without mishap. Wilson arrived very shortly afterwards with reinforcements, and led his reinforcements in a dash forward to another farmhouse nearer the picket trench. Turner at the same time, also, made a rush for a neighbouring picket trench, which he found on arrival to be full of dead men and so retired to the house he had first occupied. Within ten yards of the house occupied by Wilson was a large barn held by the enemy and, at this short range, sharpshooting was in progress the whole day. Wilson wrote:

> Some of the Boers were shooting from the trees and it was almost impossible to locate them. De la Rey had a gun with him but only fired 7 rounds into the barn, as he was short of ammunition.

The main Boer body outside the town reinforced those fighting in and around it, adding to the confusion. One of the Sherwood Rangers' shoeing smiths, Pepper, was killed and Troopers Green and Swift were wounded. Green 'did a very plucky thing': on duty as mounted orderly at an infantry picket at the corner of the town, he volunteered to take a message back to headquarters. He had not got far when he was told to hold up his hands but he fired his revolver and galloped away and was hit in two places. Luckily the wounds were not serious.

As night fell an order was issued for all outposts to withdraw but it never reached Wilson and volunteers were called for to pass the message. Although he had only a hazy idea of the whereabouts of the farmhouse, Sergeant Spooner at once responded. The gathering darkness rendered his task even more difficult but, after running the gauntlet of the enemy's fire, he reached the house in safety and the whole party retired.

A ceasefire was called for and agreed to recover the wounded; however it was threatened as the Boers breached it by firing on the garrison ambulance in which a wounded man was killed. It held well enough for both sides to gather their wounded.

Moller records that after nightfall:

> General de la Rey abandoned any further attempts, not that he felt himself beaten, but to take the town would entail useless sacrifice of life, enemy having too good cover while they were fighting, and our men having to advance along open streets, the fire being unbearable.
>
> We slept at Retriefs farm that night. Our loss was 53 killed and wounded. Reports say that the English lost 60 killed and wounded.

When dawn broke, the garrison indeed found the enemy had gone, leaving behind them twenty-five dead. The garrison's casualties were two officers and seventeen men killed and thirty wounded, of which the Sherwood Rangers lost Farrier Pepper killed and three men wounded.

Captain Wilson counted over forty dead horses round the trenches and expressed the opinion that, had it not been for a commander of Colonel Money's calibre, and a good regiment of infantry, the Boers would have taken the town. He added that he doubted they would 'try it on again, as some of them say themselves that was the biggest knock their commando had had since Modder river'. This is quite a compliment because, at the Modder river, the Boers had been outnumbered by 40,000 to 10,000, while at Lichtenburg they outnumbered the British by 2,000 to 500. For their part, the British claimed that, at some sixteen hours of intense fighting, it was the longest general action since the Modder river.

For his part in the action Wilson was awarded the Distinguished Service Order, the citation for which read:

> Captain H. Wilson 3rd Imperial Yeomanry, with only 8 men, rushed a house, losing one man killed and two wounded. By this action he rescued an infantry picket, which was commanded from the house.

Sergeants Riggall and Spooner and Trooper Stephenson each received the Distinguished Conduct Medal, and Trooper Green was promoted to corporal.

Sergeant H. Riggall's citation read:

> Sgt Riggall was foremost in rushing a house, in which rush one man was killed and two wounded; he afterwards volunteered to carry a message through the Boer's lines, he also brought a wounded man into shelter and did good work throughout the day.

Quartermaster Sergeant J. A. Spooner's citation read:

> Volunteered to carry a message to a picket through Boer Lines and managed to get through, though challenged by sentry on the way; his message enabled two pickets to be withdrawn.

Trooper Green's citation read:

> Attached to an infantry picket, volunteered to carry a message; stopped by the enemy who called on him to surrender; he however fired his revolver at them and galloped back; being wounded in two places. Had previously volunteered to search a garden where Boers were believed to be concealed.

He was promoted to corporal. The citation for Trooper W. D. Stephenson's DCM has not been found.

On 8 March Wilson reported the detail of the action to Lord Galway, adding:

> I am glad to hear that the draft has started and hope it will reach me before long as our numbers are getting reduced through sickness & casualties. ... I heard that Lord Methuen is coming up here so I expect we shall have to go on the 'Trek' again but I think I would almost sooner stay here.
>
> Things are quieter here now but they [the Boers] drove in some of our pickets this morning but we fired a few shells at them which keeps them at a respectful distance. The news seems fairly good all over the country so I expect before long they will have had enough of it.

> Horse sickness is very bad just at present. The disease is very rapid &
> sometimes horses will die in a few hours from it.

At the end of April, having served their tour of twelve months, the squadron was
relieved by the second squadron of the Sherwood Rangers, newly arrived from
the UK.

On the day of the first squadron's departure from Lichtenburg, the
Northumberlands' band played them from their quarters to the front of the
courthouse, where the excellent Colonel Money was waiting to bid them farewell.
Money thanked the squadron for so ably carrying out the work entrusted to it.
This was followed by three cheers from the garrison to the squadron and three
cheers from the squadron to the garrison after which the squadron entrained for
Cape Town.

They boarded the *Tintagel Castle* on 22 May. On landing at Southampton
they were despatched on a special train to Retford where, after a reception and
luncheon on 17 June 1901, they were disbanded, with only two officers and forty-
nine men left. The original 121 had been reinforced by a draft of a dozen men after
three months. Casualties had amounted to one officer and fourteen men killed; the
remainder had been wounded or evacuated through sickness, except for the few
who volunteered to transfer to the second squadron.

Perhaps the greatest compliment to the Sherwood Rangers and the greatest
measure of the high quality of their performance in South Africa was paid by
General Sir John French, who commanded the cavalry in South Africa throughout
the war, but who never once had 3rd Imperial Yeomanry under his command.
When he inspected the second squadron on its arrival he 'eulogized' the
outstanding achievements of the first squadron. It was clearly a matter which had
been recognized widely by those in high command.

Finally, the following piece from *His Majesty's Territorial Army*, by Walter
Richards is worth reproducing:

> Few, if any, Yeomanry contingents did more brilliant work than did [3rd
> Imperial Yeomanry]. They were the first of the Imperial Yeomanry to reach
> South Africa; and at Tweenfontein, when that gallant soldier of fortune, de
> Villebois Mareuil, met his death, they took part in the first action in which
> the Yeomanry was engaged.... From 24 March 1900 to 4 April 1901 the
> regiment was in action on thirty-nine occasions, fifteen of which were general
> engagements. Total miles marched 3,173.

Chapter 10

Second Squadron

April 1901–January 1903

Meanwhile, the second squadron had been forming, starting in autumn 1900. This created a very different set of problems. Firstly, as mentioned, the Sherwood Rangers had always struggled with recruiting. On 3 December 1901 Lord Galway wrote to Colonel Rolleston of the South Notts Hussars suggesting collaboration: 'We are only allowed to enlist experienced men and it leaves me doubtful whether we shall be able to raise as before two separate Squadrons in Notts.' Rolleston replied, politely declining, 'If we both do what we can in our own district it will, I suppose be what is wanted.' The hussars, based in the south, had always been more successful at recruiting. He assessed rightly that he could manage alone.

In the event Galway need not have worried as over 350 high quality applications were received for the second squadron which left Retford in January 1901 under the temporary command of Lieutenant T. G. B. Thomas. Given the high number of applications, it is no surprise that the fifty-eight men, many from Lincolnshire, who went via Aldershot to embark at Southampton, were a fine lot. They arrived in South Africa at the beginning of March along with many other contingents to relieve their respective first sub-units. Their quality was quickly recognized when, on 11 April 1901, Methuen inspected all newly-arrived contingents near Tango, passing the Sherwood Rangers as the only detachment on parade fit to move up country.

The squadron was then to move to Graaff Reinet in the Eastern Cape where they would meet up with Captain Dawson. He had arrived before them to take over command, having returned from convalescence following wounds received at Lindley. However, they did not arrive. Dawson ascertained that they had left Tango but had then disappeared without trace. The answer to the mystery was that Lord Methuen had liked them so much that he had stolen them!

This is the story as told by SSM Arthur Rudkin:

> We sailed the 2nd Saturday in February 1901 ... we were a month sailing, went to the Cape, stopped there three or four days but not allowed to land owing to plague. We transhipped onto the *Orient* a Troop ship ... and sailed for Port Elizabeth ... and entrained for Ellandsfontein, just outside Pretoria.

We stopped there about a week, where I was appointed SSM. We then had orders to proceed to Kroonstad, got there on the Sunday night next morning we were served out with the New Saddlery which we had done fatigue on from England. Then we drew horses. About 4 p.m. Lieutenant Thomas came and told me to get all the men & fall in as we were ordered up country entrained and went up into the Transvaal to a place called Warrenton, leaving at Kroonstadt all our horses and new saddlery which we never saw again.

Warrenton is … where Lieutenant Jennings joined us, also that man Cottell who had been Squadron Sergeant Major from the first squadron who had been captured at Lindley, and was on his way back home with the first squadron … We then entrained to Mafeking. We drew our horses off the first South Notts Squadron who were also at Warrenton and on their way home. With Horses and Saddlery which was very bad, we getting wrong for giving up our new.

We were then moved to Cowans' Farm Mafeking. Sergeant Fisher and those members of the first squadron who had stayed to serve with the second squadron was there. We then did a couple of [Treks] under Lord Methuen, leaving Sergeant Fisher and his men drilling at Cowans' Farm because they were without horses. One trek was for about a month and the other about six weeks. During these we went round by Lichtenburg, Juckolstad and Zeerust.

On 13 June 1901 we were in action at Zeerust…. We were doing rearguard that day. Mr Thomas was wounded early on. The fighting went on all day. I was in charge of the right flank screen. Oglesby was also wounded that day and lived about three weeks having six bullets in him. A few days after this we were doing the right flank guard, we had another lieutenant attached to us…. He was ordered on to a kopje with the squadron, Mr Jennings stopping back with eight of us. The Boers advanced and we went to rejoin the squadron but they were on the wrong Kopje and we got a very hot time having to cover the distance of one mile in the open under fire; consequently we had one man dropped, Sinclair, but he has since got right after being invalided home. We had about seventeen fights whilst we were with Lord Methuen who when we left spoke very highly to us and said he was sorry to lose us.

This is the end of the Sherwood Rangers' service under Lord Methuen, one of the few senior officers who served throughout. Eventually, in March 1902, he was wounded and captured by de la Ray who, due to the severity of his injuries, released him, lending him his personal cart to take him to hospital. It is said this was the start of a personal friendship between the two men but one suspects it reflects a wider respect for him on both sides for the skill and endurance with which he had fought during the campaign. This view is supported by the fact that after other senior appointments he became, successively, general officer commanding-in-chief in South Africa and governor and commander-in-chief of Natal and finally was promoted to field marshal on 19 June 1911 thus ending his military career as Field Marshal Lord Methuen GCB GCMG GCVO, a well deserved redemption.

For the 'second' and 'third' yeomanry squadrons, serving as they did in the relatively peaceful Cape, even one 'fight' was not a given, so seventeen represents a significant level of action, possibly the most for any such sub-unit. Eventually, the squadron, including those from the first squadron, having been released by Methuen, arrived at Graaff Reinet. At that point the squadron comprised six officers: Captain M. S. Dawson, and Lieutenants Jennings, Coke, Hall, Trevor-Roper and Layton. Lieutenant Thomas was recovering from his wound. Their backgrounds are as follows:

J. C. Jennings served with the first squadron: sergeant 27.01.00, QMS 01.07.00, lieutenant 27.07.01.

Lieutenant R. G. Coke was posted from the Scots Guards.

H. C. Hall was the son of Marriott Hall of Thorpe Salvin, who had been with the first squadron, and had been commissioned from the ranks: sergeant 01.11.00, lieutenant 01.11.01.

Lieutenant A. M. Trevor-Roper had served as a sergeant in Roberts' Light Horse.

Lieutenant R. C. Layton had been seconded from the Yorkshire Hussars, and continued to serve even after Lieutenant Beckett arrived.

They commanded ninety-two all ranks, and were equipped with 104 horses, two wagons, a water cart, a Cape cart, an ammunition cart, thirty mules and nine native drivers.

Third Imperial Yeomanry was also in Graaff Reinet under command of Lieutenant Colonel R. L. Birkin DSO, the decoration an appropriate recognition for his fine period of service with the SNH's first squadron. However, the plan was that the new SRY Squadron would come under command of 16th (The Queen's) Lancers rather than 3rd Imperial Yeomanry, which would, nevertheless, be made up to eight squadrons and over 1,000 rank and file.

Horses were in short supply. Although a few of the original horses brought out by the first squadron were still in use, having served for fifteen months 'and looked no worse for it', the second squadron had to make do mostly with scraggy native ponies. The second squadron moved to join 16th Lancers at Rosmead with whom they served till the end of the war. Sixteenth Lancers were to serve under Sir John French, commanding the whole of Cape Province, which was generally much more peaceful than the Free State and Transvaal where the first squadron had served. Even so, there were Boer commandos in the Cape, or infiltrating into it from time to time from the north, which had to be suppressed and captured.

The Boers, having rejected several peace initiatives offered by the British – the first in March 1901 – finally surrendered in May 1902. By that time, the second squadron had reached Clanwilliam in the Western Cape, from where they entrained for Cape Town and home on 27 June. They left South Africa on 6 August 1902, and were paid off at Aldershot on the 25th. The war was formally concluded by the Treaty of Vereeniging which ended the existence of the South African Republic (Transvaal) and the Orange Free State as independent Boer republics, and placed them within the British Empire. The Union of South Africa became a member of the Commonwealth in 1910.

All who had served in South Africa paraded at Retford on 21 January 1903 to receive their campaign medals from Lady Galway. The Sherwood Rangers had also earned two DSOs, one to Wilson and the other to Laycock, and four DCMs (three at Lichtenburg and another to T. Francis who served the whole of the first squadron's tour), a significant number of awards of such quality.

Sherwood Rangers' casualties during the war were one officer and four ORs killed, two officers and twelve ORs wounded, and six ORs died of disease.

A memorial tablet to all those from the Yeomanry and from Retford who fought in South Africa was unveiled by General Sir John French (later Field Marshal Lord French) in the Town Hall at Retford in August 1903. A Yeomanry Memorial window was unveiled in Retford Parish Church on 23 December 1903 to commemorate those who gave their lives.

A year before, Lady Galway had made a Yeoman's garden at Serlby Hall, the centrepiece being a memorial pedestal to the same gallant men. This now stands in front of the training centre at Carlton in Nottingham.

Part II

Haldane and the Territorial Force

1900–1914

Chapter 11

Khaki

January 1900–August 1914

The post mortem on the Boer War was as full of the 'fog of war' as the conflict itself and as significant for the questions it avoided as for those it addressed. Of relevance to the Sherwood Rangers were the reviews into the use, for the first time, of volunteer individuals, units and formations overseas. This process began in 1901 whilst the war was still underway. The volunteers were a resource which before the war had totalled no more than 30,000, only a third of whom were in a position to mobilize, but which cost very little. By the time the war ended, that number had risen to approximately 200,000 who had volunteered at some time, of whom over 150,000 had either served abroad or in the regular Army. The initial reaction, especially as the war was still in progress, was that the use of volunteers was a success, and to examine how best to support and reinforce them.

With this in mind, in 1901 the War Office formed a special committee of seven yeomanry colonels, including Galway, to look at the yeomanry, the main volunteer component serving in South Africa. They recommended many improvements to the home bases of serving detachments, implemented with immediate effect, the most interesting of which were:

- The re-appointment of regular adjutants
- Appointment of regimental quartermasters
- Increase in permanent staff
- Khaki uniform to be introduced for field work
- Annual training to be for 18 days, of which 14 should be compulsory
- Pay to be 10 shillings [50 pence] a day
- A decoration for long service

New establishments of 596 were introduced. In the case of the Sherwood Rangers this was instead of 250. Establishments were cut to 476 two years later, for reasons of economy, when peace was declared.

The main review into the performance of the volunteer element which served in the Boer War took the form of a Royal Commission, chaired by the 15th Duke of Norfolk and set up in 1903. The justified and spontaneous support for the volunteers had been replaced by Regular Army-led machinations, founded on its preference for a system of reinforcement based on conscription rather than formed volunteer units. As a result, the weight of evidence gathered was critical of volunteers in order to add strength to the conscription argument.

The Regular Army glossed over its own performance against a volunteer army:

- Despite an often overwhelming superiority, permitting the sieges of Mafeking, Kimberley and Ladysmith to occur and continue
- Taking three attempts to relieve Ladysmith, and three more to get north of the Modder river.
- The failure to capture Steyn and de Wet and so end the war in 1900
- Poor man management and logistics

It then conveniently forgot the performance of the yeomanry in action 'whose courage and determination have given them a place amongst the best and bravest'. As a result, a myth was created, that the problem with the Boer War was the poor performance of the volunteers, particularly the yeomanry. So successful was the creation of this myth that it remains conventional, but erroneous, wisdom today.

This revealed, for the first time, the sad truth that the Regular Army cannot manage the volunteer army when in a junior partnership with itself. This is because, ultimately at top level, it sees volunteer service as a competitor, not a partner, and is therefore conflicted in the way it leads it. For the volunteer, this partnership is essential for the access to the training he or she needs; that part has always worked well.

Worse still, obsessed with its conscription agenda, the Regular Army (and the rest of Europe) missed the key lesson of the Boer War: it was not mounted troops who had been rendered obsolete by modern weapons, particularly the machine gun, but unprotected infantry, with no defence but to dig earthworks, which then impeded the ability of mounted troops to maintain mobility over ground which, otherwise, would have been suitable. For this the nation would pay a high price in the mud of Flanders. The lesson of the Boer War was confirmed fully in Palestine in the Great War: mounted troops were still dominant when given room to manoeuvre. Might history have been changed had the power of modern weapons been countered by mounting the infantry on horses so that they could have been afforded the same opportunities as cavalry to evade the fields of fire of these weapons and to retaliate by using surprise and manoeuvre to exploit the relative immobility of modern weapons rather than merely dig trenches? We will never know. Palestine was also to confirm the battle-winning capability of volunteers, since the Egyptian Expeditionary Force was composed predominantly of British Territorial Force formations, or volunteer formations from the Empire.

However, in the new century which stretched away before it, the United Kingdom had a new problem to address in Europe, where the United States then held little influence. The problem was the longstanding matter of a unified and ever strengthening Germany, and its direction of travel. So it was that the *Entente Cordiale*, a mutual defence treaty, was created between Britain and France in 1904. Such alliances have driven much British foreign policy since.

This also added a sense of urgency to the reforms recommended as a result of the Boer War. Fortunately for the volunteer army, the person responsible for carrying out that re-organization was Richard Burdon Haldane, who was appointed Secretary of State for War in 1906 in the new Liberal government. Haldane saw all too clearly the lack of support by, or understanding in the senior ranks of, the Regular Army for the volunteers, and the harm that indifference would do. His solution to that, as well as for the lessons learned from the war, was to gather all volunteers, whether yeomanry, militia, or other volunteer units, into one force which he called the Territorial Force. It was to have an establishment of approximately 300,000, based on fourteen infantry divisions which included all other appropriate arms and services, distributed geographically throughout the country. In addition, the yeomanry provided six regiments to the Regular Army-based Expeditionary Force, and the remainder were divided into fourteen cavalry brigades, each under command of a division. Each cavalry brigade had its own battery of Royal Horse Artillery.

Briefly the terms of service were:

- War Office in control of finance, training and in command
- Director General of the Territorial Force (a new volunteer appointment) to see all papers
- Territorials to be represented on the Army Council by the Parliamentary Under-Secretary of State for War
- Four years' enlistment with opportunity to re-enlist
- Subject to military law
- Able to enlist in the Regular Army
- Between 8 and 15 days camp per annum
- Paid
- Service within the UK
- Embodiment for a year in the event of imminent national danger or grave emergency
- No role in aid of the civil power

He implemented this reform in 1908 across the whole of the UK, other than Ireland. Perhaps the most important element of all, given the Regular Army's conflict of interest in relation to volunteers, was Haldane's plan to create a civilian structure in each county which he called Territorial Associations, now called Reserve Forces and Cadets Associations. They were, and still are, presided over by the lord-lieutenant of the county, harking back to the holder's historic role as the local military commander, who traditionally called out the civilian volunteers in times of threat.

The lord-lieutenant presided over a committee consisting of civilians, past and serving volunteers and local regular commanders. Its responsibilities were premises (drill halls), recruiting, welfare and the link between the armed services and civilian population. It was an inspired solution which gave the Associations power as a counterbalance to the regular army and was a partnership which worked really well until, inexplicably, it was largely emasculated at the end of the Cold War. During the period since, the regular chain of command, unchecked and, not surprisingly, distracted by higher priorities, has chosen a number of wrong options in relation to the TA which have been damaging, and from which it is only now, as this is written, slowly, but surely, recovering.

The Boer War changed the nature of volunteer service in the Sherwood Rangers forever. They now wore khaki for all field training but the tradition of camping in turn, at or near Newark, Mansfield, Retford or Worksop, as they had for a century continued although under canvas, rather than by garrisoning the town. They also adopted the practice of selecting a country estate to host the camp near one of the towns. There was a much greater emphasis on rifle shooting, and the beginnings of the bounty system, whereby an annual bonus was paid to those who reached a high enough standard. They still tended to ride to camp, pausing at suitable hostelries to 'rest their horses' along the way, and to use the chance to carry out some basic training. Once there, the camp programme, including training, sporting and social, was virtually unchanged, compared with that which existed pre-war, save for the increased period, from one week to two, over which it extended.

The daily routine also followed tradition:

06.00 Reveille
06.30 Stables
07.20 Feed
08.00 Breakfast
09.00 Parade
13.30 Dinner
15.00 Orderly Room
17.00 Evening Stables
18.30 Guard Mounting
19.00 Supper
22.30 Watch Setting
23.00 Lights out

The rifle had replaced the carbine, a decision confirmed by the war, so that cavalry could match the infantry when dismounted. Lord Roberts, no less, gave assurance to the yeomanry at large that being equipped with rifles did not turn cavalry into infantry by the back door, a great fear of the yeomanry. Of course, there would be times when the cavalry would fight dismounted, but he emphasized the vast difference in the skills of the infantryman and the cavalryman. He said that putting a yeoman in a skirmish line did not make him an infantryman any more than putting an infantryman onto a horse made him a cavalryman. The regiment, in common with all British cavalry regiments, therefore continued to carry the sabre and sometimes the lance (the *arme blanche*), one of which was essential, if an offensive mounted action was to be attempted. Because of their dual purpose, yeomanry were not classified as cavalry.

Haldane's reforms placed a greater training obligation on the volunteer, and the onset of peace placed greater pressure on recruiting. In this the Sherwood Rangers were assisted by the creation of a Lincolnshire squadron in spring 1900, for which Lord Galway obtained permission from the War Office. It had been inspired by the patriotism generated by the raising of service squadrons for the war, which was felt no less keenly in Lincolnshire, which did not have its own yeomanry. Several individuals from the county had joined the first Sherwood Rangers' service squadron, and the new Lincolnshire squadron had been created as a result. The quality of men and horses was of the highest, and so it was a very much appreciated innovation. Although given the opportunity to raise its own yeomanry, Lincolnshire had failed to do so. The configuration of the squadrons was as follows: A Squadron consisted of Newark and Retford, B Squadron Mansfield and Clumber, whilst C Squadron was Lincoln and Grimsby.

In the run up to the First World War, Lincolnshire succeeded in raising its own regiment, which served throughout the war. However, those who had originally joined the Sherwood Rangers stayed with them. To complete the story, the Lincolnshire Yeomanry disbanded in 1920 and the Sherwood Rangers received a number of very high quality transfers as a result. This continuing connection with Lincolnshire resulted in two commanding officers and some of the finest soldiers to serve in the Second World War. It endured until the 1970s.

These are some of the notable events of the inter-war period:

In 1903 Lord Galway retired after thirty-eight years' service with the Sherwood Rangers, during which he never missed annual training. One of his many gestures was his presentation to the officers of a magnificent cup as a memento of those officers who represented the Yeomanry in the South African War. When he took command in 1882 the strength of the regiment was 138. By the time he retired in 1903 it was 380. He continued to serve as Honorary Colonel. Lord Galway was succeeded by Colonel H Denison CB of Eaton Hall. His grandfather had been commissioned into the regiment when it was raised in 1794. He had served as a regular for twenty years, holding the rank of lieutenant colonel in the Royal Engineers, and had served for twenty more in the regiment, commanding the Retford Troop.

In 1906 the regiment's four troop guidons were renovated and the battle honour 'South Africa 1900–1902' was added to each. Four years later, the Sherwood Rangers, South Notts Hussars and Derbyshire Yeomanry formed the Notts and Derby Mounted Brigade under Colonel Rolleston (late SNH). For the first time in peace, annual training was held far afield, the whole brigade going to Salisbury Plain.

Colonel A. E. Whitaker of Babworth Park, succeeded Denison in 1910. Denison handed the regiment over at full strength, a considerable achievement, and had served on the War Office committee which created the TF. He was presented with a remarkably fine silver statuette of a Sherwood Ranger, which has since been given to the regiment. Whitaker had served in the Fighting Fifth in India as a regular officer and was a well known sportsman and renowned rifle shot who had commanded the Mansfield Troop for many years.

Part III

The Great War

1914–1919

Chapter 12

Mobilization

August 1914–April 1915

The Great War was caused by the conviction of both Germany and the Austro-Hungarian Empire that they were in decline, which had to be reversed, rightly in the case of Austria, but wrongly in the case of Germany. A local conflict between Austria and Serbia, whose country included part of Macedonia, with its roots in the rise and fall of the once mighty Ottoman Empire, provided Germany with a pretext to start a war, the aim of which was her domination of Europe.

Germany and Austria-Hungary with their left flank firm, launched a right flanking attack on France through Belgium directed at Paris. Britain's Treaty obligations to Belgium and France left no choice but to declare war on Germany, as Germany well knew would be the case. The UK declared war on 4 August 1914.

One of Haldane's reforms was to create an organization for the Territorial Force in time of war. The first regiment would be formed for home defence, or would be asked to volunteer for foreign service. In the latter case, the second-line unit would be formed for home defence from those who failed to volunteer or were unfit, and a third-line unit would be established as a training cadre. These second- and third-line units would be formed into 'replica' brigades and divisions to the first line. Having rejected conscription, Haldane intended this to be the structure through which any reinforcement or enlargement of the standing army would be achieved in time of war. It was logical and followed the principles on which our armies had been successfully built for a thousand years before and since the concept of a standing army was created in the seventeenth century.

Field Marshal Lord Kitchener, newly appointed Secretary of State for War (effectively replacing 'Galloper' Jack Seeley who had started his military career with the Sherwood Rangers in 1890 and had resigned as the Secretary of State over the Curragh Incident) took the decision not to use a structure based on existing volunteers, whom, based on anecdotal evidence from other countries, he did not trust to perform in war. Both Kitchener's decision, and the pretext on which it was based, seem hard to justify, since his own experience of British volunteers in the Boer War was the opposite. It was he, of course, who was actually in command of the operations to capture de Wet at Oliphants Nek, which involved an acclaimed performance by volunteers and failed because of a heavily-criticized performance by the cream of the Regular Army.

He decided instead to form a completely new structure, which he called his New Army, through which he then proceeded to recruit the same volunteers as would have joined if Haldane's structure alone had been used, but far more slowly because he was working from a standing start and without the structure of local drill halls. The two structures each produced thirty divisions. They then operated in parallel until joined by conscription in 1916 following the heavy losses incurred by that time.

1/1st Nottinghamshire (Sherwood Rangers) Yeomanry

Orders to mobilize were received on the evening of 4 August 1914. Within twenty-four hours the Sherwood Rangers had been embodied at its four drill halls, A Squadron at Newark, B at Mansfield, C at Worksop and D at Retford, Lincolnshire having by then formed their own yeomanry. On 10 August the regiment concentrated in billets at Retford, where D Squadron was split up and absorbed into the other squadrons. The next day, troop guidons were laid up in Retford Church, and that night the regiment entrained for Diss in Norfolk, to be joined there by the other units of 17 Nottinghamshire and Derbyshire Yeomanry Brigade (1/1st Derbyshire Yeomanry, 1/1st Nottinghamshire (South Notts Hussars) Yeomanry, supported by Nottinghamshire Battery RHA). The latter was commanded by J. K. (Joe) Laycock DSO, clearly a man of many parts. The brigade was initially commanded by Lieutenant Colonel Sir Lancelot Rolleston of Watnall, commanding officer of the South Notts Hussars who had of course served with distinction in the Boer War.

In Diss the brigade reformed as 3 (Nottinghamshire and Derbyshire) Mounted Brigade of 2nd Mounted Division, which included five yeomanry brigades comprising fourteen regiments, together with supporting arms and services. At this point, Rolleston handed over command of 3 Brigade to Brigadier General P. Kenna VC, a 17th Lancer, whose VC had been earned at Omdurman. At the end of August 1914 the brigade moved to Berkshire, where it joined the other elements of 2nd Mounted Division, and started work-up training. The division was also re-equipped extensively, including new saddles and transport. During October, the division paraded in line before King George V, the first time a yeomanry division had ever been seen on parade.

At the end of October, Sir John Milbanke VC was appointed to command the regiment, taking over from Colonel Whitaker, due to the latter's temporary ill-health. Sir John was a close friend of Churchill, with whom he had been at school, and gained his VC whilst serving as a regular officer in the 10th Hussars in South Africa. At the time he was appointed to command he had retired some time before from the Regular Army.

The general assumption was that, with so much activity, the division was being prepared for deployment overseas, and this rumour was given credibility by the fact that each man was asked whether he was prepared to serve abroad.

2/1st Nottinghamshire (Sherwood Rangers) Yeomanry

At this time, the Sherwood Rangers' second-line regiment was, in accordance with the plan, forming up at Retford, under Lieutenant Colonel M. S. Dawson. The second-line regiment was taking transfers of those unwilling or unfit for overseas service, as well as the old equipment of the first regiment. Majors Fearon, Peacock and Holford were A, B and C Squadron leaders respectively. Captain Bertodano was adjutant, and Mr Hubbard was RSM. Initially, the supply of horses was on loan from riding schools. Later, a significant quantity of Canadian horses was supplied unbroken.

3/1st Nottinghamshire (Sherwood Rangers) Yeomanry

A third-line regiment was also formed under command of Colonel Willoughby and remained at Retford, and later Derby, with a strength of around 250, until August 1916. At this time it moved to Aldershot, leaving only a cadre of about forty, most of whom were employed in munitions work, initially at Retford and later at Newark. In accordance with their role as reinforcements, the arrangements in the division were that no regimental-specific sub-units existed, but that men wore regimental cap badges and lanyards.

In mid-November 1914 there was concern about possible enemy landings on the east coast, so 2nd Mounted Division was moved to cover the coast of Norfolk, the regiment being centred on Sheringham on the north Norfolk coast. They remained there till the end of March, responding to several alarms and excursions. The major dividend from this was the intensive training in horsemanship and horse management that Sir John put the regiment through. These were the key skills of the cavalryman, which they believed laid much of the foundation for the regiment's later reputation for efficiency as a mounted force for the rest of the war.

However unpleasant the east coast had been that winter, it can have been nothing like as unpleasant as the winter endured by the British Expeditionary Force in France. All hope of a swiftly concluded war of manoeuvre was exchanged for one where both sides faced each other in deadlock across a no man's land sometimes measured in yards, from the confines of two heavily fortified opposing trench systems. These offered no chance of an open flank as they stretched from the Channel to the Alps.

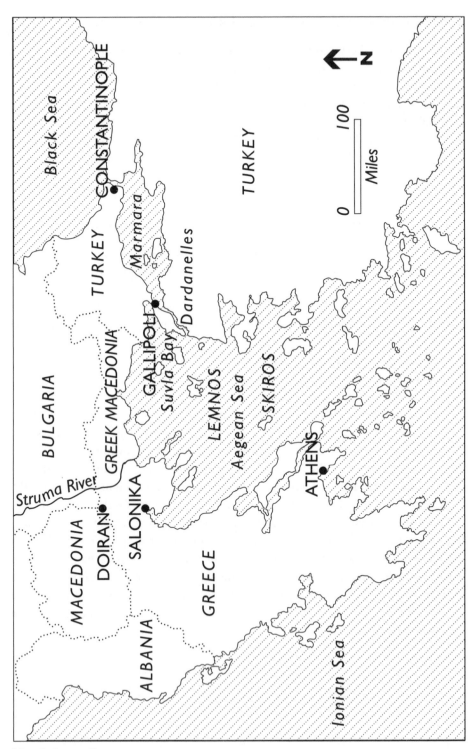

Map 4: Aegean Sea.

Chapter 13

Gallipoli

April–November 1915

By late winter, the members of the *Entente Cordiale*, consisting of France and the British Empire with Russia, Belgium and Serbia, had begun to look for ways to take the initiative against the Central Powers, Germany, Austria-Hungary and the Ottoman Empire, and break the deadlock in western Europe. The *Entente* decided to force the Dardanelles, a narrow strait held by Turkey, which led out of the Aegean Sea and linked the Aegean to the Sea of Marmara and the Black Sea, and thus to Russia via the narrow Bosporus Straits, guarded by Constantinople, now Istanbul, the capital of Turkey. This waterway was crucial, because it formed the boundary between Europe and the Middle East. If successful, the *Entente* could outflank Germany and Austria and support their own allies.

It should be added that, before the decision to force the Dardanelles had been taken, there had been two other campaigns which had conditioned the mindset of the *Entente*. In December 1914 the Turks attacked Russia in mountainous country in the Caucasus. It was a disaster and the Turks lost almost a whole army. It did, however, cause Russia to ask her allies to attack Turkey to relieve pressure in the Caucasus, and so helped precipitate the Gallipoli campaign. Then, on 1 February 1915, the Turks attacked the Suez Canal, which had been prepared as the main defensive line for Egypt. They were seen off without much difficulty and withdrew to the other side of the Sinai Desert. Because of these campaigns, the Turkish Army was mistakenly written off as a pushover by the *Entente*.

Since the Dardanelles was a waterway, the key role would fall to the Royal Navy. However, at its narrowest point, it is less than a mile wide, so it would be a very high risk strategy if attempted without the support of ground troops. Because of the shortage of such troops, the New Army still not yet operational, it was decided to take the risk using the Navy alone. The preliminary bombardment was fired in mid–February 1915, but the Navy's attempt to force the passage did not take place till mid–March, so lacked any tactical surprise or even conviction. Had it continued for even a few more hours it might have succeeded since the coast defence artillery was running out of ammunition. However, it was called off.

This triggered the decision to send a number of formations to Egypt, one of which was the 2nd Mounted Division with a view to mounting an operation to

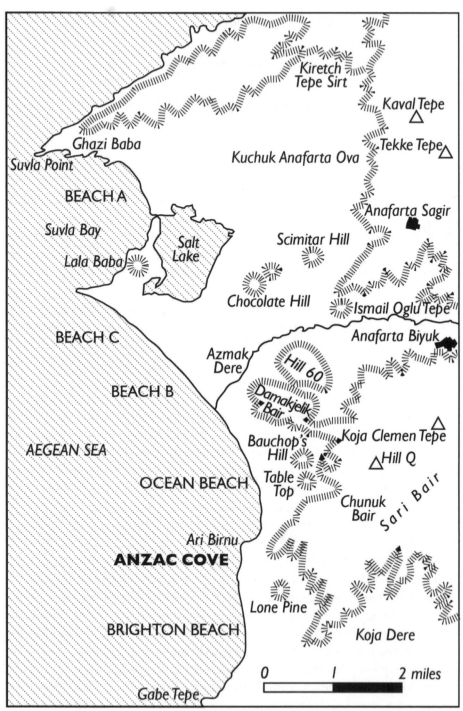

Map 5: Gallipoli.

reinforce the Navy's renewed attempt. They were relieved on the Norfolk coast by their second-line division, including 2/1st Sherwood Rangers, which moved from Retford to Swaffham, Norfolk on the19th June 1915.

By 1916, 2/1st Sherwood Rangers were fully equipped. In July 1916, the regiment moved to Essex, firstly to Narford and then Brentwood, with drafts being sent overseas at intervals to reinforce 1/1st Regiment. In 1917, the 2/1st moved to Bishops Stortford under command of Colonel Holford, Colonel Dawson having retired due to his age. On 4 September 1917 the division was renamed the Cyclist Division and the brigade became 11 Cyclist Brigade; the regiment re-organized in four companies.

In the late autumn of 1917 all fit men were transferred to 7th Bn The Sherwood Foresters (Nottinghamshire and Derbyshire Regiment) (Robin Hood Rifles) and sent into the line at Cambrai, in response to the German counter-attack made immediately after the famous tank battle. Of those who went, A. Hather and F. Harrison were killed and W. Illger was wounded, but his brother, F. Illger, served throughout and was decorated for gallantry. By March 1918 the remains of the regiment had moved to the Cavalry School at Canterbury under command of Colonel H. Thorpe on his return from commanding 1/1st in Palestine. There were no further movements until the unit was demobilized in mid-late 1919.

The remainder of this account deals with 1/1st Sherwood Rangers, who, consisting of twenty-nine officers, 454 men and 531 horses and mules, sailed from Avonmouth for Egypt in April 1915 on three ships. The journey was mostly uneventful. Their fight was to be with the Ottoman Empire, which had been born in Anatolia in the thirteenth century, and had reached a high-water mark of success in the seventeenth century, when it had dominion over all it surveyed, from the Caucasus in the east to Algeria in the west, and from Egypt and Sudan in the south, to the borders of Austria in the north. It then lost its vitality and became known as 'the Sick Man of Europe'. Turkey, the core of the Empire, was no longer strong enough to prevent this gradual break up.

On 27 April the regiment landed at Alexandria, later moving to Abbassia Barracks in Cairo. The horses arrived in good condition. Whilst they had been at sea, it had been decided by the *Entente* to support a renewed naval attack on the Dardanelles, and a Mediterranean Expeditionary Force was formed, consisting of 29th Division (a regular formation), the Royal Naval Division, a French corps, plus 1st Australian Division and the New Zealander and Australian Division already training in Egypt. The Antipodeans' force was called the Australia and New Zealand Army Corps and became known by their acronym: ANZAC. The whole force was to be commanded by General Sir Ian Hamilton with its objective the capture of Constantinople. This was the same man who stood accused of having failed to obey his orders to block Oliphants Nek in the Boer War and capture Steyn and de Wet who were being driven towards the Nek by Methuen's Yeomanry, including the Rangers.

Four landings were made by the British on 25 April 1915 at Cape Helles, on the tip of the Dardanelles peninsula forming the north-western, or European, bank of the waterway, and one by the ANZACs. Two of the landings were opposed but, despite some casualties, the troops got ashore, but failed to reach their main objectives. It is said that this was in part due to a lack of decisive action by commanders when they first landed. The ANZAC landing, due to an under-estimation of the speed of the current, had been made a mile north of the intended beach in a small cove at the foot of some very tangled and steep hills north-west of the British; it became known as Anzac Cove. Thanks to active efforts, a small beachhead was achieved before the Turks did all they could to dislodge them. In spite of valiant efforts, the ANZACs were unable to break out and capture the commanding heights overlooking them. A stalemate set in across the whole front for several months.

Meanwhile, 2nd Mounted Division continued training in Egypt, which increased in scale as time went on. A feature of their training was the thickness of the dust cloud created by mounted manoeuvres, from which all returned literally caked in the stuff. Colonel A. E. Whitaker, now recovered, had rejoined as base commandant with responsibility for all troops in the Cairo area. By August, on the Gallipoli peninsula, both sides consisted of approximately fifteen divisions, and Hamilton's plan was to reinforce with two further divisions at Suvla Bay, north of the British but south of the ANZACs, with the aim of outflanking the Turks and taking the key feature of Sari Bair. Again a successful assault failed through an inability to exploit initial tactical advantage, followed by a furious counter-attack from the Turks, which wiped out the initial advantage. The Allies' offensive was reinforced with four more divisions, the last of which to deploy was 2nd Mounted Division, minus its horses and one squadron per regiment retained in Egypt to look after them.

As a result on 12 August 3 Mounted Brigade duly handed in its horses and proceeded immediately to Gallipoli, landing there as infantry at Suvla Bay in the early hours of 18 August. The yeomen had to adapt to bitter fighting as part of an infantry division in a barren and inhospitable country, with little relevant training, since all their work-up had been as cavalry. To their front, division after division was being committed to the break-out, which involved intense close combat, generating heavy casualties. Second Mounted Division was then committed to the battle, thrown in as the last chip of a losing gambler.

Tallents, in *The Sherwood Rangers Yeomanry in the Great War*, describes this desperate affair, recounting how, on 20 August, the division marched to Lala Baba on the south side of Suvla Bay. Of the five brigades in column of sections the SRY were the third regiment of 3 Brigade; it took five hours to cover three miles.

On 21st August an attack was begun with a view to taking Scimitar Hill and the hill called Ismail Oglu Tepe lying between Chocolate Hill and Anafarta

Sagir; the MG Section was engaged in providing covering fire from the face of Chocolate Hill. 2nd Mounted Division was in reserve, but the position necessarily allocated to it, owing to the nature of the ground, was much too far back and did not afford it a fair opportunity to co-operate.

The infantry attack was pressed most gallantly (by 29th Division amongst others), but ultimately failed and at 3 p.m. our Division was ordered to be ready to move up to Chocolate Hill in support. They moved off at about 4 p.m. across Salt Lake which was then a bare dry mud flat bordered by low ground with rough grass and low scrub at intervals, the whole being in full view of the enemy who occupied positions many hundreds of feet above the level of the lake, and within easy range of his field guns.

The advance was made in a succession of waves in extended order, each wave consisting of one brigade with a distance of about 200 yards between the waves; ours was the fourth wave.

The Division was very heavily shelled throughout the advance of about two miles; the attack had failed before this and we were the only large body of troops moving so that every heavy gun was concentrated upon us, with the result that the Division suffered a great many casualties, estimated at about 500. The shells set fire to the dry scrub and grass and some of the wounded were burned before they could be saved.

The Regiment was extremely lucky and escaped with very few casualties, though Pte M. H. Colton was unfortunately killed after most gallant work as a stretcher bearer amongst the burning scrub with Ptes Spring and Smith who were afterwards awarded the Military Medal.

This was the first time the division had come under heavy fire, but the men displayed the utmost coolness. General Sir Ian Hamilton, observed:

During their march they came under a remarkably steady and accurate artillery fire. The advance of these Yeomen was calculated to send a thrill of pride through anyone with a drop of English blood in their veins. Such martial spectacles are rare in modern war. Despite the critical events in other parts of the field I could hardly take my glasses from the Yeomen. They moved like men marching on parade. Here and there a shell would take a toll of a cluster: there they lay; there was no straggling; the others moved steadily on; not a man was there who hung back or hurried ...

On arrival at Chocolate Hill we had to wait till 6.30 p.m. (writes Tallents) ... when the Division was ordered to attack the hill called Ismail Oglu Tepe mentioned earlier, our Brigade being in support.

No one had ever seen the country before, maps were inaccurate and on a small scale, none of the Regimental Officers knew for certain which of the innumerable hills was our objective or where exactly the Turkish positions were; nor had anyone the slightest idea of the position of our own infantry who had attacked earlier in the day and who were somewhere in front of us, but who were so exhausted and broken up by the failure of their attacks that they could do no more and could not even advance with us when we passed through them.

Under these unfavourable circumstances and in the rapidly failing light the Yeomanry set out upon their first attack and to attempt that which a far larger force of experienced infantry, including the famous 29th Division, had just failed to achieve.

The first and second Brigades moved forward to the attack, and about an hour later 3 Brigade was ordered to move up to attack a Turkish redoubt which was holding up the Division, but the exact position of which was uncertain, Sir John Milbanke was sent for to receive his orders from the Divisional Headquarters and when he returned he informed us that we were to take a redoubt, but that he did not know where it was and he did not think that anyone else knew accurately, but in any case we were to go ahead and attack any Turks we met.

The South Notts Hussars and the Derbyshire Yeomanry under the acting Brigadier Cole, moved out on our right making a wider sweep round, while the Regiment, led by the CO, filed along some trenches to the south of Chocolate Hill and emerged into the open at a point some way to the north of what was afterwards called Curator's House. It was now nearly dark, large numbers of wounded men and detached parties of infantry in a state of exhaustion helped to impede the way, and by some means while still in the trenches the column became broken; about three and a half troops of B Squadron followed the CO, the remainder of B Squadron followed by A Squadron halted at the end of the trench, apparently upon orders which were probably passed down by enemy snipers who were concealed in large numbers in the scrub amongst and even behind our men. After some delay Major Thorpe, who was at the head of A Squadron began to suspect that something was wrong and went forward only to find the break in the column; no one appeared to have given any orders but it was clear the order to halt had been received. He then ordered the column to move forward and advanced some way across the fields in the direction in which he thought the CO had gone, making enquiries of various infantry officers whom he met, but without success.

On the advice of a Staff Officer who said that they could not be further to the east, he tried to go to the left towards Green Hill. At the first halt after coming into the open he found that part of A Squadron who should have been following him were missing but they were soon afterwards found in a Turkish trench at the foot of Green Hill, under Lieutenant Pitt, who had been directed into a side trench.

Major Thorpe was unable to find his own Brigade during the night, but got in touch with 4th London Yeomanry Brigade, and he then put his men with others in the trench and went back to Divisional Headquarters, for orders which he received sometime later: 'To remain where he was and to get the water bottles filled as he would be required shortly to help 2nd Brigade to dig in on the ground they had taken.'

In the meantime the party with the CO passed through the lines of the men of 11th Infantry Division who knew nothing of the renewal of the attack and had no orders to advance with our men and did not in fact do so.

In spite of the darkness the CO continued to advance past the cottage which afterwards became known as Black and White House, leaving it a little on the right and then swinging slightly towards the north they reached a ditch between the house and Scimitar Hill, and some three hundred yards beyond the house. Here they were obliged to stop under cover owing to the rapidly increasing volume of fire, although the ditch was already choked with dead and wounded of both sides. The snipers here were only a few yards range and the slightest movement was greeted with several shots from them. By this time it was quite dark and shortly afterwards our very gallant Colonel, Sir John Milbanke VC, was killed and directly afterwards the acting Brigadier Colonel Cole was seriously wounded. Colonel Lance of the Derbyshire Yeomanry then commanded the Brigade.

Owing to the lack of support, the scattering of some of the men and darkness coming on directly after we left Chocolate Hill, the attack could never have succeeded and was practically a forlorn hope right from the start.

Major Thorpe, whose father had commanded the regiment in the 1850s, assumed command. Major Mirlees became second in command, Captain Tallents, the author of the above account and a future CO, took command of A Squadron and Major Francis Vernon Willey command of B Squadron. He would also be a CO of the regiment. Following his service in Egypt and Gallipoli he was, in 1916, promoted to lieutenant colonel and became Assistant Director of Equipment and Ordnance at the War Office, a position he held until 1920, during which time he was appointed CMG, CBE, and MVO. With the notable exception of Sir John Milbanke, whose body was never recovered despite every practical attempt to find it, the Sherwood Rangers' casualties were light. They had suffered three killed and twelve wounded.

Hamilton asked for reinforcements of another 95,000 men but received only 25,000. A higher priority was attributed to the impending French autumn offensive in western Europe and to a new threat. Emboldened by failures of the *Entente* in the Gallipoli Peninsula, there was now a certainty that Bulgaria would join in on the side of the Central Powers, and that, as a result, Greece might join in against the *Entente* also, something which a successful campaign in the Dardanelles had been intended to prevent. If that happened, Germany might reinforce Turkey and threaten the Allies' routes to the Far East through the Suez Canal. As a result, Hamilton was required to send three divisions to Salonica in Greek Macedonia,

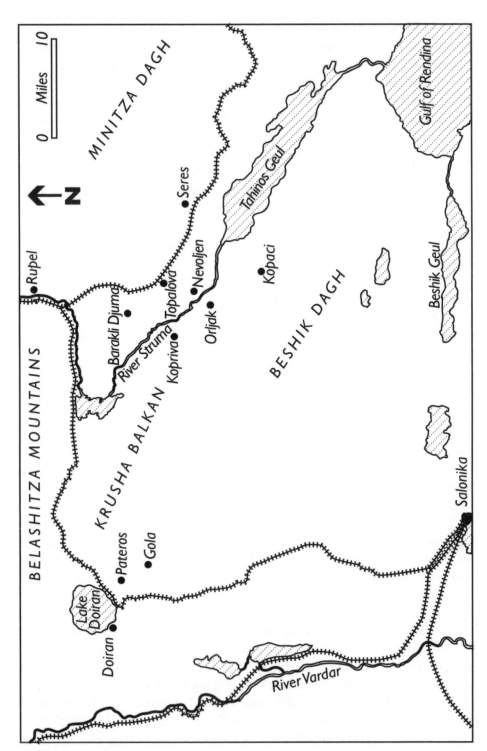

Map 6: Greek Macedonia.

of which the Sherwood Rangers were destined to form a part. With these changes, which weakened the forces available to Hamilton in Gallipoli, the game in the Gallipoli peninsula was over.

However, the suffering of the troops still on the peninsula was not finished. The deadlock, which left Turkey in a position of strength and with a re-born sense of nationhood, left the Allies hanging on in their trenches and ravaged by disease, as Tallents described:

> The awful shortage of water was beginning to tell on us, and the flies which already existed in such quantities as we could never have imagined to be possible, increased daily in numbers and persistence, they had made life almost unbearable by day and entirely prevented sleep which was so badly needed as we were digging every night. Rations consisted of bully beef, biscuits and plum and apple jam ... which never lost its well-known flavour of resembling a mixture of burnt India rubber and paraffin.
>
> There was no single spot on the whole of that part of the peninsula in which one could get away for a few minutes from the chance of being shelled, and it was very rarely that we were even out of rifle range of the Turkish trenches; in fact all the reserve trenches even to the rear most line were within that range.

By mid-October the regiment had been reduced to six officers and 151 men; they had lost ten officers and 195 men, virtually all to disease. That level was maintained to the end. As the inevitable withdrawal began to take shape, the regiment was marched out of the line to the rest camp. Tallents noted that 'It was only three miles to the Rest Camp, but even with frequent rests and at the slowest pace, it was all we could do to get there with our packs and equipment.' On 27 November the Sherwood Rangers disembarked at Alexandria and moved back to Cairo 'where our first medical inspection reduced our survivors by fully one half'.

However, if their sense of humour had deserted them during the intervening months, clearly that of the Ordnance Department had not. They demanded to know of the newly-returned regiment what had happened to the large scales of ammunition issued the previous July, why they needed their putrid water bottles replacing, and refused to provide head collars with the 300 unbroken remounts with which the regiment were to be issued, which meant there was no means by which the regiment could tie them up.

His Majesty the King later awarded the Regiment a Union Flag in recognition of its service as infantry in Gallipoli.

As for General Hamilton, the best that can be said is that, so far as the Sherwood Rangers were concerned, he had not been a lucky general.

Chapter 14

Macedonia

November 1915–June 1917

This is the Balkans where the war began, and where nothing is simple. Macedonia is a region of the Balkans of which the north-western portion is a separate landlocked nation state called Macedonia, and part of the homeland of the Serbs, the north-eastern portion is a region of Bulgaria, and the southern portion is a region of Greece. The portion of Macedonia which forms the subject matter of this campaign is that which forms the region of Greece. The combination of Greece and Greek Macedonia has a long northern border of about 400 miles from the Adriatic Sea in the west shared initially with Albania and then Macedonia and finally Bulgaria. Its border in the East abuts with Turkey in the north and then the Aegean. To keep matters 'simple', Greece and Greek Macedonia will be referred to as Greece, Bulgarian Macedonia as Bulgaria, and the nation state of Macedonia as Macedonia. (See Map 4 p. 74).

Greece was still neutral, and all sides wished that to remain the case. However Greece, living up to her Machiavellian reputation, was not impartial, since the king supported the Germans and the Government the *Entente*. This was referred to as 'The National Schism'.

The eastern portion of Greece, where the campaign involving Britain was to be centred, consists of a 200-mile strip of land east to west, but only forty-five miles in depth, north to south. Its northern border with Bulgaria abuts the Bulgarian Belshitza Mountains, and its southern boundary is the Aegean Sea. The strip of land in effect forms a coastal plain. Its lack of depth clearly makes it hard to defend against a major attack from the north. In this coastal plain the Struma River runs north-south from a gap in the mountains about fifty miles to the east of the Salonika-Doiran road, through the coastal plain, and out into the Aegean Sea. Salonika is a major Greek sea port in the Aegean Sea.

As mentioned, an *Entente* force was being put together by the French and the British. It was bound for Salonika to cover the Greek northern border with Macedonia and Bulgaria in order to prevent the Bulgarians, stiffened by some German units, from invading mainland Greece. The British force was to be re-deployed from Gallipoli with 10th (Irish) and 28th Divisions forming the initial re-deployment in October 1915. Over that winter 22nd, 26th and 27th Divisions arrived, in response to the early exchanges which favoured the much stronger

Bulgarians. The main *Entente* force was French and deployed over the same timescale, the French having overall command of the operation.

In addition to keeping the Greeks no worse than neutral, the *Entente* intended to support the Serbs, who were allies under attack by the Central Powers. Unfortunately, the Serbs had succumbed to the Bulgarian-led opposition before the *Entente* could get troops on the ground. However, it was decided to continue with the deployment to keep the Greeks neutral as mentioned, and prevent the Bulgarians securing Salonika as a submarine base for the Central Powers. Given the position of Salonika, this would have been strategically damaging for the *Entente*.

However, the campaign was considered a sideshow, as shown by events, and was to become known as the 'forgotten campaign'. That did not stop it being unforgettable as far as the Sherwood Rangers were concerned.

Both divisions in the initial deployment were infantry formations that needed cavalry to operate in the forward screen role, which fell initially to the three squadrons of 3 Mounted Brigade who had been held back in Egypt to look after the horses. They formed a composite regiment commanded by Lieutenant Colonel Gordon Ley of the South Notts Hussars. On arrival at Salonika, they were joined by twelve officers and some NCOs from their respective regiments in Gallipoli, including Lieutenant Colonel York of the Gloucestershire Hussars who took command, and Major Mirlees, SRY, who commanded the SRY squadron.

The composite regiment was to act as divisional cavalry to 10th (Irish) Division, the leading division, due to advance north and prevent a Bulgarian incursion. The division was not at full strength due to its losses in Gallipoli. The Sherwood Rangers squadron was selected to be the first sub-unit sent up-country to provide a forward cavalry screen in the area north of Lake Doiran, covering the border. The patrol area was towards the south-facing foothills of the Belashitza Mountains. It was December 1915, the weather was bitterly cold, and there were no tents.

After about a month the Bulgarians attacked at Kosturino. A combination of weather conditions and the war-weary and weakened condition of 10th Division enabled the Bulgarians to push the *Entente* south. The Sherwood Rangers formed the rearguard, thus being the last *Entente* troops to pass south through Doiran. This forced the *Entente* to enter mainland Greece but, luckily, the Bulgarians, following their own strategy regarding Greece, voluntarily and diplomatically stopped short. Although this was a poor performance by the *Entente*, in which the Sherwood Rangers had nevertheless performed their part competently, the main aim, to save the remnants of the Serb army, had been achieved, and would bear fruit two years later.

It was Christmas. There was a risk of invasion of the eastern strip of Greece up to and including Salonika by the Bulgarians, which, as already mentioned, was difficult ground to defend. The Greek Chief of the General Staff in Athens, referring to the anticipated attack, had said 'You will be driven into the sea, and you will not have time even to cry for mercy.' That surly tolerance on the part of the Greeks continued until they eventually came in on the side of the *Entente* in 1917, after the Sherwood Rangers had been re-deployed to Palestine. Salonika, and the major part of mainland Greece, could be more easily defended from an attack into the coastal strip from Bulgaria by holding the western end in strength, a task given to the British. The more likely point of attack by Bulgaria would, however, come through Macedonia, which the French were defending.

In January 1916 the main body of 3 Mounted Brigade, having been withdrawn from Gallipoli to Egypt, became an independent brigade, and was re-named 7 Mounted Brigade, as a result of 2nd Mounted Division being disbanded. The brigade still consisted of the Sherwood Rangers, under command of Lieutenant Colonel Thorpe, South Notts Hussars and Derbyshire Yeomanry, together with supporting arms. Having re-equipped and re-trained near the pyramids, the brigade embarked for Macedonia on 2 February 1916, to join its advance guard. Coincidentally, they embarked on the SS *Winifredian*, which had carried the Sherwood Rangers to South Africa sixteen years before.

By the time 7 Mounted Brigade had landed in Salonika, a major defensive position had been constructed by *Entente* infantry, who now sat safely within it. It extended around the port to a radius of about ten miles and consisted of earthworks and trenches, surmounted by copious amounts of barbed wire and, as a result of the visual effect of the barbed wire, had been christened 'The Bird Cage'.

The Sherwood Rangers, in common with the other regiments of 7 Mounted Brigade, were re-united with their detached squadrons, and the whole formation became operational, its task being to form the screen for the *Entente,* patrolling the vast mountainous area of Greece, north of the Bird Cage, between Lake Doiran and the Salonika-Seres road, a triangular area with three fifty-mile-long sides to it, effectively the no man's land between the Bird Cage and the northern Greek border. They were under command of Major General Charles Briggs, GOC 28th Division, the British commander in this campaign, a regular cavalryman, who had served with distinction in the Boer War commanding the South African Imperial Light Horse, and 1 Cavalry Brigade in the Expeditionary Force in France in 1914.

The brigade's role was to be the divisional commander's 'eyes and ears'. When the build-up of British troops was complete they were named the British Salonica Army and consisted of XII and XVI Corps. At this point Briggs took command of XVI Corps and 7 Mounted Brigade then transferred under its command. This was a classic cavalry role of patrolling, reconnaissance, and providing forward and flank screens, and, above all, accurate information about enemy strengths and movements to the corps headquarters. Because of the absence of accurate maps they also carried out map-making, another cavalry task. Finally, they were required to defend their area of responsibility from incursions and infiltration. Later, the *Entente* moved infantry north to turn the area around Doiran into a heavily-defended zone which, as a result, would draw the main fighting in the months ahead, but initially only cavalry were active outside the Bird Cage.

In April patrols by German cavalry increased in the area of Doiran, the Sherwood Rangers having the lion's share of the resulting skirmishes. During this period Corporal Bailey earned the DCM for gallantry, rescuing, while under enemy fire, a comrade whose horse had been shot from under him. Tallents' description of the most significant and frustrating skirmish gives a feel for the nature of routine contacts between the two sides:

On 17 April A Squadron were holding the outpost line, and the rest of the Regiment, with the Machine Gun Troop and two support troops of A Squadron moved out through the outpost line at 2.30 a.m. to the Gola Ridge.

At 5.00 a.m., three squadrons of German cavalry came round the end of Lake Doiran towards Pateros, supported by a considerable force of infantry; one of their squadrons came on towards Gola, their right-flank patrol passing within a few yards of Sgt Hethershaw and his troop who were lying concealed in some scrub and had been told not to fire, and approached the position where B Squadron were concealed. We disclosed only a small patrol with Pte Moore as its point, riding a specially selected horse, which would be difficult for the Germans to overtake. The Germans were cautious and approached our patrol very slowly, while Moore waited for them in the hopes that some at least of the Germans would chase him and be led into the trap; unfortunately they would not do this though they were within speaking distance of him, so after … telling him to 'go away you blutty fool', he rode slowly away to one side leaving the front of B Squadron unmasked.

The Germans stood in a bunch looking towards B Squadron's position and then turned to retire; the moment they did so it was evident that they would not be caught in the trap so B Squadron and the Machine Guns opened fire. Unfortunately both the Machine Guns which were about twelve-years-old jammed after a few rounds and consequently we only succeeded in wounding 7 of their men and 7 horses according to enemy intelligence reports obtained later.

Moore was awarded a DCM for his part in the action, 'For gallantry and coolness when sent out to try and lure a party of enemy into an ambush. He behaved in a remarkably plucky manner when in very close touch with the enemy.'

Although the regiment's role was a cherished one, it was no soft option. It is true that in spring 1916, when the brigade was operating in the area of Doiran, the situation was close to perfect, little enemy activity in a land literally flowing with eggs, milk and honey and verdant growth. The air was so clear that visibility extended over long distances. Both men and horses flourished, good health and fitness enabling them routinely to cover fifty miles in a day. However, this was about to change.

In May the 'neutral' Greeks handed over Fort Rupel to the Bulgarians. This stronghold guarded the pass where the Struma river entered the coastal plain and its handover opened the door into eastern Greece from Bulgaria. The Greek corps occupying eastern Greece then declared themselves non-combatants, presumably because the handover increased the risk of being cut off by a Bulgarian advance south. This significantly heightened the level of threat to the British and triggered the gradual easterly re-deployment of the brigade. The first unit to be sent was the Sherwood Rangers, to cover the Struma Valley, the obvious eastern stop line. Detached from the brigade the regiment came under direct command of the now formed XVI Corps Headquarters, who ordered it to move east, near to Seres on the Struma, screening the approaches to it, a task the Rangers performed for about two months.

Not only did military activity increase significantly but, much worse, due to the marshes and lakes abounding along the Struma's course, malaria was endemic. Luckily, the Sherwood Rangers had, as Medical Officer, Captain Patton, who was experienced in tropical diseases, and as a result the regiment coped best of all the units which became affected in turn. Horses also suffered during the summer months, through shortages in good quality feed and the less benign climate; heavy rainfall frequently had a debilitating effect on the ability to operate. On 1 August the Sherwood Rangers were joined by the rest of the brigade which, due to malaria, amounted to no more than a composite squadron of South Notts Hussars and Derbyshire Yeomanry, to supplement the two fit squadrons the Rangers could field.

The regiment received a letter from the corps commander, dated 2 August, in recognition of their attachment to HQ XVI Corps:

> On the Sherwood Rangers rejoining 7 Mounted Brigade, the Corps Commander wishes to express to Lieut Col Thorpe his admiration for the admirable manner in which he has carried out his orders and instructions during the period he has been attached to the XVI Corps.
>
> General Briggs considers that the good work done reflects great credit on Lieut Col Thorpe and all concerned under his command.

Given that Briggs was an experienced cavalryman, this was a valued compliment.

On 18 August the Bulgarians attacked over the whole northern Greek frontier. In the Struma Valley the brigade had obtained intelligence in the early part of August that this would happen, but the staff had not acted on it. On the Struma front the force opposite the brigade consisted of an entire corps comprising the Bulgarian 7th and 10th Divisions, with 11th Division close at hand in the Belshitza Mountains. Because no heed had been taken of the brigade's intelligence, it was fully extended on patrol on the southern flank when attacked, giving the enemy the advantage of tactical surprise. This tested the regiment to the full, as it extracted patrols totalling forty officers and men (not all on horseback) from forward positions across its entire front. The brigade then withdrew in contact.

On 19 August the brigade received new orders to check the Bulgarian advance which took it north again. Information on enemy strength and direction was also needed, this new task becoming necessary as the French division, based on Seres, and holding the whole front, moved out. The only force now opposing an entire Bulgarian corps advancing from the east in the Struma Valley was 7 Brigade at regimental strength, plus a weak company of infantry holding the bridge over the Struma at Kopriva, the main, but not the only crossing. The nearest reinforcements were fifty miles away to the west. Clearly this was a precarious situation, because it left the main British positions at Doiran exposed with an open flank. If the Bulgarians realized this, they could have struck into the British flank in little over a day.

Contact with the enemy was duly re-established. Their forward troops were, when the brigade came into contact, no more than ten miles east of the Struma. All they needed to do was secure crossings.

The brigade came under heavy fire and pressure across the front in that sector, Tallents recording:

Before daybreak on 19th we crossed the Struma at Orljak Bridge and from 5 a.m. till after dark we were incessantly operating between Nevoljen, Topalova, Elisan and Kopriva (where the infantry were positioned covering the bridge) in order to locate how far the Bulgars had advanced into the valley. We found them first between Topalova and Kumli after a long advance in open order across some miles of flat country quite devoid of cover, and a very nasty time they gave us; after driving in small parties we came under heavy fire from about a battalion ... hidden behind natural earth banks and from three batteries of field guns at fairly close range. We had to retire at the gallop across the plain to Nevoljen with shrapnel bursting all over us, which caused several casualties to both men and horses, though far less than we expected from such heavy fire.... We then moved north to Elisan and again ran into the enemy along a line covering Kumli and Barakli-Djuma; eventually we got back to Orljak after dark

At 2.30 on the 20th we marched northwards [up the west bank of the Struma] to Kopriva, crossed the bridge there, and proceeded to Ormanli ... to find out how far the enemy had advanced during the night. We held this village all day though we were being shelled and shot at from several directions and could see the enemy advancing round both flanks in order to surround us, so that we were very glad to retire as soon as it was dark enough to hide us. After re-crossing the Kopriva Bridge we dossed down just beyond it, but we had to have 100 dismounted men ready at a moment's notice to reinforce the infantry at the bridgehead.

Despite the pressure it had been under, the brigade's show of force during 19 and 20 August was so effective that it had deceived the enemy into thinking they were facing much stronger opposition. This caused the Bulgarians to check their advance for another day; they did not reach the Struma till late on the 21st.

Tallents described the 21st as 'a very anxious day, as we could see the enemy advancing in large numbers all over the plain and expected them to cross the (Struma) river at many places while we were quite powerless to stop them at more than one or two'. However the Bulgarians failed to cross and, that night, 10th (Irish) Division, after a forced march, arrived and secured the line of the Struma. The brigade continued supporting 10th Division along the river line. A good example of what this entailed occurred on 22 August when Corporal Surtees, of the regiment, was despatched to establish enemy strengths in Nevoljen, two miles beyond the east bank of the Struma. To do so he swam his horse across the swift-flowing river in the dark before dawn, slipped through enemy listening posts, and lay concealed with his horse in a *nullah* [a dry streambed] near the village till light. This enabled him to estimate enemy strength in the village at about a battalion. Galloping back under fire, he swam his horse over the river, and delivered his information unscathed, save for a flesh wound in his horse's neck.

The brigade was now relieved but re-deployed south on the Struma to Kopaci where Colonel Thorpe took temporary command, Brigadier General Lance becoming indisposed; Major Mirlees assumed command of the Sherwood Rangers. The brigade continued patrolling the Struma in their new sector, but no enemy were found in the south. On 1 September the Sherwood Rangers increased to three squadrons again on receiving a fresh draft.

The fighting in the Struma Valley was part of a general attack by the Bulgarians along the length of the northern Greek border. The Bulgarian advance, however, had been halted by a major action in August; attacking the *Entente*'s strongpoint near Doiran, the Bulgarians suffered a heavy defeat with many casualties from when the initiative switched to the *Entente*, with the main thrust being far to the west, dominated by the French. The tide having now turned the *Entente*'s way, future offensive operations, although limited in scope, were being initiated by the *Entente*. In the Struma Valley, too, the position had stabilized. In the main, for the remainder of the Sherwood Rangers' deployment in Greece, which would end in May 1917, they were committed as part of the brigade, to their core role as corps troops. They patrolled no man's land east of the Struma, which was often a considerable tract of country, which involved long days in the saddle.

In January the DSO was awarded to Lieutenant Colonel H. Thorpe, the CO and sometime brigade commander, for services in Gallipoli and Macedonia and, in May, a DSO was awarded to Major H. Tallents – one assumes for his actions in the Struma Valley.

One interesting comment by Tallents on the campaign, which relates back to the question of the continuing utility of cavalry against modern weapons addressed earlier, was:

A galloping horse is a very difficult target or we should have had far greater losses.... We found out here and confirmed later in Palestine, that if there were no natural obstacles or wire it is possible for bodies of mounted troops in open order to gallop through extremely heavy frontal fire with few casualties.

On 31 May 1917 orders were received for 7 Mounted Brigade, less the Derbyshire Yeomanry who remained in Macedonia for the rest of the war, to return to Egypt. On 23 June 1917 with Lieutenant Colonel H. Thorpe again acting brigade commander, the Sherwood Rangers embarked on the HMT *Cestrian*. After a deployment of twenty months, they sailed for Egypt that night, their strength being twenty-seven officers, 529 other ranks and 612 animals.

The Rangers' key part in one action ought to be highlighted. In the delaying action by the brigade against a corps between 19 and 21 August 1916, outlined above, the brigade was reduced by illness to three squadrons, two of which were Sherwood Rangers. The mismatch between the two sides must have been at least 30:1 in men. Armed only with rifles, with no artillery support and only a depth of ten miles in which to work, the Rangers nevertheless screened a front of twenty miles against an advancing corps, which they delayed through deception, for three days. The Bulgarians paid the brigade the considerable compliment of 'bowler hatting' their own commander (or whatever one does to a Bulgarian general).

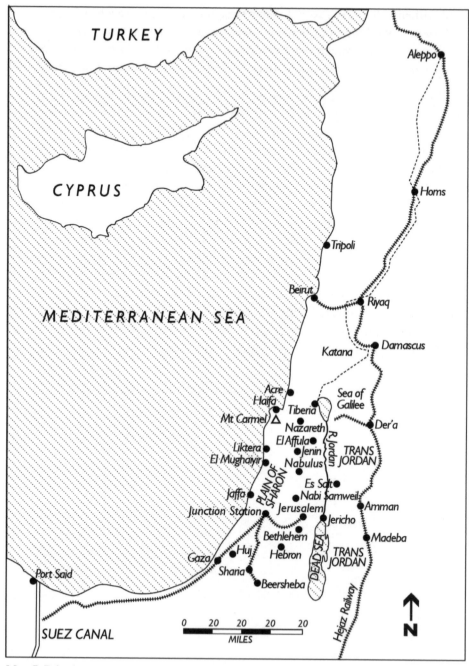

Map 7: Palestine.

Chapter 15

Palestine – Redeployment

June–October 1917

The reason for 7 Mounted Brigade's redeployment to Egypt was to form part of a significant reinforcement of the British-led Egyptian Expeditionary Force (EEF), which was now on the offensive.

The British had been engaged militarily in the Middle East since the outbreak of the war for two main reasons. The first was to defend the strategically vital Suez Canal and Egypt itself, which was a protectorate, and the base for all activity in the eastern Mediterranean; significant numbers of troops were in the country. The second was to protect the British government's investment in the Anglo Persian Oil company, a major provider of fuel oil to the Royal Navy.

Prior to mid-1916 the British and the Turks had sparred over Mesopotamia, as that area which includes Palestine and Iraq and all points in between was known generically, with not much success on either side. In truth, neither had been all that interested in Palestine, the British because the Canal and Egypt were its main interests and the Turks because they were far more fearful of Russia.

All this had changed as David Lloyd George became prime minister at the end of 1916. The government saw the stalemate in Flanders as bad politics and bad militarily and was concerned that the war was far from won. Russia was no longer fully engaged, and the Americans not yet involved. Some other allies were weakening, and a compromise favouring the Germans was becoming an unappealing possible ending. Lloyd George believed that if the Allies, led by Britain, could take Palestine, and the 'jewel' of Jerusalem in particular, this would provide a major boost to morale at home, and might then form a launch pad northwards to pose a serious threat to the Central Powers from the south. As a result, since the summer of 1916, the EEF under Lieutenant General Sir Archibald Murray had, by stages, driven the Turks out of Sinai. Given the distance of 200 miles, this does not appear all that impressive. However, with rare exceptions, the Middle East is a hostile environment in which to wage war. There were, of course, natural supplies of water, but these tended to be wells, not rivers, and widely spaced and closely guarded. This meant that, for the attacker, the next water holes, rather than the vital ground, became the main objective. As the force advanced through country where it was impossible to live off the land, re-supply became as important as the fighting itself while the lengthening distance between the force and its source of re-supply increased the problem exponentially.

Given that crossing Sinai was but the prelude to a major campaign, engineers and logisticians had built a roadway, using the ingenious solution of wire netting secured to the ground, a standard-gauge railway and a water pipeline. In March 1917 the advance came up against the well-defended Turkish position at Gaza – well defended because the Turks had suddenly become aware that the *Entente* was on the move in the Middle East. They appreciated the threat posed by a strong force advancing north through Palestine towards their southern border and their open flank with Russia, and had resolved to hold Gaza, gateway to the north, in strength.

Murray twice failed to take Gaza. Following the second attempt in April 1917, he was stood down. In July he was replaced by General Sir Edmund H. H. Allenby KCB. Allenby, born in 1861, was brought up in Nottinghamshire and knew the Sherwood Rangers well, which would certainly do them no harm in the months to come. Commissioned in the 6th (Inniskilling) Dragoons in 1882, he joined his regiment in South Africa and fought extensively and with distinction throughout the Boer War, which, as has been shown, was a war that favoured the skills of the cavalryman. He returned to Britain in 1902 to command 5th Royal Irish Lancers in Colchester. In 1910, as a lieutenant general, he was appointed Inspector-General of Cavalry. His fiery temperament and commanding presence had earned him the nickname of 'The Bull'.

During the First World War he initially served in the Expeditionary Force, commanding the only cavalry division with distinction during the early stages, when the nature of the fighting in France was still open enough to exploit his gifts for manoeuvre warfare. In 1915 he was given command of V Corps and then Third Army. Criticized for the heavy losses that both formations suffered during trench-based fighting, he is said to have lost the confidence of his commander-in-chief, Douglas Haig, was relieved in June 1917 and returned to England. In the circumstances, Lloyd George's decision to appoint Allenby to command the EEF was a brave one, destined to be fully justified by events. He was one of those rare British generals who truly understood, and was not scared to use, cavalry. More than that, the campaign was to show him to be a master of the art of all-arms warfare, and blending the strengths of the various fighting elements of an army into a co-ordinated team.

With shocking suddenness, all of this became of secondary interest to the Sherwood Rangers the day after they had put to sea for Egypt, as the HMT *Cestrian* was torpedoed off Skyros as Major E. V. Machin described:

> it got us right amidships and slap in the boilers and stopped the engines at once. I was sitting on the deck under the port lifeboat and it blew it clean in two over my head and … on the deck with all its tackle and the davits about a

yard behind me. … A perfect deluge of water was shot up and over me, which contained more coal dust than anything else. I was wet through to the skin and like a collier … most of us came off without anything…. The men are absolutely destitute. No coat, some no hats and 147 without boots. We were very lucky as we steamed off … after firing at anything which looked like a sub to keep her down. If we had had another when we were transhipping it would have been 'all up' as we were all crowded together – The other [destroyer] cruised round and picked up the men in the water, on rafts & in the lifeboats and then attempted to tow the boat towards the shore about 16 miles away but sad to say they got her within 4 miles and down she went, with all our poor horses and mules on board, 800 in all. All machine guns equipment, rifles, limbers an awful sight which I am glad to say I did not see, but the other [destroyer] did all that. Imagine 2 decks (lower decks) crowded with gees and mules tied short by the head, imagine the shambles it would be when they were mad with funk – it is cruel to think about it… The horses can never properly be replaced as they were all so fit, the men knew them and how they behaved under fire etc. … God bless the British Navy I say.

The regimental silver was also lost. The destroyer which took the regiment off was HMS *Ribble*, which put everyone ashore in Mudros Bay on Lemnos island off the Dardanelles, a major logistic base run by the Navy for the Gallipoli campaign, and still in use.

All were well looked after and were embarked on the HMT *Aragon* on 1 July, landing at Alexandria on the 3rd and entraining next day for Ferry Post on the Suez Canal. There they were met by Lieutenant Colonel Thorpe who, as acting brigade commander, had travelled with his horses and all his kit on another ship. He brought with him one horse which belonged to the regiment, which had been found by the SNH. The truth was that it was such a useless beast that it had been deliberately turned loose by the regiment before leaving Greece, so that it would wander into an adjoining camp. It was now elevated to the status of the only horse, other than the colonel's, which the regiment possessed. They joined up with the headquarters of 7 Mounted Brigade, where Brigadier General J. T. Wigan DSO had assumed command. He was aged 40. In 1898 he had joined the 13th Hussars, and served in the Boer War where he was wounded. Retiring from the Army, he joined the Berkshire Yeomanry and commanded it at Gallipoli when he was again wounded and awarded his DSO. On recovering, he was promoted to command 7 Mounted Brigade.

Luckily, while in Egypt, the Sherwood Rangers received 483 horses and thirty-eight mules, all unfit and no match for those they had lost, but capable, in time, of making decent chargers. They were also fully re-equipped, including saddles, weapons and accoutrements. The South Notts Hussars were the only other regiment in the brigade, which, in addition, had all the usual supporting arms and

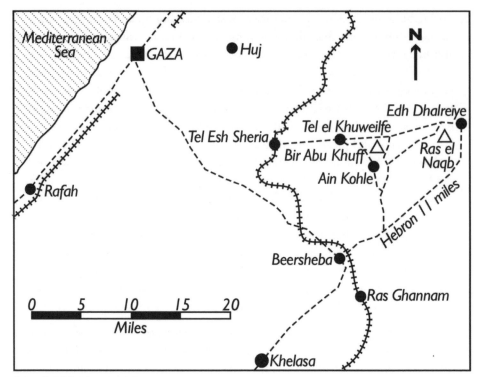

Map 8: Third Battle of Gaza.

services. On 12 August the brigade moved out to cross Sinai to join the EEF and arrived at Fukhari on the 29th.

When the brigade reported, Allenby was still planning his attack on Gaza but had already settled the configuration of the reinforced EEF:

Desert Mounted Corps

A & NZ Mounted Division (Volunteer)
Australian Mounted Division (Volunteer)
Yeomanry Mounted Division (TF)
Imperial Camel Corps Brigade (Colonial)

XX Corps

10th (Irish) Division (New Army, and nominally GHQ Troops)
53rd (Welsh) Division (TF)
60th (2/2nd London) Division (TF)
74th (Dismounted Yeomanry) Division (TF)
Four brigades of heavy artillery

XXI Corps

52nd (Lowland) Division (TF)
54th (East Anglian) Division (TF)
75th Division (Three brigades: British, Indian & S. African)
Three brigades of heavy artillery

Army Troops

7 Mounted Brigade (two regiments) (TF)

Note the small Regular or New Army component.

The EEF was opposed by Seventh and Eighth Turkish Armies on the Allied right and left respectively.

Chapter 16

Palestine – Gaza

October–November 1917

The sea to the west of Gaza and the high ground to the east of Beersheba create, to all intents and purposes, closed flanks. Any attack on the Turks would have to take place either on one of those two strongly-held towns, or the thirty miles between them. The dominant feature between the towns was an area of slightly higher ground on which sat the small settlement of Tel esh Sheria (Sheria). Two frontal attacks on the well-defended Gaza having failed before he took over, Allenby decided that XXI Corps (three divisions) would face Gaza and XX Corps (four divisions) would face Beersheba, both from the south. The battle would have the following phases:

1. XXI Corps to make a concerted attack on Gaza, supported from the sea, as a deception.
2. Desert Mounted Corps (DMC) would take Beersheba from the east following a concealed approach out of the desert; 7 Mounted Brigade's role, operating independently, was to fill and cover the gap between the DMC's left flank and XX Corps' right flank.
3. XX Corps would consolidate in Beersheba.
4. XX Corps, supported by the DMC, would strike north up the Beersheba-Hebron- Jerusalem road to secure a start line to the west of the road, facing west towards Sheria.
5. XX Corps would then attack Sheria from the east, rolling up the Turks' positions in between, forcing a fatal hole in the Turkish line.
6. On XX Corps taking the Sheria position, the DMC would be passed through to exploit north-west, bypassing Gaza, cutting off the enemy's retreat from his main position in that town, and thus defeating him.
7. Pursuit and destruction.

The DMC was commanded by General Sir Henry George Chauvel GCMG KCB, the first Australian to command a corps. The son of a grazier, Chauvel was commissioned as a second lieutenant in the Upper Clarence Light Horse, a unit organized by his father, became a regular officer in 1896 and, in 1899, commanded a company of Queensland Mounted Infantry in the Boer War. In May 1915 his formation deployed to Egypt and was sent, dismounted, to Gallipoli, where he, as its commander, assumed responsibility for some of the most dangerous parts of the line. He was subsequently promoted to command the DMC.

The ANZAC divisions did not carry sabres but the yeomanry did. All carried rifles, and the average weight carried by the horses was estimated at twenty stones, when fodder for the horse, ammunition, saddlery, weapons and the personal kit of the men were taken into account. Such an extreme weight placed a limit on the average distance covered on a daily basis.

Allenby's deception attack on Gaza by XXI Corps started on 27 October with bombardment, and then built up and continued throughout the subsequent action. He attacked in the east on 31 October following a formidable approach march by the DMC, forming a right-flanking sweep deep into the desert to avoid detection. During 31 October both XX Corps and DMC fought actions to position DMC for the final assault. When that came, it took the form of the famous and phase-winning charge of the Australian Mounted Division (AMD), followed up by other elements of the DMC and XX Corps, so that by 1800 hours they were both firm in Beersheba. Vitally they had secured the wells before the Turks could destroy them. In the absence of sabres, the heroic AMD attacked using their bayonets as hand weapons.

Later engagements by yeomanry using sabres proved more effective than bayonets; indeed on subsequent occasions, the AMD felt, by comparison, unable to engage mounted because of the lack of a suitable weapon. This failure to arm mounted formations with sabres was a consequence of the strategic failure to realize that cavalry, correctly handled to exploit firstly surprise, then manoeuvre too fast for the machine guns to track or lay, and finally fear of the sabre or lance, alone, still had the beating of the machine guns. These elements combined to achieve what was called 'Shock Action' and could be overwhelming. As will be seen, the ANZACs were eventually issued with sabres.

Seven Mounted Brigade had a satisfactory day as Tallents describes: 'Our orders were to occupy before dawn [on the 31st] a position in front of Ras Ghannam and Ras Hablein and to pursue the enemy if he retired … at 1600 a general attack was ordered.'

Their supporting 20 Machine Gun Squadron, positioned behind them, observed that:

> The Brigade at once formed up in a cloud of dust, and led by its General as if on a ceremonial parade at home, started off at the trot to attack. Soon the dust became so dense (especially in the centre of the Brigade) that it was impossible to see two yards in front.

With C Squadron leading, the regiment galloped in open order over rocky and mountainous ground to take the trenches on Ras Ghannam. The enemy fled and were captured by the Australians. The brigade followed the Australians into Beersheba at 1830 without opposition and, as Tallents notes:

watered at about 2300 after thirty hours without water.... Probably 40,000 animals had to be watered at this one place for several days, each may have taken several gallons at a time.

Allenby wanted to give the Turks time to respond to XXI Corps' deception attack on Gaza by reinforcing it with troops who had been covering their left, making the attack on Sheria easier. Unfortunately, the opposite occurred because the Turks thought that their main threat now was from an attack, which was in fact unrealistic, north up the Beersheba–Hebron road, the direct route to Jerusalem, which lay 100 miles to the north, and which they knew to be open. As a result, they started to move troops from Sheria, as Allenby had hoped. Instead of moving west to Gaza, they deployed east towards the ground Allenby planned to use as his start line for his attack on Sheria. This was bad news, particularly, as it turned out, for the Sherwood Rangers.

On 1 November XX Corps, as planned, advanced north, with DMC on their right, towards their intended start line. The ground was bare and rocky and fairly flat till it rose into the Judean Hills, where it was necessary for the start line to be established. By the end of the day, significant progress had been made, but shortage of water was becoming critical due to the wells at Beersheba becoming overwhelmed.

In the *Official History* Falls notes:

Water [now an additional need to that of securing Allenby's start line] could be found only by further advance [to reach the next nearest wells which lay in the same area as the start line but held by the Turks] and 7 Mounted Brigade with a regiment of 3 Australian Light Horse Brigade (3rd ALH) attached was ordered to move out on the morrow under the command of A&NZ Mounted Division and occupy the area Tel Khuweilfe, Bir Khuweilfe, Bir Abu Khuff and Ain Kohle.

And goes on to note that, on 2 November:

The Brigade had marched up the Khuweilfe track which leaves Hebron road near Kh. El Jubbein.... It reached the fork in the track ... without difficulty.... On the right the South Notts Hussars was ordered to seize the dominating height known as Ras en Naqb ... the Sherwood Rangers were to work up the left track and occupy the high ground at Bir Abu Khuff.... By 0300, after driving back the small bodies of enemy, it [SNH] occupied Ras en Naqb, capturing 11 prisoners and two guns.... On the other flank, however, the Sherwood Rangers was held up astride the Wadi Kohle, considerably short of its objective.

Tallents takes up the account:

B Squadron were now North of the Ain Kohle road, so C Squadron were sent to the south of it but both were quickly held up and a large body of the enemy appeared on their left flank [This was the advanced guard of the enemy re-deployment from Sheria to cover the Beersheba-Jerusalem road].

The other three troops of A Squadron were sent at full gallop to support C Squadron, whose left flank was in great danger, and the ground on this side of the road was then cleared after some fighting, during which Lt J. R. Abdy, with a few men, gallantly cleared out some Turks who were concealed amongst the rocks on the crest of one of the many steep hills. Lt Abdy was wounded in the shoulder and Lt Birchall received a slight wound to the neck, but was able to rejoin after having it dressed.

The flank guard troop of A Squadron, under Lt York, now rejoined, and a company of the Camel Corps extended our left, which relieved the situation to some extent.

The Regiment then attempted to take [the] Hill [known as] Khuweilfe, which was a very high and dominating position upon the slopes of which the enemy was established in some strength with several machine guns.

The Essex Battery RHA shelled the hill while A and C Squadrons worked forward as far as possible under cover. They were, however, still a long way from the top of the hill and separated from it by a stretch of flat ground; it was thought that this could be crossed mounted with fewer casualties than on foot, and there appeared to be some steep cliffs which would afford shelter for the horses a little way up the hill on the far side of the flat ground. Lt Moss with two troops of C Squadron, and Lts Birchall and York with two troops of A Squadron galloped forward and reached the selected places for the horses, but there were several casualties owing to the heavy and increasing rifle and machine-gun fire and from horses falling on the rocks.

All four troops dismounted but found it impossible to advance far beyond this point, owing to the heavy fire from the top and higher slopes; neither could they retire in daylight without heavy loss as the volume of fire which swept the open ground was now very heavy, so they held their position all day.

B Squadron on the right and the remainder of A and C Squadrons on the left and a section of 20 Machine Gun Squadron, held positions to the flanks and rear of the advanced troops. Strong enemy reinforcements could be seen as they reached the position and we were already heavily outnumbered apart from the strength of their position; they were continually trying to get round our left flank, and late in the afternoon the prospect for us looked very black. 5th ALH came up on the right of B Squadron in the evening but were held up by much superior forces. It was evident that the position could not be taken that day or at all without a very much larger force.

The regiment pulled back in the night, not without difficulty, and formed an outpost line, leaving the water holes, which they had been sent to secure, firmly in enemy hands. Relieved the next day (2 November) by another brigade, regimental

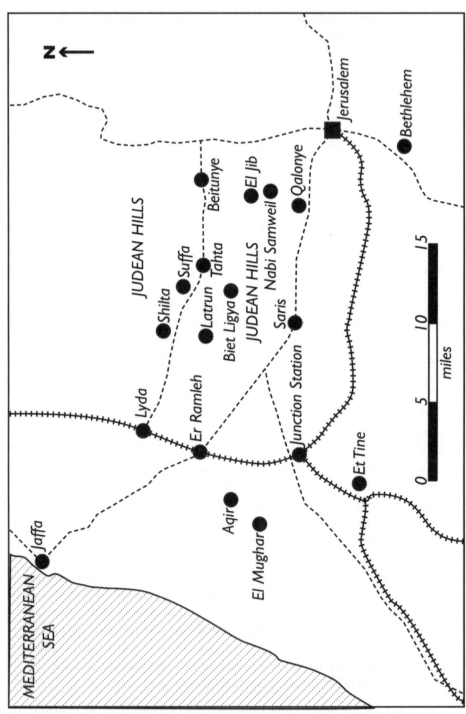

Map 9: Battles of Junction Station and Nabi Samweil.

casualties were one killed, and two officers and sixteen ORs wounded; they withdrew to Beersheba, the horses not having watered for forty hours. Lieutenant Colonel Thorpe believed that if the regiment had been two hours earlier, it would have been they, not the Turks, who would have secured Khuweilfe.

The *Official History* estimates that by nightfall on 2 November there were more than 4,000 enemy rifles and sabres (compared with the brigade's fewer than 1,000) on Khuweilfe, the vital ground opposite the brigade's position. The *Official History* goes on to credit the SNH's capture of Ras en Naqb as having cut the lines of communication of the Turkish Seventh Army Headquarters in Hebron with their left flank, and induced a state of near panic there, which caused them to make these re-dispositions in such numbers. Whilst they would have to be removed or neutralized before any attack on Sheria, they had at least been moved from Sheria, creating a valuable weakness there. This task of removing them was assigned to 53rd Division, who fought hard between 3 and 5 November to secure a satisfactory start line for XX Corps, albeit one which suffered some threat from the position at Khuweilfe.

The *Official History* sums up the fighting between 1 and 5 November:

> [It] resulted tactically in a drawn battle, satisfactory to neither side…. Yet strategically the British were to have no cause to complain of the result. They had placed themselves in a position of vantage from which to roll up the enemy's flank.…. They had drawn in his [the Turkish] reserve … division, which would otherwise have gone to Sheria. All the ground lent itself admirably to defence, as is proved by the fact that in the whole course of the fighting neither side can be said to have made a single successful attack, with the exception of the capture of Ras en Naqb.

The attack by XX Corps and DMC on Sheria from the east, rolling up the enemy's defensive positions on the way, commenced at first light on 6 November and was concluded by last light. With the capture of Sheria and the defeat of their forces in that area, the Turks commenced a full retreat from Gaza. The pursuit commenced at first light on 7 November and continued until the 10th. The pursuit was frustratingly disappointing, partly because there was delay getting the mounted formations through the breach in the line, but mainly because of the enormous difficulty and slowness in watering horses at infrequent watering places, which prevented any pressure being brought to bear on the enemy. Some baggage trains were captured, but most of the two Turkish armies escaped, albeit badly mauled.

The astonishing length of time that regiments of horses, these remarkable creatures so important to the development of civilization and warfare, were found to be able to go without watering whilst in full work was one of the revelations of the campaign; sixty hours on several occasions and, once, eighty-four hours by the Lincolnshire Yeomanry. One explanation for this may be the discovery during this campaign that horses with thoroughbred bloodlines that, therefore, reach back to the Arab horses from the Middle East, performed best. The Arab was bred by the Bedouin for beauty, speed and stamina and, logically, would have also been bred for its ability to reach scarce waterholes. However it should be added that, well-bred or not, they scattered all who dared to stand in their way once the scent of water was at last in their nostrils.

Chapter 17

Palestine – Advance on Jerusalem

November–December 1917

El Mughar/Junction Station 10–16 November

By 10 November the two Turkish armies facing the EEF had achieved some stability. Seventh Army on the left and in the Judean Hills had pickets astride the Beersheba–Hebron road as far south as Ras en Naqb, effectively unchanged at that point from its positions prior to Sheria. From there, however, its front line had been pushed to one side by Allenby's 'pursuit', which failed to cut off the retreat of Eighth Turkish Army up the coast road from Gaza to Jaffa.

Since Seventh Army had taken the main force of the fighting, it had been considerably weakened. Eighth Army, which had escaped Allenby's attempt to cut them off, had established a fresh stop line on the Wadi es Sunt and was much stronger. The inter-army boundary was the Beersheba–Junction Station railway line running north. The Turks clearly intended to defend this new stop line. XX Corps was using 53rd Division to screen Seventh Army, the remainder of XX Corps' divisions being in reserve near Gaza, unable to move up for want of the necessary re-supply capability, whilst XXI Corps and DMC faced Eighth Army.

Allenby planned to attack up the line of the Beersheba–Junction Station Railway line, with Junction Station as his objective, for four reasons. The first was that Jerusalem, his final objective for this phase, was in the high ground thirty miles to his east, and so once he had dislodged the Turks from their positions he would have to switch his line of advance in that direction. The second was that by attacking up the Turks' inter-army boundary he would hope to split them, to prevent Eighth Army interfering with his advance on Jerusalem. Thirdly, Junction Station was a key re-supply railhead for the Turks, with copious supplies of water. Finally, Junction Station would transform the EEF's logistics, giving it a railhead right back to Egypt, enabling him to re-supply XX Corps when moved up. The dispositions of EEF right to left were AMD (less 7 Mounted Brigade in force reserve), 75th Division, 52nd Division, and Yeomanry MD.

The battle for Junction Station was famous for three mounted actions, the first being the charge of 6 Yeomanry Mounted Brigade on 13 November at El Mughar. This was a three-regiment attack, with the Buckinghamshire Hussars on the right, Dorset Yeomanry on the left and Berkshire Yeomanry in reserve. It commenced from dead ground formed by the Wadi Jamus and ran eastwards over 5,000 yards to take the ridge line north of El Mughar village and was instigated in support of infantry attacks on the same feature, which had bogged down and was co-ordinated with artillery support. The regiments advanced simultaneously in column of squadrons, trotting the first 2,000 yards and galloping the last 3,000 to secure the position extending to five paces. 'Column of Squadrons' means the regiment advanced with one squadron leading, the others following behind over the same ground, in a pre-determined order. Within each squadron, the leading troop lined up facing the enemy in one or more lateral files, each numbering about three dozen cavalrymen, with the other troops lined up in the same way and in pre-determined order behind it. The CO led in the centre front with his trumpeter, and each squadron leader led his squadron in the same way. The troop leaders and senior ranks rode on either flank of their troop. The entire regimental group dressed from the centre. 'Extending to five paces' meant that there were five paces between squadrons. As for the overall distance covered, that is pretty much the distance of the Cheltenham Gold Cup. The drill book envisages a distance of a few hundred yards. The Hotchkiss sections, having followed up, were quickly brought into action to good effect once on the feature. Six Mounted Brigade's action cost an officer and fifteen ORs killed, six officers and 108 ORs wounded, and 265 casualties amongst the horses.

Later the same day, the East Riding Yeomanry and Staffordshire Yeomanry, advancing on 6 Mounted Brigade's left, took Aqir at the gallop in what was a purely opportunistic but brilliant action without orders.

The third action, on 15 November, involved the whole Yeomanry Division in a phased attack at speed onto high ground at Sidum, using artillery and machine guns in support. The Yeomanry also fought dismounted for some parts of the attack. The *Official History* comments that 'this was the second successful mounted action in the course of three days, and another good example of the co-operation of artillery and machine guns with cavalry'. Casualties were thirty-seven.

In the final stages, 7 Mounted Brigade was placed back under command AMD, and provided a flank screen to 234 Brigade of 75th Division as it made the attack which took Junction Station. The EEF pressed on and by 15 November were twenty-five miles north and fifteen miles east of the station. In this phase there was a significant amount of fighting, but nothing on 7 Mounted Brigade's front; the brigade was still under command AMD. Heavy casualties were inflicted by EEF on the Turks in this battle, which had the desired result of separating the two Turkish armies. It also meant that Seventh Army would have to defend Jerusalem with restricted re-supply by rail.

Nabi Samweil 17 November–8 December

Nabi Samweil, 'The Prophet Samuel', was the name of a peaceful hilltop town in the Judean hills above Jerusalem, said to be his resting place, a biblical name for what turned into a battle of truly biblical proportions for the city at the very heart of Christianity – Jerusalem.

Allenby, despite having had an excellent result, by splitting his enemy in two and exerting far greater attrition on them than they had on him, still had to overcome significant problems. He had to turn east into the Judean Hills, today known as the West Bank, consisting of great rounded, bare heights with deep sides into narrow treeless valleys, and almost devoid of any roads on which to advance, let alone bring supplies or reinforcements. It favoured the defender, who would be occupying the high ground where the hilltop villages, which were the norm, gave shelter and protection. This country surrounded Jerusalem, no matter from which side it was approached, and was, as a result, rightly known as the 'Judean Fortress'. Ideally, Allenby would have wanted to bring the now-rested XX Corps through XXI Corps to lead the new phase, but, because of his inability to support it logistically, as already mentioned, could not do so. It was therefore still back near Gaza. Delay was not desirable because it would give succour to his enemy. So he had to use tired and depleted, but still battle-worthy formations, whilst bringing XX Corps into the line, which he could begin to do, given his newly-captured railhead at Junction Station.

Allenby, who also had to screen Eighth Turkish Army to his north, made his dispositions as follows:

Holding Eighth Army at Jaffa were:

A&NZ MD plus 7 Mounted Brigade
54th Division

That left him with the following formations, with which he planned to advance eastwards into the Judean Hills three-up:

Yeomanry Division	Left (North)
52nd Division	Centre
75th Division	Right (South)

Fifty-third Division, part of XX Corps had, as indicated, been advancing northerly up the Beersheba-Bethlehem-Jerusalem road and was approaching the southern entrance to Bethlehem, south of Jerusalem.

AMD was in reserve.

Seven Mounted Brigade was positioned east of Lyda and, as well as facing Eighth Army, was the nearest uncommitted formation to those advancing on Jerusalem. Lieutenant Colonel Thorpe was suffering with his health at this time, as he had on and off for some time and on some days was unable to ride with the regiment.

The axis of the main eastward advance through the hills would cut the road due north out of Jerusalem, and so cut off the enemy retreating north. Allenby hoped that by enveloping the city to the north, whilst 53rd Division closed from the south, the Turks holding Jerusalem could be persuaded to surrender without a fight. The axis of 75th Division's advance in the south was Saris-Nabi Samweil; 52nd Division's axis in the centre was Biet Ligya-El Jib; the Yeomanry Mounted Division's axis in the north was Biet Ur el Tahta-Beitunye.

The front was about seven miles north to south, and the advance commenced on 19 November. It took two days to cross difficult terrain in indifferent weather whilst driving the enemy's pickets in front of them, before coming in contact with the Turks' main positions which occurred on 21 November. The enemy were found in strength in well-prepared positions on a line of hills running north to south: Bietunye-El Jib-Nabi Samweil-Qalonye.

In the south, and to the surprise of all sides, 75th Division immediately bounced the enemy out of Nabi Samweil in a brigade attack with no more than 500 rifles across a mile of open ground covered by enemy fire. Opportunism and failing light carried the day. The division then had to defend against continuous attempts to regain the ground, which inflicted significant further attrition on an already weakened division. In the north, the Yeomanry Mounted Division's objective on the 21st was Bietunye. They did brilliantly to get onto Point 2079, just one level below and within spitting distance of their objective, but were unable to dislodge the enemy. The strength of the entire division was under 1,000 sabres/rifles, and the Turks were defending with two, albeit weakened, divisions. In the end the Yeomanry were also pushed off point 2079 to Beit ur el Foqa, with 196 human casualties and 108 equine. Over the subsequent days of intensive fighting they were gradually pushed back towards Biet Ur el Tahta.

On 22 November 75th Division tried to take El Jib whilst hanging onto Nabi Samweil, and nearly lost both, just managing to retain the latter. At this stage 52nd Division entered the fight, supporting 75th Division. On the 23rd and 24th there were two determined attempts to take El Jib, now involving 52nd Division, and two gallant failures with EEF casualties running at 500 per day. At this stage, a decision was taken that success could not be achieved without reinforcements for a general attack across the front.

The new plan was that 60th Division, which had arrived in the line, would relieve 52nd Division, and take over the front covered by 75th Division. Both 74th and 10th Divisions were on the move, but four or five days away. The Mounted Yeomanry Division was to hold a position at Biet Ur el Tahta, and be reinforced by 7 Mounted Brigade on the 28th. The Yeomanry Division's left flank and left rear was acknowledged to be exposed to attack from the north. This was where the gap that had been driven between the Turkish Seventh and Eighth Armies at Junction Station still existed; 7 Mounted Brigade was to cover this area. The Yeomanry divisional commander ordered 7 Mounted Brigade to make a forced march through the night of the 27th as a precaution. This was a good decision, because the Turks, taking advantage of the short lull in the EEF offensive, were already planning to use their highly-regarded 19th Division to close the gap in their own line. However, they now saw an opportunity to accelerate the re-deployment of 19th Division, and to go further and attack the gap in the EEF's flank into the heart of XXI Corps at first light on the 28th.

Tallents notes:

> We started at 9.30 p.m. [on the 27th], and marched all night over a mountainous country, littered with rocks.... [We] reached our destination at 0445, just before dawn. When it was light enough to see we found that we were in a narrow deep valley running westwards from Beit Ur Et Tahta village where we found 22 Brigade horses.
>
> On arrival we off-saddled and began to brew some tea, thinking that the line must be some miles away and that the horses would be sent back after a short rest while we proceeded on foot.

Turkish 19th Division had indeed arrived to seal their inter-army boundary. Deployed above 7 Mounted's line of march, and ready to attack at dawn, they were unaware of the brigade's movement, which had been made under their noses. Had they but known, they could have destroyed the brigade as it passed, without adjusting their fire positions as Tallents records:

> At daybreak, to our astonishment, a sharp burst of rifle fire at close range passed over our heads, though we were quite safe in the valley as we were protected by the hill in front of us, which we discovered was held by the Lincolnshire Yeomanry. We immediately saddled up again ready for a move if necessary, and Capt Perowne, with three troops of B Squadron, was sent up the hill on foot to reinforce and extend the right of the Lincolns at Kh. Kebabe.

The ensuing battle for the gap between the Turkish armies is described by Tallents:

> The valley was choked up with animals, for besides the horses of the two Brigades, there was a Divisional Ammunition Column as well as Yeomanry Division Headquarters near Tahta village, about a mile away, and several Field Ambulances and other units.
>
> The volume of fire steadily increased, and at about 0630, the enemy began a general attack on the left of the Yeomanry Division's line, where there was a gap of about five miles, ending at Shilta village, on which the right of our infantry line rested. At about 0700 the enemy were reported in Suffa village and enveloping our left flank, so Major Tallents was at once sent off mounted with A Squadron to check this movement, but already the Turks could be seen at the mosque Sheik ab ed Din dominating the Western end of our valley.
>
> Lt Harter led the two half troops, but was unable to get far owing to the fire from the mosque hill, which was a very strong position on the top of a steep rocky hill, and already held in some force. This squadron was obliged to

take cover under the foot of a hill, a little to the East of the mosque hill, and dismount there; they then climbed the hill and took up a position on a ridge facing westwards, towards the mosque, with their right bent back at right angles so as to join up with the left of the rest of the Brigade.

Lt Harter was in charge of the Sector facing the mosque and could prevent any further enveloping movement from that direction, unless the Turks went a good deal further round. Lt Birchall was sent with his troop up the hill facing towards the north, to protect the right of Lt Harter's party, and to find out where the left of the Lincolnshire Yeomanry was; while making a reconnaissance he was unfortunately killed by a bullet through the head at close range.

Squadron-Sergeant-Major Tom East, of Newark, was then sent to take charge of that part of the line, as it was rather detached. [East received the DCM for this action: '*For conspicuous gallantry and devotion to duty. He rendered able assistance to his squadron leader, and set a splendid example to his men.* On a subsequent occasion he earned the *Medaille Militaire* to become one of the Regiment's most decorated soldiers.] Almost before A Squadron had got into position the Turks attacked the Lincolns in overwhelming numbers and drove them down the hill. The position was truly desperate, for the enemy were in possession of several hundred yards of the crest of the ridge along which our line ran, and as they were firing down into the mass of horses which were only about 150 yards below them, there were a lot of casualties and many animals broke loose, which made greater confusion. We had only one man to six horses there, so as soon as a few were hit there were many loose horses.

A Squadron were for the moment cut off from the rest of the force and had enemy on three sides of them, but retained their position on the hill.

B Squadron were on the right of the Lincolns and were just clear of the main attack, so that they were able to hold their position on the ridge and to do a lot of execution, though it seemed almost inevitable that they must be rolled up towards Tahta village and that the greater part of the Yeomanry Division would be wiped out. Luckily, the South Notts Hussars were in reserve at the foot of the hill, behind the Lincolns, and Major Barber at once led a counter-attack, assisted by fire from Lt Perowne's B Squadron on his right; this restored the position on the ridge, which B Squadron then assisted to hold for some hours, till withdrawn into reserve. General Wigan, our Brigadier, was wounded and the command devolved upon Colonel A. Calvert, of the South Notts Hussars. The Brigade Major was killed and the Staff Captain wounded.

At about 1100, 155 Infantry Brigade joined up on our left rear, though they were considerably behind A Squadron, which was still enfiladed from the Mosque and from the hill in front of Suffa. The Mosque was held by a small force of Turks with two machine guns.

At about 1130, Major Mason, who had come up to A Squadron's position, considered that the enemy were retiring and ordered an attack on the Mosque hill. Lt Harter was detailed to command, and was given all available men from Nos. 2, 3 and 4 troops of A Squadron, less the Hotchkiss-gun sections, which were required to provide covering fire and to hold the position in case of a counter attack, but the total strength of the party was very small.

To hold the line, the two C Squadron troops attached to A Squadron were brought up from squadron reserve, with every man of the horse-holders who could be spared. Very heavy covering fire was kept up on the enemy by these troops, by the machine guns, which had just come up under Lt Price, by three Hotchkiss guns and also by the infantry on our left rear. The operation was very gallantly carried out, and owing to the steepness of the hill the party was screened from direct fire from the garrison of the Mosque, for some part of the ascent, but they suffered from cross fire down the valley from the direction of Suffa.

Lt Harter and Cpl Frisby were hit when a short distance from the top, but the remainder, who were then only about fifteen strong, drove the Turks out of the Mosque and its courtyard, one of the machine guns was put out of action and several of the Turks were bayoneted.

SSM J. J. Tomkins was awarded a DCM for his part in this action:

For conspicuous gallantry and devotion to duty when two troops of his squadron were sent to seize a tactical feature. While approaching the place the squadron leader was killed, and this warrant officer at once took charge of the two troops and seized and consolidated the position, in spite of heavy rifle fire. He showed fine dash and ability.

As the battle continued:

Our covering party with the Vickers gun saw the other machine gun being carried away by its crew, and succeeded in knocking them out also.

The position was a dangerous one as the enemy could bring up supports to very close quarters under cover from Suffa, which he did and at once counter-attacked with about 70 men, with bombs and bayonets, compelling our men to leave the Mosque and retire to their starting point, as there was no intermediate position for them.

The enemy suffered considerably from our covering fire, but they were further reinforced and continued to hold the Mosque strongly thereafter.

On their return, those men who had been near Harter and Frisby, reported that they had been killed, but we wanted to bring them in to our lines if possible. An attempt to do so was very gallantly made by Sgt Ransley and others, but had to be abandoned because the face of the hill and the intervening valley were now swept by such heavy fire that it was impossible for anyone to approach the spot.

A further attempt to get them in was arranged directly it was dark, but was frustrated by the enemy advancing to attack us.

About noon half of a force which had been placed under Lt Abdy, consisting of part of B Squadron and men drawn from the horse-holders, was sent under Lt Dalziel to reinforce the right of the Lincolns at Kh. Kebabe; Lt Dalziel was wounded shortly afterwards and Lt Pelham–Clinton was also wounded.

Lt Abdy's force was withdrawn at dusk to take the horses back, though he remained with the Regiment as we were short of officers. At about 2000, Lt Perowne's force was relieved and came into Regimental reserve. The A Squadron hill was then allotted as Regimental sector of defence, with A Squadron and its two troops of C and two Vickers guns in the front line, under Major Tallents, with part of B Squadron and the South Notts Hussars on his right, the remainder of B Squadron being in Regimental Reserve.

About 2100 the enemy strongly attacked our hill from Suffa, with a force of bombers who could approach unseen through the rocks to close quarters; they drove us back about 150 yards.

The enemy at that time could easily have swept us off the hill into the valley, but for some reason he contented himself with holding the top of the hill and the cairn which was a prominent feature on it.

This enabled the men to rally and the line was then gradually pushed up again close to the enemy. Lt Abdy with part of B Squadron was sent up to reinforce Major Tallents, who sent him to protect the Vickers-gun Section, but he was severely wounded almost at once and very nearly taken prisoner, as the enemy again attacked and pushed us further down the hill. Every man was then in the line except about ten men at Regimental Headquarters under Lt Perowne.

Luckily just as the attack had been checked we were reinforced by the remnants of a company of 7th Scottish Rifles, consisting of about twenty-five men under Capt McGaffy, and a little later another twenty of them arrived; these with our own men then made a determined effort to retake the crest upon which the enemy had now installed machine guns.

The attempt failed after we had suffered very heavy casualties, amongst them being Sgt Ransley killed, and Capt McGaffy and Sgt Walster wounded. The small party of infantry was reduced to about one half in a very short time. We were short of bombs which were necessary for dislodging the enemy from among the huge boulders, while they had a plentiful supply, besides the advantage of throwing downhill, which lengthened the distance they could cover. When the enemy's machine guns were traversing, the bullets striking the rocks on the hillside made sparks fly and gave the effect of a narrow band of flash lights moving rapidly across the ground, while the flying splinters of rock considerably increased the effect of the fire.

Lt Price, who had most ably commanded the Sections of the Machine Gun Squadron on our hill throughout the previous day, was wounded during the early morning, and subsequently died. It was largely due to the steadiness and unfailing support which his section afforded to our men that we were able to retain our hold on the greater part of the hill during the night, although, just before Lt Abdy was sent to protect their flank, the section had been left practically by themselves, when A Squadron, on their right, had been temporarily driven back.

Towards morning the situation became more stable, and at 0430 on the 29th, another sixty of the Scottish Rifles arrived under Capt Nelson, to whom the left of our hill was then handed over.

Having had three officers killed and one wounded, only Major Tallents was left with his force which was then withdrawn into Regimental reserve.

Lt Perowne took over the right sector with B Squadron.

During the morning, Capt Nelson was able to make the crest untenable for the enemy by cross machine-gun fire, and retook it with twelve prisoners. He found the ground covered with the dead, both the enemy's and our own. The crest at once became untenable for him owing to cross-fire from three sides, and his losses became so heavy that he asked for and was granted permission to relinquish the crest, which then remained No Man's Land. Except for rifle and machine-gun fire, nothing occurred during the day.

From this moment XX Corps was taking over the front and 7 Mounted Brigade was gradually removed from the line down into the plain in reserve, under command the Mounted Yeomanry Division, staying there till 14 December.

The *Official History* comments:

> The enemy had little to show for his excellently conceived surprise advance against the gap in the British front. His failure to gain a great success lay partly in the fact that he was, like the British fighting in the dark. ... By the evening it was firmly held. But there was another cause: the initiative displayed by the commanders of 7 Mounted and 155 Brigades and the stubborn defence of all the troops engaged.

It is unlikely that, had the gap remained, 19th Division would have turned the battle, but it would certainly have prolonged it.

The fighting in the hills continued, but the tide had turned in favour of the EEF. The enemy were still holding out in very strong positions, but the pressure applied by fresh troops was taking its toll, till on the morning of 8 December there were white flags waving at the entrance to Jerusalem, the Turks having pulled out in the night. Sixtieth Division take the credit for the actual moment of surrender. The

Battle of Nabi Samweil was over. It had raged for three weeks. Allenby entered the completely undamaged city on foot and alone on 9 December. This campaign to capture Jerusalem is accredited as being the first defeat of the enemy by *Entente* troops in the war. It came as a beacon of light to the entire war-weary nation, at the point when the *Entente*'s key ally, Russia, had collapsed; Germany had counter-attacked successfully at Cambrai; there had been serious reverses for Italy and Rumania, and the States were yet to engage.

Allenby's astute use of cavalry played a significant part in this campaign. To imply, however, that this victory was solely down to the use of cavalry, the popular perception of Allenby's campaign in Palestine, would be wrong. It owed at least as much to the magnificent commitment and skill of the seven infantry divisions as it did to the DMC's contribution.

The regiment's strength, on returning to Gaza to rest, recuperate and retrain, was fourteen officers, 280 other ranks, 377 horses and seventy-five mules, about 60 per cent of their war establishment. The men were in such poor condition that a great many were sent straight to hospital. The horses were also in a 'deplorable' condition, scouring badly due to the absence of hay in their diet. The regiment now came under command of the Yeomanry Division.

Allenby summarized the campaign from Gaza to Jerusalem in his daily order of 15 December: 'In forty days many strong Turkish positions have been captured, and the Force has advanced some sixty miles on a front of thirty miles.' It is said that only the nature of the country saved the Turks from complete destruction. Over 12,000 prisoners were taken and 100 guns. Turkish casualties were 25,000 and the EEF suffered 18,000.

Regarding the long-held beliefs about the ability of mounted troops to deliver shock action effectively in the new era of machine guns and magazine-fed rifles, which had led to a strong disagreement over the previous thirty years between the General Staff and the mounted regiments as to whether the sabre (or the lance) should still be carried, Allenby had proved the doubters wrong. His Yeomanry Division had also proved wrong those who had doubted whether volunteer cavalry units were capable of learning the skills needed to deliver shock action, though they were yet to be permitted to call themselves cavalry. Furthermore Allenby, by delivering such a decisive campaign victory, had emphasized the lesson of Flanders, that infantry, in this new era, could no longer win conventional battles unsupported by manoeuvre troops.

Colonel Thorpe was invalided home before Christmas and Major Tallents, who gave outstanding service throughout the war, took temporary command of the regiment till, in January 1918, Major W. H. Wiggin DSO of the Worcestershire Yeomanry, and a survivor of the Affair of Huj, was, at less than 30 years of age, appointed to command. He was to serve the Sherwood Rangers with distinction.

'The Affair of Huj' was a spontaneous mounted action on 8 November during the pursuit after Gaza, by a mixture of Warwickshire and Worcestershire Yeomanries, against a retreating enemy column with an exposed flank. Although organized quickly, and executed using the best ground for concealment in the initial stages, their dust alerted the enemy, especially some Austrian gunners who were very quick to bring their guns into action. One surviving officer, who was in the van of the charge, wrote, 'A whole heap of men and horses went down twenty or thirty yards from the muzzles of the guns ... for a time I had the impression that I was the only man alive. I was amazed to discover we were the victors.' They were the victors partly because Major Wiggin commanded a squadron which miraculously passed through the Austrian guns unscathed just after they had fired, and carried the day. For that he was awarded the DSO and was destined to earn a Bar to it for his command of the regiment.

Drafts of men and horses began to arrive regularly, and the regiment turned to training them and incorporating them into its structure.

Chapter 18

Palestine – Reorganization and Repositioning

January–April 1918

L loyd George wanted more. The news from France was still bad and he clutched at a plan for Allenby to drive on to Aleppo, some 300 miles to the north, and thus force Turkey out of the war by the spring. Allenby was sceptical but willing to try if adequately reinforced. Unrealistically, sixteen divisions was the strength needed.

In February, the government sent out Lieutenant General J. C. (Jan) Smuts to agree a co-ordinated plan for the EEF, the Mesopotamian Expeditionary Force (MEF) in Iraq, and finally to address the continuing setbacks in France. He was the great South African leader who gave the United Kingdom such strong support during both world wars as to be admitted to the Order of Merit. He had also fought the British with equal commitment in the Second Boer War, including at Lichtenburg when suffering what must have been for him a rare defeat by the garrison which included the Sherwood Rangers. Maybe he asked Allenby to send his regards to the Regiment!

The following plans were finalized:

- One Indian infantry division and a cavalry brigade be transferred to the EEF from the MEF, the MEF to go into a defensive mode
- 7th Indian Infantry Division had already been diverted to the EEF on its way from India to France
- 52nd (Lowland) Division and 74th (Yeomanry) Division be transferred to France
- 14 Battalions from other EEF infantry divisions be transferred to France
- 14 Battalions from India to replace them
- 9 Yeomanry mounted regiments be transferred to France to become machine-gun battalions
- One Indian cavalry division be transferred to the EEF from France.

The Desert Mounted Corps would now consist of:

4th Cavalry (late Yeomanry) Division
5th Cavalry Division
A & NZ Mounted Division
Australian Mounted Division

The effect of this reorganization on DMC was as follows; on the minus side it had lost nine of its yeomanry regiments. These regiments were described in the *Official History* as 'first class', and the very best of them described as regiments that the divisional commander 'would not have willingly changed for any mounted troops in the world'.

On the other hand on the plus side, DMC now had four divisions, rather than three; the Indian cavalry were regular regiments, all of good quality. Finally the Australians, the arguments having been won, were due to be equipped with the sabre as well as the rifle by the end of the summer, so three of the four divisions would be equipped for shock action, up from only one before. For the six yeomanry regiments remaining in theatre, although there were differences in the interim, by the end of the summer their distribution would be:

4th Cavalry Division: Dorset Yeomanry, Middlesex Yeomanry and Staffordshire Yeomanry.
5th Cavalry Division: Gloucestershire Hussars Yeomanry and Sherwood Rangers Yeomanry.
XX Corps Troops: Worcestershire Yeomanry.
XXI Corps Troops: A composite regiment consisting of one squadron of Duke of Lancaster's Own Yeomanry and two of Hertfordshire Yeomanry.

Although the 'cavalry' divisions and brigades kept their affiliations, the brigades would be mixed in a ratio of one yeomanry regiment to two Indian regiments. In all, Allenby was clearly ahead in capability where cavalry was concerned, especially as he had retained the Sherwood Rangers. The infantry position would not be clear till he had an opportunity to assess the new formations on arrival.

Allenby and Smuts had discussed one further concern, that of the Hejaz railway which ran from El Medina in Hejaz (now Saudi Arabia), 600 miles to Allenby's south, to Beirut on the Mediterranean coast, 200 miles to his north where it connected to the Turkish railway system, which ran farther north through Aleppo, 300 miles to Allenby's north, and into Turkey. It passed about thirty miles to the east of Jerusalem, through Amman.

However, due to the terrain, the railway was out of Allenby's reach, and was controlled by the Turks. Supporting a force of 20,000 Turkish troops in garrisons along it, between El Medina in the south and Amman in the north, the railway represented a major threat to Allenby's right flank and rear. The Turks were keen to hang on in southern Arabia to retain influence there in the future. Dealing with this threat was an essential prerequisite for any advance north on Damascus and Aleppo. Luckily, there was a partial solution in the form of the Arab Northern Army (ANA) under command of Faisal bin Hussein bin Ali al-Hashimi, third son of Hussein bin Ali, Grand Sharif of Mecca (Saudi Arabia). A member of the Hashemite dynasty, he was a born leader and destined, with British support, to become king of both Greater Syria and Iraq after the war. One of the ANA's attached British officers was Captain T. E. Lawrence (of Arabia).

The ANA had three sections, British, French and Arab Regular Army, and recruited the Bedouin when it could promise them something to kill, and when it had sufficient gold to hire them. In strength it was about two brigades, its core made up of infantry and a camel corps, plus some artillery and machine guns; it also had a flight of aeroplanes and some logistic support. It had been sparring with the Turks in the vast open spaces south of Palestine and Arabia for some time with sufficient success that the Turks were confined to a couple of garrisons and some blockhouses, all based on the Hejaz railway.

The ANA's campaign had been separated from EEF operations in Egypt and Palestine by oceans of desert, and had been a sideshow within a sideshow until, on 6 July 1917, the ANA captured Aqaba, giving them a strategic port, it being the destination of the King's Highway, the major, centuries-old trade route south from Turkey, through Amman, to the sea, and also a firm base near enough to Cairo to enable Allenby to at least loosely co-ordinate Faisal's future activities with those of the EEF. They were, therefore, available to him.

Because of the restructuring of the EEF Allenby would be unable to start a major offensive north until late summer. However, since he would not lose all his experienced infantry until late spring, and the ANZAC cavalry divisions were not being re-deployed, he could take the offensive for preparatory operations immediately.

The broad plan settled by Allenby and Smuts was:

1. Consolidate the EEF's control of Jaffa and Jerusalem by improving the defensive strength of their position.
2. Tackle the threat posed by Turkish control of the Hejaz railway and through it of Trans Jordan (of which Amman was the capital), an area of high flat desert on Allenby's eastern boundary which ran from Ma'an in the south to Der'a in the north, a distance of about 175 miles with a width of some forty miles. Es Salt and Amman were its most significant towns, with Es Salt in the centre and Amman to the east. Trans Jordan was strategically important since it was an area from which the Turks, aided by the Hejaz railway, could threaten Allenby's right flank and rear. Allenby planned to deal with this by mounting a raid across the River Jordan, climbing into the high Trans Jordan country, taking Es Salt and then Amman on the other side before cutting the railway, where a major viaduct existed south of Amman, and linking up with Faisal, who would thereafter protect his right flank and rear as he advanced north.
3. Consolidate the EEF's supply lines so that they could support future army group operations.
4. When ready, but so as to finish before winter set in, to attack north, defeat Seventh and Eighth Turkish Armies to his north (plus a further army, Fourth, added, during the coming summer) with an initial objective of Damascus, and a secondary objective of Aleppo, and force Turkey to sue for peace. Fourth Army

was a reinforcement to be positioned on the left (east) of Seventh and Eighth Armies, east of the Jordan and opposite the ANA.

The following actions, which took place before the end of April 1918, did not involve the Sherwood Rangers, but provide context for those after 1 May which did. The brevity with which these events are described should not imply insignificance: some were considerable actions with important objectives; all were part of the plan. Whilst they were taking place, the EEF was doubling the capacity of the railway from Cairo on which it depended for re-supply and was building better roads, both on the line of supply and as lateral routes to aid troop movements.

Defence of Jerusalem and Jaffa: 14–30 December 1917

Whilst shepherds, no doubt, watched their flocks by night over Christmas 1917, XX and XXI Corps each exerted a concerted shove north during the last two weeks of December, to a line twenty miles north of Jerusalem and Jaffa, and also westward of Jerusalem, close to Jericho in the Jordan Valley.

Capture of Jericho: 19–21 February 1918

Allenby began to secure his right flank and neutralize the effect of the Hejaz railway. This was not a minor operation. Although the Trans Jordan feature of high desert has been described, it may help to understand the difficulty of the topography for movement west to east. First, the EEF would have to descend from Jerusalem, on the west bank of the Jordan (1,500 feet above sea level) into the Jordan Valley which ran north-south and was about twenty-five miles wide (1,400 feet below sea level), capture Jericho as a prelude to securing crossings over the river, then ascend into Trans Jordan on the east bank, (1,500 feet above) and secure Es Salt in the high country and on the main west-east axis. It then had to climb over the high ground (3,000 feet above) around Amman and down into Amman in a valley (1,500 feet above). (To provide a comparison; Ben Nevis is 4,400 feet above sea level.) All the transitions are steep in part, making for a major logistical undertaking, especially as the roads, bar the main route, were poor tracks.

As mentioned, the first step was to secure the Jordan itself. This was a XX Corps operation with cavalry support, concluded successfully between 19 and 21 February.

Tell Saur: 8–10 March 1918

This action had the effect of taking the EEF front far enough north to enable the desired raid eastwards on Amman to be launched.

Raid on Amman: 21–30 March 1918

This was a very ambitious attempt by XX Corps and DMC to take Amman, cut the Hejaz railway and link up with the ANA. Troops entered Amman and cut the railway, but were unable to consolidate, and withdrew across the Jordan without having linked up with Faisal, held up by the Turks farther south.

By March the Sherwood Rangers Yeomanry had been brought up to establishment in men and horses, and all had regained their fitness and health. Several race meetings were organized at which the regiment had many successes. They also managed to put together a bobbery pack of hounds with which they had some good gallops hunting jackals, without inflicting much damage, least of all to the jackals. With the departure of the South Notts Hussars, one of the yeomanry units destined for Europe, 7 Mounted Brigade was disbanded and the Sherwood Rangers joined 5 Mounted Brigade from the beginning of April as part of the AMD, becoming operational again on 1 April 1918.

Chapter 19

Palestine – Second Raid into Trans Jordan

April–May 1918

Gaza to Jericho: 1–30 April 1918

On 1 April 1918, under command the AMD, 5 Mounted Brigade marched past what had been the Sherwood Rangers' lines for the previous three months and the regiment marched out and fell in with the Worcestershire Yeomanry and Gloucestershire Hussars. Their destination was Jericho, deep in the Jordan Valley. The task awaiting them was Allenby's second raid into Trans Jordan. The march, with several halts, took till 28 April. Towards the end they marched at night to avoid detection by reconnaissance as Tallents describes:

> The march through Jerusalem in the brilliant moonlight was rather impressive, and after leaving the city we halted on the side of the Mount of Olives and brewed tea at 0200.... We reached Jericho at about 1300 on the 28th and bivouacked a mile or more north of the filthy little village ... which now bears that name. The view [eastwards] as we came down into the valley was very fine, the Dead Sea on the right [southwards] with its shores white with salt, high mountains in front and the valley stretching away to the left [northwards].
>
> The Jordan Valley was not at all a pleasant place. There was hardly any vegetation, and the ground was a mixture of lava rock and pure white dust which rose in vast clouds as soon as the horses moved;.... It was also extremely hot even at that time of year and the flies swarmed.

Allenby's reasons for mounting a second raid and its timing were:

- With harvest time approaching, he wished to deny the Turks the valuable quantities of barley and wheat from Trans Jordan;
- He wanted a final shot at capturing Amman, enabling him to disable permanently the Hejaz railway and link up with Faisal;
- The powerful Bedouin tribe of the Beni Sakr were camped nearby at Madeba in Trans Jordan. They had led him to believe that they would cut one of only two withdrawal routes back to Amman from the enemy positions at Shunet Nimrin. It was thought to be little more than a mountain track. They said he had to make his move before 4 May; thereafter they would have to move elsewhere because of shortage of supplies.

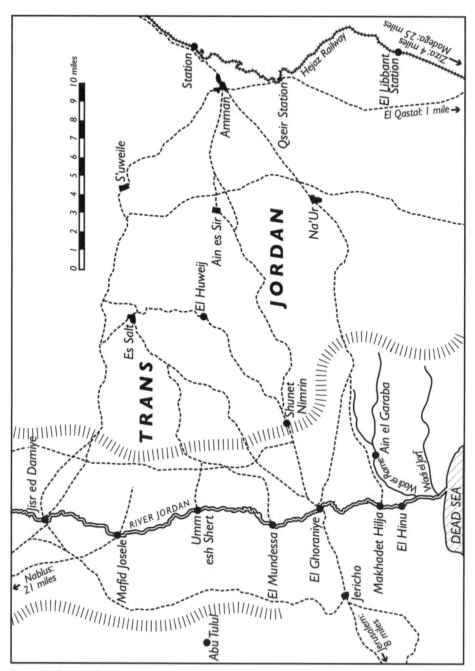

Map 10: Second Raid into Trans Jordan, The Affair of Abu Tulul.

- If the EEF could secure the high ground of Trans Jordan, it would reduce the numbers of troops who would have to remain protecting Allenby's right flank through the summer in the sweltering heat of the Jordan Valley;
- He wanted to keep the Turks on the defensive whilst he re-organized;
- Finally, Allenby was already beginning to plan the main attack northwards in the autumn. He had decided that he would break through with three cavalry divisions from his left up the Mediterranean shore and the Plain of Sharon, and therefore wanted to deceive the enemy into thinking that the attack would come up the more logical right through Trans Jordan to Der'a.

The Situation

In the Jordan Valley, looking down from atop the 'high mountains in front' was VIII Turkish Corps, consisting of what were thought to be two very low-calibre infantry divisions, centred on a narrow three-mile front at Shunet Nimrin, where the Jerusalem-Jericho-Amman road, the only significant lateral route, climbed precipitously from the Jordan Valley into Trans Jordan. The whole force was there to deny Trans Jordan, Amman and the Hejaz railway to the EEF. The Turks had detached a brigade to defend Amman. Allenby intended to encircle and cut them off, defeat them, take Trans Jordan and Amman, cut the Hejaz railway, and link up with Faisal.

There were, however, fifteen miles to the north up the Jordan Valley, Turkish forces preventing any northwards move by the EEF in that sector. These included two infantry divisions and a cavalry division, all positioned on the west bank of the Jordan facing south. They had access to the east bank via two bridges, or so it was thought (there was, in fact, a third crossing), the most northern of which, called Jisr Ed Damiye, served a significant track which ran eastward and steeply up into Trans Jordan to Es Salt. The southern crossing, called Umm est Shert, served a much inferior and more precipitous track up into Trans Jordan and on to Es Salt. Allenby planned to deploy troops to screen all three northerly Turkish divisions from the operation, by preventing their access to the east bank via the crossings, the Jordan generally being too deep to ford.

Allenby's plan was predicated on the fact that the Jerusalem-Jericho-Amman road, once on the high ground of Trans Jordan, did not run due east to Amman but north-east to El Heweij, north to Es Salt and finally south-east in a great loop to Amman. If, therefore, the EEF gained access to the high ground from the Jordan Valley from farther north of Shunet Nimrin and cut through due east to Es Salt along the two tracks just mentioned, the enemy's only adequate line of re-supply or retreat would be cut at Es Salt and, with the only other line of retreat covered by the Beni Sakr, they would be surrounded and besieged.

Access to the east bank was across the bridge near Jericho at El Ghoraniye on the Jerusalem-Amman road, the only crossing place available to the EEF.

The Plan

The raid, a DMC operation, was commanded by General Chauvel and the force consisted of the A&NZ MD, the AMD (including 5 Mounted Brigade with the Sherwood Rangers) and 60th Infantry Division.

- 60th Division would attack VIII Turkish Corps at Shunet Imrin, and seek to envelop the right of the enemy's position there. The Imperial Camel Corps Brigade would take up positions in the Jordan Valley eight miles north of Jericho on the west bank, and screen that side from a counter-attack from the north.
- 4 ALH Brigade of AMD was to be positioned with some artillery to screen the east bank of the Jordan valley from the Turkish divisions to the north.
- AMD, consisting of 5 (Yeomanry) Mounted Brigade, 1, 2 and 3 ALH Brigades, some light armoured cars, and the Hong Kong Mountain Battery of guns, but minus 4 ALH Brigade, would take Es Salt via the two northern tracks, advance south-west through El Huweij, down the main road and attack the Turkish corps at Shunet Imrin in the rear as a prelude to securing the railway.
- The corps reserve consisted of two infantry brigades, 6 Mounted Brigade and Imperial Service Cavalry Brigade.

The Raid: 30 April–4 May 1918

Well before first light on 29 April, 60th Division was covering the EEF's only crossing of the Jordan at El Ghoraniye. The crossing was then allocated to the AMD from last light on the 29th to 0200 on the 30th to enable them to cross. At 0400 on the 30th AMD on the east bank and the Camel Brigade on the west bank crossed their start lines and commenced their moves north. 'As the first streaks of light appeared in the sky, [AMD] began to move up the valley at a trot' up the east bank and by 0430 the leading elements had driven the Turkish cavalry pickets guarding the Umm esh Shert crossing before them. Five Mounted Brigade, C Squadron Sherwood Rangers, leading, was moving behind 3, 2 and 4 ALH Brigades, in that order, which were going farther north, followed by 1 ALH Brigade which was supporting 5 Mounted Brigade.

Five Mounted and 1 ALH Brigades peeled off right up the Umm esh Shert track as planned, but came under machine-gun fire from enemy pickets high in the hills. The regiment suffered several killed or wounded, including Boer War veteran Captain R. C. Layton commanding B Squadron, who was killed. Tallents takes up the story:

> The rest of the Regiment and the Gloucester Yeomanry were brought up, and the enemy began to retire, but in the meantime the Worcestershire Yeomanry found a track up the hills further to the north which was not defended, so

the Brigade followed them up [followed by 1 ALH Brigade].... The track up into the hills was very steep and rough, so much so that the pack animals had great difficulty in getting on, and several rolled down the steep slopes [the camels did not even attempt the ascent]. The whole Division had to go up in single file, and often we had to lead our horses owing to the steep gradients.

With the exception of some sniping and a little fire from automatic rifles by small parties of cavalry, there was no further opposition, and we reached the top of the hills commanding Es Salt at nightfall, and lay down till shortly before dawn, when all available men were prepared for an assault on the next ridge.

As 5 Mounted had turned into the hills, 3, 2 and 4 ALH Brigades came under light fire while advancing up the valley. They then quickened into a hand gallop as they spread out travelling north towards the crossing at Jisr en Damiye, the huge clouds of dust and surprise suppressing enemy responses. As they did so, they realized there was a third crossing, available to the enemy. As soon as the opportunity presented itself, 3 and 2 ALH Brigades bore right and were onto the Damiye track to Es Salt. The time was 0530, and they were eighteen miles north of their start line. It took them three hours to breast the ridge, where they encountered the enemy's main position, which they took with a brilliant flanking attack on foot and were in Es Salt by 18.30.

Down in the valley 60th Division's attack on the main position at Shunet Imrin had been repelled. Meanwhile, in the north, 4 ALH Brigade had failed to secure the Jisr en Damiye crossing, and the Camel Brigade had failed to secure the Umm esh Shert crossing. Four ALH Brigade asked for reinforcements because the enemy were now fully aware of the EEF's intentions towards Es Salt, and were crossing the Jordan freely to interdict AMD. This request was turned down because most reserves were already committed. The commander, therefore, concentrated his forces where the Damiye track entered the hills to prevent the enemy from pursuing 2 and 3 ALH Brigades and attacking in their rear. If the enemy were to secure the Damiye track, it could turn into a case of biter bit, because not only VIII Turkish Corps might be cut off, but the elements of the AMD holding Es Salt as well.

At dawn on 1 May, 5 Mounted and 1 ALH Brigades realized that the AMD already held Es Salt. They therefore got on with the next phase, which initially involved the Gloucester Yeomanry securing El Huweij to provide a firm base for an advance on VIII Turkish Corps' rear. However, they came under fire from strongly-held positions in high ground protecting the Turkish rear, which stopped them some way short. The Sherwood Rangers Yeomanry was in reserve at this point.

Late in the day, news reached the AMD that the second attack by 60th Division, which had gone in earlier that day, had also failed. Worse, 4 ALH Brigade had faced a full attack on its position covering the Damiye track where it entered the hills and had been forced to withdraw south down the valley to prevent being cut off by further enemy action in the vicinity of the Umm esh Shert track. In addition, the Notts RHA Battery, trapped with its back to the hills, was unable, due to the topography, to withdraw south without advancing west into strong enemy fire, and had been forced to abandon its guns. The overall effect was that there was now nothing covering the entrance to the Damiye track, and Turkish cavalry were moving into the hills towards Es Salt. Such was the pressure being brought to bear on 4 ALH Brigade that there was a risk of it being pushed south of, and thus losing control of, the Umm esh Shert track – the only remaining withdrawal route from Es Salt. Finally, the Beni Sakr had struck their tents and disappeared into the desert, leaving the secondary route to Amman open for the enemy. It is said they had been bought off.

Dawn on 2 May found the AMD increasingly stretched. Two troops had been sent down the Damiye track to hold any approach from that direction, which contained that threat for the time being. However, El Huweij was held by the enemy in strong positions that had to be forced before the main attack could start on the Turkish rear. This attack was to be dismounted over five miles of difficult and easily-defended ground. In addition, the Turkish corps was still firm and strong, was holding 60th Division comfortably, and had reserves aplenty to turn against an attack on them from El Heweij.

Two ALH and 5 Mounted Brigades had the task, and it was to be led, in the case of 5 Mounted, by the Sherwood Rangers and Worcestershire Yeomanry. Before the attack developed, the AMD's overall position suddenly became even more precarious due to new pressure on Es Salt from Amman, causing elements of 2 ALH Brigade to be re-directed from the attack at El Huweij, to reinforce those facing this threat.

The *Official History* notes that, due to the new pressure from Amman and on the Damiye track:

> the attack by 2nd [ALH] and 5th [Mounted] Brigades should [have been] broken off, so that those troops should be available in case of need at Es Salt. General Chauvel refused to hear of it ... because [if successful] ... it would have solved ... all the difficulties of 60th Division, but he gave permission for another regiment of 2nd ALH Brigade to be withdrawn. 5th Mounted Brigade was thus left to carry out, with three regiments, an operation which, to its commander, had appeared impossible with five.

Tallents records:

> We were ordered to make a dismounted attack on Hill 2750 on the [South-West] of Howeij Bridge. To approach this hill about four or five miles had to be covered on foot over extremely rough and mountainous country. The attack was [to be] in four waves, but at 1400 a heavy and accurate fire was

opened on us with 4.5-inch guns, which caused a number of casualties, including Lt R. H. Allen, whose place as Officer Commanding C Squadron was taken by Lt Dalziel. ... [They had] artillery enfilading them; strong enemy reinforcements could be seen moving along the ridges in front ... there were no troops available to support them and orders were therefore given to retire....

This was achieved, despite heavy enemy shellfire, by the leadership of Sergeant J. A. Denman, of Retford. All the wounded were, with the greatest difficulty, recovered to Es Salt by means of a captured motor ambulance driven by a German, and in various native carts. For this action, Sergeant Denman was awarded the DCM.

Sergeant W. F. Hethershaw of Retford also played a major part in the Es Salt raid and, as his citation notes, 'carried out the tasks allotted to him with great skill', especially during this withdrawal, 'when his troop was deployed to form the rearguard and to protect the evacuation of the wounded. It was largely due to his coolness, skill and energy that all the wounded were safely brought away, despite heavy shelling'. For these actions he was also awarded the DCM.

Tallents comments that 'That night we were in Brigade reserve, but rations and especially forage for the horses were practically exhausted ... nothing could be brought up the mountain path.... We were all about done up with the continuous mountain climbing with our full equipment....'

Down in the valley 60th Division had again failed to make any ground, and matters were getting close to untenable for 4 ALH in their attempt to hold the entrance to the Umm esh Shert track. At last, however, reserves in the form of the NZ Mounted Rifles Brigade and the Middlesex Yeomanry were being committed north to support 4 ALH Brigade.

Although any question of the raid achieving its main objectives on the ground had gone, 3 May was a better day because the Turkish counter-attacks had been blunted. Even the attack east of Es Salt was defeated in another brilliant flanking attack by the AMD. In addition, 4 ALH Brigade, together with its reinforcements, held the Umm est Shert track and the route back to the crossing of the Jordan at El Ghoraniye. In mid-afternoon, Allenby took the decision to cease operations.

The overriding question now was the extraction of the AMD which began immediately down the Umm est Shert track. Tallents gives an idea of how perilous the division's position was thought to be by HQ DMC: 'it was not anticipated that more than a small portion of the division would ever get back to the Jordan Valley, and a party was actually ordered to go to the bridge [at El Ghoraniye] in order to catch horses, which it was expected would find their way back in considerable numbers.' The main problem was that, even though this was the main track rather than the side track used for the ascent, and had been improved during the operation, the division could only proceed down it in single file. There were four brigades of approximately 1,200 horses each, making 5,000 horses plus, say, another 2,000 animals forming the echelon, and only the hours of darkness in which to get down: that meant ten hours at the rate of twelve animals per minute.

Tallents continues:

> at 1800 orders were received for a general retirement, and the Sherwood Rangers less C Squadron [under command of 3 ALH Brigade] left at dusk to act as reserve to the rearguard, and reported to 1 ALH Brigade.... At 2200 we were the first troops to pass through the streets of Es Salt on the way back. There was great difficulty in evacuating the wounded, who filled the Mosque which was being used as a hospital; it had not been safe to send them down during the preceding days, and there were not enough camel cacalis available for all now, but by good luck some arrived at the last minute, and rendered unnecessary the arrangements we had made for getting Lt Allen and our men away, by strapping them to horses which had been specially selected as being quiet for the purpose.
>
> The wounded must have had a terrible passage down the steep mountain path throughout that night and several of them died; for a fit man the movement of a camel, even on the level, is uncomfortable, so what it was on that path, when the greatest speed only could avoid capture by the enemy is hard to imagine. Some of the camels fell down the steep slope and the men in the cacalis were killed.
>
> All night long the Australians were passing through our line in single file at the gallop....
>
> At dawn there were still some troops to come through, and the Turks could be seen on the crest above them and also on both our flanks; much to our disgust, when we thought that nearly everyone had passed, some camels appeared and another regiment; those camels never travelled so fast in their lives as they did when they reached us and the Australians went through at full gallop.
>
> This left us the rearmost party with the enemy on the last ridge above us and pressing on very fast, but it was too soon for us to leave as the troops below were delayed by having to pass through a narrow gully. There was little or no cover for our horses, and they began to suffer from rifle and machine-gun fire and had to be moved back, for a lot of casualties amongst the horses would have meant leaving men behind. Luckily, owing to cover afforded by the rocky ground, our casualties were slight, as it was impossible to get serious cases away.
>
> We succeeded in checking the enemy till the Division was out of danger, and just as things were looking really bad and the enemy were close up to us on all sides we were able to retire through 1 ALH Brigade who held a ridge about two miles below us; A Squadron, forming the rear party, only just got away as the enemy captured their rearguard position.

On the way down we were bombed by aeroplanes, which also strafed us with their machine guns from a very low altitude and caused a number of casualties to horses but luckily only a few to men. The rear of the column was overtaken shortly before reaching the valley by some snipers who caused some inconvenience but only hit one man. The Regiment then re-crossed the Jordan after coming under shell fire while traversing the valley, and returned to bivouac north of Jericho....

It was 0600 on 4 May.

The DMC withdrew to the west bank, leaving only a strongly-held bridgehead in place at El Ghoraniye.

When I tread the verge of Jordan
Bid my anxious fears subside
Death of death and hells destruction
Land me safe on Canaan's side
Amen.

Almost certainly the operation was not sufficiently supported. In particular, another division assaulting the Turks' main position at Shunet Nimrin would have helped. The *Official History* gives the Sherwood Rangers an honourable mention for its part in assisting 1 ALH Brigade with the task they were given, namely picketing the heights covering the Umm esh Shert track all the way down the mountain.

British casualties were 1,649, over 1,000 of them in 60th Division. Turkish casualties are thought to have been higher. The Sherwood Rangers' casualties were one officer killed, two officers and sixteen ORs wounded, seven horses killed, four missing and twenty-eight wounded.

Chapter 20

Palestine – Affair of Abu Tulul

May–September 1918

On 10 May the Sherwood Rangers, under command of XXI Corps, marched out of the Jordan Valley to bivouac on the sand dunes close to the sea, north of Jaffa, and enjoy a rest period badly needed by both men and horses.

The Indian cavalry units were arriving in theatre and so 7 Mounted Brigade, under command of Brigadier General Clarke, was reconstituted. The Sherwood Rangers rejoined, and the South Notts Hussars were replaced by the 20th Deccan Horse and 34th Poonah Horse redeployed from the ravages of the Somme; the brigade became part of SRY's old division, 2nd Mounted, which had been disbanded after Gallipoli. The other brigades were the Imperial Service Cavalry (Jodhpore, Mysore and Hyderabad Lancers) and Imperial Camel Corps Brigades. Brigadier General Goland V. Clarke DSO was 53 and had originally joined 18th Hussars, earned the DSO during the Boer War, left the Regular Army in 1907 and subsequently joined the City of London Yeomanry (Rough Riders). He was the Rough Riders' CO when war began, served in Gallipoli, and was promoted to command the brigade.

The summer's heat carries with it disease of all sorts, for both man and horse, throughout Palestine which was minimized by the EEF with a massive programme of human and equine healthcare and attention to sanitation to restrict losses; this was a remarkable success. The Turks on the other hand suffered increasing casualties to disease, as well as steady attrition from desertion, and a rising loss of morale among those who stayed. This divergence proved a significant factor when the main attack took place in September. Throughout the summer there was constant minor activity by both sides across the front which, for the EEF, served to bed in the newly-arrived troops. These skirmishes were extremely valuable to Allenby because they yielded vital information about the Turks' declining levels of strength and capability. It also informed him of the capability of his newly-arrived regiments and formations.

On 6 July, after a period of work up training, 2nd Mounted Division was ordered to the Jordan Valley for outpost duties in the El Ghoraniye bridgehead. Whilst the climate in the coastal plain of Palestine in summer was hot, it was cooler in the Judean Hills. However the Jordan Valley was a 120-degrees airless cauldron of heat, dust and mosquitoes. Because the conditions were so hostile, Allenby rotated troops on month-long tours, and it was to meet this obligation that 2nd Mounted Division marched into Jericho under cover of darkness. The *Official History* states:

> The retention of the bridgehead over the Jordan was necessary to secure the right flank of the Force, and also to maintain that threat against the Hejaz Railway which was always vital to the plans of the Commander in Chief. The defence of it, and of the approach to it from the hills, [was] much the most ungrateful task which any troops in Palestine were set to perform during the hot season.

In addition to 2nd Mounted Division, the A&NZ MD was also assigned to this task, carried out mostly by the cavalry because they could hold the bridgehead, and the vital ground around it, with fewer troops than the infantry; this meant that fewer troops need suffer the conditions. However, there were also two battalions of infantry providing the close protection for the bridge. Second Mounted Division was allocated the El Ghoraniye bridgehead itself. It was not a routine task, the Turks always being able to shell the bridgehead from the Trans Jordan Hills, and probe and challenge its extremities. The cavalry countered this with constant patrolling.

The A&NZ MD was responsible for the Abu Tulul feature, the other main position in the Jordan Valley. Lying north of Jericho on the west bank, roughly opposite the crossing at Umm esh Shert, it was the key to that defensive line, and was in the foothills of the Judean Hills lining the valley's western edge. It blocked the Turks in the north from being able to observe troop movements around Jericho in the bridgehead area. More to the point, possession of it would give the Turks the very field of observation and fire they needed, preventing the organization of any future raid on the Hejaz Railway by the EEF.

These were the tasks with which 2nd Mounted Division and the A&NZ MD were becoming familiar, when they found themselves caught up in the most significant action of the summer, the Affair of Abu Tulul. At 0100 on 14 July and, given it was considered an 'affair', without much by way of foreplay, the Turks, including numbers of Germans, commenced a night attack on the Abu Tulul position. Fighting went on all day, but whilst this was undoubtedly the main attack, this account must concentrate on the enemy's significant but diversionary attack, part of which fell on Sherwood Rangers.

At about the same time as the attack on Abu Tulul, numbers of enemy contacted both the Imperial Service Cavalry Brigade, covering the southern sector of the bridgehead, and the Sherwood Rangers, at that time deployed in the bridgehead east of the Jordan during darkness. The regiment was covering the northern, 7 Mounted Brigade's sector, and Tallents tells us:

> Two Troops on patrol were heavily fired on ... by two machine guns and about 40 rifles. Two more Troops from the night outpost line were sent up

in support, and it was found the enemy were holding the line of the Wadi er Rame ... in some strength with machine guns at the three fords ... and it was reported he was advancing North West [towards the bridgehead].

At 0645 the Imperial Camel Corps Brigade reported 1,200 enemy on their front, whereupon we took up a defensive line along the Wadi er Rame. An Officer's Patrol was sent out to locate the enemy's right flank, and found them extending Northwards along the edge of the cultivation; the patrol was shelled for some time. The remainder of the Regiment and two armoured cars now arrived in support.

At 0930 orders were received to act vigorously against the enemy's Northern flank, and to assist Imperial Service Brigade who were to attack his South flank.

From the *Official History* we learn:

At 0330 a squadron of the Jodhpore Lancers crossed at El Hinu and one of the Mysore Lancers at Makhadet Hilja.... [The ISB commander sought and received approval] that the rest of the Jodhpores with two machine guns should cross at El Hinu and attack the enemy's left flank from the south, while the Mysore Lancers advanced from Hijla [to] attack north of the Wadi er Rame from the West, the Sherwood Rangers ... co-operating from the north west.

At 1030 [CO Jodhpore Lancers] was ordered to cross at El Hinu with two squadrons. The objective ... was the ford over the Wadi er Rame at Ain el Garaba.... He conferred with ... A Squadron of the Jodhpores, which was already east of the Jordan ..., arranging for its co-operation. ... as soon as he was seen to charge the high ground on the enemy's left flank, the Mysore Lancers and the Sherwood Rangers were also to attack.... The Mysore Lancers had meanwhile been reinforced by two troops and two machine guns.

[The Jodhpores moved] down the east bank of the Jordan and under cover of the low hills, reached the mouth of the Wadi el Jorfe ... and there turned north eastwards. The two squadrons trotted along the wadi unobserved by the enemy ..., extended to an interval of two horses' length on coming under fire, swung left-handed in column of troops, and galloped due north.

Two or three troops on the enemy's left flank incontinently turned about and fled eastward towards the hills, but the Jodhpores dashed into a large body on the next ridge, spearing a number with their lances. They then advanced to the ford, capturing more prisoners, but coming under machine-gun fire from the right bank, swung round to rally a mile to the south.

On seeing the Jodhpores charge, the Sherwoods and six troops of the Mysore Lancers advanced at 1315.

Tallents notes that the enemy began giving way, those 'on our front being able to slip away by the Wadi as we advanced to the ford'. The *Official History* recounts how some thirty Turks 'were speared before they could reach the shelter of some scrub' while the Jodhpores had sustained twenty-eight casualties from the 125 who rode in the charge; they had fifty prisoners and a large number of horses in their hands. 'Horses and men, moreover, were exhausted by the terrific midday heat and so now withdrew.' Cavalry on horses that are 'done up' are notoriously vulnerable if counter-attacked by fresh cavalry. Tallents confirms that the Mysore Lancers had also withdrawn 'after warning us'.

The *Official History* goes on:

> This left the Sherwood Rangers strung out in a big semi-circle facing Ain el Garaba, the right on the wadi about a mile west of it and the left flank in air. The enemy still held a trench on the north bank covering the ford with some seventy rifles and two machine guns.
>
> At 1430 the Poonah Horse ... had been ordered to get in touch with the Sherwoods. The regiment advanced rapidly down the track leading to Ain el Garaba under considerable shellfire, but presenting such a fleeting target that it suffered few casualties.... The CO ordered a halt on the Sherwoods' left; but the leading troop, not receiving the message, dashed straight forward and charged the Turkish trench ... [the troop leader and six men were killed] ... the bloody swords and lances on the trampled ground bearing witness to the desperate bravery with which they had sold their lives. An advance by the Sherwoods south of the wadi and of the Poonah Horse on the north bank [and by the Imperial Camel Corps Brigade along the wadi] caused the enemy to evacuate the position at 1730 and fall back eastward, covering his retreat with machine-gun fire.

Casualties were 100 Turks and eighty-six EEF. It was later learned that the enemy had fielded three cavalry regiments. Meanwhile, back at Abu Tulul, the battle had been won decisively by the A & NZ MD. Turkish casualties from both actions were estimated at 1,000 to the EEF's 189.

The *Official History* concludes:

> The action proved how valuable a striking force was the reconstituted Desert [Mounted] Corps, with its regiments of resolute and experienced Australians and New Zealanders, of well-tried and dashing Yeomanry still in the country, and of the almost over-eager Indians.

On 23 July, 2nd Mounted Division became 5th Cavalry Division, 7 Mounted Brigade and the Imperial Service Brigade becoming respectively 14 and 15 (Imperial Service) Cavalry Brigades. The division was completed by the substitution, in August, of the Imperial Camel Corps Brigade by 5 Mounted Brigade on transfer from the AMD; it was renamed 13 (Imperial Service) Cavalry Brigade. The Sherwood Rangers Yeomanry were cavalry at last.

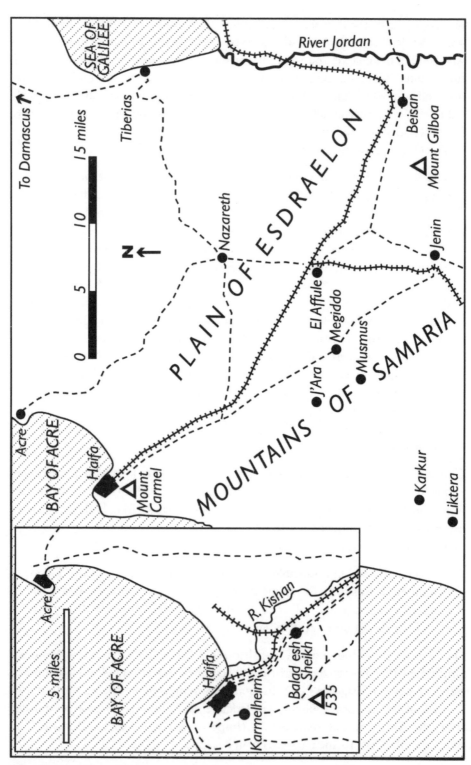

Map 11: Megiddo and Haifa.

Fifth Cavalry Division was relieved on 14 August and marched back to the coast north of Jaffa.

The significant toll on the health of the regiment extracted by the Jordan Valley can be judged by the fact that, between 1 and 14 August, 314 men reported sick, eighty-six of whom were admitted to hospital, and, in the second half of the month, the figures were 256 and seventy, most of the cases being a form of high fever. On the other hand, during late August and early September, the Sherwood Rangers received a strong reinforcement of officers and men, totalling ninety-six ORs and ten officers. On 10 September the Commander-in-Chief, General Allenby, presented MCs to Captains Perowne and Moss and DCMs to SSM Tomkins and Sergeant Woodcock. Presumably these were all for gallantry at either Nebi Samweil or Es Salt.

Chapter 21

Palestine – Final Campaign

September 1918–November 1919

llenby was about to march his army into battle on a piece of ground
which, in the course of several millennia, has been fought over by some
of the most renowned warriors known to history: Pharaoh Thothmes III,
Vespasian, Saul, the Philistines, Ibn Raik, Salah ad-Din, the Mongols, Marmaluke
Sultan Kutuz, and even Napoleon, and deliver a victory which would be the envy
of them all.

Preparation and Planning

This campaign is a textbook study in good battle procedure:

- Back in March, Allenby had chosen mid-September to take advantage of the
  amelioration in the extreme summer heat, before the coming of the heavy rains
  from November onwards.
- His last reinforcements arrived in August.
- He had determined that his plans would not depend on any support from Britain,
  because he knew that Britain could not deliver due to overriding commitments
  in Europe.
- The work to double the capacity of the road and rail system connecting the EEF
  to its base in Cairo was complete and carrying 2,000 tons of supplies a day.
- Ever since his arrival, Allenby had been building Egypt's capacity to generate
  food for both the men and horses he needed to feed his army of 340,000 men
  and in the order of 60,000 animals, mostly horses. In so far as Egypt could not
  supply him, he sourced his re-supply from the east, particularly the Empire, out
  of reach of enemy submarine action.
- Water was always short once movement commenced, but a sufficiency was
  available where the troops were concentrating.
- The medical services were first class, especially regarding sanitation, protection
  and prevention, including suppression of mosquitoes in the vicinity of troops.
  In contrast, the state of Allenby's enemy had deteriorated in every way with
  cholera and typhus making their appearance in the Turkish armies.

- The German element of the army had increased and became unpopular with the Turks. Allenby used propaganda to drive a wedge between them, and convey the impression that captured Turkish prisoners were better fed than Turkish soldiers.
- He created many deceptions to pre-condition the Turks to expect the main weight of the attack to fall in the east, astride the Jordan, allowing forged documents with misleading information to be captured. In addition to the raids, he built false camps in the east and made dummy horses; troop movements eastwards were exaggerated and made obvious, whereas troop movements west took place at night into concealed camps. In particular, the cavalry in the west were moved up close behind the infantry before the attack, and concealed in orange groves.
- Air superiority was used to ensure overflying by the enemy was minimized.
- Last, but not least, horse management was crucial if each horse was going to be in a condition to carry close on twenty stones of man and equipment, averaging twenty miles a day for long spells of, say, forty-eight hours continuously, or several weeks with periodic rest, and living off the land over terrain hostile to horses in every way. For this he ensured extensive veterinary support close behind the cavalry divisions so that horses were quickly and successfully treated.

Own Forces/Enemy Forces

Allenby had a ration strength of 340,000 in the equivalent of eight infantry and four cavalry divisions, representing about 12,000 sabres, 57,000 rifles and 540 guns. Faisal's Arab Northern Army (ANA) was in addition. Allenby estimated the equivalent ration strength of Fourth, Seventh and Eighth Turkish Armies opposing him at 247,000 consisting of 3,000 sabres, 26,000 rifles and 370 guns. The troops south of Amman, estimated at 6,000, were cut off and unable to make an impact on the coming battle. As the Turks had more heavy machine guns on a formation-for-formation basis than the British, their firepower still had to be respected.

Deployment of EEF

Left to right:

- XXI Corps: from the sea twenty miles north of Jaffa to the left flank of the Judean Hills;
- XX Corps: astride the Judean Hills;
- Chaytor's Force, the key component of which was A & NZ MD: in the Jordan Valley, with its left flank on the river adjacent to Abu Tulul;
- ANA was lurking in the desert close to the Hejaz Railway near Der'a, tasked with taking out the railway;
- DMC, with three divisions, 4th, 5th and Australian, was on the Mediterranean coast, north of Jaffa, hidden in orange groves immediately behind XXI Corps.

The Battles of Sharon and Nabulus

At 0430 on 19 September an EEF artillery barrage of over a thousand shells a minute opened up. The carefully-planned EEF counter-battery fire quickly degraded the accuracy and density of the Turks' reply.

With the breaking dawn barely apparent, the infantry divisions advanced across the front attacking north and swarmed into the Turkish trenches. Having overwhelmed the initial enemy positions, the infantry divisions all had objectives: to seize key road and rail junctions some five to ten miles to their north within their boundaries, and degrade the capability of the enemy to withdraw, all of which they were destined to secure.

On the extreme left, against the Mediterranean shore, 60th Division, XXI Corps' left division, and 7th and 3rd Divisions respectively on its right, drove east from the coast, rather than due north, pivoting on 54th Division, opening up a gap between the Turks' most westerly positions and the shore. By 0700 the gap was sufficient to allow the leading elements of DMC, having watered its 10,000 horses in the river which formed the start line, to be released unopposed, as planned. This force represented one of the largest concentrations of cavalry seen under the British flag. The order of advance was 5th Cavalry Division (including SRY), 4th Cavalry Division and AMD. Initially, they travelled due north, literally up the shore through dunes, which was hard going for the horses, and into the Plain of Sharon. They were moving with their guns and machine-gun sections and some light armoured car sub-units, all followed by their echelons. Surprise was total, and they were to encounter nothing that was expecting them nor, once they contacted them, nothing which contemplated for more than a moment any option other than surrender.

Once level with El Mughaiyir, the divisions began diverging towards their respective tasks. Fifth Division continued due north to take Nazareth and 4th, on their right, to take El'Affule and Beisan. AMD was corps reserve, following 4th Division, but ordered to take Jenin. These were all objectives over sixty miles distant, and incapable of being reached until some stage on the 20th, irrespective of whether resistance was encountered.

The objectives of the DMC during this initial phase were all north-east of the corps start line and were key strategic locations; taking Nazareth would involve cutting the main road and rail links to the port of Haifa, and Nazareth itself was on the main road to Damascus and therefore critical to the capture of that city which was this phase of the campaign's ultimate objective. El'Affule and Jenin were on main rail and road junctions, and Beisan was on the Jordan. Having thus passed to the north of Seventh and Eighth Turkish Armies, they would have completely enveloped them, trapping them in the open, in mid-flight from Allenby's unstoppable infantry divisions. To get to these objectives, each of the two routes were challenging, including a very difficult crossing of the Mountains of Samaria at night, using almost invisible and tortuous single file tracks to reach the Plain of Esdraelon.

Focus now returns to the Sherwood Rangers' formation. By noon, 5th Cavalry Division was at Liktera, having separated from the other divisions and moved in well-dispersed squadron columns due north along the coast road. Hodson's Horse, the lead regiment, had executed three spontaneous squadron charges without waiting for covering fire, suppressing three minor enemy positions. At Liktera, the division off-saddled, watered and rested till 1800. They had covered twenty-five miles, were already a dozen miles behind enemy lines, an hour up on their timetable, and had taken fifty prisoners. They also realized that if their horse power was to last, they had moved too quickly, especially as the next stage was the night crossing of the Mountains of Samaria.

Megiddo

It was already apparent that neither the armoured cars and other vehicles nor their camels, forming their echelons, could match the rate of movement of the division's horses; therefore the division moved on with 13 and 14 (including SRY) Cavalry Brigades leading, leaving 15 Cavalry Brigade to bring on the vehicles the next day. Thirteen Brigade's commander, Kelly, wisely led the vanguard over the mountains. The *Official History* notes that:

> The tracks … were bad at best, and at worst indistinguishable even in the bright moonlight. The greater part of the ride through the hills was carried out in single file. Silent and gaping with astonishment, a few villagers watched the long column pass.

At J'ara, on the apex of the watershed, 13 Cavalry Brigade left two squadrons to screen 4th Cavalry Division, crossing five miles south-east of them, from intervention by the Turks from the direction of Haifa. Fourth Cavalry Division was using the Musmus Pass, the historically important route across the mountains, past its pinnacle, a mountain called Megiddo, which had lent its name to battles down the centuries.

Now in the Plain of Esdraelon and, having paused to allow the mounted columns to close up as dawn broke, 5th Cavalry Division pressed on – pausing only to blow a 100-yard section of the Beisan-Haifa railway – 13 Cavalry Brigade still leading, and entered Nazareth at 0430. The division had been given El Affule, 4th Cavalry Division's primary objective, as a secondary objective, and 14 Cavalry Brigade diverted south down the El Affule-Nazareth road, the Deccan Horse leading and Sherwood Rangers following up. At 0715 the Deccan Horse charged a body of enemy before taking the station. Tallents notes that 'Affule was captured by our Division about half an hour before 4th Cavalry Division arrived there travelling by a parallel route on our right', while:

A large number of motor lorries were seen trying to escape, and most of these with 988 prisoners were captured, of whom the Regiment accounted for about 250. 4th Division then proceeded for Beisan, leaving our Division at Affule.

In a mere thirty-six hours the Turks had been surrounded and defeated, with minimal loss of life. The key was an all-arms battle in which each had been used correctly. Incredibly the defeat was so complete that not even a pursuit phase followed, only exploitation and mopping up. In short, this was one of the finest examples of the capability of horsed formations to achieve shock action ever achieved by that arm in modern times, and achieved against two admittedly weakened but nevertheless well-armed modern armies. Trumpeter Timmons was awarded the MM for gallantry in action at El Affule.

There was now a painful pause of twenty-four hours whilst all the armoured cars, the divisional artillery of both divisions and their respective echelons, whether coming by camel, horse, vehicle or rail, struggled to catch up with the horses. However, the DMC had its hands full as Tallents relates:

> The entire Turkish Army was completely routed and in full retreat, and knowing the enormous force of cavalry in their rear they surrendered in thousands whenever they encountered our men, without any serious fighting. It became merely a matter of rounding them up into groups of about 100 and sending them back under escort....

At 0420 on the 21st the Regiment marched as advance guard to the brigade, moving due south to Jenin to support the AMD, who had collected about 10,000 prisoners. There they screened Mount Gilboa to prevent the Turks escaping in that direction. This work extended into the 22nd, and included searching surrounding villages and rounding up prisoners. That night the entire division concentrated at El Affule.

The Capture of Haifa

Whilst the Sherwood Rangers were searching for prisoners on the 22nd, General Chauvel, commanding DMC, ordered 5th Cavalry Division to capture Haifa and Acre on the 23rd. Both, but especially Haifa, were important ports for the EEF, which had to be captured intact so that they would be able to re-supply the EEF quicker and in greater volumes than the echelons could. However, they were, according to the *Official History*, both formidable fortresses, Acre having defied Napoleon, held in strength by over 1,000 fresh troops with high morale.

On receiving a report that Haifa was being evacuated, Chauvel issued fresh orders to secure its capture that day by the division's armoured cars. This failed, given a bloody nose by an enemy who clearly was not planning to leave. Chauvel then reverted to the original plan. As soon as 5th Cavalry Division's mounted

Officers of the Sherwood Rangers (L)
and the larger Yorkshire Dragoons at
Serlby Park on 5 May 1899 following
the inspection by the C-in-C, Field
Marshal Viscount Wolseley. Lords
Galway and Scarbrough are seated
centre (L and R).

The C-in-C taking the salute at Serlby.

7 January 1900 on the eve of
deployment to South Africa. (L to R)
Col J. Thorpe (CO SRY 1880-82), Lt
A. C. (Job) Williams (KIA), Capt M.
. Dawson (OC SRY Service Sqn to
une 1900 and OC 2nd Service Sqn to
an 1902), Lt H. O. (Hop) Peacock,
t Col Lord Galway (serving CO SRY 1882-1903), Lt R. T. O. (Bertie) Sheriffe (OC SRY Service Sqn
une-Sep 1900), Major A. E. Whitaker (CO SRY 1910-14), Lt H. Thorpe, (CO SRY 1915-17 and
9/20 and son of Col Thorpe) and Lt Col H. Denison (CO SRY 1903-10).

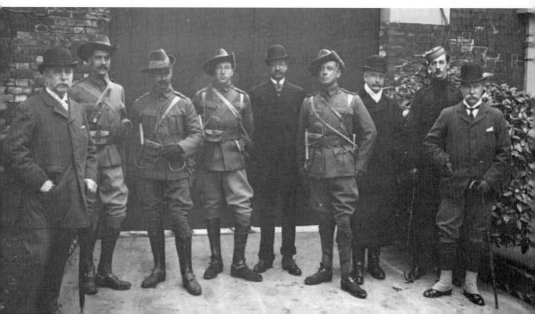

Lt H. H. (Bertie) Wilson DSO, OC SRY Service Sqn Sep 1900-May 1901.

Lt Gen Lord Methuen, Commander 1st Division. (*History of 3 IY*, Birkin)

The shell that was said to have killed Major General le Comte de Villebois-Mareuil at Boshof on 5 April 1900 (By kind permission of Captain Mick Holtby)

Lt Col G. J. Younghusband CB commanded 3rd Imperial Yeomanry 1899-1900. (*History of 3 IY*, Birkin)

The Sherwood Rangers Yeomanry and their ladies at Serlby Park, Bawtry, at their Camp and Field Day in 1903. Lord Galway's last camp as CO, this was attended by Lord Roberts and Lord Chesham, the inspecting officer; all three are seen seated.

The Sherwood Rangers marching past at Camp between the Boer War and First World War. Note the new prominence given to the rifle, demonstrating the tactical emphasis on the cavalry being able to fight both mounted and dismounted and the priority given to rifle shooting.

The Sherwood Rangers parading in Retford Market Square at Easter 1915 just prior to embarking for Egypt.

Gallipoli, October 1915. Lala Baba from Nebrunsi Point.

Gallipoli, October 1915 (L to R) Maj H. Tallents DSO, CO of SRY 1928-34, Maj H. Thorpe DSO, CO SRY 1915-17 and 1919-20, Lt R. E. Brassey, Lt E. Davies.

Struma Valley, Greek Macedonia 1916. SRY Patrol. Note the man in the tree. The country in the Struma Valley was very close which led to many surprise contacts with the enemy. (Percy Laws, SRY archives)

River Struma 1916 from an SRY Observation Post. (Percy Laws, SRY archives)

On 23 June 1917 the HMT *Cestrian* was torpedoed off Skyros whilst transporting the Regiment from Greece to Egypt. All the men were saved but the horses and baggage were lost. (Percy Laws, SRY archives)

Wells were the 'vital ground' of the advance from Gaza to Jerusalem. Troops fought from well to well but, even so, they and their horses sometimes went days, rather than hours, without watering.

April 1918. 5 Mounted Brigade (including the Regiment) resting at midday during the march from Gaza to Jerusalem prior to the Second Raid into TransJordan.

Elements of 14 (Imperial Service) Cavalry Brigade on parade in 1918, prior to Allenby's final advance.

Lt Col Francis Vernon Willey CMG CBE MVO TD, later 2nd Baron Barnby, (CO 1920- 28) and dog, which has clearly mastered the 'laidback yeoman' look.

The senior ranks of the Regiment at a post-First World War Camp. The very heroes for whom the land was to be made fit?

The Sherwood Rangers Yeomanry in 1937 marching past at Brocklesby Park, Lincolnshire, ancestral home of the Earls of Yarborough.

Lt Col the 5th Earl of Yarborough MC (commanded 1937-40) and on his left Lt Col the Marquis of Titchfield, later 7th Duke of Portland KG (commanded 1934-37).

In Palestine there was good shooting to be had. Second left Lt P. J. D. McCraith MC and CO SRY 1953-57 and, extreme right, Donny Player.

(L) Col E. O. (Flash) Kellett DSO MP commanded the Sherwood Rangers Yeomanry 1940-43, KIA on 22 March 1943, and Lt Col J. D. (Donny) Player who took over from him on 6 March 1943 and was KIA on 24 April 1943.

Lt Gen Bernard Montgomery (Monty), commander of Eighth Army, revered by the Sherwood Rangers in the desert for giving them deliverance. He is wearing his multi-badged bush hat, clearly bearing the Regiment's cap badge. The hat is now displayed in the Australian War Memorial (Museum) in Canberra, complete with SRY badge, albeit in need of a polish. (Imperial War Museum)

1941. Tobruk had a substantial network of tunnels providing protection from the daily air raids. However, Flash Kellett believed that using the tunnels during air raids would damage the Regiment's offensive culture, and instead ordered that, when under attack, the Regiment should return fire.

Lt Col Michael (Mike) Laycock MC TD took command of the Sherwood Rangers on the beach on 6 June 1944 and was KIA on 11 June 1944 in St Pierre.

Lt Col S. D. (Stanley) Christopherson DSO MC and Bar TD commanded the Sherwood Rangers Yeomanr 1944-46. He was A Squadron Leader in the Desert and early on in NW Europe, when the Regiment won 14 Battle Honours, and he commanded in NW Europe when the regiment won 16 Battle Honours.

March 1943 at Tebaga Gap. (L to R) Tprs Ken Ewing, John Stephenson, Jigger Lea, Paddy Ryan and their 75mm Sherman.

Padre Leslie Skinner, revered regimental padre in NW Europe. (SRY archives)

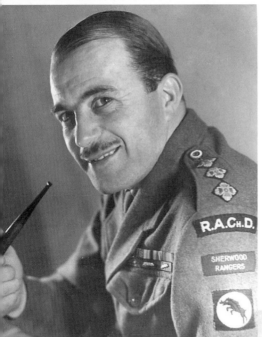

Sherwood Rangers' tanks entering Tripoli on 26 January 1943 after the fight for Libya, which had included Wadi Zem Zem, where they suffered their heaviest losses thus far in the war.

This encapsulates the logistical challenge created by modern warfare: trucks are almost more important than tanks and certainly outnumber them many times over, putting unbearable pressure on inadequate road systems to deliver the capacity that enables the armour to advance and fight.

Investiture London 1944: (L to R) Cpl Derek Lenton MM, MQMS John Scott MM, Sgt Erny Thwaites MM, SSM Henry Hutchinson MM, KIA April 1945, Sgt Guy Sanders MM, KIA at Berjou August 1944, Sgt George Dring MM and Bar and Cpl James Loades MM.

Asnelles-sur-Mer taken at noon on D Day showing a troop of the Regiment's amphibians advancing to contact, southwards, apparently without infantry support having just broken out of the beachhead.

(L to R) Maj Gen D. A. H. Graham, GOC 50th (Northumbrian) Division, Lt Gen Sir Brian Horrocks, Commander XXX Corps, Maj Gen or Thomas, GOC 43rd (Wessex) Division.

(L to R) Capt Jack Holman MC and Captain Jimmy McWilliam.

The first DD tank of the Sherwood Rangers to enter Bayeux at 10.50 on 7 June 1944. The non-amphibious tanks of A Squadron had already taken the town at first light, the first major town liberated by the Allies.

Sgt George Dring and his crew on *Akilla* in Normandy: (L to R) Sgt Dring, Tprs Hodkin, Denton, Bennet and Cpl Gold.

Gheel 11 September 1944. The 17-pounder Firefly Shermans of Cpl Burnett (KIA the next day) and Sgt Stan Nesling DCM advancing through the main square in Gheel with the 75mm Sherman of Stuart Hills MC in support. Note that, despite being in action, all three commanders have their heads out.

(L to R) Capt John Gauntley MC and Capt Neville Fearn DSO.

Geilenkirchen November 1944. The Regiment in rain and mud supporting 84th US Division breaching the Siegfried Line.

Issum, 6 March 1945. The Regiment had linked up with Ninth US Army in the town two days earlier and was advancing east out of Issum supporting 71 Brigade. During the day the Regiment won two MCs.

At an investiture 30 November 1944. (L to R) Maj John Semken MC, Lt Col Stanley Christopherson DSO MC and Bar, facing centre Maj Jack Holman MC, next right Capt Stuart Hills MC.

formations had been relieved by AMD from their tasks in Nazareth and El Affule, they moved out for Haifa, and prepared to attack on arrival, but now without the benefit of surprise.

The *Official History* records:

> 5th Cavalry Division advanced in two columns: the right consisting of 13 Cavalry Brigade ... moving on Acre ...; the left consisting of the remainder of the division, 15 Cavalry Brigade ... less Hyderabad Lancers, with B Battery HAC, and 1st Light Car Patrol as advance guard, by the main road to Haifa. The right column met with but trifling opposition and the renowned fortress of Acre ... fell into British hands almost without resistance.
>
> Haifa ... has a splendid site at the foot of Mount Carmel on the southern shore of the Bay of Acre. Though it is very open to attack from the sea, the approach to it from the Plain of Esdraelon is easily defensible; for the road is commanded from the south by Carmel while to the north the country is broken by the swift and swampy River Kishon, and its tributaries. Carmel is a long narrow ridge, [between 1500 and 1000 feet above sea level] running from the coast to the south east....
>
> 15 Cavalry Brigade met with no opposition until the leading squadron of the Mysore Lancers passed through Balad esh Sheikh at 1000 and came under fire from guns on the heights west of the village and from guns near the Karmelheim [on Mount Carmel]. More Turkish artillery opened fire from the eastern end of Haifa, and an aeroplane dropped a message that the place was strongly held. One squadron [Mysores] was then despatched ... to Tell esh Subat, 4½ miles east of Haifa, with orders to advance on the town from the north-east. A second squadron, with two machine guns, climbed up on to Carmel from a point south of Balad esh Sheikh with the object of advancing along the track following the crest-line against the guns at the Karmelheim. B Battery HAC came into action, and the Jodhpore Lancers halted in the open east of Balad esh Sheikh with orders to advance mounted.
>
> At 1154 the Sherwood Rangers (14 Cavalry Brigade) joined [15 Cavalry] Brigade, and one squadron [A] was ordered to move up and assist the Mysore squadron on Carmel. Brigadier General Harbord postponed the attack until 1400 in hopes that the force on the hill would by then be ready to attack the guns simultaneously. ... At the appointed hour the Jodhpores trotted forward in column of squadrons in line of troop column ...

Tallents takes up the narrative, noting that the regiment, less A Squadron, 'was in close support but did not have to come into action'. As they crossed the Acre railway the enemy's fire increased, but they quickened their pace and suffered little loss riding straight for the Kishon.

Nearing the bank it was seen to be precipitous,.... It was only too clear that no crossing was possible.... [The] regiment swung left, across the narrower wadi beside the ... railway and charged the machine guns on Carmel's lower slopes. This was a critical moment as the regiment was being raked by fire from front and flank and horses were falling fast. But the leading squadron rallied swiftly, turned and got amongst the machine guns and speared the detachments thus opening the defile through which ran the main road to Haifa. The second squadron thereupon galloped up the road, wheeled half right and charged a mount east of the road on which it captured two more machine guns. Lieutenant Colonel Holden then led the two remaining squadrons straight into the town ... the passage of the defile had practically decided the issue and there was little left to do but round up the prisoners.

Almost at the same instant as the main attack was launched the left-hand detached squadron of the Mysores charged the enemy's guns south of the Karmelheim. In course of a very difficult ascent there had been some casualties and a number of this squadron's horses had dropped out exhausted or lamed so that after [some members] had been dropped [to give covering fire] from a flank only about fifteen men were left for the actual charge.

Benefiting from a fine record in horse management throughout the war, A Squadron had caught up with the Mysores without as many losses. Both were now ready to charge the guns south of the Karmelheim at almost the same moment as the attack below was being pressed home. Corporal Law, SRY,

> was in charge of the advanced patrol of [A Squadron ... and was] approaching Karmelheim, when heavy rifle fire was opened from a garden. He at once attacked, and took seven prisoners by himself. By his dash and initiative [he] greatly assisted the advance of both squadrons.

Both squadrons pressed home the charge 'and were completely successful and broke through the enemy position'. One 150mm naval gun, two mountain guns and seventy-eight prisoners were taken. Relics of the captured guns were liberated and later mounted and presented by Lieutenant Colonel Wiggin to the Sherwood Rangers who hold them to this day.

In the valley, on the Jodhpores' right, 'The right squadron of the Mysores ... mounted and advanced as soon as the Jodhpore attack was seen. A strong body of Turks was charged and dispersed. Two more guns and 100 prisoners were taken.'

The *Official History* commented:

> No more remarkable cavalry action of its scale was fought in the whole course of the campaign. The position was naturally formidable with a precipitous hill and an impassable river on either side of the defile; it was held by a well-armed force about a thousand strong, which had not yet been engaged.... It

was taken in a few hours by a cavalry brigade of two weak cavalry regiments. Undoubtedly only the boldness and dash of the cavalry combined with the skilful flanking movements, made success possible, and there is little likelihood that a dismounted attack by a force of this strength would have had equal fortune.

This almost unheard of mounted action may well be, historically, the last brigade-level cavalry charge involving a British regiment. The date was 23 September 1918.

For his decisive part in the action, Corporal C. G. Law, of Bawtry, received the DCM. Between 19 and 24 September the Sherwood Rangers had suffered no casualties, but evacuated seven men to hospital. One horse was killed and twenty-eight either died or were evacuated. They now bivouacked on the beach north of Haifa with 15 Cavalry Brigade, where they were joined by 14 Cavalry Brigade.

Advance on Damascus and Beirut

Seventh and Eighth Turkish Armies had ceased to exist as fighting forces, save for two weak columns east of the Jordan, scuttling north. Fourth Army, which had been centred on Amman, was not destroyed but was in full retreat, with nothing better than Shanks's Pony for transport, desperately trying to get north of Allenby before being cut off at Damascus. It had been denied the use of the Hejaz Railway by Faisal's ANA, which had destroyed a section at Der'a. The Turks would have fared better had their infantry been mounted.

Allenby was now moving elements of his infantry north to the line Haifa-Nazareth, partly to relieve his cavalry from garrison duties in the towns they had captured so that they could advance again, and partly to support the next phase of his campaign, the capture of Damascus and Beirut. Once again the task of leading the next phase fell to the DMC. Chauvel's plan to achieve this was for 4th Cavalry Division to advance on Damascus via Der'a, where it would link up with the ANA to catch and destroy Fourth Turkish Army. Meanwhile 5th Cavalry Division and the AMD would march straight on Damascus. An infantry division of XXI Corps was to capture Beirut.

On the 25th, 5th Cavalry Division marched out of Haifa for Tiberias to be ready for the advance on Damascus. The Sherwood Rangers were to remain and garrison the town till relieved by the infantry, marching north to assume that role. The regiment was relieved on the 27th, and immediately marched in pursuit of the division. They were not destined to be re-united with it until 5 October, four days after Damascus had fallen. Haifa to Damascus is in the order of ninety miles. They marched to Tiberias, where 5th Cavalry Division had started the advance to Damascus, and then followed their centre line, travelling at their normal rate of march, about twenty miles per day. In spite of adverse ground, they were outside

Damascus on 1 October, the day the town was captured and came under command of the AMD for four days.

The Sherwood Rangers missed some actions by 14 Cavalry Brigade as the Turks put up some semblance of a fight for Damascus. Meanwhile, the remnants of Fourth Army, having been heavily attacked by the ANA, blundered into DMC's positions outside Damascus from the south, with the points of 4th Cavalry Division's lances uncomfortably close behind them. The battle fought on the east bank of the Jordan between the retreating Turks and the rampant ANA had been heavy with retribution. The ANA had conducted a savage slaughter of Fourth Army in Der'a, as 4th Cavalry Division discovered on arriving there. The capture of Damascus was, like that of Jerusalem, a symbolic moment, particularly for the ANA, who ceremonially entered at the gallop, rather a different affair to Allenby's entrance to Jerusalem.

The health of the EEF was beginning to suffer with malaria, and the influenza epidemic which affected the whole world at that time. Also, the EEF was outstripping its re-supply, due to the rapid rate of advance, which had carried them 140 miles from the start line. The greatest success story was the resilience and toughness of the horses, which had out-marched everything and had only suffered relatively limited rates of attrition. The attention paid to the arts of horse-mastership had paid off in fitness and endurance, and water had been more freely available than during the advance on Jerusalem.

The Sherwood Rangers finally caught up with 5th Cavalry Division at Sasa which it had reached by leaving Damascus on its right. On their march from Haifa, the Sherwood Rangers had lost to hospital one officer and twelve yeomen, four horses dead or destroyed and eleven evacuated. It was at Sasa that the division's guns and echelon also caught up.

Riyaq

Fifth Cavalry Division was now to take Riyaq, the town at the junction of the Turkish rail system with the Hejaz Railway. This they did on the 6th, finding the enemy had retreated north, leaving a key rail centre full of destroyed equipment and a population which offered a warm welcome.

Homs

The division's next objective was Homs which it entered on 16 October. The nature of the experience was changing, as the division passed through beautiful country with adequate supplies of food and water for men and horses, to an enthusiastic welcome by the inhabitants in the wake of the enemy's departure. The regiment did not think much of Homs, which it described as a large dirty town. Their casualties, since leaving Damascus, were five officers and twenty-five yeomen admitted to hospital, and eleven horses or mules either dead or evacuated. From Damascus another 100 miles had been covered.

Aleppo

Whilst the fighting strength of 5th Cavalry Division was 2,500, which meant they were still operational, that of 4th Cavalry Division was half that, and so it was non-operational. AMD were still in Damascus. Allenby was concerned that, although his Intelligence was telling him that the enemy was evacuating Aleppo, the risks of advancing another 100 miles with only one division were significant. However, the ANA was able to support and protect 5th Cavalry Division's right flank with a force of 1,500 and Allenby allocated all available armoured cars, and so the decision was taken to go. Aleppo was reached and taken on 26 October 1918, and the Armistice with Turkey was signed on the 30th.

Thus, with the conclusion of one of the finest displays by British cavalry ever seen, did the Great War in the Middle East come to an end. As this account implies, the Sherwood Rangers were in the thick of the fighting in Palestine. Indeed it seems that, of the infantry and cavalry regiments that fought at the Third Battle of Gaza at the start, only the Sherwood Rangers Yeomanry and the Gloucestershire Hussars were amongst those who took Aleppo at the finish.

A tribute to the horses is in order; in thirty-six days, 540 miles were covered. The horses out-marched by some way everything else on the battlefield, whether human, animal or machine. They displayed impressive levels of availability, suffering less than 20 per cent attrition through injury, and few fatalities.

This feat of arms by cavalry bears comparison with those later achieved by tanks. For example Operation COMPASS, O'Connor's advance to El Agheila in 1940/41, covered a similar distance, but in two months rather than one. Also Montgomery's 200 mile pursuit from the Seine to Antwerp in 1944, said to be the fastest advance by armour in history, was achieved at a rate of thirty-three miles per day over six days against Allenby's partially opposed fifteen miles per day over thirty-six days. For armour to advance for thirty-six days would be unlikely given the heavy toll on resupply and basic maintenance that would be extracted. It is worth mentioning Methuen's mounted pursuit of de Wet which included a spell of eighty-four miles in three days, an average of twenty-eight miles per day, at the end of an overall advance of 160 miles which had also included five fights. Interestingly the Sherwood Rangers were the only regiment to take a leading role in both the advance to Aleppo and to Antwerp. To avoid any concerns as to where this is all leading there is no suggestion that horses be preferred to tanks; for a start, unlike with tanks, there is no facility on a horse to make a hot brew whilst on the move.

Allenby described 5th Division's advance from Damascus to Aleppo as 'a brilliant feat of arms. The record of casualties to horses shows the 5th Cavalry Division to be as good horsemen as fighters'.

Occupation and Home

Many months remained during which the Sherwood Rangers performed occupational duties around Aleppo and Killis. The regiment proper dwindled during this time, so that it was scarcely recognizable leaving Syria twelve months later, and was suitably welcomed home to Retford on 5 November, 1919.

A memorial window to the seventeen officers and seventy-seven men of 1/1st Nottinghamshire (Sherwood Rangers) Yeomanry who gave their lives in the Great War was unveiled by Lord Galway in East Retford Church in May 1921. This formed a fitting companion to its predecessor of the Boer War, unveiled in the same church eighteen years before. Members of the regiment who lost their lives are also commemorated in a special chapel in Newark Parish Church.

Part IV

Inter-War Years

1919–39

Chapter 22

A Peace Fit for Heroes

November 1919–September 1939

The First World War had, for the most part, been fought on the Western Front in Flanders, even though the Sherwood Rangers had not been there. In Flanders the lack of manoeuvre had made the cavalry of little value. Therefore, when the British Army was re-organized in 1919, cavalry was out of favour in spite of its magnificent performance in Palestine. Only the ten senior yeomanry units remained cavalry, the remainder becoming artillery or armoured car units. The Sherwood Rangers had the seniority to remain cavalry.

Lieutenant Colonel Thorpe resumed command, and the regiment, now entitled The Notts Sherwood Rangers Yeomanry, was brigaded with the Yorkshire Hussars and Queen's Own Yorkshire Dragoons, each allowed to recruit three squadrons with a total strength of 329.

The squadrons were:

A Squadron (Newark and Retford)
Major H. Tallents of Coddington

B Squadron (Mansfield)
Major D. Warner Turner of Cuckney House

C Squadron (Worksop)
Colonel F. V. Willey

However, by 1920, Colonel Willey had assumed command. He was the son of Francis Willey, of Bradford who had a very successful wool merchant's business there with agencies all over the world. The father was a great field sportsman and had bought the Blyth Hall estate in North Nottinghamshire, which he had made his seat. Colonel Willey was born in Bradford and, before the war, joined his father's wool business, which later became Francis Willey & Co. Ltd. In the immediate aftermath of the war he had been elected the Unionist (Conservative) Member of Parliament for Bradford South serving until 1922. He, too, was a hunting man and Master of the Blankney between 1919 and 1933. He had a significant career as a businessman. In addition to running the family business he was President of the Federation of British Industries (a predecessor of the CBI), 1925–26, a member of the Central Electricity Board 1927–46, a member of the Overseas Settlement

Board from 1937, and *Chevalier* of the Legion of Honour. He was also a director of Lloyds Bank. Throughout his life he had interests in Africa.

Major Tallents was his second-in-command. Major C. Wilson took over A Squadron, whilst Major the Marquis of Titchfield, later 7th Duke of Portland, resigned from the Horse Guards and took over C Squadron.

By 1923 the organization had evolved:

A Squadron (Newark)
Major the Marquis of Titchfield of Welbeck

B Squadron (Mansfield and Worksop)
Major C. W. Bennett of Kirklington Hall

C Squadron (Retford)
Captain R. H. Allen

Captain Allen, wounded at Es Salt, was succeeded at the end of 1927 by Major Lord Conyers, later 5th Earl of Yarborough of Brocklesby Park in Lincolnshire. In 1924 Regimental Headquarters moved from Retford to Newark. The three-year tenure of command of Colonel Willey was so successful that he was five times extended by a year, finally relinquishing command in October 1928. His father had been ennobled as 1st Baron Barnby in the 1922 Honours list and Colonel Willey succeeded to the Barony on his father's death in 1929. He led an active and long life, dying in 1982 aged 98, having attended the Regimental Dinner at Claridges firing on all cylinders a couple of years previously. Lieutenant Colonel H. Tallents DSO, the outstanding regimental officer in the Great War, and by now a very successful solicitor, took over. In the next year, out of an enlisted strength of 297 men, 283 attended annual camp. This high proportion was the best that year in the Territorial Army, and won for the Sherwood Rangers the *Daily Telegraph* Cup. The next few years continued to be good for recruiting. This is particularly remarkable because the Army was, at that time, little liked by the British public as a whole. In 1930, at the Town Hall in Retford, the first Yeomanry Old Comrades' Reunion Dinner was held.

Colonel The Marquis of Titchfield succeeded Tallents in command in 1934. He, in his turn, was followed by Major Lord Conyers, by this time the Earl of Yarborough, in 1937. C Squadron at Retford was taken over by Major A. Massey (Bob) Gamble and B Squadron was under Major E. O. (Flash) Kellett. In 1936 a 10 per cent increase in strength was authorized and each sabre squadron raised a fourth troop while a Headquarters Squadron was formed under Captain C. Tonge alongside A Squadron at Newark. This new squadron consisted of a medium machine-gun troop under Captain H. R. Trotter and a signal troop under Captain M. Denison. Early in 1939 a further increase was authorized to bring the regiment up to full war establishment which meant finding an extra 230 recruits in one year. This was accomplished, together with a waiting list of almost forty.

Part V

The Second World War
1939–42

The Beginning

Chapter 23

Unhorsed

September 1939–December 1940

The Sherwood Rangers mobilized in September 1939. Their commanding officer was still Lord Yarborough, known as 'Sack'. Although a Territorial, his military experiencwe had been obtained in the Regular Army. A true countryman, and man of few words, his apparent shyness concealed a very real sense of humour. It was said that he judged a subaltern solely on the condition of his horses.

The following officers were serving at the outbreak of war; those marked * were posted elsewhere within twelve months of mobilization; those who later became prisoners of war or were killed in action are noted:

Regimental Headquarters:

Commanding Officer	Lieutenant Colonel the Earl of Yarborough MC
Second in Command	Major Wilfred Bennett
Adjutant	Captain Gerald Grosvenor (9th Lancers) (later 4th Duke of Westminster and CO of 9th Lancers at El Alamein)

Headquarters Squadron:

Squadron Leader	Major Jack Abdy
Quartermaster	Major Bob Knight MBE
MG Officer	Captain Henry Trotter
Signal Troop Officer	Lieutenant Max Denison
Medical Officer	Captain Geoffrey Brooks RAMC, a GP from West Bridgeford
Chaplain	Canon Hughes MC (later Chaplain General)
Veterinary Surgeon	Captain V. G. Hinds RAVC

A Squadron:

Squadron Leader	Major R. H. Bush *
Second in Command	Captain Basil Ringrose
Troop Leader	Lieutenant Dennis Le Marchant *
Troop Leader	Second Lieutenant Joscelyn Abel Smith (PoW)
Troop Leader	Second Lieutenant Roger Sutton Nelthorpe
Troop Leader	Second Lieutenant Derick Warwick

B Squadron:

Squadron Leader	Major Flash Kellett (KIA, having just relinquished command of the regiment)
Second in Command	Captain Tony Holden (PoW)
Troop Leader	Lieutenant Dandy Wallace *
Troop Leader	Lieutenant Sidney Morse (PoW)
Troop Leader	Lieutenant Patrick McCraith
Troop Leader	Second Lieutenant Myles Hildyard
Troop Leader	Second Lieutenant Michael Riviere (PoW)

C Squadron:

Squadron Leader	Major Donny Player (KIA in command of the regiment)
Second in Command	Captain Peter Laycock *
Troop Leader	Lieutenant Michael Laycock (KIA in command of the regiment)
Troop Leader	Second Lieutenant Stephen Mitchell
Troop Leader	Second Lieutenant Michael Gold
Troop Leader	Second Lieutenant Michael Parish
Troop Leader	Second Lieutenant Dan Ranfurly (PoW) (Earl of Ranfurly)

Many were away from home on holiday at the time, including Lord Ranfurly who was stalking in Scotland with the Laycocks in the same party. On returning to his London home, having heard the declaration of war, he, in common with everyone else, received a telegram requiring him to report immediately to RHQ in Newark.

He asked his Bunteresque cook-butler Whitaker if he would like to go with him. Whitaker looked over the top of his spectacles and said:

'To the War, my Lord?'
'Yes.'
'Very good, my Lord.'

Thus has the Yeomanry been recruiting for generations.

In October the regiment moved to Malton in Yorkshire and, whilst there, was joined by Stanley Christopherson, Lawrence Biddle and John Walters, who had all been in the Inns of Court Regiment, which was at that time in part an officer cadre for the cavalry. Yeomanry regiments being the tribal organizations that they are, their unsolicited arrival was not all that welcome. However, somehow they were allowed to stay, one of the regiment's better decisions: Christopherson was posted to C Squadron, Biddle to the Signal Troop, and Walters to the MG Troop.

The regiment, now fully recruited, included members from a wide cross-section of occupations, ranging from those with rural and agricultural backgrounds to coal miners, and merchants and people who worked for the major employers of the larger towns. Because of the strong family connection with the regiment, Players supplied it with free cigarettes for the duration of the war. Those under 19 years of age were not allowed overseas, and those in reserved occupations, for example coal mining, were claimed by their employers. They were replaced by former regulars, from the regular reserve, mostly from 7th Hussars, whose culture and ethos was quite different to that of the yeomen. These were mostly older married men, having previously had at least six years' service in the Regular Army, who brought a strong nucleus of skill and professionalism that they passed on to the regiment, and which was greatly valued.

The regiment remained brigaded with the Yorkshire Hussars and Yorkshire Dragoons, with the usual supporting arms and services, including their sister regiment, the South Notts Hussars, as the gunner regiment. It was to tie up with the rest of the brigade, and draw their horses, that they had moved to Malton where the brigade formed part of 1st Cavalry Division, which included two Yeomanry and a regular brigade, which was serving in Palestine.

With the division assigned Lincolnshire in which to form up and carry out its training, the regiment moved back south in November. Lord Yarborough asked to be given the northern part of the county and 'as he owned it, this was agreed'. Although an exaggeration, his estate, Brocklesby Park, covered several thousand acres of north Lincolnshire, and every troop was indeed billeted in a farm he owned. RHQ moved to his home, Brocklesby Park itself.

The assumption was that the division's Territorial elements would move to Palestine to join the regular brigade. Britain had significant interests in the Middle East, particularly oil, and had troops stationed in Egypt and Palestine where there was an internal security situation involving Arabs and Jews. Germany posed little or no direct threat to the Middle East. Turkey, the greatest regional threat in the Great War, was now neutral. However, as an ally of Germany, there was a threat from Italy, which had a presence in both Libya and Abyssinia.

However, France also had significant interests in North Africa, in Tunisia, Algeria and Morocco. Since France was Britain's ally, it was not thought likely that Mussolini would seek to move against British interests in the Middle East. In the light of all this, the rationale for moving the division to Palestine was primarily preventative to ensure that a backwater remained stable, and to free regular units from their peace-keeping role. The reason for choosing a cavalry division was the success under Allenby of British cavalry, including the regiment, in Palestine at the end of the First World War. Military thinking was that, although in general cavalry had had its day, it could still be effective in that region.

On 31 December 1939 there was a New Year's Eve Dance at Brocklesby Park given by Lord and Lady Yarborough for the regiment. Lady Ranfurly wrote 'The Ballroom looked splendid, filled with officers in their Sherwood green tunics with yellow facings and chain epaulettes, and their wives in long beautiful dresses.'

Their preparations were now complete and they feared this was a farewell party. In January 1940, as widely expected, the division received orders to move to Palestine and the regiment left England on 12 January. This was the period of the phoney war and no British troops had yet been engaged by the enemy on land. The deployment was therefore more akin to a peacetime one and many creature comforts associated with such deployments were taken.

The Earls of Yarborough have for centuries been masters of the Brocklesby, one of the country's finest packs of purebred English foxhounds. A significant number of the regiment hunted, many of them in Leicestershire, then the legendary 'ocean of grass', quartered by fly fences, and guarded by ditches. This combination, mixed with a straight-necked fox on a good scenting day had been described as 'The image of war without its guilt and only five and twenty per cent of the danger'.

Nor was it just the officers and their wives who were field sportsmen. A number of the yeomen were in hunt service or were grooms or farmers or countrymen, and all were horsemen. Some had hunted with the Brocklesby in their spare time whilst based in Lincolnshire. This was by no means as frivolous as it sounds, since foxhunting gifts to the cavalryman skilled horsemanship and 'an eye for country or ground', the latter being the most precious of all military skills required of soldiers of all kinds, but especially tank men. This would prove one of the regiment's strongest suits in the years to come. For these reasons, it was logical to Lord Yarborough to take some of his hounds with him, to hunt the devious Palestinian jackals they knew from the Great War. However, whilst passing through France with them, the French caused indignation when they complained that the regiment was not taking the war seriously enough. It was not even as though it was a full pack! However, they had to be returned home.

In addition, the regular brigade, already in theatre before war had been declared, had had the usual rules applied to it, including officers being accompanied by their wives. The rules permitting this related only to the Regular Army and the privilege was denied the yeomanry brigades, even though mobilized as though regulars. Lady Ranfurly put it, not without a hint of exaggeration, 'Grannies, sisters, mothers mistresses and Regular Army wives may go – only Yeomanry wives are banned.' One wonders which of these refused requests, to take their wives or their hounds, caused the greater disappointment.

The regiment travelled with its horses across the English Channel and then by railway across France to Marseilles, in an exceptionally cold wintry spell, said to be the coldest since 1815. They re-embarked at Marseilles, and encountered severe storms during the passage, from which the horses suffered badly, some falling and becoming cast, a real crisis on a cramped ship. They landed at Haifa in Palestine on 29 January, the scene of one of their finest hours in the Great War (See Maps 7 p.92, 9 p.102, and 11 p.134). Some yeomanry wives, including six from the regiment, amongst them Ladies Yarborough and Ranfurly, had one of those periodical attacks of selective deafness that has traditionally afflicted their husbands, and found their way out to the Middle East anyway, becoming known quaintly as 'the illegal wives'. They did not bring any hounds with them, but did bring their husband's shotguns, since it had been discovered that very good shooting was to be had.

For the first five months the regiment was used on internal security duties, initially in and around their old stamping ground, Jaffa (Tel Aviv), where recent land legislation, of which the Jews disapproved, had led to some rioting. The regiment patrolled the streets and, on some occasions, had to charge with drawn swords to disperse crowds. In particular, this activity included a mounted charge by A Squadron down the main street of Jaffa. On 13 March the regiment was ordered to move north from Latrun to Karkur where an event occurred, which arguably altered the regiment's entire destiny. Lady Ranfurly wrote an account, gleaned from her husband, of what then happened:

> Dan said it was a fine sight – seeing the Regiment paraded by squadrons below Latrun and file away across the plain. ... They rode all morning, plagued by flies and halted at noon for lunch in a narrow lane with a hedge on one side and a line of trees on the other. Dan had dismounted and given his Troop the order to take bits out and prepare to water when suddenly, without the slightest warning, two squadrons of horses which were standing in the rise beyond him, charged down the track at full gallop. Dan flung himself into a ditch. They swept by like an avalanche; some of them crashed headlong into two army trucks which were parked in the lane, others hit the telegraph poles which fell like ninepins and, as they passed, Dan's troop broke loose and went with them. When the dust cleared Dan saw an incredible scene of destruction – injured men, dead horses and a tangle of equipment lay everywhere and,

far away, a moving trail of dust showed the horses were still racing madly on. Doctor Brook, who had been dressing a soldier's foot in the middle of the lane, had a marvellous escape; when he saw the horses charging down on him he flung himself over his patient and the whole cavalcade passed over him. Neither of them was hurt. [In fact he suffered damage to several ribs].

For that remarkable piece of courage the good doctor, a Nottinghamshire GP in real life, was awarded the George Medal and became the first person in the regiment to be decorated, his citation noting that 'In spite of this and though in great pain, he continued to attend to more than 30 men injured in the stampede. It was not until this task was performed that he admitted to having received any injury himself.'

> They collected the casualties and then set off on foot to find the horses. It took ages. Some had gone back to Latrun; two days later some are still lost. Dan found his chestnut mare covered with blood – all the skin torn off her shoulders and flanks. She had galloped through a barbed-wire fence. But many other horses were worse and several had to be shot. Gradually the regiment reassembled and started out again. When evening came they put down horse lines and bivouacked. A special watch was kept in case of more trouble.... Dan put his bed two hundred yards from the horse lines and went to sleep. He was woken by the thunder of hooves. It was terrifying – in the dark he could not see which way they were coming till one horse crashed into the cookhouse tent and sent it up in flames. The poor cook had both his legs broken.

Twenty-four men were injured, including Lawrence Biddle, who was galloped over, and four horses were killed in the stampedes. Over 100 horses were admitted to Ramleh Veterinary Hospital. No one knows what causes stampedes like these. Whatever the cause, the stampedes damaged seriously the regiment's reputation, since it was felt to reflect on its standards of horse management, which, to that point, had been considered one of its greatest accomplishments. As a result, the regiment became regarded as among the worst in the division, being dubbed the 'Stampede Rangers', which both angered and humiliated them.

As the seasons turned from spring to summer, the news from home turned from bad to worse. Germany invaded the Low Countries and France. The British Expeditionary Force in France was driven back to Dunkirk, and evacuated. France fell. Thus emboldened, on 10 June, Mussolini entered the war under Germany's protection, completely altering the balance of power in the Mediterranean and North Africa. With France out of the war, Italy's fleet became a major player in the Mediterranean, and its troops in Libya were no longer threatened by the French in Tunisia. Accordingly, Mussolini now felt free to pursue his ambitions, and began to plan an attack on Egypt.

The backwater had become the principal theatre, at least on land, so that when the eyes of the free world were not transfixed by the Battle of Britain, as it rolled and looped in a silent deadly struggle high above the South Downs, they looked anxiously down on Egypt. In addition to the threat to Egypt, Italy, through its troops in Abyssinia, created a further threat to central Africa, thus tying up many thousands of Allied troops which were, as a result, unable to reinforce British forces in Egypt and the Middle East.

The one non-sequential but beneficial result of the fall of France and Italy's entry into the war was that the troubles between the Jews and Arabs quietened down and, as a result, there was little for the division to do. Most people became bored. On 2 July, the regiment had the ignominy of being first in the division to receive orders to hand in all its horses. This was undoubtedly a consequence of the stampedes. As many horses were the personal property of the officers, this decision was felt most deeply by them. The yeomen cheered however; they were ready to move on. Some weeks later the regiment received a formal written enquiry: 'Please state whether The Unit under your command is "Horsed" or "Mechanised".' Kellet wrote 'Unmechanised', then deleted it and wrote 'Answer – UNHORSED'. The real blessing, but one that remained well disguised for several months to come, was that, as a consequence of being the first regiment in the division to lose its horses, it was given a head start on the others in the major task of conversion to a mechanized role, which would in the end give them a vital edge.

The regiment received even more unpleasant news when they were ordered to become coast artillery, seen at the time as just about the lowest form of military life, particularly for a cavalry regiment. They spent a miserable two months manning some antiquated guns guarding Haifa, which they had famously helped to take in the Great War, against the non-existent (as they believed) threat posed by the Italian Fleet. September found the regiment promoted to guarding prisoners of war, and training to become a motorized infantry battalion, with the exception of Y Battery, under command of Tony Holden, which was sent to Cyprus as coast gunners.

On 18 September there was a momentary quickening of the pulse as Italy attacked across the Egyptian border from Libya (See Map 13 p.162), making the first move in the struggle for control of Egypt and Cyrenaica, which would last for the next two and a quarter years, and which became known as the Benghazi Handicap. The Italians halted their advance at Sidi Barrani and the regimental pulse returned to normal.

Also in September, Lord Yarborough handed over command. He had commanded for four years, during which he had prepared the regiment for war, and recruited it up to full strength when few other TA regiments found that possible. He must, nevertheless, have felt keenly the fact that he was leaving at a low point. However, he undoubtedly left the regiment containing the seeds of its future greatness, for amongst those recruits (in addition to Nottinghamshire, also from his own estate and Lincolnshire) were many of the young men who formed its backbone when it became armoured. From their ranks came the young and fearless tank commanders through whom it gained its great reputation. Undoubtedly, the time was right for change, and for somebody to take command who could look to the future and prepare the regiment for it: that man was Lieutenant Colonel E. O. (Flash) Kellett MP.

Kellett had learnt his soldiering in the Irish Guards. Immaculate in his turn-out, he was equally exacting in relation to everybody else's turn-out and discipline. Energetic, far-sighted and a brilliant trainer, he eventually got the regiment to such a high pitch that ever after they went into battle with an unbreakable will to prevail, which became their hallmark, and was responsible in equal measure for their success in battle, and their heavy losses, both of which endured to the very end.

As MP for the Aston division of Birmingham, Kellett was also extremely well connected, and knew everybody of importance in theatre. His position gave him the ear of Winston Churchill, and he used his advantages shamelessly to protect the regiment from threats of disbandment and to further its interests.

The question of 'the illegal wives', which had been simmering, now came to a head. At the end of September they were all ordered to return home on the *Empress of Britain*; Lord Yarborough was also on board. The ship was bombed and sunk off Ireland, and Dandy Wallace's wife was killed. The other wives survived, save for Lady Ranfurly who did not need sparing: she had jumped ship in Cape Town and returned to the Middle East. Evading captivity, despite every effort to send her home, eventually, because she could type, she went to work for SOE and later became personal assistant to General Sir Henry (Jumbo) Wilson, Commander-in-Chief, Middle East and earned the accolade of 'having outmanoeuvred every general in the Middle East'. Thus she was allowed to stay, legally, at the very centre of events, for several more years.

On 9 December the Allies counter-attacked the Italians at Sidi Barrani and drove them out of Egypt. They attacked again on 3 January, and by 21 January had taken the vital ports of Bardia and Tobruk. Only Benghazi and Tripoli remained in Italian hands. The ports on the coast of Cyrenaica, particularly those of Tobruk and Benghazi, were crucial. East to west Cyrenaica is some 600 miles across and, without control of the ports, it was impossible for the Italians to re-supply their forces for an attack on Egypt, or for the Allies to re-supply theirs for an attack beyond El Agheila.

Meanwhile, the regiment remained in Palestine on security duties, but had been training hard as motorized infantry. At the end of January 1941, a report from Headquarters 1st Cavalry Division expressed itself 'very pleased with the appearance and turn out' of the Sherwood Rangers. The standard of training already reached was 'particularly praiseworthy'. External perceptions concerning the Stampede Rangers had begun to change.

Chapter 24

Abyssinia, Tobruk, Benghazi and Crete

January–July 1941

Among officers joining at this time was John Semken, another posting from the Inns of Court Regiment complete with riding boots, to find there was nothing to ride, while some existing officers went on attachments to other units or staff appointments.

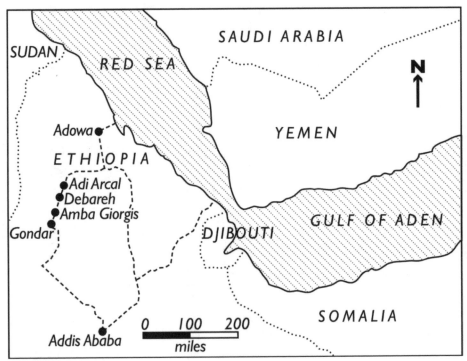

Map 12: Ethiopia.

Abyssinia

Major Basil Ringrose was one of the latter who, in early 1941, left with a bag of gold Maria Theresa dollars and two regimental sergeants bound for Ethiopia, becoming one of a number of officers and senior NCOs known as Gideon Force, under the overall command of Brigadier Sandford and the operational command

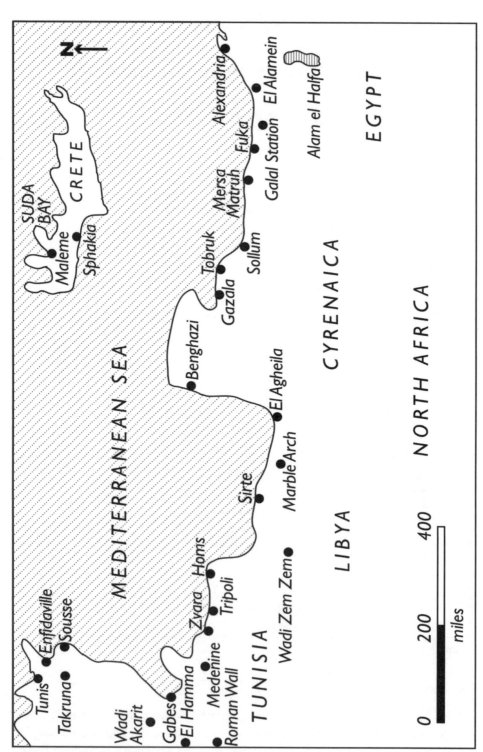

Map 13: North Africa.

of Lieutenant Colonel Orde Wingate. They were to assist conventional forces in the defeat of the Italians through guerrilla action, and thus bring Haile Selassie, Emperor of Ethiopia, back into power from which position he had been removed by the Italians. The only account of Ringrose's exploits is recorded in the citation for the fine DSO he earned:

In February 1941 Major Ringrose with two SRY SNCOs was sent to Adi Remoz with the instruction to raise a patriot force and attempt to cut the Adowa-Gondar road in the vicinity of Adi Arcal.

Acting independently, he raised a large patriot army [said to number 20,000], which by the beginning of May, was astride the Gondar road from South of Debarech to Amba Giogis, and had mined the road in several places. These operations cut off the enemy garrison of Wolcheffitt from Gondar.

On 28 May his force captured Debareh, and although the enemy counter-attacked and twice retook the town on 31 May, it remained in our hands. 400 enemy dead were left on the ground and 150 deserters came in.

On 16 June Maj Ringrose's Patriots found the enemy sentries of one of his forts asleep. They entered, threw a hundred grenades at a given signal and caused 100 casualties.

On 22 June Maj Ringrose was overwhelmingly attacked at dawn. Ras Ayalu was captured, and the patriot army dispersed, taking with them all his mules. Treachery is suspected. He himself was wounded.

Immediately he was released from hospital he insisted on returning to his base at Zareima to re-organize his army, which he effected rapidly. Having again assembled his forces towards Debarech, he was on 1 August heavily attacked by 500 white Italians with guns and mortars. The enemy were routed, leaving 43 dead including 3 officers, also 13 prisoners.

Major Ringrose has been for a long period under conditions of considerable privation and personal danger. He has shown throughout great gallantry and resolution, and the eventual reductions of the enemy garrison at Wolchefitt will be in a large measure due to his efforts.

The outcome of these actions, and those of others, was the defeat of the Italian Army in Abyssinia, removing the threat Italy posed to east Africa, and releasing many thousands of troops to reinforce Egypt. Ringrose returned to the Sherwood Rangers, but had a personality clash with Flash Kellett so was eventually posted elsewhere but returned in north-west Europe to end the war as second-in-command.

Tobruk and Benghazi

On the capture of Tobruk, part of the regiment received orders to man the guns protecting the port; when Benghazi fell similar orders arrived. Now able to see such an order as a challenge, the regiment was reconfigured:

Sub-unit	Personnel	Location
RHQ	CO: Flash Kellett	Tobruk
	2i/c Donny Player	
A Battery	Stephen Mitchell	Tobruk
C Battery	Henry Trotter	Tobruk
	Derick Warwick	
X Battery	Peter Laycock	Benghazi
Z Battery	Michael Laycock	Tobruk

In February A and C Batteries manned guns protecting Tobruk harbour, whilst Z Battery manned the boom defences. In early February Benghazi and Cyrenaica as far as El Agheila fell to the Allies and Tenth Italian Army surrendered; the Allies took 130,000 prisoners and captured 400 tanks and 1,290 guns, a magnificent victory.

X Battery immediately deployed to man Benghazi's coast defences. A further detachment had a lively time as shore observation teams to the monitor HMS *Terror* until she was sunk by enemy air attack. The primary purpose of all these gun positions was to defend their locations from attack from the sea.

In late February Germany announced its entry into the war in North Africa for the first time, with the arrival in Tripoli of General Erwin Rommel. He brought with him some German reinforcements, two elements of which would become all too well known to the regiment over the coming years. The first was 21st Panzer Division (initially 5th Light Division) and the second was the 88mm gun, an anti-aircraft gun used as an anti-tank gun. It could, in some but not all variants, be dug in flush with the ground, and threw a 20-pound shell which, assisted by an excellent sight, could knock out a tank at 3,000 yards. Its significance can best be illustrated by the fact that most tank-on-tank engagements took place at half that range, or even less.

Rommel's aim was to retake Cyrenaica without delay in preparation for an invasion of Egypt. His timing, as would become the norm, was excellent. The Allies' hold over Cyrenaica was tenuous with their lines of communication stretched over 800 miles

The ability of the Allies to generate reinforcements and stocks of armour, men, ammunition and fuel in the Middle East was constrained by the slow if steady build-up of momentum of the war effort in the UK. In addition, it took between six weeks and three months for a ship to travel from the UK round the Cape of Good Hope to Port Tewfik or Port Suez in Egypt. The direct route through the Mediterranean originally taken by the regiment was too hazardous and not until late summer 1942, still eighteen long months away, would the Allies have available to them the build-up of *materiel* necessary for victory.

Initially, the regiment were about the only combatant troops in Tobruk and had the task of building up the defences, which took up all their time. At first, the assessment was that it would be early summer before Rommel would be able to attack, and there was no assumption that he would be successful. Apart from incessant air raids, several times a day, which continued throughout the regiment's tour, the immediate danger was thought to be from airborne landings. Even so, there was a feeling that once the defences were complete, Tobruk would become almost as peaceful and boring as Palestine, the first of a steady stream of similarly inaccurate attempts at regimental soothsaying.

In late March all Flash Kellett's diplomatic initiatives (scheming?!) on behalf of the regiment paid off when orders were received that it would become an armoured regiment at the end of its time in Tobruk. From then on, at every spare moment, Kellett focused on training the regiment in the key skills of gunnery, mechanics, signals and logistics that would be vital as an armoured unit. Instead of selecting those who could be spared to attend the relevant courses, he chose those with the greatest aptitude. Many gained glowing reports from these courses. For example, under Lawrence Biddle's leadership, and tapping into the existing skills of some of the reservists, the regiment became recognized as having the division's best signals troop. Radio was to become for the armoured regiment what the trumpet had been to the cavalry: then 'no trumpeter, no cavalry', henceforth 'no signals, no armoured regiment'.

However, when the news of the new role first came through, there was little time to relish it, because Rommel launched his attack on 27 March, significantly earlier than expected. The Allies, for the reasons mentioned earlier, were unable to resist his attack. X Battery had to abandon Benghazi on 3 April, re-joining the regiment at Tobruk next day. As Rommel swept forward, his boldness was immediately rewarded by the capture, on 7 April, of both Lieutenant General Neame VC, who was C-in-C Cyrenaica Command, and Lieutenant General O'Connor, at the time the most experienced British desert commander who was with him. This capture was a great blow. The significance to the regiment was that General Neame's ADC was Dan Ranfurly, who was travelling with him, and was also taken prisoner.

Two regimental flying columns, together with others in an assortment of vehicles with a variety of weapons, sallied forth from Tobruk to El Adem and El Gubi airfields, but were not committed to battle. By 11 April, Good Friday, Rommel's advance had taken him east of Tobruk and the town was cut off completely and invested by the enemy. However, Tobruk had been reinforced by 9th Australian Division with a number of other units. During the period 11 to 14 April the enemy mounted several major attacks on the perimeter, which included the regiment's first meeting with the German 5th Light Division. The German and Italian forces included four full divisions and over 200 tanks. The garrison was to 'hold Tobruk to the end'. By the end of the fighting, the regiment's coastal defence guns had been turned about to support the shoreward defences. Every attack was forcibly repelled. By 14 April German survivors were referring to 'the hell of Tobruk'. One German commanding officer, having lost half his tanks in an attack, wrote 'the regiment went into battle with an unbendable will determined at all costs to break the enemy and take Tobruk. Only the vastly superior enemy caused the regiment to fail in its task.'

There was no renewal of the German attack on 15 April. Major General Lavarack, GOC 9th Australian Division, issued a special order of the day: 'Stern determination, prompt action and close co-operation by all arms ensured the enemy's defeat – Well done, Tobruk.' This action was significant, as the first defeat inflicted on the might of Germany in the war and provided a major boost to morale back home. Those in Tobruk were not displeased either. Although Rommel's advance took him only just beyond Tobruk, overall it represented a significant defeat for the Allies.

From the moment that Tobruk was besieged, the garrison had to contend not only with incessant air raids, but also with shelling. The enemy made some 300 air raids on Tobruk during the next three months, a daily average of three. Tobruk had a substantial network of tunnels providing ample protection from the air raids. However, it is an insight into Flash Kellett's approach that he believed using the tunnels during air raids would damage the regiment's offensive culture, and instead ordered that slit trenches be dug; the regiment, when under attack from aircraft, should return fire, even small-arms fire. He also typically sustained morale by insisting on a high standard of dress, a practice which did not pass the notice of the Australians without prompting comment!

The Sherwood Rangers left Tobruk early in July when they were relieved by a specially trained gunner regiment. The siege lasted until November.

Chester Wilmot wrote of Tobruk:

the final streamlined garrison from early May to late August averaged little more than 23,000 men. Of these nearly 15,000 were Australians and about 500 were Indians. The rest came from Great Britain, and she has probably never been served by finer troops.

Crete

At the same time that RHQ, A, C, X and Z Batteries deployed to Tobruk and Benghazi, the remainder of the regiment, B Battery from Palestine and Y Battery from Cyprus, deployed to Crete to man coastal guns defending Suda Bay (See Map 13 p.162).

The batteries were configured:

B Battery   Sidney Morse
                             Michael Riviere
                             Myles Hildyard
Y Battery   Tony Holden
                             Jocelyn Abel Smith
                             Michael Parish

Italy had invaded Greece at the end of the previous October. Britain had treaty obligations to Greece and, in addition, Crete was strategically important to the defence of Egypt because of Maleme aerodrome and the naval fuelling base in the excellent natural fjord-like harbour at Suda Bay on the north coast. Despite the inadequacy of resources in the Middle East, not even sufficient to cope with the threat on the North African mainland, it was decided that Greece must be supported. B and Y Batteries moved to Crete in early February, B Battery being sited at Khelevis in the old prison overlooking the entrance to Suda Bay where they manned four coast defence guns. Y Battery manned two guns in a position on top of St John's Hill, one and a half miles west of Suda Bay.

Initially this mission seemed to be a forlorn backwater. Tony Holden wrote to Flash Kellett with another regimental foresight, 'We are absolutely certain that we shall never see any action here.' Both batteries occupied themselves by exploring and admiring the beautiful island and its spectacular wildflowers, and recalling its place in history as the site of the great pre-Doric Aegean civilization of the Minoan kings. But the ever-present influence of Kellett was also in evidence, and they trained assiduously in signalling and other skills relevant to an armoured role, despite the doomed efforts of their local commander and his staff to make them resign themselves to their fate as gunners.

After three tranquil months they were rudely awakened on 1 May by the unwelcome news that Greece had fallen to the Germans. Crete was now in reach of German air power. The time to take stock had arrived; Crete's only decent harbours were in the north, thus exposing Allied shipping, which was using and re-supplying them, to a threat from the Greek mainland.

The defenders were under command of General Freyberg VC, a legendary British-born New Zealander and a hero of the First World War, of whom more later. However, the New Zealand troops holding the island were poorly equipped with few supporting arms and little anti-aircraft protection while little had been done to improve the ability of the island to resist attack.

Germany attacked Crete on 19 May with 400 bombers and fighters followed by a full-blown airborne landing at Maleme airfield. The landing was contested fiercely and the regiment was in action day and night for the next nine days, its guns eventually turned inland and onto the German DZ at Maleme. During this phase, Sergeant George Clark of Newark gained a fine MM engaging enemy aircraft for an extended period with his Vickers machine gun. By the end, when the Germans finally prevailed, the regiment was already exhausted through lack of sleep. To this was added hunger, once they were ordered to abandon the gun positions. They would get little sleep or food during the next four days as they withdrew across the island to the south coast where they were told that they would be evacuated by the Navy from the beach at Sphakia. The Sherwood Rangers were amongst the last troops to reach the beach because they fought as part of the rearguard.

The Navy itself was exhausted and had suffered heavily with two cruisers and four destroyers sunk, and two battleships, an aircraft carrier, a cruiser and a destroyer so badly damaged as to be out of action. They had only a cruiser and seven destroyers to spare for the evacuation. On 1 June the regiment was informed that the Navy could do no more, and that all troops then still on the island would be surrendered. When the news came through, B Battery was waiting only twenty yards from the embarkation stage. The only Sherwood Rangers to be evacuated were those, fifty-two in number, who had been injured or wounded or had collapsed in the arduous process of crossing the mountains. The remaining 110 had no choice but to surrender, with the rest of the garrison.

There were some gallant escapes by captured boats through the Aegean to Turkey, notably by Captains Myles Hildyard and Michael Parish, who were both awarded MCs, and Lance Corporal Edwin Peacock, who earned the MM. Those members of the regiment who fought in Crete did so with great courage and tenacity and to great effect. The Germans had suffered approximately 50 per cent casualties, and were only once more to attempt a major airborne operation. Myles Hildyard went on to join the staff of 7th Armoured Division where he served until the end of the war and was to be described by his commander as 'the best GSO III (I) whom I have met in this war'. He was joined by another Sherwood Ranger, Captain Martin Lindsay, as Intelligence Officer, after the latter had served throughout the Desert campaign. Both were awarded the MBE for their service and after the war both worked on the regimental history of the war, though Lindsay is rightly credited with the lion's share of the work on what is an acclaimed account. Ending his service with an MC and an MBE, plus a couple of Mentions, Hildyard must have been one of the more highly decorated officers of his rank in the war. He also wore another badge of honour, namely that he was 'gay', in an age when that was against the law. Post-war regimental balls at his home Flintham Hall had plenty of style anyway, but all the more so because they were enjoyed as much by himself, his life-long companion and their friends, as by the rest of the regiment and, indeed, Nottinghamshire.

Chapter 25

Armoured Training

August 1941–August 1942

Back at Karkur Camp in Palestine in August 1941, the Sherwood Rangers Yeomanry found themselves all together for the first time for a year. The regiment had reached a watershed in its history as, after a short period of leave, it began to train in earnest as an armoured regiment. Major Donny Player was second in command with the squadrons commanded by Major Stanley Christopherson (A), Major Michael Laycock (B), Major Stephen Mitchell (C) and Major Lawrence Biddle (HQ). The regiment was to join 8 Armoured Brigade in 10th Armoured Division, being formed out of 1st Cavalry Division. The other regiments initially posted to the brigade as armoured units were the Staffordshire Yeomanry, who stayed with it throughout the fighting in North Africa, and the Royal Scots Greys, who were later replaced by 3rd Royal Tank Regiment, an experienced armoured regiment. The Sherwood Rangers would stay with the brigade for the rest of the war, the only major unit to do so.

What then, was the role of an armoured regiment for which the Rangers were about to train? After the war, Stanley Christopherson wrote:

In tank warfare there are two distinct types of fighting which are:

- the deliberate frontal attack against prepared enemy positions in order to make a hole in the enemy's line, through which an armoured column can pass, and,
- the pursuit battle, which follows the piercing of the enemy's line.

In the deliberate battle, generally speaking, the armoured regiment is placed in support of an infantry brigade with each squadron supporting an infantry battalion, and the attack is preceded by intensive artillery concentrations on the enemy strongpoints, during which time the sappers clear lanes through the minefields for the tanks to pass. The armoured CO works with the infantry brigadier and the squadron leaders with the battalion commanders.

The pursuit battle is altogether more satisfactory and follows the breaking of the enemy's line. The armoured regiment is sent off on its own together with its company of motorized infantry and battery of guns and works independently to exploit successes and cause havoc in the rear of the enemy; light opposition is brushed aside or, if too strong, is bypassed. It is an ideal command where the armoured regiment commander can use initiative, speed and is entirely independent of his brigade commander.

... as, throughout the war, only a limited number of armoured divisions existed, 8 Independent Armoured Brigade [initially part of 10th Armoured Division but independent following the battle of El Alamein] was continuously called upon to support the very numerous infantry divisions who [did not have integral armoured support] for a deliberate attack and then again for the pursuit battle....

Not often in Europe did [the armoured brigade commander] command his whole brigade operating as one unit in a pursuit battle, although he did so in the desert....

This appears contrary to the descriptions likening armoured formations in North Africa to 'fleets of ships manoeuvring in an ocean of desert'. That was prior to Alam el Halfa, after which both sides were large enough to leave no open flanks. John Semken explained: 'After Alam Halfa there [was not] any naval manoeuvring – just a careful approach followed by a heavyweight boxing match. We just kept fighting all day edging forward as best we could.'

All that, however, was in the future. For the next twelve months the regiment's efforts were devoted to converting to and training as an armoured regiment. Of the initial phase of this process and its effect, John Semken wrote:

The first sign of the new order of things was the arrival of Capt Wrangham, lent to us by the Royal Tank Regiment to be our first Technical Adjutant. After him came Ned Leakey and AQMS North, with their Light Aid Detachment of the [what was to become] REME. Then came the first tanks – Little American 'Honey' tanks with radial engines, and American Top-Sergeants to tell our new-fledged fitters how to maintain them. Then came new officers – Ronnie Hutton, Keith Douglas (KIA), John Bethell-Fox, John Masefield (KIA), Ken Graves (KIA), and Freddie Cooper (KIA), all tank men with not a saddle or spur in sight. Trade classes, trade tests, new titles and new rates of pay were the order of the day.

These new officers had been carefully selected by Kellet, using his customary attention to detail.

Notwithstanding the shortage of armour, the regiment continued to train unabated. The young yeomen, recruited by Lord Yarborough in the lead up to war, now came into their own. Young, intelligent and adaptable, their strengths began to show through, as did their ability, in comparison with those of the older cavalrymen, to cope with the demands of an armoured regiment. Indeed Lieutenant General Sir Brian Horrocks wrote that the key element which gave the regiment, and other yeomanry regiments converted to armour, a decisive edge in performance, even over regular armoured regiments, was the fact that man for man they were that much younger and therefore that much less risk averse.

During this period the regiment was issued with battledress, which seems to have been used as a parade dress, shorts and shirts being worn on an everyday basis. They even wore shorts when they went into action for the first time but never thereafter, as they learned a hard lesson: tank crews must wear coveralls or, at least, long trousers and long sleeves in action. Berets were also issued, and were worn by all in the field. Officers continued wearing service-dress hats at other times. Desert boots were the universal footwear. Yeomen, as a breed, would be devastated if ever accused of being compliant with Dress Regulations.

The regiment not only needed equipping with tanks, it also needed reinforcing, not just with officers, but also with crewmen. It had lost a significant part of its strength in Crete, and there was also a significant turnover of the older members. Flash Kellett applied all his energy, skills and influence to this selection process, as to all others. These reinforcements mostly came by ship round the Cape of Good Hope. Philip Foster, who joined as a trooper before El Alamein, described the experience:

On each side of the deck which was the width of the stern, were six mess tables for eighteen men each. It would have been sheer impossibility to have seated more than nine a side…. It is worth adding that the space separating the bench belonging to one table from the bench belonging to another was so microscopic that … [A person] was obliged to edge his way sideways….

Directed upwards my gaze was attracted by multitudes of hooks welded in even rows on the steel girders … we soon discovered that their purpose was to receive the ring on each extremity of a hammock….

The overcrowding was positively oppressive during the night as hammocks had to be slung in such close proximity; although staggered they were actually touching each other. Nevertheless they were moderately comfortable,…. Men were literally everywhere, in the hammocks on the entire floor space, on the tables and under the tables.

Whilst the regiment trained, the battle for control of the Western Desert continued. In June 1941 General Wavell twice counter-attacked Rommel in the Sollum area but ultimately failed due to a hallmark counter-stroke by Rommel into his left flank.

Following this setback, Wavell was replaced by General Auchinleck who, in September 1941 and in acknowledgement of the steady build-up in the size of the forces deployed in the Western Desert through reinforcements, created an Army Headquarters designated 8th Army, set in overall command of a force which now comprised two Corps; XIII, which was the former Western Desert Force and XXX comprising newly assigned units and formations. Since Wavell's departure, there had also been a further reinforcement consisting of the delivery of 300 tanks through the Mediterranean at great risk. It sounds a lot but it is in fact no more than two brigades' worth.

Auchinleck attacked on 18 November 1941, timed to pre-empt Rommel's own attack on the still unrelieved Tobruk due later that month. Auchinleck achieved surprise, but ferocious fighting continued with the advantage swinging one way then the next until, on 29 November, a corridor to Tobruk was opened, and it was relieved on 10 December. The battle ended with Rommel in full retreat. Eighth Army captured 33,000 prisoners and 300 tanks, compared with its own losses of 18,000 all ranks and 278 tanks.

Auchinleck, having pursued as far as El Agheila only to have to yield some of his gains, consolidated his position some twenty-five miles west of Tobruk. Considerable additional reinforcements would be required before he could contemplate a further move. Rommel's reinforcements were anticipated to arrive first, and therefore the next most likely event would be a counter-attack by Rommel in early summer 1942.

Rommel attacked on the night of 26/27 May in what became known as the Battle of Gazala. Although there was fierce fighting, he successfully turned Eighth Army's flank from the south, and inexorably forced it back, farther than had been anticipated, right back to El Alamein, where Rommel was finally held, less than seventy miles from Alexandria. Worse still, on 21 June, Tobruk unexpectedly fell to Rommel, providing him with the vital port facilities he needed to mount an attack on Egypt and with supplies for 30,000 men for three months and more than 10,000 cubic metres of petrol. The loss of Tobruk was so grievous that it cost Auchinleck his job. In August General Alexander was appointed to succeed him and General Bernard Montgomery, in due course, was appointed to command Eighth Army in succession to General Ritchie.

In March 1942 the regiment had left Karkur and Palestine for the last time and moved to Khatatba in Egypt, a tented camp in the desert within striking distance of Cairo and much closer to the front line. The regiment played no part in the operations described above but, by June 1942, it was reasonably well equipped with tanks. Following the Gazala battles it was deployed south of Matruh and its tank strength increased: A Squadron was equipped fully but B and C combined as a composite squadron. No sooner had this occurred than orders were received to hand over its tanks and to return to Khatatba.

Finally, all the frustration and training came to an end when, in mid-August, the regiment was equipped from the latest consignment of over 300 tanks. A Squadron received Crusaders, light, fast tanks with a low profile but mechanically unreliable; B and C Squadrons re-equipped with Grants, a good tank, but one which, due to its main gun being mounted low down in a side sponson could not be fought in the hull-down position.

The regiment had been at war for three long years. Once again in late August, almost fully equipped and fully trained, as part of 10th Armoured Division, the Sherwood Rangers moved up to the Western Desert.

Part VI

The Second World War
1942–43

The End of the Beginning

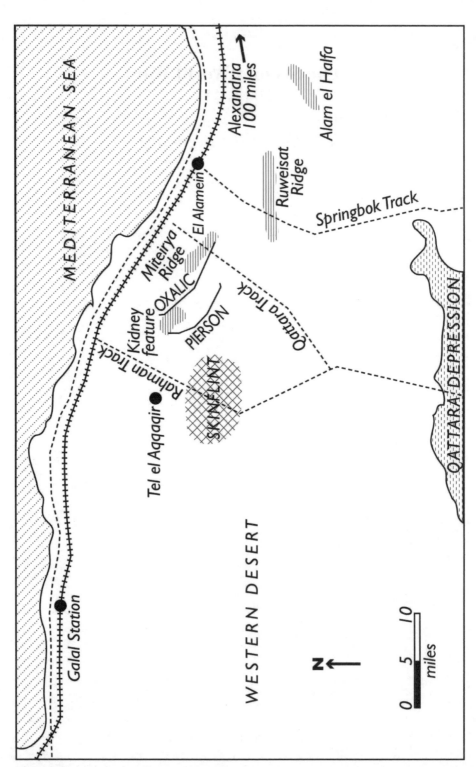

Map 14: Battles of Alamel Halfa and El Alamein.

Chapter 26

Battle of Alam el Halfa

August–October 1942

In the evening of 30 August 1942 Major General Gatehouse's 10th Armoured Division took up positions on Eighth Army's stop line at El Alamein, which stretched between closed flanks formed by the sea in the north and the impassable Qattara Depression in the south. This was in anticipation of Rommel's attack which he launched at 0200 next morning, the 31st, in his attempt to defeat the Allies and win the massive prizes of Egypt, the Suez Canal, the Middle East and control of its vital oilfields. The vital ground was the Bare Ridge feature; the action became known as the Battle of Alam el Halfa.

John Semken was acting adjutant in RHQ:

> I shall never forget that Sunday [31st] when I sat by the rear-link set and took down the German dispositions ... nor the report of German tanks and MT which were reported some three miles East of us and in our rear.... Soon afterwards we were diving into tanks and roaring away into the evening sun. However, we did not meet the Hun that night....
>
> Next morning as soon as it was light we started the approach march to our new positions post-haste and then I saw the Germans for the first time. We crossed a ridge and there as far as the eye could see were his dispersed transports.... Something was afoot so I went to Steve Delmar-Morgan to find out what.... He said quite calmly 'the Germans have got that ridge there and we are going to take it'. I said 'thanks' and walked back to my own tank. Then the advance began.

Major Steve Delmar-Morgan was a Sherwood Ranger but at that time was on the staff of Eighth Army responsible for the forward control of its 'J' Service (staff information), for which he would be appointed MBE.

An initial attack by 3rd Tanks failed. The regiment, supported by the Staffordshire Yeomanry on their left, then attacked enemy tanks which had established themselves on the ridge to their front by a right-flanking manoeuvre. By attacking from a flank the regiment exposed its own flank to the enemy's gun line hidden on the reverse slope 150 yards in front of its panzers' fall-back position. The gun line held its fire until the regiment was on top of its positions as John Semken recalled:

I shall not forget the moment when I first saw one of our tanks in flames but my meditations were cut short because the next moment it looked as if the majority of the Regiment was ablaze. And still we were advancing. The tank first in front was now flaming and then the order from Brigade 'WFA you may withdraw'. The manner in which the Colonel got the remains of the Regiment out was a masterpiece of calm ability. The stuff was still falling round us and I could see the devil who was firing at us and I could even see his gun recoil and the smoke rise each time he fired with such fiendish regularity. But we were putting down smoke for all we were worth and soon it was dense and safe. 'Good old WFA well done' came over the air – I felt more like weeping....

That night the Hun, who had been within an ace of the Bare Ridge and the command of Egypt, withdrew. We had succeeded.

This was both a bloody nose and a wake-up call, although the regiment had proved its staunchness, determination and gallantry by gaining, in spite of suffering twenty-eight casualties, two immediate Military Crosses and two immediate Military Medals in its first day in action as armour. The first MC went to Michael Laycock, wounded in command of B Squadron, when his first tank was knocked out, and then in respect of his actions to save his second tank from brewing up. The second MC was to Lieutenant Sam Garrett, commanding the Recce Troop, who led his troop forward under fire to rescue the regiment's wounded. The two MMs went to Trooper Lenton for rescuing his crew when his tank brewed up, and Trooper Robertson of Recce Troop, who rescued a crew member from another brewed-up tank and was wounded whilst carrying him to his own vehicle.

After two more days of manoeuvre, Rommel had no choice but to break off the engagement due to lack of re-supply, and his inability to overcome or bypass the Alam el Halfa position. He withdrew on 3 September, 10th Armoured Division's presence and the tenacity with which it had fought having been a complete surprise to him. On 8 Armoured Brigade's front, twenty-one enemy tanks were subsequently found destroyed.

The battle was crucial, because at the start of it the threat that the Axis Panzerarmee Afrika posed to Egypt and the whole of the Middle East was considered to be both real and imminent. However, by the end of it, the tide had turned, and it was clear that, with reinforcements to Eighth Army arriving daily, Rommel would never again be able to threaten Alexandria. Indeed, he would never take other than backward steps till trapped and defeated. It only remained for Eighth Army to force that ending.

It was now that the regiment learned, as mentioned earlier, the key lessons when fighting in the Western Desert. Where there was no set-piece defence, it was an environment that was extremely favourable to armour, since the degree of freedom of manoeuvre possible gave opportunities to achieve surprise and shock action induced by encirclement of the enemy. Where, however, the enemy had had time to prepare a strong defensive position with no open flanks, and had to be attacked from the front, the open and bare terrain favoured the defender, and was extremely hostile to attacking tanks.

The normal tactic of the defender was to site his anti-tank screen or 'gun line' a short way in front of its own armour, well dug in, in concealed positions. It then used its armour to tempt the enemy into attacking. Alternatively, the tanks could fight from hull-down positions or behind reverse slopes. The enemy had several capable anti-tank guns, probably the best being the PAK 75 and 76. Ironically the PAK76s were captured Red Army pieces that had been supplied to the Soviets by the UK as redundant 3-inch heavy anti-aircraft guns. Of all the guns, however, the one the armoured regiments feared the most was the 88mm. It mattered not that it was rarer than conventional wisdom believed. After the North African campaign was won, the regiment came to realize the Achilles heel of the 88s, which was that their crews had no overhead cover, and were therefore vulnerable to artillery fire using airburst. Some regiments knew this but the regimental system hindered the sharing of this type of information.

Both sides learned techniques designed to improve the odds of the attacker in such situations, and used them against each other on a regular basis. The first lesson was not to try and charge the gun line or expose your flank as the regiment had just done. This was bound to fail, probably disastrously.

The principal tactic became use of the light squadron fanning out ahead of the regiment until it contacted the enemy. It then went to ground and continued to report all enemy movement and identify targets, while the regiment's battery of supporting artillery and the heavy squadrons took over, and engaged in the heavyweight boxing match of tank-gun and artillery fire. Sometimes, when the enemy became impossible to spot, the light squadron would manoeuvre in front of their positions, using dead ground to try and locate them, and often in doing so their dust drew the enemy's fire, so that it could be identified and engaged. Although the foregoing described reality, the only order that any tank commander, no matter at what level, can actually ever remember receiving was 'Get on!'

The second was to advance to form a salient, which the enemy would be tempted to counter-attack, and thus himself be caught in the open. A third was to attack out of the setting or rising sun, where the attacker became extremely difficult to spot, whilst the defender could be seen by the attacker with much greater clarity, not least because of the chance to catch reflections of the sunlight on shiny surfaces. The counter to such attacks was laying smoke, to silhouette the attacker as he emerged through the screen. This was used only rarely because of the difficulty of controlling the smoke and its limited effect.

Night was of only limited use because it was not easy for tanks to fight in the dark, since nothing could be seen through the gun-sight; therefore darkness was usually only used to shroud approach marches. Any movement at night, however, required a lot of practice, unless a lighted centre line was used. It meant moving nose-to-tail, at a crawl, eyes fixed on the convoy light of the tank ahead occulting through the dust. To lose sight of the light would spell disaster. Night moves were usually only attempted when out of contact, since if caught in an ambush one brew-up could light the rest, making them easy prey to an enemy still concealed by darkness. In addition, night movements often took much longer than planned, leaving the possibility of being caught out of position in the open as dawn broke.

In the middle of September, the regiment was withdrawn, and for five weeks trained for its task in the next battle. This involved endless practice at night movements through minefields. New tanks began to arrive, the long-awaited Shermans with a 75mm, a tank regarded as a match for the German Mark IIIs and Mark IVs. There were also Crusaders with the much improved 6-pounder guns, but still mechanically unreliable. The regiment was now equipped with thirteen Crusaders in A Squadron, eleven Shermans in C Squadron, which could fight hull-down, and twenty Grants which could not, and which were assigned to both B Squadron and RHQ. The RHQ tanks were appropriately named 'Robin Hood', 'Little John', 'Friar Tuck' and 'Maid Marian'.

On the night of 21 October, the regiment left its staging area occupied by dummy tanks. Its tracks obliterated by harrows towed by jeeps, it laagered close to its start line and concealed its tanks with canvas 'sunbonnets' to make them resemble lorries. Captain Patrick McCraith, having trained with the Long Range Desert Group, was the regiment's navigation officer, and was about to have the opportunity to put his skills to the test.

Chapter 27

Battle of El Alamein

October–November 1942

The Break-in (Operation LIGHTFOOT)

B oth sides had secure flanks and a front of over thirty miles. 'Since there is no open flank, the battle must be so stage-managed that a hole is blown in the enemy's front', wrote Alexander. Eighth Army had three corps: XXX Corps (Leese) in the north, with five infantry divisions; XIII Corps (Horrocks) in the south; and X Corps (Lumsden). X Corps included 1st (Briggs) and 10th (Gatehouse) Armoured Divisions. Tenth Armoured included 8 Armoured Brigade (Brigadier Custance) which, of course, included the regiment, and 24 Armoured Brigade.

Eighth Army was stronger than Panzerarmee Afrika but did not possess anything like the conventional superiority of three to one that an attacker needed to be reasonably sure of victory. Montgomery would have to conserve his resources. Both sides were deployed behind minefields of up to five miles in depth, between which was a no man's land of about one to two miles. Montgomery planned to attack in the north, the centre line running westerly about ten miles south of the coast, using the infantry divisions of XXX Corps, supported by X Corps' armour; XIII Corps would make a feint attack in the south, the centre line of which was also westerly and about five miles north of the Qattara Depression.

During the first night, XXX Corps' infantry divisions in the north would pass, four up with one in reserve, through their own minefields, across no man's land and the enemy's minefields. Once the infantry had secured the enemy's minefields and gone firm on that line, called *Oxalic*, Montgomery planned to pass both armoured divisions of X Corps through the infantry positions and out into open country onto objectives farther west, identified as line *Pierson*, 1st Armoured Division on the right and 10th on the left. The objective on 10th Armoured's front was 4,000 yards to the west of the infantry's objectives. This was a night attack and, for the reasons stated earlier, an extremely dangerous operation for the armour to attempt, once clear of the minefields.

Montgomery was well aware that the enemy's anti-tank screen represented the greatest threat to his armour. Tank commanders were instructed that tank strengths were not to be dissipated against the anti-tank screen, but reserved to destroy the enemy armour. Therefore, once in open country, the armoured divisions were to 'deploy well forward on ground of their own choosing and prepare to meet the enemy's armoured counter-attack'. He was seeking to exploit Rommel's well-known liking for the counter-attack. If the forward deployment onto the objectives was untenable, the armour should go firm with and protect the infantry from attack by panzers.

The infantry and the armoured divisions had interlinking but quite separate missions. The armour was not either in support of or under command of the infantry. The infantry division through which 10th Armoured Division, the left armoured division, would pass, was 2nd New Zealand Division (Freyberg), with 9 Armoured Brigade, a British independent armoured brigade, under command. The main feature on the New Zealanders' front was the northern end of Miteiriya Ridge, running northwest-southeast, believed to mark the western extremity of the enemy's minefields. It was therefore identified as 2nd NZ Division's objective.

Each armoured division would pass through corridors some three to five miles apart, prepared for their use in both Eighth Army's and Panzerarmee Afrika's minefields. The corridors in Eighth Army's minefields had, of course, not only been pre-cleared, but had been strengthened to take the anticipated weight of traffic. Even so, during the battle sand became ground into such fine dust that troops passing through the minefields became covered in it.

The order of march between armoured brigades in the left corridor through which 10th Armoured Division was to pass, was 8, 9 and 24 Armoured Brigades. The corridor had three separate tracks, the right called Bottle, assigned to the Staffordshire Yeomanry, that in the centre called Boat, assigned to the Sherwood Rangers, and the left called Hat, assigned to 3rd Royal Tanks. The enemy's minefield could not be cleared until the attack started which was to be done under cover of darkness. All of this was to be preceded by an artillery barrage of approximately 900 guns of which there were on XXX Corps' 12,000-yard front 432 field and forty-eight medium. These opened up at 2140 on the night of 23 October. The din was unbelievable, and the fire co-ordinated to address both counter-battery and suppression.

X Corps moved after dark up from its concentration areas to the start line, a track called Springbok, running south from Alamein station, where the armour topped up. At 0200 on 24 October, the Sherwood Rangers Yeomanry moved off behind their sappers, guided down the track by lighted petrol tins with the shape of a boat cut into them. Although there was little communication between the regiment and the infantry, who were advancing across no man's land and through the enemy's minefields, everything went broadly to plan, until the regiment secured Miteiriya Ridge, even though by that time it had moved ahead of the infantry.

Instead of being able to debouch as expected, the regiment was held up as the sappers found that, contrary to expectations, the minefield recommenced on the far side of the ridge, continuing down the forward slope. Mine-clearing became extremely hazardous, and the operation fell behind schedule.

It is important to understand what dawn looks like in the Western Desert. All deserts are different. This one is relatively flat compared to most other deserts, and hard. To someone standing in the middle of it looking east, dawn takes the best part of an hour to pass from dark to sunrise. Throughout that period, a loom of light rises above the flat horizon to create the sharpest of contrasts, so that even a radio antenna, let alone a tank, creates the clearest silhouette from first light. Even though dust on the day would have reduced the effect it, too, would have been a giveaway. Once the sun crests the horizon that effect ends and the glare of the sun reverses the advantage. Looking west, on the other hand, during the whole of that hour until the sun lights it with its first beam, it is pitch black.

An hour before daylight on the 24th, dangerously later than planned, the regiment was given the all clear by the sappers, and advanced with A Squadron (ten Crusaders) under Stanley Christopherson leading in the dark until, when they had cleared the minefield by about a mile, and as the effect of first light kicked in, all hell broke loose.

Trooper Philip Foster recalled from his vantage point in the echelon:

> As dawn broke the flood of battle burst with staccato fury.... The tanks … had fallen foul of savage cross-fire from 88mm guns and machine guns. Everywhere there was a crisscrossing of coloured tracer, accompanied by the ear-splitting crescendo of explosion, and the bark of small-arms fire. Green, red, and whitish balls of brilliant fire raced through the air at colossal speed, seeking their targets. The whole column on the track through the minefield had been forced to halt owing to this powerful opposition. Tanks began to 'brew up' right and left. I glanced forward at other lines of tanks extended in battle order like ships of a fleet. It was extraordinary how in this half-light of dawn these armoured monsters suggested the silhouettes of battleships floating dispassionately in a calm sea. Armour-piercing thermite shells ricocheted close to the echelon, cracking viciously as they smacked the deck.

A Squadron took the brunt of the fire, but fought back and knocked out two enemy tanks in reply. Michael Laycock's B Squadron also deployed clear of the minefield but took losses as well. By the time the sun had risen, switching the advantage, for a time, in favour of the regiment, sixteen Sherwood Rangers tanks had been hit, seven of them from A Squadron. The regiment then withdrew a little way back onto Miteiriya Ridge, where the infantry had dug in, re-organized and held firm. Both the infantry and the armour now withstood a continuous bombardment by the enemy artillery.

Many tank crewmen now lay wounded by their knocked-out tanks on the forward slope of the position, and Stanley Christopherson organized their rescue through the invaluable help of SSM Hutchinson and his driver, Trooper McDonald. Using a jeep and making many journeys under continuous enemy shell and machine-gun fire, they rescued the wounded and bought them back. SSM Hutchinson was wounded once and Trooper McDonald twice, the second wound breaking his leg. For this they received MMs.

Including those of the regiment, there were now some 400 tanks holding Miteiriya Ridge, rendering it impregnable to the enemy. They could see 10th Armoured Division's original objective, some high ground across the valley to their front beyond the minefields. That afternoon, the Germans counter-attacked and were beaten off by the regiment, with the loss to the enemy of seven tanks. The regiment deployed a fighting patrol from C Squadron (Stephen Mitchell) which knocked out a couple of lorries and possibly a tank before returning. During the enemy's counter-attack, Stanley Christopherson was wounded in the face and temporarily evacuated.

Tenth Armoured Division now received orders for another night attack, beginning at 2200, on the ridge that had been their original objective. The plan was for 8 Armoured Brigade to take the ridge with their left flank protected by 9 Armoured Brigade, and their right by 24 Armoured Brigade. As the regiment was forming up to move, it was attacked by enemy bombers. Regimental Headquarters and the B1 Echelon, which, for protection, was positioned within the armour, were hit.

Trooper Foster wrote:

> Deafening detonations crashed through the column of vehicles.... I found myself in the midst of an immense inferno. Every vehicle was afire. It became as light as day. Survivors were scattering in all directions from the ring of flames. For nearly two hours the entire illuminated area was subjected to the most intense fire. The noise was augmented by the blowing up of the ammunition lorries in the echelon. Two lorries hurled their contents and the best part of themselves about 100 feet into the air in a tangle of colourful sparks and glowing metal. Scores of shells and small ammunition went off like giant squibs as the heat of the conflagration set off the explosive fillings.

During that night Padre Hales earned an immediate MC rescuing wounded from within the minefield whilst under constant enemy fire, and restoring order when the Regimental Aid Post (RAP) received a direct hit which caused multiple casualties.

Captain Warwick, despite the fact that he was himself wounded, jumped from his tank and organized the evacuation of badly wounded officers and men, then led the undamaged B vehicles back in good order, and took the wounded to the RAP, before having his own wound dressed. For this he received an immediate MC.

Captain William Scott was the OC of the B1 Echelon, part of his role being to drive about the battlefield, organizing the replenishment of the regiment, in nothing more than a jeep. On his echelon being blown up, he made it his business to collect survivors, and salvage vehicles. He worked through the night and managed to produce a new echelon and supply the regiment on the following day. He also received an immediate MC.

The brigade had been on the receiving end of a concerted enemy aerial and artillery bombardment; the regiment's B1 echelon was destroyed and some tanks were disabled. The brigade managed to commence its attack on time through the Staffordshire Yeomanry alone, both the regiment and 3rd Tanks being affected by the bombing. However, both were able to join the attack by 0400.

As dawn broke the brigade was almost on its objective when, once again silhouetted, it became under heavy fire from near the high ground, the other two regiments taking significant tank losses. The brigade was ordered to withdraw to Miteiriya Ridge. The regiment was close to the objective, concealed by mist, and had not come under significant fire, and Flash Kellett requested permission to stay and seek to secure the objective, but was refused permission. This was shown to be a wise decision when the mist cleared. The enemy's dispositions on the objective at the time rendered it unassailable.

In the evening the enemy counter-attacked Miteiriya Ridge with 100 tanks out of the setting sun. The centre point of their attack was the regiment's positions onto which they brought down intense artillery fire. As the enemy came within range, the entire regiment opened up. Flash Kellett called down smoke to silhouette the enemy, but on this occasion it drifted so as to obscure the enemy from 9 Armoured Brigade, positioned 2,000 yards south-west of the regiment, hampering their shoot and was therefore discontinued. The attack was driven off, large fires on the enemy side indicating the damage done to him.

The air raid on the brigade's positions on the night of 24 October had wider repercussions; the bombing had taken out land-line so that when Major General Gatehouse was required to communicate back to Corps Headquarters and Montgomery, he was forced to move from his Tactical HQ to his Rear HQ. He was then unfairly accused of fighting the battle from too far back to be in control of his division. This also gave birth to the myth that the armour was fought with too little aggression during this phase of the battle, which is hard to justify given the events just described.

During that night, 25 October, the brigade was withdrawn. The Sherwood Rangers had suffered eighty-five casualties in two days, including every officer in A Squadron. In addition, the regiment had lost about 50 per cent of its tanks and all its echelon. This reflected 10th Armoured Division's losses, estimated to be 1,350 as at 31 October, equal to 50 per cent of its tank-crew strength. These losses were only exceeded, at that point of the battle, by 51st (Highland) and 9th (Australian) Divisions, who had each lost approximately 2,000. The enemy had also suffered; their records indicate that only ninety-one tanks remained of the 235 deployed on X Armoured Corps' front at the beginning of the battle. However, his reserves, not included in these figures, and not yet committed to battle, were still intact.

On 26 and 27 October the regiment rested and re-equipped. During those two days, 2nd NZ Division conducted further attacks in the Miteiriya Ridge, which finally stabilized that part of the front, but could not secure the platform for a breakthrough. Montgomery then decided that his best chance of securing the required breakout was in the area of the right tank corridor and Kidney Ridge, some five miles north of Miteiriya Ridge and on 1st Armoured Division's centre line. It is not generally known that Kidney 'Ridge' is really a depression, the 'ridge' description coming from the use of the wrong map symbol.

On 28 October 8 Armoured Brigade returned to the line, relieving 1st Armoured Division around Kidney 'Ridge'. By then, 1st Armoured Division had been in continuous action for four and a half days. Between 29 October and 1 November the regiment was involved in several skirmishes in this area, whilst the infantry continued to exert pressure on the enemy, as part of the crucial attritional part of the battle known as a 'crumbling' process. Montgomery also used the infantry divisions to the north of 1st Armoured Division's corridor to open up a salient by pushing towards the sea. They were successful, despite meeting the strongest resistance, drawing substantial enemy reserves to the north, away from 1st Armoured Division's corridor.

Keith Douglas, a troop leader in A Squadron, had missed the first days of the battle due to his attendance on a camouflage course from which he now returned, having gone AWOL, to take his place in his depleted squadron. He was the very opposite of a typical yeoman; he was already a gifted writer and poet (in the yeomanry poetry didn't count, unless it was about something important, such as the death of a fox) with a radical and intense outlook, who, due to what can only be explained as a particularly perverse example of the 'fog of war', found himself posted before Alamein to such a regiment as this, which delighted in a pretence of insouciance about all things life threatening, which irked him as much as it amused them. He wrote *Alamein to Zem Zem,* the iconic account of armoured warfare at troop level in the desert, and in it he described his going into action for the first time with the regiment as it moved out on one of these skirmishing operations. As was his genius, it strikes a chord:

> Someone shook me out of my sleep at 4 o'clock in the cold morning. Somewhat to my surprise I woke immediately with the full consciousness of where I was; for I had feared as I dropped asleep the morning might surprise me unpleasantly at my least heroic hour. The moment I was wakeful I had to be busy. We were to move at five; before that, engines and sets had to be warmed up, orders to be given through the whole hierarchy from the Colonel to the tank crews. In the half-light tanks seem to crouch, still, but alive like toads. I touched the cold metal shell of my tank; my fingers amazed for a moment at its hardness, and swung myself into the turret to get out my map case. Of course, it had fallen down on the small circular steel floor of the turret.

In getting down after it, I contrived to hit my head on the base of the six-pounder and scratched open both my hands; inside the turret was less room even than in an aircraft, and it requires experience to move about. By the time I came up, general activity had begun to warm the appearance of the place if not the air of it. The tanks were now half hidden in clouds of blue smoke as their engines began, one after another, to grumble and the stagnant oil burnt away. This scene with the silhouettes of men and turrets interrupted by swirls of smoke and the sky lightening behind them was to be made familiar to me by many repetitions. Out of each turret, like the voices of dwarfs, thin and cracked and bodiless, the voices of the operators and of the control set come; they speak to the usual accompaniment of 'mush' morse, odd squeals, and peculiar jangling, like a barrel organ, of an enemy jamming station.

On the morning of 29 October, as the regiment was taking up position, Sergeant Kenneth Lee's C Squadron Sherman struck a mine, damaged a bogey wheel and was immobilized. It was soon realized that the enemy had guns of all calibres concealed in the sand dunes in the immediate vicinity. B and C Squadrons were withdrawn some 400 yards to a position from which they could get better observation and not run unnecessary risks. Sergeant Lee's tank was therefore left some 400–500 yards in front of the main line. Recovery vehicles were sent for but did not immediately appear. At 1700 Sergeant Lee reported that infantry in fairly large numbers were advancing towards him with the obvious intention of capturing the tank, and he was subjected to heavy attacks from mortars and hand grenades. He engaged the infantry with his Browning and with his 75mm gun, thereby killing some thirty to forty of them. At this time the recovery section arrived and Sergeant Lee, under intense small-arms fire, jumped from his tank and assisted in fastening the tow rope.

While this was in progress, a tank attack developed, the objective being to destroy Lee's tank. He remounted and again vigorously engaged the enemy. The result of the action was that five M13s were destroyed and his tank was saved, recovered and back in action the following day. He was awarded the DCM.

The Break Out – Operation SUPERCHARGE

The regiment received orders for the next phase for which 8 Armoured Brigade was to regroup under command of 1st Armoured Division (Major General Briggs). This new phase, codenamed Operation SUPERCHARGE, was to be the *coup de grace*. The plan was for a three phase operation:

Phase 1: the creation of a 4,000-yard-wide and 4,000-yard-deep salient beyond Kidney 'Ridge'. This task was under command of Headquarters 2nd NZ Division but included only a portion of Freyberg's own troops. The attack was preceded by an artillery barrage from 340 field and medium guns. As part of this phase,

9 Armoured Brigade would drive forward beyond the infantry's final objective and break through the enemy anti-tank screen astride the Rahman Track, running north-south some two miles west of Kidney. It was anticipated that the anti-tank screen was strong, and therefore 9 Armoured Brigade would suffer heavy losses.

Phase 2: the deployment of 1st Armoured Division, now consisting of 2 and 8 Armoured Brigades, into the salient to defend it from the expected panzer counter-attack, and with the intention of destroying the enemy armour.

Phase 3: the breakout by 1st and 7th Armoured Divisions. The latter had been held in reserve throughout the battle especially for this phase, but also because it was Montgomery's most valued formation and his insurance policy against any unexpected setback; however it had, as part of XIII Corps, more than just warmed its barrels whilst taking part in the feint in the south.

Flash Kellett praised the regiment for the way it had fought to that point, congratulated it on having been given the honour of inflicting the *coup de grace*, and promised everyone a bath in Cairo when it was all over.

The artillery barrage opened up at 0100 on 2 November and 2nd NZ Division crossed their start line on time. By 0400 the division had secured all its objectives. At 0615, 9 Armoured Brigade attacked west and became involved in a ferocious battle against the enemy gun line, during which it lost 110 of its 132 tanks. As a fighting formation, it had ceased to exist. Unfortunately, the gun line, although depleted, was still very much a going concern. At 0700, 1st Armoured Division advanced into the salient, 2 Armoured Brigade leading. Once in the salient, 2 Armoured deployed to cover the south, west and north perimeters; 8 Armoured provided the mobile reserve.

As anticipated, the enemy armour counter-attacked. First the regiment was in action facing north-west and then south. On one occasion a column of enemy tanks came down the Rahman Track in profile and were heavily engaged. The whole division fought well and skilfully, as evidenced by the numerous columns of smoke on the enemy's side. The Axis kept attacking the salient from different approaches; each attack was defeated as the battle ebbed and flowed. By the end of the morning the enemy's armour was defeated. It is estimated that over 500 tanks were involved. Rommel's tank losses were estimated at between 120 and 130. First Armoured Division's losses were placed at fourteen knocked out and forty damaged. However, by the end Montgomery still had 400 tanks while Rommel was left with thirty German and 155 Italian light tanks.

At dawn on 3 November 1st Armoured Division attacked the depleted enemy anti-tank screen astride the Rahman Track that had inflicted such damage on 9 Armoured Brigade. The Sherwood Rangers were on the left, A Squadron scouting well forward, taking out enemy positions themselves and spotting for the heavy squadrons and 1st RHA.

Veterans of desert warfare from the beginning, 1st RHA had supported the regiment closely and brilliantly throughout the whole battle. Through Jack Tyrrell, their FOO attached to the Regiment, they also gave great advice on desert fighting to what was still a novice regiment. He worked closely with Stanley Christopherson throughout the battle. It was their fast and accurate indirect fire that had accounted for many of the kills made by the regimental group. It was a day of constant fighting, during which the regiment produced one of its best performances thus far, Stanley Christopherson earning a well-deserved Immediate MC, both for his handling of A Squadron during the break-in battle, and on this occasion before being wounded for the second time in the battle. The regiment, however, still took losses: Flash Kellett called to A Squadron Leader (at that moment Keith Douglas, only a troop leader) 'Control your squadron and stop it wandering'; Answer: 'The squadron now consists of my own tank and one other.' By nightfall the outcome of the fighting was still unclear.

> At first light on 4 November the enemy gun line was again attacked by 8 Armoured Brigade. The Sherwood Rangers were pushing south-west of the Tel el Aqqaqir feature, A Squadron, with Stanley Christopherson back in the saddle, again leading. At this point, as the book *8th Armoured Brigade 1939–45* states:
>
> Here the Sherwood Rangers distinguished themselves by finding a gap in the enemy defences; as a result an attack was made which completely broke through and started the rout of the Afrika Korps.

The *Official History* also states that the moment of victory was first light on 4 November. This is further endorsed by the citation for Kellett's immediate DSO, signed by both Montgomery and Alexander:

> On November 3rd, by skilful handling, he initiated a Regimental attack which found a hole in the enemy defences and which possibly turned the scale in our favour on the Tel el Aqqaqir feature.

After eleven days of intense and bitter fighting what had been achieved the day before was plain for all to see. Alexander's hole had finally been 'blown in the enemy's front'. Alamein was won, albeit at the cost of 13,500 Allied casualties. The echelon came up to join the regiment. It found a euphoric atmosphere and the regiment drinking some captured champagne. Refreshed, the brigade pressed on past Tel el Aqqaqir, coming up against another stop line. The assumption was that this would withdraw in the night and so they halted. Kellett was called to receive congratulations from Generals Lumsden and Gatehouse for the regiment's performance on the previous day. An attempt was made by 8 Armoured Brigade to continue the advance after dark, but this difficult manoeuvre had to be abandoned because the moon had set, the night was overcast and it was impossible to see.

Galal Station

On 5 November the pursuit began in earnest, Eighth Army spreading out across the desert, each formation with a separate objective, 8 Armoured Brigade directed north-west for Galal Station on the coast road. After advancing rapidly, the brigade got astride the enemy line of withdrawal along the coast road: fifty-four tanks were destroyed by the three regiments of the brigade, twenty-six by the Sherwood Rangers, together with some guns and many lorries. A thousand prisoners were taken, 300 by the Sherwood Rangers. All this was accomplished in one day, a stunning day's work by any standards: 8 Armoured Brigade was the only formation sharp enough in the pursuit to catch such a significant portion of the retreating enemy. However, they may also have been assisted by luck in the way in which they were tasked.

If, as mentioned, the enemy's tank force was down to thirty German and 155 Italian tanks by the end of SUPERCHARGE, Galal Station would have further reduced that number to 130 in total. Montgomery wrote to the regiment: 'the Army Commander congratulates all ranks on their magnificent victory at Galal Station which has done much to help in the final destruction of the enemy forces.' As mentioned, Kellett was awarded an immediate DSO, the citation covering the break-in battle, SUPERCHARGE, the break-through at Tel el Aqqaqir and Galal Station.

Next day the regiment pushed on again. At Mersa Matruh an attack was found necessary which was led by the Commanding Officer, whose tank was hit twice and two of his crew killed. The town fell on 8 November and the brigade was withdrawn for a well-earned rest, having done the hard part, leaving the pursuit of Panzerarmee Afrika across Cyrenaica to 7th Armoured Division. That pursuit continued until finally being brought to a halt at El Agheila, where the enemy turned and took up fresh positions.

Of the twenty-two officers with whom the regiment had begun the battle, sixteen had been casualties while the regiment was awarded one DSO, one DCM, five MCs and two MMs.

For the Sherwood Rangers, as for many others, this had been a battle of shocking intensity, to the extent that few survived who did not think that it was against all the odds that they had done so. None had imagined before just how total would be the experience. The way they reacted was typical. The experience had taught them that the only way they would survive what was ahead was if they accelerated their evolution into becoming as good if not better than the best in the desert.

Churchill said 'It could almost be said that before Alamein we did not have a victory, after Alamein we did not have a defeat.' For the second war running the Sherwood Rangers had fought prominently at the battle which had delivered to the Allies their first major victory.

Chapter 28

Advance on Tripoli

November 1942–January 1943

Move to El Agheila

Following the battle of El Alamein 10th Armoured Division was disbanded and 8 Armoured Brigade became an independent armoured brigade, not part of any division, other than to give support, until the end of the war. Initially, it was attached to 7th Armoured Division and used by that formation to break into the enemy's defences and weaken them. Seventh Armoured would then follow up and break through. Alternatively, when later attached to an infantry division, its role was to provide dedicated armoured support. Because of this, whenever Eighth Army encountered a Panzerarmee Afrika stop line, on almost every occasion it was 8 Armoured Brigade that was deployed to make the initial attack.

It should be remembered that 7th Armoured Division had been fighting in the desert for the previous two years while 8 Armoured Brigade had been operational for only two months and was therefore more expendable. There did quickly emerge, however, a formation with a reputation for fighting qualities of durability, skill, and hardness second to none. Because of its role the brigade was given its own dedicated slice of the integral logistic support for which it had formerly relied on its division, and so it became an armoured brigade group.

The divisional sign of 10th Armoured Division, a red fox's mask on a black background, had been retained on conversion from 1st Cavalry Division. When the division was disbanded, 8 Armoured Brigade took over the sign but, to make it more visible, the background was changed to yellow.

Although the fighting ceased for a while, clearly the bath in Cairo had been postponed indefinitely. The regiment now learned how to make the routine of life in the Western Desert bearable. When halted for significant periods in the same place the officers in each squadron erected a tent for a squadron mess. The regiment had acquired several black tents for this purpose and which each squadron did its best to make like home. That apart, the regiment lived off its vehicles for the duration of the campaign.

Keith Douglas described how this was done:

We often had to exist on half a gallon of water a day for washing, cooking and drinking. We had almost all our food from tins, eked out with occasional issues of flour, oatmeal, rice, or papery dried vegetables captured from the enemy. Bread we did not see for many days on end sometimes, and then only a slice or two each of the stalest, even mildewed. The water, what there was of it, tasted so strongly of disinfectant and salt that even whisky was lost in it. In some areas flies were almost unbearable – even one Egyptian fly can take up all one man's attention. They return persistently to the attack on eyes, mouth and nostrils, and are devilishly agile.

Nine in every twelve men were covered with inflamed, swollen, and painful sores, on hands, faces, or legs, which took weeks or months to heal and left deep red scars. Every man was coloured under his skin with dirt, and eyes were bloodshot with continual dust and sandstorms. But everyone shaved and washed, at least superficially, at reasonable intervals. Everyone had a mug of strong heavily sweetened tea three times a day. We were warmly clothed in the cold nights. We built comfortable latrine seats, in little houses of petrol tins filled with sand, whenever we were static for two or three days. We had papers, magazines and books throughout the journey; [and] were within reach of reasonably equipped and competent doctors and even dentists, albeit not so competent or well-equipped. Canteens reached us at regular intervals with a little chocolate, tobacco, beer, whisky, or gin. There was an occasional cigarette issue with rations, though these 'V' cigarettes were very bad.

We were always a little sorry when we began to eat in the black tent again, and no longer had the right to eat the delicacies cooked by our crews, although the officers' mess cook fed us very well.

[Each tank crew cooked for itself, and enjoyed using their originality on the limited rations.] If we stopped more than two days in an area, ovens, cooking pots, fireplaces, frying-pans and washbasins were made out of cut and hammered petrol tins. Extra mugs and mess-tins were made from empty tins with wire handles fitted to them. Everyone wanted to cook, and took turns in trying out new recipes. From biscuits, we made porridge by smashing the biscuits to powder with a hammer, soaking them overnight and boiling the result for breakfast in the morning. When it was made with oatmeal biscuits, this was indistinguishable from real porridge. It was always warm and filling, with sugar and condensed milk added to it. From biscuits and jam, cakes and puddings were made, well browned on the outside and doughy in the middle. Sometimes there were currants to add, and a sort of duff was made. Biscuits were fried in the fat of American tinned bacon. There were immense stews of tinned meat and vegetables, Worcester sauce, onions, tinned potatoes, fried bully shreds, brown and crisp, with potato chips or crisps, and fried and flavoured rice cakes. If there were a flour issue, we had bully fritters, in batter, or fritters of dried fruit, or batter dumplings, or meat, jam, or treacle pies and pastries – we had plenty of margarine. Cheese fritters, flapjacks, pancakes, angels on horseback – the triumphs of these menus were endless. Occasionally gala feasts of eggs or sheep bought from the Senussi for, sugar, bully or biscuits, or on one occasion, for the two halves of an old Italian map, handed over with an air by an Irishman. Sometimes an ill-fated gazelle or two crossed our path.

News now came through that the British First Army had landed in Algeria on 8 November. Rumour had it that the two armies would meet in Tripoli. This was never the intention, however, and underestimated the fact that First Army initially consisted of little more than an infantry division of two brigades, and two armoured regiments of an armoured division. Further, the build-up of additional units, formations and of the massive logistic infrastructure was slow. To that should be added the difficulty of the terrain, the effect of winter, and the strength of the Axis forces (these became *Heeresgruppe Afrika*, an army group, in February 1943). In the end, it would not be until March that First Army, by then at something like full strength, would be able to exert decisive pressure on the enemy from the west.

The regiment left Mersa Matruh on 24 November for El Agheila, 600 miles to the west through the whole of Cyrenaica, being lifted by tank transporter. Michael Laycock, as second-in-command, commanded the move, and resisted attempts by the RASC to move tanks as individual vehicles rather than by troops and squadrons. This identified an unbridgeable cultural gulf between teeth-arm units and the movers, which exists to this day. The distinction was that the regiment saw itself as a fighting unit during this phase whereas the movers saw it merely as a mixture of hardware and personnel to be processed. There is no doubt that the movers are wrong. Once formed, the structure of a unit must never be broken up or overridden since it must be ready to fight at any time.

El Agheila

On 14 December 8 Armoured Brigade attacked, the regiment on the right, and gained contact with the long established wire and mine defences of the old El Agheila stop line running north to south for many miles. At the time it was expected that the enemy would make a significant stand but Rommel had already withdrawn, leaving only an armoured rearguard supported by anti-tank guns covering the minefields with fire. A Squadron took the brunt of the enemy's opening salvo and then the enemy launched a quixotic counter-attack on the brigade with a dozen or so M14 tanks, no match for the Shermans. The attack was a disaster for the enemy and the brigade claimed thirteen tanks, six of which fell to the regiment, three destroyed by Sergeant Nelson. The regiment also destroyed twelve anti-tank guns and took fifty prisoners.

The finest individual contribution to this action was by Lieutenant John Bethell-Fox of A Squadron, just returned having been wounded in the battle for the Rahman Track. His was the right-flank troop of the Crusader squadron. In the afternoon, having been in contact all day without losing a tank, he saw what he thought to be a movement of enemy tanks around his right flank. He moved forward, destroyed two tanks, and then, seeing an anti-tank gun in action on the far side of a ridge, engaged and destroyed it in the face of fire from this and other guns in the vicinity. During this period his tank was hit more than once. On his return, seeing that the track of another Crusader had been split, and the tank itself under shell and machine-gun fire, he went alongside, adjusted the tow rope and pulled it out of action. He was awarded an immediate MC but was wounded by shellfire that evening.

Next morning the enemy had withdrawn. The brigade pressed on, hoping to trap the enemy in a pincer movement in which 2nd NZ Division had made a deep left hook into the desert around the enemy positions, but the enemy escaped the trap. The advance continued, still hampered by enemy mines and booby traps, past Mussolini's monument, erected to mark the border of Libya with Cyrenaica and to commemorate the opening of the Tripoli-Benghazi road, which Eighth Army christened Marble Arch. However, Eighth Army was finding it difficult to arrange for supplies to reach forward 900 miles from Cairo, and the advance halted for the time being at Merduma near Sirte. This delay was welcome since it was Christmas, which the regiment celebrated with carols, church services, and a Christmas lunch served, in accordance with tradition, by the officers to the whole regiment in a large tent. The meal consisted of turkey, pork, Christmas pudding, iced cake, a bottle of beer and fifty cigarettes per man. The officers dined in the evening.

At Christmas Donny Player was sent on a long patrol in jeeps behind German lines as far as Misurata to reconnoitre the going because there was little knowledge of the country ahead. He was captured whilst returning from this successful reconnaissance and was interrogated by two staff officers but demanded to see Rommel instead. As he later expressed it 'Rommel could not be produced' but his chief of staff, Bayerlein, did appear. The Regiment would next meet him as General Bayerlein of the Panzer Lehr Division in Normandy, five days after D-Day. In Donny Player's opinion he was 'a frightful type of jovial bounder'.

Player eventually escaped by sharing his wine with his Italian guard who then obligingly played his part in the cunning plan by falling asleep. Living off some bread he had stored, off the land and the offerings of friendly Arabs, he walked back towards the British front line, which he met after covering about 150 miles, rejoining the regiment on 20 January.

Wadi Zem Zem

After Sirte was taken, the enemy fell back to defend Tripoli to a position at Buerat and on the line of the Bu Ngem Road (known to the regiment as 'Bung 'em' Road') and by 15 January Eighth Army was ready to attack. The plan was that whilst the Highland Division attacked towards Tripoli along the coast road, 2nd NZ Division, 8 Armoured and 22 Armoured Brigades would execute a left hook to attack Tripoli from the south-east. This was achieved by two night approach marches into the desert along a lighted centre line. Eight Armoured Brigade would attack in the centre with 2nd NZ Division on the left and 22 on the right. The principal feature on Eighth Army's front was the Wadi Zem Zem, a substantial steep-sided valley lying across their path, about two to three miles wide and about 100 miles long, and so impossible to avoid.

The brigade attacked at daybreak on 15 January from out of the rising sun with the regiment leading. This is Keith Douglas's description of an armoured regiment in action. Nothing reveals the personality of armoured/armoured recce regiments, especially, more completely than their radio nets:

This, then, is how the battle goes.

Piccadilly Jim [the name given to Kellett by Douglas in his book] is accustomed to say – and in sanguine moments we believe him – that we have a good wireless discipline. That should mean that no one interrupts or speaks at unnecessary length, and that every vital message gets through in one. In fact, it means that we keep off the air when Piccadilly Jim is speaking, while he interrupts, dilates, or ignores messages entirely. No one ever interrupts or ignores him. For this offence, no stress of battle, except death, is an excuse. The result of this is clearly that, whatever happens, Piccadilly Jim retains absolute control of the air, and, therefore, of the regimental group.

From the first appearance of the enemy, a Crusader troop leader well out in front of the regiment, sees and hears the whole action, almost as if it were a pageant prepared for his entertainment: for hours on end it may continue to be exciting in quite an impersonal way. He sees a suspicious blob on the horizon; halts, his squat turret almost level with a ridge, and scrutinises the blob through his glasses.

Each speaker has his own codename, shortened, after the initial netting calls, to a letter and a number, or simply a letter in the case of a control station.

Pressing the switch of his microphone, releasing it a moment to see if someone else is talking, and pressing it again he says:

'King 2. Something that looks like a tank to my front about three miles, I am on your right. Over'.

'King 2. OK off to you. King, did you hear King 2's message?'

'King. Yes. Let him keep bumming on. But be cautious. Off,' says Piccadilly Jim to Edward [the name given by Douglas to Stanley Christopherson].

'King 1,' says Edward calling the Squadron 'slow down a bit and have a good look from hull down before you go swanning over the ridges. Over'.

'2 OK off'.

'3 OK off'.

'4 OK off'.

'King 2, 3, 4, okay off to you. King 5, did you get my last message?'

'King 5. Yes. Over'.

'King 5, well bloody well wake up and acknowledge. Off.' 'Off' caps the rebuke, like a telephone receiver being hung up.

We have two main sources of allusion, horses and cricket. 'Uncle Tom, what is the going like over this next bit? Can we bring the, er, unshod horses over it?' 'Uncle Tom, I'm *just* going over Becher's myself, you want to hold 'em in a bit and go carefully, but after that it's good going for the whole field.' 'King 2 Ack', says someone who has broken a track. 'I shall need the farrier, I've cast a shoe'. Someone else is 'having trouble with my horse's insides. Could I have the Vet?'

Metaphor changes: 'King 2. Someone is throwing stones. I can't see where from yet. Over.' And a little later Piccadilly Jim asks:

'King 2. Now that that chap has retired to the pavilion, how many short of a full team are you?'

As the action goes on, metaphors, direct speech, codes, sequences of messages are intermingled, and a good deal of concentration is needed to disentangle them.

'King 2. There are a couple of 88s on that grey ridge to my right. One is near the brew up, and the other to the left of it, about two degrees. Over.'

'King 2. OK. Off to you. Orange Pip, can you see those 88s of King 2's? Over?'

'George 4, is that a vehicle moving on your right front? Over ?'

'Orange Pip. Yes. Getting gunfire on now. Over.'

'George 4. Yes, I reported it just now. Over.'

'George 4. Can you bring fire onto it?'

'King. Have you anything to report? Over?'

'George. one of your children came up in the middle of my transmission and when I was trying to talk to King. It's most difficult and annoying and I won't have it.... Tell him to bloody well keep off the air when I'm trying to fight a battle. Off ... er, to you. King, King have you anything to report? Over?'

'King, King. Signals. Over.'

'King 2. I think one of those guns is being towed away. Over.'

'King 2 or whoever that is, GET OFF THE BLOODY AIR when I am trying to talk to somebody. Off. King, King, signals over.'

'King, strength NINER. I'm sorry, I was talking to my jockey. Could you say it again? Over?' And so on.

Every turn of events is recorded on the air. Someone asks for 'the little fat man' – this means they are hopelessly broken down and want the technical adjutant, known officially over the wireless as 'Tock Ack', to arrange their recovery. ... Now and then an awkward hesitating transmission creates a short silence –

'Nuts 3 calling. We 'ave, er, 'ad a misfortune. The horse 'as fallen, driver is no more. Can we have Monkey Orange?' The gunner of the tank which has been hit, shaken by the impact of the shell, the sight of one of his friends beheaded, of another bleeding from a great wound, has forgotten his wireless procedure, if he ever knew it. If the MO is not already attending to someone, he will try and reach the tank in a scout car. Meanwhile the gunner must try to get the unconscious corporal out, because the tank is burning, and bandage him roughly, because he is bleeding to death.

As the regiment crossed the 'Bung 'em' road, A Squadron leading, it came under fire from anti-tank guns. All morning the squadron stalked and tried to pinpoint the enemy positions, but these had been beautifully laid out by an old enemy of the regiment, Hauptmann Dr Zahn of 33rd Anti-Tank Battalion. Nor was the regiment able to tempt the enemy into a counter-attack. Three Mark IV Specials nosed their way forward, were engaged, and withdrew. In the end, the regiment had no choice but to take the initiative. C Squadron (Stephen Mitchell), on the right, and one troop of B Squadron were ordered forward, deep into the bottom of Wadi Zem Zem, where they were soon swallowed up by folds in the ground. The enemy held their fire until C Squadron was at close quarters, and then let fly from the high ground on the far side of the wadi. There was an intense fire fight that lasted all afternoon and until dusk.

As dusk was falling, the regiment had managed to push forward onto the high ground on the other side of the wadi, but armour-piercing shells were bouncing all around, and the situation was very confused. Ominously, many call signs were not answering and clear information was scarce. The regiment pulled back into laager, not knowing the outcome of the battle. In the dark they could see tanks still burning and feared the worst. It was plain that C Squadron had been mauled badly.

Captain Hubert Churchman was 'Tock Ack', or 'the little fat man', in fact the Technical Adjutant. His job, irrespective of the intensity of fire, was to travel the battlefield in a jeep to organize repair or recovery of disabled vehicles. During this night following the battle he, accompanied by WOII John Scott, the MQMS, proceeded in the dark through the minefield to find the missing vehicles.

They found and reported back that many tanks had been knocked out and the crews killed and wounded by machine-gun fire as they bailed out. As they moved about they too came under heavy machine-gun fire. Undeterred, they organized a relief party and got the wounded men back before dawn. All in a day's work, but this time Hubert Churchman was recognized by an immediate MC.

Among those killed that day was Lieutenant Ken Graves who had always been able to make that vital opiate, laughter, which the regiment survived on, and was loved by all for it. He is immortalized for his rendition of certain humorous/ unprintable soldiers' songs and his own description of armoured warfare, specifically in a Grant:

> The 75 is jammed. The 37 is firing but is traversed the wrong way. I'm saying: 'Driver reverse' on the regimental net; and the driver, who can only hear me if I remember to switch to the intercom, is advancing. As I look over the top of the turret and see 12 enemy tanks 50 yards away, someone hands me a cheese sandwich.

By first light next day, 16 January, it had been established that the previous day C Squadron had destroyed three Mark IV Specials, but themselves lost seven of the eleven regimental tanks destroyed, about half the squadron – mostly to 88s. There had been many casualties, with Keith Douglas among the wounded.

However, C Squadron had taken the key enemy position and the enemy had withdrawn. Stephen Mitchell was the C Squadron Leader and, despite his tank brewing up, leaving him wounded, he retained command of his squadron. This was the second tank to have been knocked out under him in North Africa. He was awarded an immediate MC. For his role in laying out the enemy positions at Zem Zem, Hauptmann Dr Zahn was awarded the Knight's Cross with Oak Leaves. But for the regiment, this is remembered with bitterness and grief as one of the worst day's fighting, in terms of losses, suffered by it in the war.

The pursuit north-west was led by the regiment and lasted for three days, till the mountains which ringed Tripoli were reached. During this pursuit the regiment fought well. Next day the infantry forced the passes and the brigade debouched onto the coastal plain and, after more sporadic fighting 11th Hussars, under command of 8 Armoured Brigade, entered Tripoli on 23 January. In due course, a small detachment from the regiment, commanded by Flash Kellett, attended the victory parade in Tripoli.

During this break from action Eighth Army organized a seminar on armoured warfare, attended by commanders not just from North Africa, but from the UK and the USA, to teach the lessons learned in battle. The main presentation at regimental level was given by Flash Kellett and a team from the Sherwood Rangers, a remarkable tribute to the respect the regiment had earned. From reading their diaries and other accounts of this campaign, it is easy for anyone who has served in armour to see them developing drills and procedures which are now basic standard processes, for example, radio procedures, battlefield security, semi-indirect shooting practices with tanks, the echelon system, including replenishment on the battlefield.

Chapter 29

Battle of Tebaga Gap

February–March 1943

Medenine

Following the fall of Tripoli there was a brief respite for the brigade; its place in the line was taken by a composite regiment supplied from all three armoured regiments. On the return of the composite regiment a month later, the brigade was brought back up to establishment with tanks taken over from 22 Armoured Brigade and, after a brief period of work-up training, moved out to join in the successful defensive battle of Medenine. The brigade was mostly in reserve.

This was Flash Kellett's last action commanding the regiment since, on 6 March 1943, he was promoted to full colonel and became second-in-command of the brigade. Lieutenant Colonel J. D. (Donny) Player of Friars Wells, Wartnaby, near Melton Mowbray, took over. Everybody loved him – always beautifully turned out, feudal in bearing, fearless in battle, but with a reputation for being perhaps a little too reckless and not a good logistician.

Mareth and Tebaga Gap

The enemy, now without Rommel who had returned home due to ill-health, withdrew behind the Mareth Line, a substantial series of defensive positions prepared by the French in Tunisia to protect them from Mussolini. It ran for twenty miles from the coast in the north-east to the Matmata Hills in the south-west along the border between Tunisia and Libya. Because it was realized that it might be difficult to take the Mareth Line with a frontal attack, Montgomery's Staff had, some weeks previously, tasked the Long Range Desert Group to reconnoitre a route to outflank the position to the south which, based on a reconnaissance by the French in 1938, was thought to exist and which they had confirmed.

Montgomery issued preliminary orders to force the Mareth position in February. They were for a co-ordinated attack on two fronts: a frontal attack by XXX Corps on the Mareth Line itself through which, once success was achieved, he intended to pass X Armoured Corps to exploit. At the same time, he planned a secondary attack from the south by 2nd NZ Division, supported by 8 Armoured Brigade

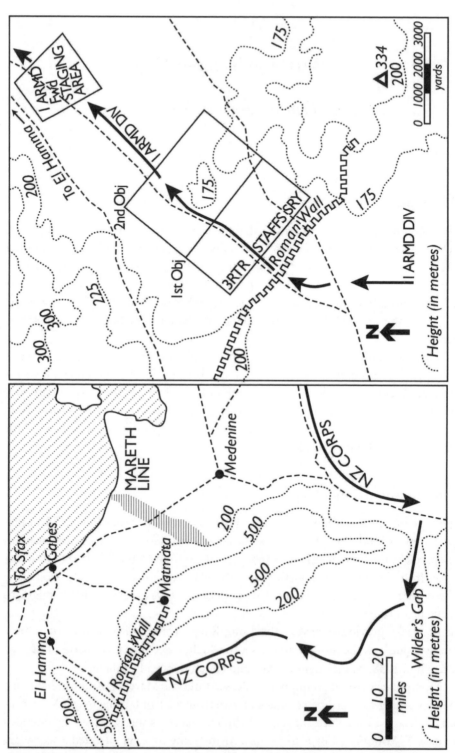

Map 15: The Advance and Battle of Tebega Gap.

and a medium artillery regiment. They were to be joined, during the operation, by L Force, a formation of Fighting French under the elegantly-attired General Leclerc, described as 'a motley group' who were nonetheless effective and had battled their way north from Chad.

The grouping was called New Zealand Corps. Montgomery intended it to force a gap which formed a valley running north between the Matmata Hills and the Djebel Tebaga, thus outflanking the Germans' main positions at Mareth. The valley was the Tebaga Gap. This left-flanking manoeuvre by the New Zealand Corps covered a distance in excess of 200 miles 'over uninhabited regions of salt lakes, sand, and abject wilderness' without a single road (the equivalent of Nottingham to Exeter). The first leg was eastwards from Medenine for fifty miles before a southward turn could be made. The move was accomplished over the period of 12–17 March.

Given the difficulty of the ground, it would be a very challenging logistical operation to re-supply such a large formation during what turned out to be two weeks of continuous fighting. Whilst on the subject of logistics, it was at this time that the regiment developed what Donny Player called a 'snack bar' system of re-supply, made possible by the capture of sufficient jerry-cans, containers far superior to the British petrol cans, which leaked much of their content before it could be poured into a petrol tank. Now with sufficient jerry-cans to make it possible, Captain Ronnie Hutton, commanding the B1 Echelon, was able to deploy two or three lorries from the echelon to follow as close behind the regiment as possible in action. Any tank that ran short of fuel or ammunition could go straight to the 'snack bar' for re-supply.

The move of the armour was accomplished under radio silence, mostly at night, down a lighted centre line, as usual, the tanks on transporters until the going became impassable for the lorries, and then continuing on their tracks.

On 19 March, following a day of maintenance after the completion of the move, the New Zealand Corps advanced to contact with the enemy who were deployed along the feature known as Roman Wall, an ancient fortification, erected by the Romans to mark the southern limit of their dominions in North Africa, at this point running across the southern end of the Tebaga Gap. Although now but an eighteen-inch-high earthwork, when it had been built, 2,000 years before, the wall had been a substantial structure designed to control the access of desert tribes with warlike intentions to Roman possessions but to permit trade.

The enemy was holding the Roman Wall feature, and the nearby Point 201, in some strength and had to be dislodged. Although the enemy had anticipated the left-flanking move, they did not detect it until 20 March after which, with surprise lost, movement took place in daylight. Part of Montgomery's plan was that the New Zealand Corps' attack on the Roman Wall position would be co-ordinated with that of XXX Corps on the Mareth Line itself, which would be the main effort. Both would take place on 21 March. In the event, for some unknown reason, XXX

Corps attacked the Mareth Line a day early, on the night of 20 March. Freyberg stuck to the original plan.

Initially, the New Zealand Corps was facing an Italian infantry formation, the 136th *Giovani Fascisti* Division, covering a minefield astride the Kebili-Gabes road in the area of Roman Wall. However, intelligence reports indicated that they were due to be relieved by the German 164th Light and 21st Panzer Divisions, who were moving to take up positions at Roman Wall in the area of Point 201. At the same time, 10th and 15th Panzer Divisions, with between them 169 tanks, were taking up depth positions at the northern end of the Tebaga Gap valley, near El Hamma.

At first light on the 21st, the New Zealand Corps attacked, with 8 Armoured Brigade (171 tanks) leading, the regiment on the right. The enemy position on the Roman Wall was strongly held. The Sherwood Rangers used the Crusaders to spot for the heavy squadrons, and achieved significant attrition on the enemy. Although advances were achieved, the final breakthrough was not secured by last light. This was despite a notable contribution at one stage by Sergeant George Dring, moving his Crusader under fire to take up a crucial observation position, for which he received an immediate MM. Sergeant Erny Thwaites also made a valuable contribution.

That bitterly cold night there was a successful attack by the New Zealand infantry which secured the minefield by 0200 on 22 March, before first light. Then, the Sherwood Rangers, with C Squadron leading, passed through a gap in the minefield, watched by Flash Kellett in his red hat, standing by his tank waving them on. In what Freyberg described as a 'brilliant attack', once clear of the minefield, the regiment deployed forward onto Point 201. It was then found that many of the Italian troops were concealed in large caves in a wadi side. The regiment's Shermans were able to fire most effectively into these caves thus causing large numbers of Italians to give themselves up. Eventually the whole regiment crossed the wadi into the jaws of the Tebaga Gap feature, the objective. The valley was only two miles wide at that point and the enemy held the high ground on either side. From that advantageous position, they could bring both direct and indirect fire to bear, making it extremely uncomfortable for the regiment.

The ground was hotly contested all day. Philip Foster, now the gunner in Sergeant Thwaites' Sherman, recalled:

Four Crusaders had gone forward to the road and lay in observation. We were called up to their support. As our tank approached the telegraph poles it was greeted with accurate fire from a 75 assault gun emplaced at the foot of a hill some seven hundred yards away. Its crew had a deadline on us. The first two shells burst a few feet in front raising such a cloud of dust that we were each time temporarily screened from view. The third shell landed on the front of the tank, smashing and twisting all the two-gallon water cans which had been loaded onto a metal ledge specially constructed for their accommodation. Our presence among the Crusaders attracted a disconcerting amount of armour-piercing shells. The position was open and exposed from all directions. Our opponent's guns were presumably firing from a great range; otherwise they ought to have brewed us up. I distinctly recall seeing one AP shell, at least 88mm in size, dashing over the ground at the speed of an express train obviously on its last legs. Spasmodic tremors in the hull warned us that we had received minor hits in the nether regions.

The regiment, having lost two tanks, pressed on, but now there were signs of significant numbers of enemy tanks manoeuvring in the dead ground beyond the objective (presumably 21st Panzer Division announcing its arrival); these were engaged by RAF tank-busters. The whole battlefield was still strongly contested, there was heavy shelling everywhere and individual tanks were stalking each other. Stanley Christopherson stalked an enemy tank on foot, and came face to face with its commander doing the same to him. Lieutenant Neville Fearn was knocked out twice, once by the enemy and again by friendly fire. Lieutenant Archie Stockton stalked and knocked out a Mark IV. At last light, the enemy tanks put in a counter-attack which petered out. After a long vigil against the risk of the renewal of the attack, during which an Italian lorry with rations for over 1,000 men was captured, the regiment withdrew into laager, dog tired, but with booty from the lorry to look forward to, and in the knowledge that the Roman Wall feature was now securely held. Erny Thwaites was shrewd enough to identify a container from the Italian lorry, dismissed by others as containing liquorice water, as holding Arak. That and some Chianti were duly liberated and sustained his crew in battle for the next few days.

Tragic news was now passed down through the regiment that Flash Kellett had been killed earlier in the day by a shell splinter from a stray shell whilst he was shaving in the turret of his command tank at brigade headquarters. A brother officer wrote:

A fine soldier and a gallant leader.... He was a man possessing to a marked degree a sense of public duty and an inventive and resourceful brain. He was, moreover, a true and reliable friend at all times. A strict disciplinarian, he yet had a great affection for the men under his command and was forever concerned for their comfort and for the well-being of their relatives at home:.... He proved himself a gallant leader, completely indefatigable and an inspiration to all.

Keith Douglas wrote:

He was an institution.... He had embodied in himself all the regimental characteristics he had been at pains to create: that assumption of superiority, that dandyism, individuality, and disregard of the duller military conventions and regulations that made the Regiment sometimes unpopular ... but always discussed and admired. We knew we were better than anyone else and cared for no one....

Not bad coming from Keith Douglas, the ultimate egalitarian, but now falling under the regiment's spell. The cap badge of the regiment now appears in its own panel in the west-facing stained-glass window of Westminster Hall as his memorial. All who have died in action as a serving Member of Parliament have this honour. Few have deserved it more than he.

By 22 March it became clear that the attack by XXX Corps on the Mareth Line itself had failed due to a combination of the strength of the enemy's position and bad weather flooding the Wadi Zigzaou, which Montgomery had planned to cross dry. Montgomery, in a significant adjustment to his original plan, now switched his main effort to the New Zealand Corps' front, and decided to reinforce it with 1st Armoured Division and X Corps, under Horrocks. It would take these additional forces three days to make the move round. Therefore Freyberg decided to delay the main effort to force the Gap until they arrived. He spent the intervening period securing observation and gun positions in the hills on either side of the start line. This, of course, meant capturing the very positions from which so much accurate enemy fire was now being directed against his corps.

In what were described by Freyberg as 'brilliant attacks' over 23–24 March, 3rd Tanks and the Sherwood Rangers, particularly B Squadron secured the vital high ground where the enemy 88mm guns had been sited. These actions provided important observation points for the artillery in the main attack.

B Squadron was now commanded by Major Michael Gold who had taken over from Michael Laycock, when the latter was appointed second-in-command in succession to Donny Player. In the regiment since before the outbreak of war, he was a courageous leader with a flamboyant and colourful personality and a great sense of humour. Always immaculately turned out, in the post-war era he sported a black eye-patch from a wound he was to receive at Gheel later in the war. As was the norm in those days he was a heavy smoker, using a stylish cigarette holder. For years the Loyal Toast at the Regimental Dinner at Claridges took place after the first course, so that he and others could have early permission to smoke, which they then proceeded to do between courses. When asked many years later by a Cold War warrior how he coped in a fierce battle he replied 'I kept asking myself *what am I supposed to be doing?* then doing it'. There you have it: maintain the Mission, simple!

Following these attacks the regiment laagered on the objective. No sooner were they in than they discovered an enemy laager within 500 yards which opened up on them. A fire fight then raged for two hours, the pyrotechnic display from which was visible to Patrick MacCraith from across the valley, and which he used to guide the echelon into the regiment's laager (one of the many tasks of a regimental navigation officer, and for which, on this occasion, he earned an immediate MC. A successful Nottingham solicitor, he was destined both to command the regiment after the war and serve as its Honorary Colonel. He served in all for sixty years and was the regiment's talisman for the whole of the Cold War era). Eventually the gunfire died down, but enemy movement continued all night, as they recovered knocked-out tanks. The regiment's position was exposed, and it remained stood to till dawn, never more glad of the protection afforded to it on this, as on many similar nights, by its attached company of 1st Buffs. No one slept. Before dawn they heard the enemy withdraw, apparently well beaten.

The regiment continued to hold the ground taken in the attack the previous night, until late on 25 March, when it was relieved and gradually thinned out into laager south of Point 201 which, in common with the locations given to all units and formations taking part in the main attack, was carefully sited in a position concealed from the enemy. It was now confirmed that X Corps' artillery had arrived and was moving into the New Zealand Corps' gun lines and that 1st Armoured Division was expected next day, 26 March, in time for the main attack on the Tebaga Gap, SUPERCHARGE II, to proceed on schedule.

The regiment woke on the 26th to find a *khamsin* blowing, under cover of which the battle procedure for the attack followed its familiar course. Orders were given to the brigade by Lawrence Biddle, now the brigade major of 8 Armoured (posted from the regiment). They had been written by him on the morning of the battle on one page, distilled from six pages of divisional orders. The plan was for the New Zealand Corps to force the Gap with a frontal attack straight down the two-mile-wide valley behind a heavy creeping barrage, laid down by the divisional artillery. It was the first time such a tactic had been tried by Eighth Army.

At 1530 the operation commenced, when formations of day bombers attacked from low-level and dropped their bombs in pattern on the enemy. Then came the fighter bombers, about thirty Kitty-bombers every fifteen minutes, protected by Spitfire patrols in squadron strength. These attacks, to provide cover to the ground forces, continued until 1800 hours, by which time it was planned that the brigade would be firm on the second, and main, objective. Over 400 sorties were flown, the first in support of a ground attack in such strength and whilst also being fully integrated with the ground arms.

Ground attacks went in on the high ground on either flank of the start line to secure additional vital ground; that on the right was carried out by the Fighting French. At 1600 hours the artillery programme, which incorporated the creeping barrage, opened. The tanks of 8 Armoured Brigade emerged from their hides, passed through the infantry, who were still lying hidden, and crossed the start line. The brigade deployed three regiments up, Sherwood Rangers on the right, Staffordshire Yeomanry in the centre, tasked with co-ordination, and 3rd Tanks on the left. Each regiment had its two heavy squadrons leading, mostly Shermans, in line abreast about twenty yards apart stretching across the valley floor. The Crusader squadrons were in a second rank, not more than 200 yards to the rear. One company of the supporting battalion of New Zealand infantry rode on the Crusaders, and the other two on Bren-gun carriers behind. The Crusader squadrons were ordered not to fire unless certain of the identification of their target. In the third rank were 1st Buffs, mounted in their Bren-gun carriers. Donny Player rode in a Crusader Command tank at the centre of the second line.

The New Zealand battalion supporting the regiment was 28th (Maori), memorably described, after the war, by Michael Gold:

> Up to this moment I don't think I'd ever seen a Maori before. When I saw Col Bennett (the Commanding Officer) he terrified me. He was a wonderfully built chap. When he took me and introduced me to his other Maoris I became more and more nervous. They were enormous great fellows, very young and any of them could have taken me in their left-hand and thrown me through the blooming Gap.

The rate of advance was set at 100 yards per minute to the first objective, a line of rising ground approximately 2,000 yards-plus of the start line, on which there was to be no pause. Thereafter, the rate of advance was to be 100 yards per two minutes between the first objective and a second objective, Wadi Hernel, approximately 2,000 yards farther on.

The main enemy positions to be taken out by the attack were known to lie between the first and second objectives. The brigade was ordered, on taking the second objective, to rally and assume battle positions facing north-east and east, prepared to deal with pockets of resistance or any enemy tanks still in the area. However, it was anticipated that this would be hard to achieve because, in addition to the main positions already described, the enemy was holding, in some strength, the ground on the brigade's final objective, where it was supposed to re-organize.

Meanwhile, 2 Armoured Brigade of 1st Armoured Division (which only arrived in the nick of time to do so) would pass through the brigade, and laager a further 3,000 yards on, re-organize, and wait for the moon to rise at midnight. At that point, it would immediately push on using the moonlight. It was anticipated that this would also be difficult to achieve, since the enemy was holding its proposed laager areas. Indeed, it was anticipated that the whole battlefield could become very broken up and confused.

The advance to the first objective would have made a frightening sight, when viewed by an enemy already partially blinded by the setting sun; two ranks of armour spread across the valley floor, firing their machine guns on the move as they were fleetingly viewed behind the creeping barrage, which was throwing dust a hundred feet in the air. The poor visibility must have made our strength difficult to estimate, and target acquisition a nightmare for the enemy. The attack went well as far as the first objective, apart possibly from some initial confusion within the regiment, in distinguishing the creeping barrage from enemy fire. It was impossible to see more than twenty yards in any direction. It was also difficult to keep the speed of the tanks down to the rate at which the creeping barrage was moving. This meant the front rank of tanks kept moving disconcertingly in and out of the barrage as they sped up and slowed down.

Philip Foster described the initial advance from the vantage point of his gunner's seat:

> Explosions occurred all around us, giving off dirty grey smoke. Wishful thinking at first laughed them off as the product of our own guns; but we knew from the texture of the smoke that their authors were hostile.
>
> We were in hill-scrub covered ground; there was little else I could see through my periscope, although the area was alive with enemy. As we advanced, we raked the opposing slopes with machine-gun fire, expending one belt after another without pause. I was kept perspiringly busy changing the belt boxes and reloading; at all costs the heads of the enemy had to be pinned down. I also had to press the Browning trigger as the remote control solenoid from the gunner's footplate had faulted. The gun was soon far too hot to touch.

In B Squadron, on the right, Michael Gold's radio went 'dis', forcing him to change tanks in order to retain command. As well as engaging any opposition with their machine guns, the tank commanders were throwing grenades into enemy weapon pits as they passed, to counter snipers. Once through the first objective, however, whilst the other two regiments were able to make progress as planned, the Sherwood Rangers, particularly B Squadron on the right, were funnelled into the very broken steep ground at the right edge of the valley, and into heavy enemy tank and anti-tank opposition. This ground, full of deep wadis and boulders, was overlooked by the enemy from Point 209 which commanded perfect observation of the whole plain, the Roman Wall and Point 201. For the regiment, once the first objective had been achieved, it was very soon the case that every squadron, troop and individual tank was fighting its own battle.

Philip Foster:

> German tanks and anti-tank guns began to take a toll of our tanks. Through my periscope I observed two Sherman tanks of our own Squadron [B] burning furiously within a few yards of each other …. AP was now lashing at us with formidable accuracy. Any further advance would have been sheer suicide until the authors of the shooting had been located and silenced. We reversed engines and pulled back a vital 20 yards while Erny hastily warned Mr Williams to copy our example. It was too late. His tank was hit and both Mr Williams and his gunner were instantaneously killed.

Meanwhile snipers were dangerously energetic, making it highly precarious for Erny to put his head out of the turret. 'Zip, zip,' one heard each time he peered furtively outside. … We altered our tactics by swinging forward half right and gained the brow of the slope on which a section of Maoris were already perched. After adopting a suitable hull down position.… Here was an opportunity for our 75mm gun to soften the offending targets. From outside Erny directed Harold and gave his fire orders but it soon grew too dark for efficient observation.

Last light was about 1900. The three knocked-out tanks observed by Philip Foster had all been engaged by the enemy's anti-tank screen just beyond the first objective.

Trooper Evers earned himself free drinks for life at post-war regimental OCA dinners from his commander, Lieutenant Colin Thomson, by managing to stall his engine, thus preventing his tank from being the first to breast the rise where the other three were knocked out. They then worked their way round the ambush into a better fire position. Major Stephen Mitchell's tank knocked out two tanks, a Mk III and a Mk IV, with a left and right, thereby saving Donny Player who was about to be engaged by them in his Crusader, which was of the command tank variant, having a dummy gun instead of conventional main armament in order to provide room for more radios and operators.

In another incident, Major Micky Gold fought a tank-against-tank battle at thirty yards in which each missed on numerous occasions while dodging and manoeuvring against each other either side of a ridge until his gunner, Trooper Mills, finally won the duel. Major Gold had long regarded Mills as the worst gunner in the squadron. Having changed tanks he had no idea who his gunner was, until he ducked down inside the turret when they came under fire to plan his retaliation. Trooper Mills went on to elevate himself to the best gunner 'in the western desert' by knocking out a second. By nightfall the regiment had fought back from its initial losses and accounted for six tanks, two 88mm guns and two 50mm guns.

Night fell with the brigade not firm on the second objective, particularly on the regiment's front. The enemy's main positions, between the first and second objectives, had been heavily engaged and all around there were blazing hulls with considerable confusion in the dark as friend and foe intermingled. However, the position was judged firm enough to pass 2 Armoured Brigade through. This was achieved successfully, leaving 8 Armoured to fight through to the second objective in support of the Maoris, and then laager on the battlefield as best it could.

The Maoris were meanwhile fighting a pitched battle in the high ground on the regiment's right to take Point 209. They had found that the objective had a false crest, strongly held by the enemy, which doubled their task, but they fought with breathtaking courage, Second Lieutenant Moana-Nui-a-Kiwa Ngarimu gaining a quite stunning posthumous VC in the process, but by nightfall they had only managed to secure the forward slopes of the false crest. This they held against repeated counter-attacks throughout the night. When the grenades ran out they threw stones, accompanied by the war cry 'E Koe!' Corporal James Loades, a medic, had been with the tanks and, throughout this desperate action, under fire from all sides, he had carried in the wounded, both from the tanks and from the Maoris, and driven them back to the ambulances. His fearlessness was described as 'extraordinary'.

Eventually, the signal to laager was made by RHQ, but it was not until 0200 that the manoeuvre was complete. The regiment laagered beside a knocked-out German tank, the engine of which ran all night, with the beheaded torso of its commander hanging from the turret. Even then, there was no rest, since the replenishment arrived an hour later. It was no sooner complete than the regiment stood to, moving before first light to seek to secure the final objective.

Meanwhile, 2 Armoured Brigade had exploited forward of 8 Armoured, starting their move on time at 1800 down the centre of the valley. They went firm in the 1st Armoured Division concentration area, 3,000 yards-plus of 8 Armoured Brigade's second objective, as planned. In an afternoon 8 Armoured Brigade had decisively broken through the enemy's positions. As a result, unknown to the brigade, orders were being issued by the Germans to withdraw from the Mareth positions. Wind and dust increased as darkness fell and the moon, due to rise at midnight and light 2 Armoured Brigade's further advance, was obliterated by cloud. Notwithstanding this, at midnight General Briggs, commanding 1st Armoured Division, ordered 2 Armoured Brigade to advance on El Hamma, fifteen miles to the north-east. This move was catastrophic to the enemy defending Tebaga Gap, who were forced to withdraw in disarray alongside and sometimes even intermingled with the advancing armour. Racing the tanks, the Germans scraped together an anti-tank screen of three 88s, four 50mm anti-tank guns and four 100mm field guns, three miles south of El Hamma. These, with remnants of 21st Panzer, finally checked the British armour. First Armoured Division was then held throughout the 27th. On the 28th they found the enemy had withdrawn from El Hamma and pressed on, reaching Gabes by midday but unable to prevent the enemy withdrawing the last of his forces from the Mareth position.

Meanwhile, as already recorded, the regiment re-deployed forward before first light on the 27th, taking up positions alongside the Staffordshire Yeomanry on the second objective. The Staffordshires were coming under counter-attack from enemy tanks on their left, which they fought off. The SRY was still supporting the Maoris, who were fighting to secure Point 209 on the right. At dawn, the Maoris finally managed to secure the false crest, forcing the Germans to withdraw onto Point 209 itself. As they were seeking to do so, 300–400 Germans were caught in the open by what was left of B Squadron, who inflicted a terrible slaughter on them. After a short truce, to allow the Germans to recover their dead and wounded, D Company of the Maoris attacked Point 209, their final objective.

They did so chanting the rhythmic *Haka 'Ka mate Ka mate'*. Their history states: 'The remainder of the Maori battalion stood up and watched the attack from the rim of the bowl, each section attack and surrender being cheered as if it were a contest for the Ranfurly Shield,' a rugby tournament named after Dan Ranfurly's grandfather, who had been Governor of New Zealand.

No sooner was the regiment in position on the second objective than, on the right, in the sector covered by the heavily-depleted B Squadron, there was significant movement and dust on the skyline, over which came an 'enormous' number of tanks, later established to be a combination of 15th and 21st Panzer Divisions. They were in behind 1st Armoured Division. The squadron looked as though it was going to be overrun. It opened fire. The force stopped short 1,500 yards away. After about an hour the cloud of dust went up again, and the squadron prepared itself for the attack. Instead the panzers withdrew.

Philip Foster describes how, later that day:

> When Erny moved the tank onto ground which commanded an excellent view of the plain, he espied two stationary German tanks, a Mark III and a Mark IV, in observation at the foot of the slope some 1,500 yards away. Without delay we knocked out both of them, reducing one to a pukka 'brew up'.

Meanwhile, all day, the regiment was recovering wounded and dismounted crews from tanks knocked out the previous day, some from under the guns of the enemy.

Stanley Christopherson, in an action typical of him, had become aware that Captain McGowan, one of his officers, who had been missing overnight, was lying wounded close to the enemy's position. He took a party to recover him, but then went on himself under fire to bring him back to the party and was awarded an immediate Bar to his MC. In the afternoon the regiment was withdrawn into reserve for twenty-four hours of rest. The tanks and men were badly in need of repair, replenishment, sleep and food. No sooner had they begun to relish the thought of twenty-four hours' rest than the order was changed to a move at 0100 next morning up the Kelibi-El Hamma Road. The Germans were in full retreat from the Mareth positions, and the brigade's task was to strike north to the right of where 1st Armoured Division was held south of El Hamma. Their objective was to take 1st Division's place and cut off the enemy's retreat from the Mareth Line along the coast road. In the event 1st Armoured themselves were able to break through.

At 0100 on 28 March the regiment moved. Considerable difficulties were encountered all day with the ground, particularly in the area of Wadi Mataba, which was strongly held. Two enemy tanks were destroyed as well as one 88mm and three 50mm guns, both tanks and two of the guns being destroyed by Sergeant Guy Sanders, for which he received an immediate MM.

The regiment moved at first light on the 29th, having had the first reasonable night's rest since the operation began. The enemy had withdrawn and the brigade pushed on to cut the El Hamma–Gabes road although the regiment was held up in the rain by heavy gunfire. During this action Sergeant Thwaites' troop destroyed an 88 and two 50mm guns. For this, coupled with his left and right on the 27th, he was awarded an immediate MM.

On 30 March the brigade pressed on and encountered heavy shellfire, but was finally rewarded by securing observation positions over the enemy's retreat. They could be seen streaming along the coastal valley and into Fatnassa Bauman. Sadly they were unable to bring down fire on the enemy, due to the fact that the brigade artillery had become bogged and was not in position. Next day the brigade went firm on the ridge overlooking Wadi Akarit, and there tied up with 50th Division, which had moved up from the Mareth positions. This, together with the appearance of many generals, signalled the end of the battle of Tebaga Gap. The brigade received a message from General Montgomery:

> My very best congratulations to the NZ Corps and 8 Armoured Brigade on the splendid results achieved by the left hook. The results have led to the complete disintegration of the resistance of the enemy and the whole Mareth position is now in our hands. Give my congratulations to all your officers and men and tell them how pleased I am with what they have done.

Lawrence Biddle was awarded an MC:

> It is largely due to his efficiency and hard work that the operations in which the Bde took part were carried out smoothly, efficiently and successfully. In battle he has no regard for his personal safety and is always cool, unperturbed and a fine example to all ranks. In every way this officer has given exceptional service which I strongly recommend should receive recognition.

He was always proud of the fact that the citation had been for a DSO, downgraded to an MC by Montgomery in his own handwriting.

Including Flash Kellett, the Sherwood Rangers suffered twelve killed during the action and many wounded. Amongst the dead was Captain Sam Garrett MC, who had been second-in-command of A Squadron during all the previous battles, and something of a talisman for the regiment. Sergeant King had also been killed when his tank was knocked out on the 24th. The majority of casualties were suffered during the main action on 26 March.

Captain Ronnie Hutton was awarded an MC. As mentioned he operated the 'snack bar' battlefield replenishment for the regiment throughout this action, which involved him coming forward in a jeep with the trucks to re-supply tanks in action. MQMS John Scott was awarded an Immediate MM. During the initial advance through the Gap he followed directly behind the tanks and in front of the New Zealand infantry and, under heavy machine-gun and mortar fire, was responsible for the evacuation of one Sherman tank, as well as bringing back five wounded men. This award was also in recognition of the fact that, throughout the campaign, and always under fire, he had been responsible for the salvage of many tanks which would otherwise have been destroyed by the enemy. In addition, it was for his contribution at Zem Zem which has already been mentioned.

Freyberg has been criticized for not ordering 8 Armoured Brigade to attack and break through the Gap before first light on 22 March. The correct appraisal of the battle should be one of praise of Freyberg. That move would have been too high risk. Also it was the first time that armour, infantry, artillery and airpower all worked collaboratively together, which would have been impossible with a piecemeal approach.

Chapter 30

'From a Scent to a View ...'

April–May 1943

First Army had been reinforced during the winter and had fought for and secured the many hilltops held by the enemy to clear an access to the coastal plain. Furthermore, the going on their front had improved, enabling them to attack eastwards and south-eastwards to cut off the retreating Axis forces and join up with Eighth Army. Unfortunately, the American corps in the south, showing their inexperience, had been caught in a classic armoured ambush in the Kasserine Pass.

Not until 6 April had sufficient re-supply been moved forward to put Eighth Army in a position to continue operations. Wadi Akarit, which was backed to the north by hills in which the enemy had set out its positions, was a strong defence line, and the next obstacle to be overcome. The main assault, Operation SCIPIO, went in at 0400 on 6 April with 51st (Highland) Division on the right, 50th (Northumbrian) in the centre and 4th Indian on the left. Supporting armour was provided by 8 Armoured Brigade, the regiment supporting 50th Division.

There was bitter fighting by the infantry in which, as General Alexander later claimed, '15th Panzer and 90th Light were fighting the best battle of their distinguished careers'. However, by the afternoon, Eighth Army had taken the two key pieces of high ground and 5,000 prisoners. The Germans immediately counter-attacked and lost a further 4,500 captured. During the fighting both Sergeants Dring and Thwaites were wounded.

On the back of this fine performance by the infantry the brigade broke through the Roumana Gap on 7 April. Now, once again leading Eighth Army's advance, 8 Armoured Brigade exploited north, intermingled with and giving chase to retreating enemy columns. For the next seven days the brigade spread out laterally with the rest of Eighth Army strung out behind. It was able to move at speed across open country, which gradually turned from the beige of the desert to a more fertile green, and from scrub to olive groves, becoming increasingly civilized and welcoming. During this phase Stanley Christopherson found time to pursue a fox he came across in his tank, running it to ground. Donny Player, who kept his Purdy loaded beside him in his jeep, had a left and right on a brace of partridge.

The brigade was moving by night as well as by day, from time to time fighting off armoured counter-attacks and the regiment was taking the risks inherent in such tactics. On the one hand the air was full of the scent of victory, but on the other there was a succession of major and minor casualties and narrow escapes, as tanks hit mines, or were suddenly caught in accurate artillery or anti-tank fire.

On 13 April the brigade came up against the enemy in his final position at Takrouna, in the impregnable hills north of Enfidaville, a mere twenty-five miles from Tunis. Taking these hills would be primarily an infantry task. For the rest of the month the regiment supported bitter but hopeless attempts to take them. All attempts to bypass them were thwarted.

On 20 April the regiment moved past Takrouna at dawn in support of 23rd New Zealand Battalion. Many tanks were lost by fire or on mines and the Medical Officer's scout car was blown up on a mine; he and Corporal James Loades were stranded for two and a half hours under heavy mortar fire before escaping to safer ground, only to hear that there was a wounded man in the area they had just vacated. Loades went back on his feet and, under fire from Takrouna, dressed and brought in the wounded man.

The following day, with the regiment halted by shellfire, Corporal Loades came up in a jeep to dress a casualty in one of the squadrons. While he was there the intense enemy fire forced the squadron to withdraw. Loades, on his feet, had been walking from tank to tank attending to wounded men and loading them onto other tanks, and he remained by the knocked-out tanks when the squadron withdrew, aiding and encouraging the men who could not be moved. He remained in that area under consistently heavy shell and mortar fire till the last man had been evacuated. For this, and his bravery at Tebaga Gap, he was awarded the MM.

During this fighting Donny Player was wounded by shellfire whilst reconnoitring fresh positions and died later that night. During his short command he had handled the regiment with considerable skill. It had fought its most successful battle in North Africa, and had suffered relatively few casualties in the process. He had fully justified the faith put in him.

Keith Douglas, by now one of the war's finest poets, was moved by his death to write the following:

Aristocrats

> *'I Think I Am Becoming A God'*
> The noble horse with courage in his eye,
> clean in the bone, looks up at a shell burst:
> away fly the images of the shires
> but he puts the pipe back in his mouth.
> Peter was unfortunately killed by an 88;
> it took his leg away, he died in the ambulance.
> I saw him crawling on the sand, he said
> It's most unfair, they've shot my foot off.

How can I live among this gentle
obsolescent breed of heroes, and not weep?
Unicorns, almost, for they are fading into two legends
in which their stupidity and chivalry
are celebrated. Each, fool and hero, will be an immortal.
These plains were their cricket pitch
and in the mountains the tremendous drop fences
brought down some of the runners. Here then
under the stones and earth they dispose themselves,
I think with their famous unconcern.
It is not gunfire I hear, but a hunting horn.

'Peter' was Donny, and Keith Douglas was writing, in despair, of his regiment and its members, not least himself.

Lieutenant Colonel the Viscount Cranley, later Earl of Onslow, who had been second-in-command of 4th County of London Yeomanry (the Sharpshooters) in 22 Armoured Brigade, took over command in the middle of battle. The Sharpshooters had been in the desert as an armoured regiment long before the Sherwood Rangers. He, and they, had seen a great deal of fighting, and he was said to have had more tanks shot from under him than any other officer in the desert.

The impregnable nature of the positions at Enfidaville was at last acknowledged, and First Army, which was attacking from the west, was given the task of making the final assault on Tunis. To do so, it was reinforced by formations from Eighth Army, not including the regiment. The final assault on Tunis was successfully launched on two axes.

Heeresgruppe Afrika, the Axis forces in Tunisia, under Colonel General Jürgen von Arnim, capitulated on 12 May.

Eighth Army was now able to move north and join up with First Army. It was a symbolic moment; these men had been cut off in the Middle East, for nearly four years. Although they had been reinforced and re-supplied, they had not been relieved. They had had to fight their way out through 2,000 miles of inhospitable desert and against a formidable foe, until they finally re-found green and fertile civilization.

It was a story full of Biblical analogies. Their pride and self-belief was almost tangible. During that time they had effectively evolved into a different strain, separated and distinguished by a new vocabulary, their unique experience of the war and their shared hardships, triumphs and tragedies. Nothing illustrated this ethos more than the unconventional desert camouflage of their tanks, now incongruous against the olive green of the countryside through which they were travelling. Then there was their desert-weathered look and their unconventional dress, which was anything but uniform, when compared with the relatively spick and span military appearance of First Army, whom they dubbed *Inglese*.

There was no triumphalism. John Semken probably reflected the emotions of them all when he wrote shortly afterwards:

These last pages may appear disconsolate when written by a member of a victorious army....

I had four great personal friends.... They were all killed between October and January.

The reader may not have seen the mutilated corpse of a man he knew, but in contemplating it, it is difficult to remember that Death is natural and beautiful and that its owner died Gloriously....

He was 21.

Thus ended the war in North Africa.

Chapter 31

Return Home

May–December 1943

After relaxing for a month, during which the Sherwood Rangers hosted a party for the brigade, the regiment returned to Tripolitania. Lieutenant Colonel the Viscount Cranley went back to command his own regiment and Lieutenant Colonel Ian Spence, North Somerset Yeomanry, arrived to take his place. He was well known to the regiment, having been brigade major of 8 Armoured Brigade before Lawrence Biddle, who had commanded 3rd Tanks during the CO's absence whilst wounded.

Three months were spent near Leptis Magna, whilst many took much overdue leave. During this time the regiment took part in many sports; even a race meeting was held. Whilst this was happening, the regiment's future was being discussed in high places: remain in theatre or return to England for the opening of the long-anticipated Second Front? Because of the high regard in which the regiment was held, it was chosen for the latter, more critical, theatre. One of the requirements made whilst they were relaxing in Leptis Magna was that every man should learn to swim. No one gave it a second thought.

The regiment moved back to Egypt and, on 17 November, having handed in all their equipment, sailed from Alexandria for Britain. They disembarked in the Clyde on 11 December. Next day they reached camp at Chippenham near Newmarket, judged by some a one-horse town, which, to their surprise, turned out to contain quite a lot of horses. They immediately broke up for a month of leave, home at last and in time for Christmas, indifferent for the time being to what lay ahead.

After Tobruk, Peter Laycock had transferred to the commandos. His cousin, Robert Laycock, had preceded him into the same force and, by 1943 had been promoted major general as Chief of Combined Operations. In 1942 Peter became second-in-command of No. 10 (Inter-Allied) Commando, a unit with personnel from many German-occupied countries, later divided into two sub-units, the second under Peter's command known as Layforce II. Based in Newhaven, it carried out deception raids on German-occupied Europe. These were discontinued when they had the unintended effect of having the coastline reinforced. Peter Laycock ended the war as a lieutenant colonel with decorations from three Allied countries.

Part VII

The Second World War
1944

The Beginning of the End

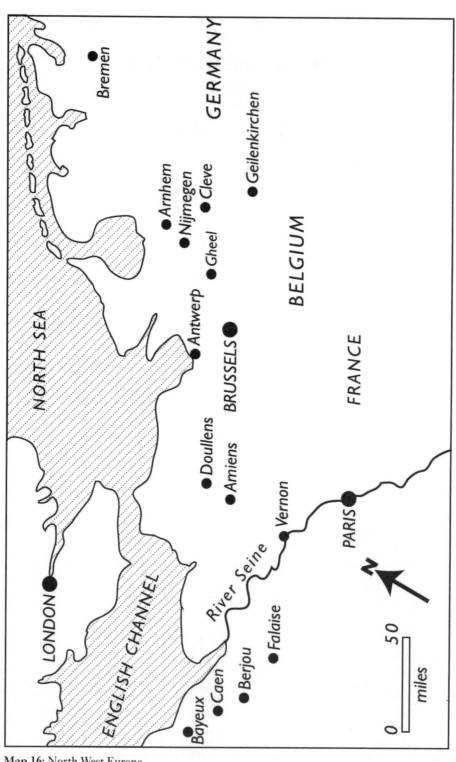

Map 16: North West Europe.

Chapter 32

D Day

January–June 1944

The regiment re-assembled at the end of January in Chippenham. Ian Spence was required for a job on Montgomery's staff and was replaced by Lieutenant Colonel John D'A. Anderson DSO, a highly regarded regular officer who went on to have a distinguished military career, culminating in the rank of general in his final appointment as Deputy Chief of the Imperial General Staff. At that time he had limited operational experience which made, for him, the critical task of establishing his credibility as Commanding Officer extremely difficult amongst such a battle-wise group. The regiment would, undoubtedly, have preferred one of their own to be appointed.

It did not help that one of Anderson's first tasks was to ensure that the regiment was weaned off its unconventional desert dress, worn almost as a battle honour, and thus to become *Inglese* in appearance, even to wearing boots and gaiters. A draft of over 100 men, mostly from the Lancashire Fusiliers, made up for losses from various causes and brought the regiment up to its increased establishment. Major Michael Laycock MC was still second-in-command while the adjutant was Captain George Jones, son of the head woodsman on the Laycocks' estate at Wiseton. Recruited as a trooper before the war, he had been commissioned on merit, and was greatly admired and respected for his efficiency. The squadron leaders were: A Squadron – Major Stanley Christopherson MC; B Squadron – Major Hanson Lawson (ex-24th Lancers; he and Major Michael Gold had swapped regiments); C Squadron – Major Stephen Mitchell MC; Reconnaissance Troop – Captain Patrick McCraith MC; HQ Squadron – Major Roger Sutton-Nelthorpe.

All three squadrons were eventually to be equipped with Shermans, armed with the 75mm. The remaining Shermans, issued, in due course, on a ratio of one per troop, were equipped with the 17-pounder; these were called Fireflies. Each squadron had four tanks in SHQ and four sabre troops, each of four tanks three 75mm and one 17 pounder. The Reconnaissance Troop was equipped with the Honey light tank with two tanks in HQ and three troops each of three tanks. The echelon consisted of about 100 supply vehicles.

Also re-organized was 8 Armoured Brigade so as to include 4th/7th Royal Dragoon Guards, a famous and able regular regiment, 24th Lancers, re-raised during the war, with strong links to 17th/21st Lancers, and the Sherwood Rangers.

The motor battalion was 12th King's Royal Rifle Corps and the Essex Yeomanry was the gunner regiment, equipped with Sexton, self-propelled 25-pounders on a Grant or Sherman hull. The regiment's FOO (forward observation officer) was Captain Arthur Warburton. The support provided by the Essex Yeomanry, and Warburton in particular, became legendary. Coincidentally, Warburton came from North Nottinghamshire, and after the war commanded the South Notts Hussars. So special was the regiment's regard for him that he was the only non-Sherwood Ranger to have been made a member of the Officers' Dining Club, until it became part of the Royal Yeomanry.

This change in brigade configuration was part of Montgomery's plan to ensure that the Army was strengthened by mixing experienced regiments and individuals with less experienced ones. The regiment's first task was to draw some of its tanks and all other equipment, which was extensive, a massive task, due to the fact that everything had been handed back in Egypt.

Much of the responsibility for re-equipping fell on the shoulders of John Semken, who, at 22 years of age, was technical adjutant. As mentioned he had joined when the regiment was losing its horses, and had been a troop leader at Alamein, going into action in a tank on which he had painted the Eye of Horus as a good-luck sign. Promoted to captain he remained a troop leader. The Eye of Horus kept him safe but not his successor, who was knocked out at Zem Zem.

When the tanks and other vehicles came, the regiment had neither spares nor tools with which to maintain them which made re-equipping a nightmare. No necessities had ever arrived and they were not allowed to use petrol to go and fetch anything. For want of spares, cannibalization was the order of the day, which meant at least twice the work.

The regiment also began rebuilding its training, starting with individual training, working up through troop, squadron and regimental to brigade-level. Stanley Christopherson later wrote:

> I am convinced that the most important and essential part of our training was the original 'Individual Training', especially the gunnery and wireless part. The success of any tank v. tank battle depended on accurate and quick fire, and it was quite impossible to fight any kind of battle … unless wireless communication was good….

Operation OVERLORD: The D Day Landings

The regiment knew that it had been brought home to take part in the liberation of North-West Europe. The purpose of the operation was to establish the 'Second Front' that the USA and the UK had promised the Russians, so taking pressure off the Russian Front and hastening the defeat of Germany. Planning of the Second Front had been underway for a long time and, by early 1944, had reached an advanced stage.

It was known that the enemy dispositions in North-West Europe in summer 1944 consisted of sixty divisions under the command of Field Marshal von Rundstedt. They covered the coast from the Low Countries to the Bay of Biscay, and from Marseilles along the Southern French shore. Rundstedt had Rommel under his command, who in turn commanded Army Group B which included Seventh Army, consisting of fifteen infantry divisions positioned in Normandy. Crucially, although Germany had nine panzer divisions in North-West Europe, their deployment was widely dispersed from the Low Countries to the South of France instead of being concentrated for a counter-attack; they also were held too far back from the coast because the difficulty of moving them under a state of air inferiority had been heavily underestimated by all in the chain of command save Rommel.

The Channel itself was heavily mined. On land there was a line of concrete works with all-round defence, incorporating fixed guns of a variety of calibres encased in reinforced concrete up to ten-feet thick, covering extensive minefields, wire, anti-tank ditches, and walls. Field artillery also covered the beaches. In addition, on the beaches themselves was a variety of obstacles positioned below the high watermark, including the gate-like C Elements, tetrahedrons, hedgehogs, and curved steel rails, designed to hole or prevent landing craft from getting ashore. There was no formal second line of defence but some villages inland were fortified strongly.

The Allied landings in North-West Europe were under command of the Supreme Allied Commander, General Dwight Eisenhower. The plan was to land two armies, under command of General Bernard Montgomery, on approximately twenty-five miles of beaches in Normandy, north and north-west of Caen. Second British Army under General Dempsey was on the left (east), and First US Army under General Omar Bradley was on the right (west).

Second British Army had a three-division front with 3rd British Division on the left, on the section of beach codenamed Sword; 3rd Canadian Division was in the centre on Juno beach and 50th Northumbrian, a TA Division back from Africa, was on the right, on Gold beach. In addition, 6th Airborne Division was to be dropped some hours before the landings, north-east of Caen, to capture bridges over the lower Orne and secure the left flank.

First US Army had a two-division front with 1st Division on the coast east of the Vire estuary on Omaha beach and 4th Division north of it on Utah beach on the Cotentin peninsula. First US Army would be aided by the drop of 82nd and 101st Airborne Divisions.

Each army would have one division in ships for immediate reinforcement. For the British, this was 49th (West Riding) Infantry Division, another TA formation, back from guarding Iceland where it had adopted the Polar Bear as its divisional sign. The first objectives of the attack included Caen, Bayeux, Isigny and Carentan. With these gained, the Americans would advance across the Cotentin peninsula and also drive northwards to liberate Cherbourg. The British would protect the American left flank from counter-attack, gaining ground south and south-west of Caen, where they could create airfields and use their armour. It was hoped to reach the line Falaise-Avranches three weeks after landing: in the event it took nine weeks. Then, with the strong reinforcements that would, by that time, be ashore, the Allies would break out eastwards towards Paris, north-eastwards towards the Seine, and westwards to the Brittany ports.

To achieve these aims, it would be necessary to put ashore 326,000 men, 54,000 vehicles, and 104,000 tonnes of stores within the first six days of the operation. Effectively this would be across open beaches, since the capture of a major port as a prerequisite had been abandoned following the unsuccessful Dieppe raid. Instead, two artificial harbours (one for each army), called Mulberry, were to be constructed from floating concrete sections, towed across the Channel immediately following the landings, and sunk in place. In the event, storms in the Channel on 19 June destroyed the US harbour: only the British harbour at Arromanches survived. Fuel was to be supplied through an underwater pipeline called Pluto to be laid under the Channel, once the Allies were firmly ashore.

The operation was preceded by several months of extensive activity by Allied air forces, which had first secured command of the skies. Such was the measure of Allied air superiority that, in the twenty-four hours of the day of the invasion, the Allies flew 14,600 sorties to the enemy's 100. At the same time, in the months before the invasion, Allied air forces destroyed all but one of the enemy's radars, rendering him operationally blind. They also wrought damage and destruction to a significant proportion of his critical oil plants, refineries, factories, rail junctions, airfields, roads, bridges and canals, all of which severely restricted the ability to re-supply forces already in position, or bring in reinforcements in a timely and effective manner.

In addition, the landings themselves were to be supported by massive tactical bombing both prior to and on the day itself, together with bombardment from the sea, aimed at taking out all enemy gun positions. The Allies, assisted by the capture of an Enigma machine which enabled them to break the enemy's codes and many other stratagems, managed to identify and turn all Germany's agents in this country so as to leak to and convince the Germans that the landings would take place in the Pas de Calais. To add to the deception, an entire phantom army was represented as being sited in south-east England, opposite the Pas de Calais. This was achieved by all manner of tricks, including mock-ups and false radio transmissions.

The enemy had also overestimated both the number of Allied divisions in England and the amount of shipping available, so that they assessed, wrongly, that a second big landing was easily an option. It was not until the third week in July, six weeks after D Day, that reserves from Fifteenth Army were sent from the Pas de Calais to Normandy. By that time it was much too late to defeat the landing.

The selection of D Day and H Hour were both critical decisions relating to getting the troops ashore as safely as possible. D Day could not be before the end of May because that was the first moment at which everything would be physically available and ready for the invasion; prior to that date there would not be sufficient ships, military equipment or appropriately trained troops with which to proceed.

The following factors determined the choice of H Hour: it was decided to approach the enemy coast by moonlight, because this would help both ships and airborne troops. A period of daylight before H Hour was also needed to give order to the deployment of the small craft, and accuracy to the covering bombardment. But, if the interval between first light and H Hour was too long, the enemy would have more time to recover from their surprise, and fire on the troops while landing. Tides were also a factor, since if the tide was too low, whilst obstacles would be fully revealed, there would be too great an expanse of open beach to cross; if the tide was too high obstacles would be concealed, and would come fully into play.

For these complex and interlinking reasons, it was decided to land about three hours before high water, at half flood, which was to prove significant, since it meant that the tidal current would be flooding from west to east along the coast as normal, and would carry vessels eastward of their intended point of landing, unless the helmsman aimed off to hold his true course. Tidal variations meant that H Hour would vary by up to eighty-five minutes between the various beaches to be used, the earliest being on Utah, the most westerly beach.

There were only three days in each lunar month when all these conditions were fulfilled. The first such period, after the end of May, was 5, 6, and 7 June and 5 June was therefore chosen, with the 6th and 7th as fall-back options. Once established, this fact became the most closely guarded secret of all.

Little of the foregoing was known to anyone, and indeed much of it would not become generally known until after the war. However, the Sherwood Rangers were about to become aware that there were few units for whom this massive attention to detail was to be of greater importance than to them. They learned that during the landings, B and C Squadrons' Sherman tanks were to be Duplex Drive amphibians (DD tanks) issued on a scale of sixteen per squadron to be, literally, the first troops to land on their allocated beach. These two squadrons were chosen for such a role, ahead of A Squadron, as an acknowledgement that it was A Squadron that had led the regiment throughout the North African campaign.

However, as they became familiar with the characteristics of their new equipment, they could have been forgiven for thinking that they had been placed beyond the help of mere good planning by the General Staff. An intervention from the Almighty Himself would be required to procure their survival: the tanks were described as 'amphibians' because each had a fifteen-foot-high canvas screen attached to the hull which was held erect by compressed air pillars and none-too-strong metal struts. When the tank was 'afloat' it looked like a small canvas boat because it was suspended under the canvas screen, about eighteen inches of which showed above the waves. This canvas screen alone ensured that the tank did not immediately sink.

Medium-term survival depended on the sea being relatively calm, the screen remaining in place, even though prone to collapse, and the waterproofing of the tank itself and its engine, which was down to the crew, having been skilfully applied. The screen failed if holed by enemy fire. The tank came fitted with a hand-operated bilge pump in its bowels, described by tank crews as 'useless'. In the event that the tank sank, there was a rubber dinghy large enough to accommodate the entire crew in some discomfort and which, when broken out, inflated automatically. Self-evidently, given the tank weighed thirty tons, the crew would need to be quick.

They were described as 'Duplex Drive' because, whilst afloat, each tank was driven off the main engine by two screws at the stern, whilst the tracks were also turning at speed, to enable the tank to be steered as if on land. As it came ashore, the driver had to change from third gear to first just before the tracks grounded to slow the speed at which the tracks were revolving. If he failed to do so, the engine stalled and, in earlier variants, this was wont to cause a blow back, normally through the turret, which was no doubt a memorable experience for those in the way.

Whilst at sea the commander stood on a special platform behind the turret to see over the screen. It follows, therefore, that the driver and the rest of the crew were an unpleasantly long way below the surface. In practice the tank was defenceless

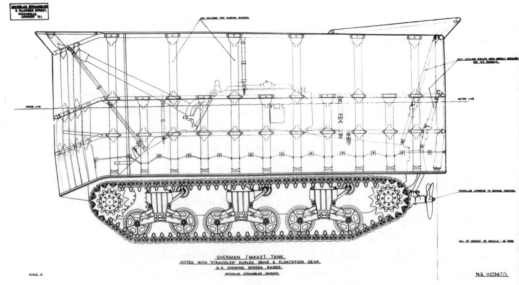

A diagram of a DD Sherman with its flotation screen raised. When 'swimming' only a very small portion of the top of the screen was visible.

whilst at sea, since it could not fire its weapons effectively with the screen up, and therefore yet another thing that the driver had to accomplish, on coming ashore, was to activate a small electric charge which collapsed the screen.

The two squadrons were to be launched in their tanks from landing craft up to 6,000 yards (yes, three and a half miles!) offshore and, having 'steamed' initially in 'line ahead' and latterly, on an arm signal from the squadron leader, in 'line abreast', 'navigate' the tank to the correct point on the 'beach' (all naval expressions). These tanks were considered crucial to the success of the landings, because one of the lessons learned from the Dieppe raid in 1942, was that if the infantry landed before the tanks they lacked the benefit of essential covering fire. Only four British regiments (ten in all) were equipped with DD tanks and so it was a singular compliment to the regiment, but one that, on the whole, they would have happily foregone.

As for A Squadron and RHQ, they would land at H Hour plus 90 minutes behind the initial assault, followed sometime later by Headquarters Squadron and the Recce Troop. The B Echelon would not land until some weeks later.

With the basic training complete, including a spell of live firing in Kirkcudbright, B and C Squadrons went off to a row of boarding houses on the front at Great Yarmouth in Norfolk. From there they were transported daily in enclosed lorries (to keep their destination secret) for intensive practice in their new role at the Water Assault Wing situated on some lakes concealed by woodlands at what they eventually discovered was Fritton, a short distance inland from Yarmouth and adjacent to the Norfolk Boards. If there was any lingering sense of optimism concerning the seagoing qualities of their new craft this was quickly removed when they found that their initial training was to take the form of instruction on the Davis Escape Apparatus, which each man had to wear and learn to use. The basic apparatus was a variant, for the use of tank crews, specially adapted from that which had been developed by the Navy to help submariners escape from a submarine that had foundered.

Training in its use consisted of descending twelve feet into a specially-constructed concrete circular structure at the bottom of which the hull of a Sherman tank had been set. Each man was required to seat himself in the fighting compartment. Ten water cocks were opened, and the tank hull and the whole system rapidly flooded with water. The Davis Escape Apparatus provided sufficient air to last a man twelve minutes. He then had to breathe through the equipment, whilst operating the controls in the tank hull, for a specific time, before escaping and surfacing. It was a very unpleasant experience. Initially between thirty and forty yeomen refused to do this. As veterans of the desert they had repeatedly demonstrated courage of legendary proportions, but 'to be a bloody sailor in a bloody tank' was different. Who can blame them? However, it would become a serious matter for the regiment if they continued to refuse. The irony of coming from a situation of extreme water shortage to that of an overwhelming surfeit was not lost on them.

Lieutenant Colonel Anderson asked Michael Laycock, who knew them best, to try to persuade those who had refused. Laycock went there and talked as only someone who had shared their experiences could do. He went in the thing himself and, having got the procedure slightly wrong, came up spluttering to universal silent amusement. But almost to a man they followed his lead.

Having done basic and specialist training, the regiment moved into specially isolated and separate security camps close to the Channel. Southern England had become an enormous training area and encampment, ready for the final phases of preparation. B and C Squadrons went initially to Lee-on-Solent where they worked with the Royal Navy's landing craft tanks (LCTs). They, no doubt, did a lot of 'steaming', perfecting the launching, operation and landing of the tanks, including normal lateral ebb and flow of the tide along coast lines, often on the beach below Osborne House on the Isle of Wight, during which they found that the tanks worked fine if it was calm. Their final destination was a tented camp in the woods at Fawley, on the shore of the Solent opposite Cowes, where it rained most of the time. They were under strict security, and were fed 'like turkeys for the pot'. They called the rest of the regiment who were not under canvas 'base wallahs'.

The rest of the regiment went in April, first to Sway in Hampshire, where they were based in a large house, to continue their work-up training and then to what they later realized was their assembly area for the operation at Hursley Park near Winchester, from the comfort of which they called B and C Squadrons 'backwoodsmen'.

Finally, in the last few days before embarkation, the regiment, less B and C Squadrons, went to their final concentration area, a well-organized camp identified as C10, a few miles outside Southampton, completely sealed off from the outside world and full of other units, mostly Canadian. As a result, although each part of the regiment trained extensively on landing craft and with the infantry and other arms, the regiment only trained together as a unit on a couple of occasions before D Day. Increasingly, as time went by, each time they deployed on exercise, they did so not knowing whether it was to be the real thing. For everyone tension and pre-match nerves began to build inexorably. With all training finished and all camps sealed off, briefings and O Groups took place. These went down to every possible detail, except the actual location of the landings, and the names of the towns and villages that were their objectives. In practice, no doubt, many guessed the true location in a similar way that the regiment had. John Bethell-Fox recognized from the initial maps that, despite the altered names, Normandy, the location of his childhood summer holidays, was to be the area of the landings.

Eight Armoured Brigade was to support 50th (Northumbrian) Division, recruiting from East Yorkshire as well as from the north-east, and a veteran, like themselves, of Eighth Army and the desert, whom they had supported in Tunisia.

By the end of the North African campaign the division consisted of two brigades, 69 and 151. It was then assigned the role of an assault landing division for Operation HUSKY, the Sicily landings in 1943. For that it had attached 231(Malta) Brigade, liberated from its task of defending Malta. It was not only, at that point, a fresh brigade, but also a 'crack' one consisting of 2nd Devons, 1st Hampshires and 1st Dorsets. Fiftieth Division's landing on Sicily, in the dark before dawn, is described, even by its supporters, as 'chaos', with, at its worst, platoons landing with the wrong companies and companies with the wrong battalions. Worse, whole battalions landed miles from their intended destinations. However, due to the soft defence by the Italians, it got away with it: 231 Brigade, which had performed best of the three brigades, was then used, as an independent brigade, to mount another landing on the toe of Italy. Again 'chaotic' was the description, but was also ultimately successful.

The division had caught Montgomery's eye for having twice plucked triumph from disaster. So it was for that reason, having given due credit for the huge difficulty of opposed amphibious landings in the dark, and the many lessons learned, that 50th Division was selected to land on D Day. It was his most experienced amphibious landing division and contained within it 231 Brigade, his most experienced amphibious landing brigade. In addition to the three brigades mentioned, for the landing itself a fourth infantry brigade, 56, was attached.

The entire coastline, from which the five landing beaches were to be selected, was divided into sectors of about two miles in length, each given a separate codename. Only a select few formed part of one of the landing beaches. The five operational beaches were not directly adjacent to each other and, due to terrain, not all of each beach selected was fit to be used. Fiftieth Division was to assault the centre of the five beaches codenamed Gold. Each division was allocated two adjacent sectors, those on Gold being King on the left and Jig on the right. Each sector was allocated to a brigade and subdivided into the left half, always called Red and the right half, always called Green, each roughly equating to a battalion front. They were further sub-divided, for example Jig Green East/West.

King was to be assaulted by 69 Brigade, supported by 4th/7th Royal Dragoon Guards with the Sherwood Rangers supporting 231 Brigade, the right brigade assaulting Jig. Unlike 69 Brigade, which was to land with one battalion on King Red and another on King Green, 231 Brigade was to land on Jig Green with B Squadron, under command 1st Hampshires, on the right, or Jig Green West, and C Squadron, under command 1st Dorsets on the left, Jig Green East. For reasons to be explained Jig Red was not to be used. 'Under command' rather than 'in support', because initially neither SRY RHQ nor superior armoured headquarters would be ashore. 'Under command' meant the armoured squadron became part of a mixed infantry/armour battle-group, further enhanced by the ability to call for close support from, not only the division's artillery, but from the Essex Yeomanry's SP guns. This meant that each battalion CO had a very powerful command, if used as a unit. Of the remaining two brigades, 151 was to be the follow-up on King, and 56 the follow-up on Jig.

Once their respective assaulting brigades had gone firm on their initial objectives on high ground behind the beach, each follow-up brigade was to pass through to further tasks to the south. The final objectives of 231 Brigade were three villages on the high ground behind Jig, but it also had a second phase, which was to send 2nd Devons, its reserve battalion, west to link up with the Americans on Omaha Beach, the assault beach ten or so miles west of Gold.

In addition, 47 Commando was to land on Gold to take Port-en-Bessin, ten miles to the west and close to Omaha.

Fiftieth Division was briefed that Jig beach consisted of sand but also, over the whole of Jig Red, had areas of soft blue clay along the foreshore in which vehicles could bog easily. Further, Jig Red led into low turfed dunes, all of which were mined; the beach was not. Behind the Jig Red dunes, to the south of a lateral road and railway, was a marsh. These were the reasons why Jig Red was not to be used. Behind Jig Green, there was a village and some higher ground.

Gold was covered by a full selection of beach obstacles and also by fire from strongpoints. Two in particular enfiladed the whole beach, number 36 from the east and 37 from the village behind Jig Green.

These briefings were followed by endless conferences to tie up with the units with which the regiment would be working. The key units not so far mentioned were those that would operate the variety of devices to clear the various beach obstacles, based on tank hulls and collectively known as 'Funnies'. The sub-units operating the Funnies allocated to Jig were B Squadron, Westminster Dragoons, operating flail tanks, and 82 Assault Squadron RE, who would operate the remainder of the equipments. These had all been designed, developed and tested in secrecy at various locations, including Brancaster in Norfolk and Orfordness in Suffolk, where the tide flooded along the coast to the south and ebbed to the north.

Naturally the Sherwood Rangers were keen to discover from the sub-units what equipment they had and what each did. The answer was:

- Flail tanks, known as 'Crabs', were Sherman tanks with a 75mm gun, to the front of the hull of which was mounted a horizontal drum with chain flails attached and wire cutters to clear minefields and wire.
- The Petard mounted on an Assault Vehicle Royal Engineers (AVRE), could throw a 'dustbin' filled with high explosive to breach beach obstacles and knock out reinforced defended locations. 'General Wade' and 'beehive' charges could be placed to achieve the same effect.
- Various types of bridge-layer could span concrete walls and anti-tank ditches, and fascines could be used to fill craters or ditches.
- AVREs were also equipped with a dozer blade which could be used in a variety of ways, including the removal of beach obstacles.

- In addition, there were various items of equipment designed to overcome the soft going and therefore the risk of bogging, in particular Bobbin AVRE which could lay a matting road.

Both specialist sub-units were to land dry in the second wave, very shortly after the regiment and before the leading infantry. They were to clear three lanes about 250 yards apart due south, avoiding the bad ground, over Jig Green which had the soundest going for vehicles to the lateral coast road and beyond until clear of the obstacles and minefields. These lanes were initially for the regiment's tanks and the infantry, and thereafter for the use of all follow-up echelons. The equipment necessary to clear each lane was to be self-contained in a single LCT, so there were three LCTs. Each load consisted of a standard mixture of the vehicles from each specialist squadron to provide a balanced capability and was called an RE Armoured Assault Team. Clearly they were vital to the success of the operation.

It is worth appreciating, notwithstanding the massive nature of the invasion, the relatively small number of fighting men, 'bayonets', actually delivered onto the beaches in the first wave by each assaulting division. For example, 50th Division was assaulting a beach about four miles long. Assaulting 'two-up' this meant that the first wave consisted of only thirty-two rifle sections totalling about 250 bayonets and four sabre squadrons totalling sixty-four tanks, or sixty soldiers and twelve tanks per mile. Of course, as has been indicated, the build-up of reinforcements, even within the division itself, was fully planned and rapid, but even so it can be seen why getting ashore securely, the task assigned to the division, was the most hazardous part of the whole operation with strategic and tactical surprise essential.

Following these briefings, the squadrons moved from their various locations, as part of a massive, but superbly co-ordinated, operation which included final rationing, replenishment and bombing up. The backwoodsmen went straight from their beach at Fawley onto their landing craft, reversing their vehicles off the beach up the narrow ramp in a carefully pre-planned sequence, so that they could later disembark forwards, and in the right order, and secured them with chains. The base wallahs, on their wheels and tracks, proceeded through the streets of Southampton to a wonderful welcome from the people, and many cups of tea and cakes, to Southampton docks where they embarked, again in reverse order, on their various pre-allocated LCTs. In the case of the regiment these were from 15 and 45 LCT Flotillas.

Each craft was flat-bottomed, and therefore rolled considerably in a seaway and, apart from a small but comfortable ward-room at the stern and a canvas canopy when fitted, was completely open to the skies. Each was commanded by a sub-lieutenant and had a crew of three or four, and could take up to six tanks and their crews. With a full load it was almost impossible to move, let alone find a space on deck on which to stretch out to sleep. Having been loaded, each craft moved to tie up farther down the quay alongside another, which was already laden. The harbour was filled to capacity with a vast number and variety of craft, a sight repeated in every harbour and cove throughout southern England. The date was 2 June and the regiment was fully embarked by last light. On 4 June, as part of the inexorable process, all the craft moved away from the quay and anchored in Southampton Water.

The invasion had been timed for 5 June, but the weather was very bad, the worst in the Channel at that time of year for twenty years, gusts of close to hurricane strength in places being mentioned. This caused a postponement, the entire force remaining embarked and at anchor pitching uncomfortably along the whole of the south coast. After a delay of twenty-four hours, the Supreme Allied Commander took a significant risk and trusted his 'Met', which indicated a break in the bad weather covering much of 6 and 7 June. He ordered the invasion fleet of over 4,000 ships and several thousand smaller craft to sea at midnight on 5 June 1944, with Montgomery's apt quotation from '*If*' ringing in their ears:

> *He either fears his fate too much,*
> *Or his deserts are small,*
> *Who dares not put it to the touch,*
> *To win or lose it all.*

After two days pitching at anchor in Southampton Water, what most Sherwood Rangers had lost was the contents of their stomachs. The regiment's LCTs were described by Leslie Skinner, the padre, as having 'great quantities of grease, water and vomit swishing about. Everything dirty and crowded. Cold and wet.' However, they were on their way, a tiny part of a huge fleet that had set sail from every port and cove from Felixstowe to the Bristol Channel. Their orders were to converge five miles south of the Isle of Wight at what was called Point Zero, a mile-wide circle on a chart, before turning south down what was called the Spout, two gradually widening, but broadly parallel lines on the same chart, for the Normandy coast, in five parallel columns, one for each beach.

In the vanguard of the centre column were the two flotillas of landing craft carrying B and C Squadrons of the Sherwood Rangers Yeomanry, the very tip of the point of the largest amphibious operation the world has ever seen. A small, but remarkable place in history. It was only now that they were at sea, with the operation in progress, that commanders were handed their sealed orders by the commanders of their landing craft. Those orders confirmed the landings would take place in Normandy and that, in the case of B and C Squadrons, Jig Green had a front of 1,000 yards from the village of le Hamel on the right (west) to some coastal gun emplacements on the left (east). Jig Red extended east for about a mile and a half, to a point midway between le Hamel and the village of la Rivière. The three villages comprising 231 Brigade's objectives were Asnelles-sur-Mer, Ryes, and Meuvaines, on the rising ground half a mile south of the lateral coastal road,

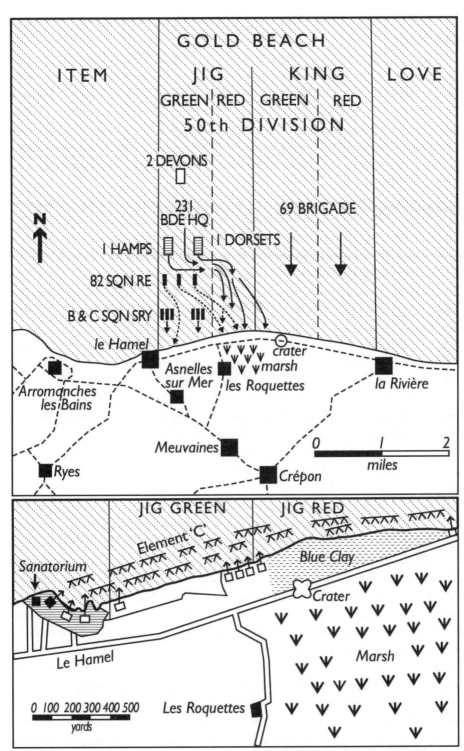

Map 17: Gold Beach.

which itself ran through le Hamel and la Rivière, about a quarter of a mile south of the beach.

Of the lanes to be cleared by the three RE Armoured Assault Teams assigned to Jig, the axis of Lane 1, the most westerly (right), was to be through le Hamel itself, the axis of Lane 2, approximately 250 yards to the east (left), pointing towards Asnelles-sur-Mer, and the axis of Lane 3 a further 250 yards east (left) of that, pointing towards les Roquettes and on to Meuvaines. This meant that all three axes were confined to Jig Green as were 231 Brigade's left and right boundaries and therefore missed the worst of the blue clay and marsh land just to the east (left) in Jig Red.

The timings were that B and C Squadrons would land first at H – 5 minutes, take up fire positions on the beach and provide covering fire, firstly for the RE Armoured Assault Teams, who would land at H hour, and secondly for the first wave of assaulting infantry, landing at H + 5. On Gold Beach H Hour was 0730. The Essex Yeomanry, and their SP 25-pounders, despite being still at sea, would be providing close fire support to the assaulting troops on Gold, firing from their landing craft, until they stopped briefly whilst they came ashore, when they would take up gun positions and then carry on.

As an aside, 4th/7th Royal Dragoon Guards changed this sequence in respect of their own landing shortly before making their final approach, probably in response to the adverse weather conditions, so that they landed last, giving the RE Armoured Assault Teams on King time to clear the beach obstacles for them; they also elected to land dry. Whilst this got them ashore, the infantry of 50th Division claimed that this adversely affected operations on King, in that the tanks were prevented from providing support to the infantry, who relied instead on the Crabs' main armament. This did not happen on Jig where the Sherwood Rangers stuck to the plan.

In the first phase the infantry would pass through and secure the beach defences themselves, in particular numbers 36 and 37 which enfiladed the beach, 36 from south of Jig Red and 37 from the sea front at le Hamel. In the second phase, B and C Squadrons were to move through the gaps breached by each RE Armoured Assault Team, behind the infantry, and support them in the operation to secure le Hamel and various adjacent known strongpoints, including Asnelles-sur-Mer and Meuvaines. The 231 Brigade units would take up positions to prevent counter-attacks and mop up any enemy left behind. B and C Squadrons would be released at that stage and revert under command RHQ Sherwood Rangers, which would by then be ashore, and rally at a predetermined RV at Buhot. They would then prepare for further operations in support of 56 Brigade, the follow-up brigade due to liberate Bayeux by last light. Next day the Sherwood Rangers were to be available to set up patrol bases south of Bayeux in the area of Villers Bocage.

It is hard to imagine the thoughts that entered the heads of the members of B and C Squadrons as dawn broke, finding them sleepless, cold, wet and in many cases with empty stomachs, and green with sea sickness. They found a considerable sea, with five- to six-foot waves, running, and from time to time the LCTs would take solid water over the side. Never can there have been a dawn more likely than this one to 'surprise them unpleasantly at their least heroic hour'.

Padre Skinner recalled: 'Up 0500 cold wet, sea rough'. The padre was probably the only person amongst the assaulting troops on the whole of Gold Beach who had the time, let alone the presence of mind, to make regular checks of his watch. His timings are used, therefore, as the basis for fixing the sequence of events on yet another chaotic day for 50th Division.

Stuart Hills wrote:

> When dawn first broke we found ourselves rather disconcertingly in the lead and apart from the other landing craft bearing the squadron there was not another ship in sight. However, as it became light as far as the eye could see over the very rough, and very grey sea, there were boats and ships of all descriptions.

Suddenly the drone of the bombers flying north, having done their best to take out the sea defences, was drowned out by a mighty clap of thunder as the warships' guns opened up at 0521 and then fired incessantly shoreward, incorporating smoke in the ammunition mix from 0545 onwards to baffle the enemy's long-range guns. Their key targets were the gun positions covering the beaches. As B and C Squadron's flotillas passed through, their spirits must have been raised by the sheer power of the bombardment, although a glance towards the coast of Normandy, emerging shrouded in mist and smoke in the stormy dawn, must have filled them all with a fear of the unknown.

Quickly, however, other problems would have become uppermost in their minds. One look at the sea state and they would have realized that to launch their tanks at 6,000 yards would be suicidal. The decision to launch did not lie with the Sherwood Rangers, but with the commanders of each LCT flotilla, probably aged no more than twenty-five, whose LCT was carrying each squadron leader, with whom he would liaise. The nearer he went before giving the order to launch, the greater the risk of losing ships.

There was much else to accomplish, however. Good regiments wash and shave before stand to, and this was one of the best, the balance of the water heated for that purpose also making a hot sweet strong brew of tea. Food of some sort would have been taken by those who could cope with it. First parade had to be carried out on the tanks (checking engine levels and track tensions); personal weapons to be checked and loaded; a round fisted home into the breach of the 75mm and the base clips eased on half a dozen more; the first round of a new belt clamped in the breaches of the three .30s and safety catches applied; screens needed erecting; chains securing the tanks removed; muzzle covers removed; engines warmed up; personal kit stowed; the Escape Apparatus 'donned'. Because radio silence was lifted for the DD units, their 19 Sets, which were HF radios, had to be netted. This complex procedure involved tuning the set to a transmission from the control station in SHQ sent at a pre-arranged time, which culminated in the operator holding the tuning dial, now correctly adjusted, still with his thumb whilst he used a coin as a screw driver to lock the dial by tightening two screws in balance with each other. The setting was so sensitive that, if the radio was to transmit or receive, not the slightest movement of the dial could take place once tuned, until locked. Just the thing to attempt wearing your Escape Apparatus, crouched awkwardly in the turret, on a pitching and rolling landing craft as it stood into the shore under fire, and with the rest of the crew swarming over and through the tank as they completed their own tasks.

The SHQ tank had an additional radio, an 18 Set, issued specially for D Day, pre-tuned to a selected frequency, that of the battalion they were supporting. So, all the squadron and the battalion had to do was switch on.

Padre Skinner: 'Stand To' for 0700. This is it. Land visible through mist by 0630. Rain cleared. Running for beach by 0700 under fire by 0710'.

In the event, thanks to the courage of the commanders of the landing craft flotillas, and in consultation with the squadron leaders, both squadrons launched at approximately 800 yards.

The drill was that the LCTs went from line astern to line abreast, facing the beach, and came to a halt before lowering their ramps. The tanks then, one by one, slid off the ramps into the sea which had to be done as slowly as possible lest the screen's bow wave would over-top the screen and sink the tank. Once each tank had steadied itself in the water, there was a brief hiatus before the driver could engage drive and the tank began to move away. It was important that the LCT had no forward movement at this point, since if it had, it could overrun the tank, catch and rip the screen and sink it. Once moving, the tank, hopefully, when viewed by the enemy, assumed, as advertised, the aspect of a harmless fragile canvas boat.

Once at sea the DDs were not left entirely to their own devices to navigate to the shore. They were in the hands of a Combined Operations Pilotage Party (COPP) whose role was assault force navigation, the task of ensuring that all vessels actually landing themselves, vehicles, equipment or troops on the beach did so in the correct place. They were part of an organization raised in 1942 under Lieutenant Commander Nigel Clogstoun-Willmott, had much leading-edge equipment to aid navigation, and were represented on D Day on the leading landing craft and offshore in X-craft (midget submarines) and, once launched, alongside the DD tanks in assault boats, to pilot them right onto the beaches using torches and infra-red beacons.

Lieutenant Stuart Hills writes:

Our LCT was in the van of the assault, and our tank was at the front of the LCT. We were 700 yards out. I gave the order for the canvas screen to be inflated. The LCT lowered its ramp. A shell slammed into the water just in front of us then one on the side of the ramp. I gave the order: 'Go go go' and we flopped into the sea.

Lindsay in his official history records Stuart Hills stating at this point that 'The landing craft carrying the Flails came past us'. This would have been one of the RE Armoured Assault Teams apparently ahead of the other two.

Lieutenant Jack Holman notes:

> Johnny Mann's tank which was the front tank would not inflate [its screen] so it was pushed off the front to allow the others to launch. We swam in but had difficulty in steering between the closely packed obstacles so I had to stand on top of my turret to see like an Aunt Sally at a fair ground.

Even 800 yards was too far for some tanks which foundered, so that the first Sherwood Rangers to die in this campaign were drowned. Stuart Hills was lucky:

> The tank was shipping water from the bottom. It was clear we had no chance of making it to the shore. I gave the order to abandon ship. Cpl Footitt inflated our small rubber dingy and we piled into it.

They bobbed about in the midst of the invasion for some time before being picked up and eventually came ashore next day in a rowing boat. 'My, this will swing the balance in Montgomery's favour!' said the beach-master.

Trooper Philip Foster, still a gunner, was a member of Sergeant Bill Digby's crew, one of the best of the regiment's tank commanders from the desert, whose tank was the second onto the beach after his troop leader. Foster later wrote:

> It was ... evident that the Germans were now greeting us by pounding the sea with their shells as we swam forward.... We had a nasty moment when one of the forward steel struts, holding firm the canvas structure, collapsed with the side caving inwards. Bill ... managed to force the strut back into place.
>
> We safely proceeded through the rain of shells right onto the beach as we had so often done in practice. Now we were on firm ground and turned up the beach. I could see through my periscope over the dunes the little village of le Hamel intact and seemingly deserted. Of course the Germans had the beach covered with their guns and there must have been a strongpoint ahead enfilading the beach. Over the wireless tuned into the regiment's frequency I heard our Troop Commander Lt Horley say in an anxious voice that his tank was on fire.... Then we heard no more as the tank was knocked out and he was killed. We continued on and fired our first shell, but then things went wrong for us. Ahead the Germans had an anti-tank gun that started firing at us at fairly short-range.
>
> The next moment we were hit by an armour-piercing shell, probably a 50mm, which penetrated the three-inch thick turret just in front of the

gunner. The shell smashed through the knee of the gunner, took both legs off the commander above the knees and then hit my foot. Mercifully we did not catch fire as Shermans were prone to do. The next thing I knew was that Bill lay on the floor of the turret with his two legs severed except for a few strands of flesh. Bill asked me for morphine which we carried and I injected him. Later he wanted me to shoot him dead. Meanwhile the driver started backing the tank but could not see where he was going through his limited vision. Very inconveniently he drove into the sea where we got totally stuck, neither able to move forwards or backwards.

Bill Digby died that night from his wounds. Philip Foster's war was also over, but his post-war ministry as a Roman Catholic priest still lay ahead.

Lieutenant Jimmy McWilliam remembered that 'We swam in from about 1,000 yards and on landing put down a lot of covering fire for the infantry'. One LCT had a collision during the crossing which prevented the ramp being lowered, did not launch and so beached before unloading. That meant that five or six tanks landed dry; the rest swam.

Because the tide was reasonably high, the beach defences themselves did not seem to come into play. Therefore B and C Squadrons, less three B Squadron and five C Squadron tanks that had foundered, landed on Jig Green, well up the beach within about 100 yards of the promenade. Padre Skinner wrote in his diary 'Beached 0725'.

Even at this early stage problems aplenty were building up. There were two 88s on the high ground south and south-west of le Hamel which had not been knocked out by the preliminary bombardment and had the beach covered, initially inflicting losses. The gun to the south-west took the scalp of an LCT, possibly that seen by Stuart Hills, carrying the RE Armoured Assault team of 82 Assault Engineer Squadron, assigned to Lane 1, the western lane. It hit the LCT several times, disabling its engine. The LCT drifted ashore sideways-on, so its ramp lowered into deeper water. One AVRE endeavoured to disembark, but drowned in the swell and nothing else was able to get ashore until early afternoon when the tide had finished flooding and then ebbed sufficiently.

In fact, few of the guns covering Jig Green had been taken out before the landing commenced. Particularly of concern to the tanks, was a Polish 77mm anti-tank gun in a reinforced concrete emplacement on the le Hamel seawall, number 37, still in action and which the regiment's guns could not knock out. It was an infantry/engineer task and there were, as yet, no infantry or engineers. This anti-tank gun had the whole of Jig Green in enfilade. As soon as a tank drove sufficiently far up the beach, the gun in the emplacement, which had limited traverse, could be laid. It then knocked the tank out. Those that stayed back were safe from it but could be engaged by guns on the higher ground behind, facing seaward.

The absence of engineers was caused by the fact that neither of the remaining two RE Armoured Assault Teams landed on Jig Green. As 82 Squadron's war diary notes, 'The landing points differed considerably from the original intention with the net result that the breaching teams were dispersed on too great a length of beach and dispersed too far to the east'. The fate of the LCT for Lane 1 caused the other two to land east of and away from the trouble.

The problem was now compounded, because historians of 50th Division state their research reveals the infantry landing craft flotillas carrying the Headquarters of 231 Brigade, 1st Hampshires and 1st Dorsets, the two lead battalions, landed not on Jig Green, but partly on Jig Red and on King Green, upwards of a mile to the east, completely outside their brigade boundaries as set out in 50th Division's orders, and leaving 231 Brigade with no hope of taking command of and directing the fighting on Jig Green as ordered, at least for the time being. They were also partly in that section of the beach unsuitable for tanks and other vehicles, so even if the tanks knew where they were, they could not have joined them. The easterly set of the tide was an explanation suggested for this after the war, but it involves, for the fully qualified naval helmsmen steering all the landing craft, an elementary error of seamanship, avoiding which had been incorporated in all their training, and may be discounted. Poor visibility is also blamed, but was not mentioned by the Sherwood Rangers and the many other units who all reported le Hamel as visible.

There are photographs of the shore taken from the starboard side of a 231 Brigade landing craft indicating it was deliberately steaming easterly and parallel to the clearly visible shore, which requires a different explanation. It is inconceivable that a brigade of 231's experience would deliberately breach its clear orders. Almost certainly, therefore, this was a kindly act of their COPP who, seeing the hot reception being meted out to the Sherwood Rangers and engineers on Jig Green, did his best, in ignorance of the implications of his decision, and sought for them a safer landfall. Lieutenant Edward Wright, 1st Hampshires noted that, 'When I had time to look at my map we had landed two or three hundred metres to the east … that proved fortunate because … those who landed closest to le Hamel got the worst of it.'

Despite supposedly having radio communications with the Sherwood Rangers, there is no record of either battalion having used that means. B and C Squadrons were, as a result, fighting on the beach in ignorance of this turn of events, and with no higher command and control. The whole command and control function of the brigade had broken down at battalion HQ level, which meant the Brigade HQ was not in contact with the rifle companies. This was partly because the COs of both battalions were casualties, and in one of them its second-in-command as well. This prevented any compensating correction that could have brought them back within their boundaries and to the key tasks, particularly taking out the guns, needing to be carried out on Jig Green. To add to the problems, the OC of 82

Assault Engineer Squadron was killed, which also delayed any response from that direction that would assist the Sherwood Rangers for the time being.

Alone on the beach and trapped there by the gun position 37 at le Hamel, the Sherwood Rangers had lost a number of tanks and were in some difficulty. During this phase, it seems that most of the other guns covering this part of the beach were neutralized, presumably by either the regiment, or their artillery or the shore bombardment, thus containing the attrition.

Meanwhile the invasion was continuing behind them, and congestion on the beach was threatening to become a problem. Padre Skinner, who, typically, was on the beach dealing with the wounded at a much earlier time than he should have been, commented, 'Chaos ashore. Germans firing everything they had'. Solutions were beginning to emerge for this was now, perforce, a sub-unit commander's battle of the infantry, armour, engineers and indeed artillery units tasked with taking Jig Green, who began to remember their missions, use their initiative and follow their orders.

At company level in 231 Brigade they knew exactly what they were supposed to do and set about doing it, ironically lamenting the lack of availability of armour and artillery to help them, though it was the armour and artillery that had landed in the right place. From where they were, an assortment of rifle companies started to do three things from their start point on Jig Red/King Green. The first was that elements tried to get down the lateral route to le Hamel which ran just inland from the beach. This was thwarted for some considerable time because of a large crater in the road, roughly at the boundary of Jig Red with King Green. The second was for other elements to work their way south-westerly inland to the villages on the high ground that were their secondary targets. Neither action was, initially, much help to those on Jig Green. The third was, however.

That there were infantry fighting on the correct sector of the beach with the regiment is clear from several contemporary accounts quoted here. Their identity is not specified but they must surely have been elements of the lead battalions of 231 Brigade who had made the correct landfall, despite what the research says, or had traversed the beach to get back within their boundaries. The only other options were 2nd Devons and 47 Commando, but records reveal that neither touched Jig Green on the day, their orders notwithstanding.

The next key event was the landing of the Essex Yeomanry. Arthur Warburton, the regiment's FOO attached from the Essex Yeomanry, who landed just behind the tanks at H Hour recalled that, 'Also there was a gun … in concrete and steel …. This position at le Hamel had excellent fields of fire.' He was referring to Number 37, the gun enfilading the beach. 'I'm bloody sure that thing is pointing at me at that very moment the thing hit me. I then saw one of the regimental self-propelled guns coming ashore [this could not have been before 0900, the time they were due to land] so I got hold of him. I said "blow that damned thing up".'

Sergeant Robert Palmer, Essex Yeomanry, responded:

We flew across as fast as we could ... we caught them by surprise ... the driver stopped ... and immediately turned 45 degrees to the right ... the gunlayer fired immediately and the first round actually hit but it had not gone in the narrow slit that we wanted ... he fired again and would you believe the next one was kind enough to go right in the actual aperture ... and exploded inside and put the gun out of action.

He was awarded an immediate MM. 'The Guns, the Guns, Thank God the Guns' springs to mind!

This did not solve all the problems for the tanks on the beach, nor for the, by now heavy and increasing, build-up of men and vehicles of all types. They were still under fire, but at last the Sherwood Rangers could begin to take on the remainder of the anti-tank threat and fight their way inland:

When his Squadron was held up by heavy fire on the beach at le Hamel, Sgt Bracegirdle pushed along a secondary beach exit towards le Hamel which had not at that time been entered by other allied troops. He came under heavy anti-tank gunfire from guns at close ranges and, although his tank was repeatedly hit, he silenced one anti-tank gun, and after his gun had been put out of action temporarily, he directed the fire of a supporting tank on to other anti-tank guns, while he himself pushed forward. Through his action it was possible to penetrate the enemy positions and drive a wedge into the defences.

For this action he was awarded an immediate MM.

It was now well into the morning, probably between 1000 and 1100. Nos. 2 and 3 RE Armoured Assault Teams had managed to disembark during the morning, and were beginning to react, particularly Team No. 2. One of their Crabs had found its way onto the lateral road west of the crater and had advanced along it into le Hamel, where it was knocked out. A second Crab and two AVREs then came onto Jig Green to try and clear Lane 2 in accordance with the plan. The Crab was blown up in the lane by a mine which its flail had failed to detonate. The first AVRE also struck a mine while trying to pass the Crab. The second AVRE towed the Crab out of the lane. This must have been just south of the actual beach since it is known that there were no mines on the beach itself.

Colin Thomson, commanding what had been one of the first troops on the beach, was waiting at the entrance to Lane 2 and providing covering fire. Although many larger calibre guns had been taken out, the beach was still covered by small-arms fire. The Royal Engineers, with no other mechanical and armoured mine-clearing resources available, were clearing the lane by hand, using a Polish Detector provided by the infantry. Thomson was later to describe the man doing this dangerous task, and for whom he was providing covering fire, but whose name he never knew, as 'The bravest man I ever saw'. Lane 2 was the only lane of the three planned for Jig Green to be opened for use, and carried everything off Jig Green. Lane 3, the eastern lane, was too badly affected by the blue clay and other bad ground, and Lane 1, due to the loss of the LCT due to clear it, was not tackled.

Colin Thomson was the first through Lane 2.

> Capt Thomson commanded one of the first troops to land on 'D' Day ... with the assault troops. In spite of the beach defences, he successfully landed and guided his troop up the shore in order to engage the beach defences. In spite of heavy opposition, causing casualties to other tanks in his Squadron, he succeeded in forcing a gap and leading his troop into le Hamel, which, at that time was strongly held by the enemy. His offensive action cleared the town of the enemy and enabled a route to be made through the town down which our infantry were able to pass, and destroyed a 50mm A/Tank gun which had knocked out his leading tank.

The Sherwood Rangers had thus taken le Hamel. Colin Thomson was awarded an immediate MC, in part, for this action. Lieutenant Jimmy McWilliam recalled that 'We cleared the beach up a fisherman's ramp near the gun emplacement which had knocked out Monty Horley. I had infantry on my tank and took prisoners from a slit trench at which point a gendarme appeared and asked what was going on.' On the basis of Padre Skinner's diary notes, at some point before midday, 'Regt. clear now and moving well', indicating that the battle for Jig Green had been won and the regiment had moved inland. Colin Thomson's troop must have led the advance off the beach at about 1100 so that all were clear by 1130.

C Squadron, on the left, was now able to link up with the major part of 231 Brigade on their left which was trying to move west along the coastal railway line to mop up in le Hamel, whilst other elements, as mentioned, were moving south-west inland to reach and take the three villages which were the brigade's secondary objectives:

> Lt Ian Greenway commanded a troop of tanks on D Day in the assault on the beaches at le Hamel in support of 1 Dorsets. On advancing from the beaches, this officer immediately appreciated that the capture of the feature Pt 54, which dominated the area and which was strongly held by the enemy, was vital to our advance. By using ground and clever manoeuvring and the use of the full fire power of his troop, he soon dominated the feature and enabled the infantry to clear the position of enemy at the point of the bayonet.

However, as described, one of the AVREs which had been assigned to Lane 2 was able to support another C Squadron Troop in leaving the beach via Lane 2. The troop and the AVRE, during the afternoon, then tied up with and supported 1st Hampshires in clearing Asnelles-sur-Mer before moving on to destroy the Sanatorium, a prominent building to the west of le Hamel, and belatedly attacking the gun emplacement, number 37, already neutralized by the Essex Yeomanry, but which was still manned, taking some prisoners.

Later in the day, Colin Thomson and his Troop helped 231 Brigade to clear the ground which overlooked the beaches between le Hamel and Arromanches so they could join up with the Americans. Despite the fact that the enemy had fought with great tenacity, 231 Brigade was able gradually to overwhelm their resistance and to secure its objectives. At that point B and C Squadrons were released to move on to their rallying point at Buhot, less than a mile inland. In addition to the three B Squadron and five C Squadron tanks that had sunk, the regiment lost eight tanks once ashore.

About 320 DD tanks were used on D Day. Some 250 were launched to swim varying distances and, of those, about seventy sank. Eisenhower later wrote:

> despite the losses ... suffered on account of heavy seas, on the beaches where they were used they proved conspicuously effective. It is doubtful if the assault forces could have established themselves without these weapons.

If these matters are judged by the inherent danger in operating the tanks at sea, and the other risks taken by the individuals concerned, this action by the DD regiments that swam must surely rank as one of the supreme acts of collective courage of the Second World War.

During the landing there were some further casualties, including the Sherwood Rangers' Commanding Officer, John Anderson, who was wounded as his tank came ashore. During the hold-up on the edge of le Hamel, he dismounted to seek to move things on and was wounded by snipers. Stanley Christopherson took over until Major Michael Laycock got ashore. Lieutenant Colonel Anderson's wounds were so severe that he was unable to take any further part in the war.

A Squadron came in ninety minutes after the first two squadrons. Because the hold-up in le Hamel had been noted, they were directed by the beach-master to land farther to the right [west], and were able to bypass the village and meet up with the rest of the regiment in Buhot. Then, whilst B and C Squadrons laagered and dismantled the amphibious equipment on their tanks to prepare them for further action, Stanley Christopherson went forward to find 2nd Devons, the reserve battalion of 231 Brigade, who had also found an alternative landing point to the east, to support them in capturing Ryes, which fell without much opposition, and moved back to Buhot.

A Squadron's next task, as planned, was to support 2nd Essex Regiment (The Pompadours) in taking the high ground outside Bayeux, and Bayeux itself. The Essex were a battalion of 56 Brigade, 50th Division's follow-up brigade, which was now also ashore. Stanley Christopherson therefore needed to find and tie up with them. It must have come as something of a surprise to them when he arrived on a horse which he had found already saddled and liberated, as a better means of transport for the purpose, than his tank. A Squadron then supported 2nd Essex in taking the high ground north of the town and laagered with them for the night.

Padre Skinner wrote:

> Caught up with the Regiment 2 miles north Bayeux, west Sommervieu. One Squadron had taken Sommervieu while other two Squadrons approaching outskirts of Bayeux shooting two companies of infantry into the suburbs and railway station. Command tanks leaguered in Sommervieu. 40 casualties to date, including 'missing' [later corrected to 8 KIA and 20 Wounded].

Major Stanley Christopherson notes that:

> Bayeux could have been attacked and captured that night. The Essex CO preferred to move in at first light. [By last light] All units of 50th Division were in exact positions as planned. After replenishment of the tanks and various 'O Groups' for the next day's battles most of us managed a few hours' sleep.

Chapter 33

Battle for Normandy

June–August 1944

Point 103

A t first light next day A Squadron moved alongside the leading company of 2nd Essex. Stanley Christopherson leant down from his turret and said to the company commander 'Would you like us to lead then?' 'Oh yes please!' Thus a precedent was set for the Sherwood Rangers which endured on a recurring basis for the rest of the campaign. They led the battalion into the town at first light to find that the enemy had almost entirely withdrawn during the night. Bayeux was the first town liberated by the Allies.

Now 8 Armoured Brigade advanced south, its axis to the east of Bayeux, on a line of Meuvaines-Audrieu, still in support of 50th Division. Villers Bocage was their objective but the regiment was ordered to divert to the south-east and take an area of high ground called Point 103, overlooking Tilly-sur-Seulles Fontenay-le-Pesnel and St Pierre, lying in the shallow valley below. There they came face to face with the Panzer Lehr Division under the skilful and committed command of Donny Player's 'frightful type of jovial bounder', General Bayerlein.

Between 8 and 12 June the regiment supported units of 50th Division in the struggle to control the valley and the three villages in that part of it. They became intermingled with the enemy in close fighting, during which several tanks were knocked out, and a number of key members of the regiment were killed or wounded, including Keith Douglas who was killed. At one point they seemed to have secured Fontenay, but it was not to last. During this fighting Captain Neville Fearn did particularly well, breaking up two of Panzer Lehr's counter-attacks without infantry support, the first by clever use of ground and speed, so that he could attack from the flank. As a result, the counter-attack was stopped and casualties inflicted on the enemy tanks and infantry. The second was on the same night, when his troop fought throughout the hours of darkness and was instrumental in breaking up another counter-attack against St Pierre.

On 11 June Lieutenant Ian Greenway's troop was leading his squadron through St Pierre in support of 7th Durham LI. An enemy OP was located which was bringing down fire on infantry positions. His tank knocked out the OP and advanced still further through very enclosed country so that he established himself

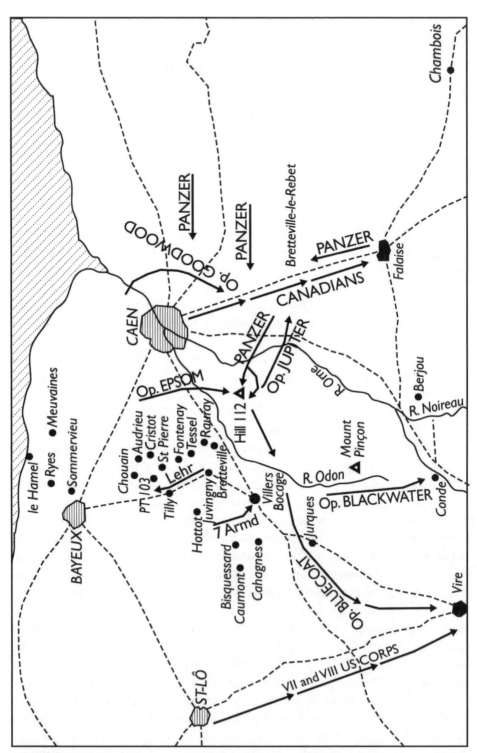

Map 18: Battle for Normandy.

in such a position that he was able to direct the fire of the supporting artillery on enemy positions as he identified them. He remained in the position throughout the day in spite of intense enemy fire until his tank was eventually set on fire by an enemy SP gun. In spite of enemy opposition he led the whole of his crew to safety. For this action and for D Day he was awarded an immediate MC.

Later that fateful day the precarious nature of the regiment's tenure was all too starkly demonstrated when RHQ, located in a farmyard in St Pierre, received a direct hit from an artillery shell, killing Michael Laycock and George Jones, the Adjutant. The Intelligence Officer was also killed, and Patrick McCraith, Recce Troop Leader, who had just arrived up the centre line, was wounded. With little time to recover, Stanley Christopherson took over command, with Stephen Mitchell MC standing aside to be his second-in-command.

Fiftieth Division was now counter-attacked with great determination by Panzer Lehr and driven back onto the high ground around Pt 103 and the regiment had to leave many of their dead, including their deceased commanding officer, buried in territory held by the enemy. This was one of the few backward steps forced on them in the entire war. Even 8 Armoured Brigade HQ came under fire, and both Cracroft, the brigade commander, and Lawrence Biddle, still brigade major, were wounded.

On the evening of 12 June the regiment was withdrawn to the Bayeux area for two days to replenish and re-equip, a welcome respite from an exceedingly unpleasant initiation into fighting in the bocage. Casualties between 7 and 12 June were six officers and three ORs killed with six officers and twenty-two ORs wounded, a total of thirty-seven. These figures should be judged against the total number of tank crew in the regiment, where the majority of casualties fell, which was about 300.

Stanley Christopherson later wrote of Michael Laycock:

> His manner was abrupt and sometimes rude and his temper, which he often lost, was fiendish and this, together with his dark and swarthy complexion, caused him to be nicknamed 'Black Michael' by men in the Regiment. But beneath this superficial exterior he had a great, kind heart and a simple, serious and most lovable nature. He had the courage of a lion and would never issue an unpleasant order in battle which he himself would not be prepared to carry out.

During this period of rest Stanley Christopherson was confirmed in command of the regiment. 'Command', however, had, all of a sudden, become an unenviable task in the climate that now prevailed. Such was the desperation to force a breakout that huge downward pressure was applied on commanders at all levels to succeed. Any failure to be seen to measure up was likely to result in dismissal. Even very distinguished regular commanding officers, some with several medals for gallantry only recently won, were summarily sacked during this period. However, this never seemed to come close to happening to Stanley Christopherson, incredibly so, since he was the very antithesis of the sort of intense hard driving commanding officer that regular commanders seemed to favour, and worse still, was both an amateur and a yeomanry officer. Christopherson was able, not merely to overcome these perceived disadvantages, but to win sixteen battle honours whilst in command. This is believed to be a record for a CO's tour of command.

Furthermore, the regiment was never to be subjected, during his tour, to the accusation of battle-weariness that was placed at the door of almost every other unit and formation that had fought in the desert campaign. Indeed, it gained a unique reputation, and was often to be asked for by name by battalions about to go into action.

Perhaps the best starting point for an assessment of Stanley Christopherson at the start of a remarkable tour in command, which outlasted the war, is the description of both Christopherson and the regiment provided by Major Anthony Cotterell who, in his capacity as a war staff writer for the Army Bureau of Current Affairs, attended Christopherson's first O Group.

> The CO of the Regiment explained the situation to me from his maps which were set up on some ammunition boxes in the three-ton lorry which he was using as an office. He was a creditably bemedalled young man with a twinkling personality and an attractive air of unassuming expertness. The expertness was not surprising because his Regiment had been pretty constantly in action for several years and the atmosphere of professionalism extended through all ranks.

His most immediately apparent qualities did not constitute a promising starting point, given the times, since they were charm, good nature and enthusiasm. A man for whom conversation full of laughter and a relaxed and easy style was always a part, he fostered and enjoyed a wide range of friendships. His approachability created an easy-going atmosphere within the regiment, enabling him to get across his ideas on how an armoured regiment should be fought, about which he was deadly serious. Perhaps it also made men want to fight for him and do their best. However, these qualities alone would not have been enough, and there was indeed more. He was a brave man, firstly in the sense that he possessed physical courage in battle which he had demonstrated so many times in the desert. The other sense in which he had courage was in his seeming ability to endure repeated periods of combat without it wearing him down. This is described as the insidious dripping of a tap. It is a rare quality, even amongst the bravest of men, and a vital one in a commanding officer. One of the regiment's great strengths was its tactical awareness and ability to adapt to changing situations. He created the climate which enabled good new ideas to be heard and adopted, no matter who had thought of them.

Both the regiment and its CO had much to absorb. They had already learnt, from the first few days in action, that the Normandy countryside could hardly be more hostile to the attacker. The bocage consisted of a combination of small fields, tall hedges set on top of banks, sunken lanes and small villages. Armour could not use the natural shape of the ground to take up hull-down positions, as it had in the desert, because the banks and narrow sunken lanes were impassable to tanks and obstructed their fields of fire when they did so. If they took up positions with adequate fields of fire and observation, they were invariably too exposed.

Another factor was the short range of engagements so that the German *Panzerfaust*, the handheld anti-tank weapon, could be used to devastating effect against armour. Snipers could be placed where they could, and did, shoot tank commanders in considerable numbers. This was because commanders could not fight closed down since the tanks were then too blind. They were too valuable to lose.

The tanks that the regiment met were, firstly, the Tiger with its massive armour and 88mm gun, but fortunately both ponderous in all it did and only relatively rarely seen. Secondly, the more often encountered Panther, with a 75mm gun and better armour than the Sherman, and, thirdly, the prolific Mark IV. Of those it was only the Mark IV for which the Sherman was a match. There was still the 88mm anti-tank gun which had lost none of its venom by being transferred to a new theatre, and indeed was now often found mounted on an armoured hull as a ground-hugging self-propelled gun.

The short range of most engagements meant the Germans were not able to exploit the significant overall superiority of their tanks, compared with those of the Allies. Furthermore, the comparatively short barrel of the Sherman's 75, its speed of traverse, and significantly faster rate of fire, compared with that of the German's tanks gave it some advantages at close range that would not have existed at longer ranges. Above all, since the Allies were now some ten miles inland, the extent to which terrain favoured the defender would make it almost impossible for the outnumbered Germans to reverse the roles and advance, as they would have to do, to push the Allies back into the sea.

The old rules of 'stay in the tank' and avoid showing your thinly armoured flank to the enemy still applied, nonetheless, it was clear that new tactics needed to be adopted if the regiment was to impose its will on the enemy. Work on these now began, adapting the skill of stalking the enemy, developed in the desert, to the present situation; some commanders, particularly Sergeant George Dring, began stalking enemy tanks on foot along the close cover of the hedges and then, by using the tele-handset, guiding the tank into position for the kill. Commanders took to setting their helmet and goggles on the machine-gun bracket on the turret as a deception. Even in the desert the officers wore berets like their men and not service-dress hats. They also used their infantry to protect them against the *Panzerfaust*.

Perhaps the most critical change of all made to the way the regiment operated was that it became mandatory to lay down heavy suppressive fire before any forward movement. This applied to tanks as well as artillery. All likely enemy positions and OPs were targeted. Although not new, and a tactic recognized by many, there was a natural tendency amongst tank crews in other regiments to give it only lip service to minimize the arduous and lengthy task of bombing up the tank during the short summer nights. Exhausted crews found this an unappealing prospect after an endless summer's day in action.

Philip Foster wrote:

> Those who have operated in Shermans know only too well what an awkward task it is to replace rounds into the side magazines. It is necessary to distort oneself into all imaginable shapes and angles in order to reach them, while the rest of the crew pass the shells from the ground through the turret into the bowels of the hull. I was invariably barking my hands on the multitudes of rough metal edges, which accordingly sharpened the edge of my temper.

The brief hours of darkness were already crowded with re-fuelling, maintenance, O Groups and personal administration. Better not to fire too much ammunition and save oneself from one more drain on time desperately needed for rest. Finally, good crew skills and tactics, as described by Stanley Christopherson earlier, played a full part.

The command structure of the regiment was now: Commanding Officer – Lieutenant Colonel Stanley Christopherson MC; Second-in-Command – Major Stephen Mitchell MC; Adjutant – Captain Terry Leinster; A Squadron – Major John Semken; B Squadron – Major John Hanson-Lawson; C Squadron – Major Peter Seleri; HQ Squadron – Major Roger Sutton-Nelthorpe; Recce Troop – Captain Ian McKay.

Villers Bocage

On 16 June the regiment was back in the line, supporting 69 Brigade of 50th Division. Until now 50th Division's objective had been Villers Bocage, but it had been unable to break through. Instead, whilst the regiment had been out of the line, 7th Armoured Division, now ashore, had been ordered to complete the task, and moved through 50th Division as it swept round to the right to approach Villers Bocage from the west. After heavy fighting, 7th Armoured Division withdrew with the honours no more than even.

Operation EPSOM

Progress to date was deemed to have been a great success, in that the landings had been achieved, and were secure, whilst six German divisions had been destroyed, and two others badly depleted in the process. However, the failure of the Allies to secure as deep a penetration as had been originally hoped for, brought about a change in approach. This change was from a battle based on infantry divisions supported by armour to a major armoured confrontation, one of the largest tank battles the world has ever seen. This meant that the battle for Normandy became a single huge co-ordinated struggle by tanks.

Montgomery had three armoured divisions ashore, and the Germans had six in Normandy, two having been re-deployed from Russia. From now on the build-up of armoured divisions on both sides would be relentless. When the Falaise pocket was closed, there would be no fewer than thirteen Allied armoured divisions in action against twelve German.

The role of the infantry divisions changed to holding their sectors whilst applying constant southward pressure, thus creating a stable platform. The armoured divisions on both sides then manoeuvred to and fro across the whole front, striking, parrying and counter-attacking each other, seeking the weak spots and the decisive breakthrough or killing zone. The first of these armoured attacks was Operation EPSOM which involved the newly-landed VIII Corps, consisting of two infantry divisions, 15th (Scottish) and 43rd (Wessex), and two armoured divisions, Guards and 11th. It was to be centred on a single divisional front, immediately on what had been 50th Division's left boundary, and supported by pressure along the whole front. The objective was to achieve an anti-clockwise encirclement of Caen and cut the Caen-Falaise road at Bretteville-le-Rebet.

As mentioned 50th Division had been forced back to an approximate line just north of Pt 103-Cristot, and its positions were taken over by 49th (West Riding) Division with 8 Armoured Brigade in support and therefore fighting over ground now familiar to it. The division's initial task was to retake the ground to the north of Fontenay-le-Pesnel, including St Pierre, as a prelude to EPSOM. Neither side had total control over this ground. Having secured that ground, 49th Division would then cover the right flank of the main attack by taking Fontenay before striking south to Tessel and Rauray on the left, and Vendes and Bretteville on the right.

Between 17 and 20 June the regiment supported 147 Brigade in some fierce fighting over the disputed ground, already strewn with the dead of both sides, to secure the start line for the main offensive. Success in this task came with the inevitable casualties and some alarms, in particular when one of the battalions being supported failed to hold steady under a heavy air-burst attack on the woods known as le Parc de Boislonde, south-west of Cristot. This left the regiment temporarily without protection. Sergeant Joseph Butler, a veteran of the entire North African campaign, was one of those left exposed, but he held his position under strong fire. He then heavily engaged the enemy when they began to attack. His fire broke up the counter-attack and restored the position.

There was now a delay due to the very bad weather that destroyed the Mulberry Harbour incorrectly constructed by the Americans.

Fontenay-le-Pesnil

The attack on Fontenay-le-Pesnil finally commenced, as part of the main offensive, at first light on 25 June, following an intense artillery barrage which had opened at 0300. As it happened, the attack was just in time to pre-empt an enemy armoured offensive at almost the same point, intended to drive the Allies back into the sea, and so was opposed heavily. The division's initial attack was planned as a three-phase operation: Phase 1 was to secure Fontenay itself; Phase 2 the high ground immediately to the south of Fontenay; and Phase 3 to secure the line of the Venres-Rauray road, some 2,500 yards further south.

The regiment was supporting 147 Brigade, on the left once more, and the rest of 8 Armoured Brigade was supporting 146 Brigade on the right. Rain was falling incessantly and the valley was shrouded in mist; visibility at times was nil. The division attacked down the forward slope towards Fontenay. As it came under direct fire, the infantry went to ground, and the fighting became confused and intense. Contact between armour and infantry was difficult; this was a constant problem. Fierce fighting went on all day but by last light 147 Brigade's attack had ground to a halt short of Fontenay. However, 146 Brigade had done better, capturing their objectives in Fontenay and Tessel Wood.

During this fighting Padre Skinner was wounded by shrapnel and invalided back to the UK. This was a catastrophe because this very special man had taken it upon himself to ensure that no Sherwood Ranger was posted missing and all received a proper burial. In addition, he alone cleared the knocked-out tanks of those who had died inside, to ensure that none but he knew that harrowing sight. In extremis he completed his tally by counting the pelvic bones, vomited and moved on. The positive impact that he had on regimental morale was beyond price. He was ten years older than the CO and twenty older than the youngest. The pastoral care he was able to provide to every single person was exceptional. He recovered and returned after about a month, discharging himself from hospital to do so. The only members of the regiment posted missing in the entire campaign were during his absence. The regiment wrapped its arms around him when he returned, and never let him out of its sight again.

At 2130 a further battalion attack, supported by C Squadron, was launched from Point 102, almost the same point as the initial attack had started that morning. The attack started in the dusk and continued into the night. Despite the risk inherent in night operations, a firm foothold was secured in the village. The next day this was extended bit by bit until, by the evening of 26 June, the entire village, including the St Nicholas Farm feature the key position immediately to the south of it, had fallen, thus completing the first two phases. During the action Sergeant Robert Sanders took out several machine-gun positions on the first day. On the second day, he helped the infantry secure St Nicholas Farm, before pushing on through its orchard to account for the enemy rearguard transport.

He was awarded an immediate MM. Lieutenant Johnny Mann was commanding the leading troop on that attack and his tenacity and determination to press home the attack, combined with the extremely close support he gave to the infantry, enabled his squadron to secure all but the south-eastern fringe of the village by midnight. Showing great leadership he remained, in spite of the darkness, in support of the infantry and after they had been withdrawn, entirely without them, in a most difficult and exposed forward position until ordered to withdraw at 0700. The following morning, after only two hours' sleep, he again attacked with the infantry and brought about the final capture of the village. Three hours later he was engaged in an unsuccessful attack on St Nicholas Farm south of the village. Finally, in the afternoon, he secured the farm and the surrounding area without any assistance from the infantry and earned an immediate MC. Colin Thomson was also prominent in defeating an enemy counter-attack at one key moment.

Rauray

The regiment was now ordered to complete Phase 3, the 2,500-yard advance from Fontenay to Rauray. Infantry were to advance with the tanks for the first thousand yards and dig in, the regiment then continuing alone. Having fought well, the infantry were exhausted. Continuously in action since first light the day before, they had suffered considerable casualties and so were relieved from this phase. H hour was fixed for 1730, and an artillery barrage onto suspected enemy positions was laid on. The attack got off to a disconcerting start. As John Semken led A Squadron through Fontenay to the start line, he suddenly confronted a Tiger tank, the first the regiment had encountered, face-to-face in the narrow village street. Much to his relief, he knocked it out in a tank duel at almost point-blank range during which the Sherman got the vital first shot away which hit, and the Tiger became shrouded in smoke from the Sherman's rapid follow up accurate gunfire. Since John Semken had just passed by RHQ, there was relief all round.

C Squadron led initially and then A Squadron passed through. The line of their attack ran parallel and to the west of the Fontenay-Rauray road, immediately behind where the monument to 49th Division stands today. The ground was much more open and favoured armour, and therefore gave the regiment a much-needed opportunity to display its skills. The first stage of the action was a long-range shooting duel between the regiment and elements of 12th SS Panzer Division *Hitlerjugend*, positioned mainly to the left of centre, which went decisively to the regiment. The sun had finally put in an appearance, and was conveniently now setting behind the regiment, reflecting off the surfaces of the enemy armour and betraying their positions. During the action, a lone Panther sought to withdraw from right to left across the regiment's front, but was engaged by virtually every tank in A Squadron for its trouble, and destroyed. The Panther expelled fumes when moving at speed which could be ignited by enemy fire. A Squadron then attacked across the open ground towards Rauray. Due to lack of infantry support, the regiment, having reached the outskirts of the village, could not secure Rauray and withdrew, handing over to a battalion that later came up and dug in on the northern edge of the village.

This had been the most decisive and successful tank-on-tank action for the regiment so far in the campaign. They had knocked out approximately thirteen tanks, of which Sergeant George Dring in his Firefly (named *Akilla* by his crew, a name they deemed more appropriate than the intended *Achilles*) claimed four, and for which he received a Bar to his MM, downgraded from a DCM, nevertheless making him one of the highest-decorated soldiers of the war. The regiment had lost two tanks in return. The regiment accords Sergeant Dring the distinction of having knocked out more tanks than anyone else. He was one of a select group of British 'aces', possessing, to a rare degree, a sixth sense on the battlefield coupled with an eye for ground learnt in the hunting field, and a rare coolness, which gave him an edge. Johnny Mann was once again prominent in this phase.

John Semken earned an immediate MC for the skill with which he handled A Squadron. He was exceptionally bright, qualifying as a lawyer and destined to enjoy a successful career in the Civil Service, culminating in the award of a CB. Being bright can be a disadvantage for someone fighting the dirty end of a ferocious war, but it gave him an instinctive understanding of tactics and the eloquence to pass on what he understood to his tank crews who credited him with achieving a better rate of survival for them as a result. He was hottest of all on using heavy suppressive fire, as he had just demonstrated, which meant that most of his squadron's kills went unattributed below squadron level. It should perhaps be added that he led a series of battlefield tours in later years which were brilliant due to his clarity and ability to explain how armoured regiments function in action. The later ones were particularly memorable because by then his eyesight had reached the point where he could no longer read normal print and were therefore delivered over several days without a note. It is fair to say that what he was able to impart forms a thread throughout this account.

The next morning, B Squadron renewed the attack on Rauray. This time the advantage lay with the enemy. Sergeant Birch was the leading tank of the centre troop of the squadron. The enemy was encountered at 1000 hours and a sharp battle took place, during which the three tanks of the right troop of the squadron were destroyed and set on fire by a Tiger. Birch edged his way forward, pinpointed the Tiger, and engaged it with fire, although only the top of its turret could be seen. After his second shot, the tank withdrew, thus allowing the squadron, well supported by their infantry, to re-occupy Rauray. B Squadron suffered heavy casualties, but captured several tanks, including the first undamaged Tiger taken in battle in Normandy. Sergeant Birch was awarded an immediate MM.

Sporadic but intense fighting continued for several days as the division sought to protect the right flank of the main right hook across the Odon, in which the regiment supported various units in local attacks. During this, Sergeant Doug Nelson, a Recce Troop section leader, who had done well earlier in June when he had accounted for an anti-tank gun that had knocked out another tank, was himself knocked out. In the aftermath, he rescued both his crew and that of another disabled tank whilst under fire, for which he earned an immediate MM.

Meanwhile, on the regiment's left, Operation EPSOM, the right hook, was partially successful, and the armour secured Hill 112, east of the Odon. However, this created a significant salient which was heavily counter-attacked twice at the end of June by the Germans, on Hitler's direct instructions, using the five panzer divisions they had intended to use in their own attack at the outset of the battle. On receiving those orders, von Rundstedt was asked by Keitel, who was on Hitler's staff, 'What shall we do?' 'Make peace, you idiots,' he replied. It was not to be.

Intense fighting continued in the area of Hill 112. However, on 4 July, the regiment was withdrawn north, to the area of Chouain, south of Bayeux, for much-needed rest and recuperation. B Squadron had suffered particularly badly, having lost all but two of its officers, and all but seven of its tanks. The regiment was exhausted, and on arriving in laager 'slept the clock round and then shaved off the stubble'. The petrol and ammunition lorries had landed on the first day and, now, the remaining administrative vehicles forming B Echelon arrived, having just landed; the regiment was united for the first time since embarkation five weeks before.

Major Makins, from the Royals, took over A Squadron, to release John Semken to his original task as Technical Adjutant and, better still, Major Michael Gold returned to command B Squadron, Major Hanson Lawson, regrettably, having been wounded at Fontenay. Micky Gold found the squadron sadly depleted. Losses of both commanders and crew arising from the heavy tank battles were now becoming a matter for concern. Many had irreplaceable experience of armoured warfare. The tanks could be replaced, but not the crews.

It helps to put the intensity of the armoured fighting in North-West Europe into some kind of perspective, to understand that during the period June 1944 to May 1945 approximately 1,200 battlefield replacement tanks were supplied through the Armoured Delivery Regiment to 8 Armoured Brigade, which had a war establishment of less than 200 tanks.

The Sherwood Rangers' casualties for Fontenay, Rauray, and their role on the flank of Operation EPSOM, included two officers and twenty ORs killed and seven officers and thirty ORs wounded.

Operation MAORI II

On 11 July, after five days' rest, the regiment was again in action. The intense tank battles arising from German counter-attacks in the area of Hill 112 had continued throughout the period that the regiment had been resting, causing the Germans to be severely defeated with heavy losses. This effort, coupled with other operations by the British farther east, had at last, on 10 July, brought about the fall of Caen.

Operation EPSOM was now to be succeeded by Operation JUPITER, a renewed attempt to break out in the area of Hill 112, seize crossings over the Orne and cut the Caen-Falaise road. The regiment was to support 50th Division once more, this time for Operation MAORI II. Fiftieth Division was fighting with 49th Division on the left, and the boundary between Second British Army and First US Army on their right. They gave 8 Armoured Brigade, and especially the regiment, a warm welcome, saying quite firmly that they had given them better support than other armour with which they had fought. The respect was mutual, their commander, Major General Graham, being as popular with the regiment as he was with his division.

Hottot

The task was an attack on Hottot, about four miles west of Rauray, to straighten the line. It was also part of operations, across the whole front, to support Operation JUPITER. The divisional objective was the line of the Juvingny-Hottot-Landes road and the high ground 500 yards to the south. The regiment moved up to an assembly area at Folliot on 10 July and then onto the start line during the night, encountering a lot of congestion on the roads, and arriving just before the attack was to start at first light. The ground was typical bocage, almost impenetrable to tanks; parts of it were wooded.

This was another hard two-day-long battle, B and A Squadrons once again supporting 231 Brigade; C Squadron was supporting 70 Brigade of 49th Division on the left, in what was initially a reserve role. So pressed were the infantry that the tanks stayed in the line through the nights as well. At the end of the action, the regiment was withdrawn to Chouain once more. In the fighting for Hottot the regiment knocked out seven enemy tanks, but lost four of their own. Major Makins was killed in his first action, putting John Semken back in command of A Squadron. Other casualties were two ORs killed and three officers and fifteen ORs wounded. Whilst out of the line, the regiment worked hard on cadres to replace the loss of skills they had suffered through their heavy casualties.

Although 50th Division broadly achieved its local objectives no breakthrough was secured around Hill 112. Something new was required. The plan had always been that the British and Canadians would draw the main enemy effort, thus forming the hinge on which the Americans could break out in the west. The Americans believed that they would be in a position to make the attack southwards in the west by mid-July and so it was planned that Second British Army in the east would attack southwards on a broad front, to keep the main enemy concentration committed against them. VIII Corps, consisting of three British armoured divisions east of Caen, would force a break-out of their own to threaten the Seine basin, thus completing the encirclement from the north. VIII Corps' operation was named GOODWOOD.

There were now thirty Allied divisions in theatre, divided equally between the United States and British/Canadians. This triggered a re-organization of Second Army into three corps with 8 Armoured Brigade coming under command XXX Corps, and their old friend Lieutenant General Brian Horrocks.

The fighting strength of Seventh German Army was estimated at no higher than sixteen divisions which the Germans clearly thought inadequate, as they now sought to reinforce it with fresh divisions from their Fifteenth Army, east of the Seine.

Operation GOODWOOD

On 17 July, as part of the re-positioning taking place as a prelude to the new offensive, the regiment moved to Caumont, a few miles west of Hottot to relieve a brigade of 2nd US Armored Division. These moves represented an adjustment to the inter-army boundary between First US and Second British Armies. The new area, yet to be fought over, was unspoiled, the line only thinly held with no more than a recce regiment and an infantry battalion, 12th KRRC, to the regiment's front as it settled into its hides.

On 18 July Second British and First Canadian Armies together attacked south-east with three corps in an operation with the Caen-Falaise road as its axis and the aim of enlarging the bridgehead in the area of Hill 112 to a point well eastward of the Orne. Good progress was also made initially east of Caen by VIII Corps' armoured divisions, in Operation GOODWOOD, until clouded skies began hampering the air support. This in turn gave an advantage to the Germans, which they used to bring the British armoured attack to a halt, using a numerically inferior, but superbly deployed anti-tank screen, consisting of tanks and anti-tank guns.

Operation GOODWOOD eventually failed in the sense that a breakthrough was not achieved, but arguably succeeded because it prevented the Germans from executing their own plan, which was to transfer the weight of their armour, at least two divisions, to attack the weakly-held inter-British/US army boundary at Caumont, and drive north for the coast right through 8 Armoured Brigade's positions and which could have delayed the American breakout. Most important of all it saved 8 Armoured and the Sherwood Rangers from a very unpleasant experience.

On 18 July the brigade was informed that 24th Lancers would be disbanded, two complete troops coming to strengthen B Squadron. They chose the regiment because 'it wasn't as full of bull as some of the armoured units'. This was part of a more widespread re-organization of the forces now in theatre, an inevitable consequence of the heavy losses suffered by many units in the fighting since D

Day. From now onwards Allied forces in Europe would cease enlarging. Whilst the US still had fresh formations not yet in theatre that was not the case for the other Allies. Overall, from this point, numbers would shrink as attrition took its toll. In the brigade 24th Lancers were replaced by 13th/18th Hussars.

Towards the end of July, 43rd (Wessex) Division, the Wessex Wyverns, moved into the same sector as that occupied by 8 Armoured Brigade, which was to support them. The division had been moved to the Caumont sector as part of the preparations for operations in support of the American breakout delayed a week by rain. Destined to become well known to the Rangers, the division was commanded by Major General Ivor Thomas, 'a small, fiery, very determined and grim gunner without a spark of humour'. The regiment nicknamed him 'von Thoma' after the German general captured during Alamein.

On 25 July, on the regiment's right, VII US Corps struck south from St Lo, followed the next day by VIII US Corps. After an initial assault by infantry, which involved some fierce fighting, the American armour, with little German armour on their front, broke through and swept south to Coutances, cutting the German escape route down the coast of Normandy and bringing chaos to the German defences west of the Vire. Simultaneously the Canadians again attacked from Caen down the Falaise road.

The Wyverns' role was to attack south within their boundaries to support this wide-ranging operation, their attack preceded by sustained heavy bombing attack by the RAF, commenced five days later on 30 July. The regiment supported 130 Brigade, with the initial objective Bricquessard, where A Squadron, in particular Lieutenant David Render's troop, knocked out one *Panzerfaust* and captured a new type of infantry anti-tank weapon, a type of Bazooka called a *Panzerschreck*, the first such weapon it had encountered. The troop, following some improvised mine clearing by its leader, went on to take out an entire enemy platoon.

Sergeant Butler, after a good show at Hottot, was also in action. His tank received a direct hit from a very heavy mortar and one of the crew inside was wounded. The aerial and base were shot away but, in spite of extremely heavy enemy fire from mortars and machine guns, he re-organized his troop, improvised an aerial base and was back in action within a few minutes. For the combination of Hottot and this action he received an MM.

On 31 July the regiment supported the division in a further advance south against relatively light opposition and took the division's objective, Cahagnes. The main difficulties encountered during the first two days was the bocage country, which was particularly impenetrable to tanks in this area. Another was that the whole area was dominated by a wooded feature to the south, called Mont Pinçon, the other key feature on Second Army's front, apart from Hill 112. It gave the Germans command of the country for miles around, enabling them to bring viciously accurate indirect fire to bear as the division came in range of it in the coming days.

On 1 August A Squadron came under command of 214 Brigade to make an advance of about 7,000 yards south of Bois du Homme, which they achieved by evening, Sergeant Dring destroying one Tiger and capturing two others when they became bogged down.

Operation BLUECOAT

It now became clear that the main effort, the Canadian attempt to force their way down the Caen-Falaise road, had been stopped by no fewer than four Panzer divisions. The Canadians had even been driven back 1,000 yards at one point. Unfair comparisons were levelled at Montgomery by the Americans with their massive gains compared to the apparently modest achievements of Operation GOODWOOD and this current operation.

Montgomery recognized that his plan had worked and he had attracted a very large percentage of the enemy's armour onto his original main axis. He therefore switched his main effort to the west onto Second Army, now concentrated between the Canadians on the left and the Americans on the right, and ordered six divisions to strike south-west to Vire, also one of the Americans' objectives; their axis was to run south-westerly to by-pass the heavy concentration of armour on the Canadians' front.

This was Operation BLUECOAT, and 43rd Division was one of the divisions selected for the task. Orders for BLUECOAT were received on the evening of 1 August. The division's task was to press south towards Mont Pinçon, so allowing 11th Armoured, 50th and 3rd Divisions, the latter supported by 4 Armoured Brigade, to pass behind them on the south-western axis to Vire. The regiment was to support 130 Brigade. Between 1 and 6 August it fought its way south with very little rest, taking the villages of Jurques, la Bigne, and Ondefontaine, the latter on the slopes of Mont Pinçon.

Operation BLACKWATER

On 6 August 43rd Division received orders for Operation BLACKWATER, a three-divisional operation to take Conde-sur-Noireau, fifteen miles farther south, and east of Vire. The switch of the objective away from Vire was due to it having fallen to the Americans and 3rd Division the day before. Because 43rd Division now had 11th Armoured Division, 3rd and 50th Divisions on its right and 59th and 53rd Divisions on its left, it was effectively in the centre of Second Army's line. Between the 6th and 15th the Wyverns, supported by 8 Armoured Brigade, continued to fight on south. During this phase Mont Pinçon was taken by 13th/18th Hussars. On 7 August the regiment, shattered after six nights without sleep, was withdrawn from the line for four days of much-needed rest. The advance of nine miles, south from Caumont to this point, had cost two officers and nine ORs killed and three officers, including Major Peter Selerie, OC C Squadron, and twenty-two ORs wounded. Six tanks had been lost, of which three would fight again.

Meanwhile the Americans had broken into Brittany, and had passed Patton's Third US Army through them. Patton's orders were to turn and drive eastwards, with the north bank of the Loire as his right boundary. The objective was Paris. By 9 August they were in le Mans. The risk to the Allies was that Patton's lines of re-supply had to pass through the Atlantic coastal town of Avranches. The enemy understood this, so under direct orders from Hitler, the Germans struck westerly on Mortain, in a counter-attack codenamed Operation LUTTICH, with the objective of breaking through and re-capturing Avranches. Five Panzer and two infantry divisions were used, most of which were only newly-arrived from Fifteenth Army east of the Seine, but much depleted after a horrific journey carried out under continuous attack from the air.

By 7 August the counter-attack had been ruthlessly defeated short of Mortain by the Americans, using a combination of nearly 300 sorties from ground-attack fighters, and three divisions moved with speed from the north, to support the single US division on which the initial blow had fallen.

Noireau Crossing

The Sherwood Rangers were back in the line on 12 August, 43rd Division still forcing its way south. On 14 August Sergeant Leslie Cribben earned a particularly fine immediate MM, downgraded from a DCM, reconnoitring crossings over the River Noireau. He was in command of a section of the Recce Troop, attached to C Squadron, and was to find out whether a bridge across the river was still intact.

To reach the river, the section had to pass through country strongly held by enemy armed with anti-armour weapons. He got within 300 yards of the crossing but could go no farther by tank because the road was mined; he also saw the crossing was held by about a company of infantry. Cribben decided to carry out a foot recce with one other man; they each took a Bren gun. After100 yards they were engaged by a machine gun from the high ground beyond the river crossing and by snipers from the thick wood on the left of the road. They went to ground, moved under cover to a position of observation and saw the enemy trying to withdraw a 50mm anti-tank gun across the bridge. Both men engaged the party and, as a result killed both horses towing the gun and wounded practically half the infantry, who were in platoon strength. They could not stop the bridge from being blown, but they did prevent the enemy from getting the gun across before doing so. Both men withdrew to their tank, under fire and reported back to the squadron with full details of the crossing point.

On 15 August preparations were made for crossing the River Noireau, five miles north of Conde, with the village of Berjou just beyond as the objective, itself still held by the enemy.

Berjou

The river was set in a steep valley with Berjou having to be approached up a four-mile-long mountainous, heavily-wooded incline. The regiment was supporting 214 Brigade, which was to take Berjou and create a bridgehead out of which the division could attack onwards. B Squadron was supporting 1st Worcesters on the right and C Squadron, now commanded by Captain Jack Holman, 5th Duke of Cornwall's LI on the left. It is hard to imagine country less suitable for tanks. Moreover, the whole area was dominated by the high ground adjacent to Berjou, held by the enemy, from which they were able to bring accurate fire to bear throughout the operation.

Crossings were secured over the Noireau during the night of the 15th/16th. Once the infantry had formed a small bridgehead, and while Sappers were clearing the mines and making a ford for the tanks on 5th DCLI's axis, Jack Holman led an infantry patrol for three miles to find a way up the exceedingly long and difficult incline onto the high ground. In spite of mortar fire and snipers and every conceivable kind of mine, he found one and, as dawn broke, C Squadron crossed the river, carrying the DCLI on their tanks, and started the long climb.

They had to fight their way up a single and exceedingly steep track with thick woods on either side. The track had not been cleared of mines or infantry and the squadron was continually attacked by bazookas and crew commanders shot at by snipers. Holman had to spend much of the time on foot to find a way up for the squadron. In spite of having seven tanks knocked out by bazookas, the squadron pressed on, destroying five machine-gun nests on the way, until it reached the top, when Jack Holman was able to extend what remained of his squadron into fire positions to cover the bridgehead. The troop that bore the brunt of the fighting was that of Lieutenant Stuart Hills; despite having become separated from the infantry they were supporting, they finally reached the top. They had been fighting since dawn, and the light was now fading.

C Squadron remained in position until after darkness had fallen when the infantry arrived to clear the village, but not before the squadron had driven off an enemy infantry counter-attack.

Meanwhile B Squadron, commanded by Major Micky Gold, was supporting 1st Worcesters, who had simultaneously secured a second small bridgehead over the Noireau on the right of the line. The battalion's axis for the attack on Berjou ran through the wooded country already decribed. As a result of this, and mortar and machine-gun fire coming over the ridge, the squadron became separated from the infantry who were compelled to take cover.

Micky Gold detached one troop to cover the infantry advance with the remainder of his squadron continuing the advance. On many occasions they were attacked by bazookas and crew commanders fired upon by snipers but, in spite of casualties to crew commanders and damage caused to the tanks by bazookas, the squadron continued the advance, and attacked a battalion of German infantry on the Berjou ridge. His squadron surrounded the battalion on which he inflicted severe casualties. The remainder gave themselves up to the infantry when they arrived on the scene; 214 Brigade then cleared Berjou.

The action by the Sherwood Rangers was rightly described as a triumph of determination and grit over almost impossible country. The commander of 214 Brigade later wrote: 'no Infantry Brigade had ever had better tank cooperation.' Brigadier Prior Palmer added 'Your chaps really did do a super-human job up that ruddy mountain'.

The casualties during the five days following the regiment's return to the line were one officer and nine ORs, including Sergeant Saunders MM, killed and two officers and fourteen ORs wounded. Ten tanks were knocked out, but eight would run again.

For their part in the attack on Berjou, Major Micky Gold, Captain Jack Holman and Lieutenant Stuart Hills were each awarded immediate MCs. In addition, Sergeant John Kirman was awarded an immediate MM for his part in the fighting in Normandy, during which he commanded a tank which swam in on D Day, and then had four tanks knocked out under him during the fighting inland. He went on to be an outstanding signals sergeant in C Squadron.

The Mace

No tanks had been encountered during the assault on Berjou due to events taking place farther east. As Second Army was forcing its way south towards Vire and Conde, First Canadian Army, using improvised armoured personnel carriers for the first time, had at last been able to overcome the resistance on the Caen-Falaise road and were closing inexorably on Falaise, which they reached on 17 August, the day after the regiment took Berjou.

Meanwhile Third US Army had, belatedly, swung north from Alençon to Argentan, only a few miles south of Falaise. The Germans had responded by throwing their full effort into holding open the jaws of the gap between Falaise and Argentan. The Allies now unleashed the armoured divisions: 11th Armoured followed by 50th Division, supported by 8 Armoured Brigade, prepared to strike east on Chambois through the length of the pocket from Conde; 4th Canadian Armoured Division striking south-east from Falaise to Trun and 1st Polish Armoured Division, on the Canadians' left, attacking south-east towards Chambois.

In Chambois the Polish Armoured Division met with 2nd French Armoured Division, fighting with the Americans, attacking from the south, and closed the jaws on 20 August. The Poles then fought magnificently to keep the Gap closed against determined German counter-attacks from the east, by managing to hold the vital ground, a feature a few miles north-east of Chambois. Until that moment it had been called Hill 262, but for ever after known as 'The Mace'. It was also the moment of victory in Normandy.

Overall the battle for Normandy was a great feat of arms, in which thirty-four Allied divisions had destroyed eleven of twelve German armoured divisions including 2,200 tanks, leaving them only 120 tanks. In addition, of the forty-eight infantry divisions under von Rundstedt's command at the beginning of June, only twenty-one remained, of which eight were classified as remnants. Effectively, therefore, a total of forty-six divisions were destroyed and 500,000 German soldiers had been wiped off the order of battle as killed or captured.

The only other battle of comparable size was the destruction of the German Army Group Centre by the Russians, which commenced on 22 June 1944, in which 140 Russian divisions destroyed twenty-eight German divisions, and during which 300,000 German soldiers had been killed or taken prisoner.

The regiment was also left to count the cost of the fighting in Normandy. It lost over 200 killed or wounded, of which approximately fifty were tank commanders, virtually one for every tank in the regiment and thirty-six were officers, a number equal to the establishment of the officers' mess. The total killed was sixty all ranks.

Since landing, the Sherwood Rangers had been in the line for an astonishing fifty-five of seventy-two days of the battle.

Chapter 34

Pursuit into Belgium

August–September 1944

Operation KITTEN

The Sherwood Rangers now gathered themselves together ready for the pursuit, Operation KITTEN. At 0650 on 23 August, 8 Armoured Brigade crossed the start line, the Sherwood Rangers leading. This advance had three stages: pursuit to the Seine, the crossing and pursuit into Belgium.

The chase started as a traffic jam, the sheer weight of numbers of Allied units and formations seeking to get forward overwhelming what was left of the road system. If that was not enough, there was the need for one entire corps to cross the tracks of another. Whilst the Regiment was waiting, Major Lord Leigh, posted in from the Royal Gloucestershire Hussars, took over as second-in-command to replace Stephen Mitchell. The regiment moved at last, closing with the Seine at Vernon on 27 August. Paris had fallen to le Clerc's Free French and the Americans on the 25th. Micky Gold had sought permission to visit his former unit, 23rd Hussars, and had taken his SSM and squadron clerk with him. They must have become disorientated because instead they found themselves pulling up outside the Ritz in Paris in their jeep, where they were mobbed by a crowd of hysterical Frenchmen, who led them into the hotel and plied them with champagne for the rest of the night. They claimed yet another first for the regiment: that of the first British troops from a combat unit to enter Paris!

Vernon

The plan for the Seine crossing was that 8 Armoured Brigade would support 43rd Division. The regiment was in reserve during all the serious fighting over a three-day period when the Wyverns took significant losses. By the time the regiment crossed on 28 August, they did so virtually unopposed, save for some sharp small-arms engagements in the woods beyond.

The Pursuit

Then, as the ground opened up into the rolling countryside of northern France, they adopted the desert formation of one squadron up, in open formation, followed by RHQ and the other two on either flank, with their infantry and battery of guns moving behind. They rejoiced in the exhilaration of having the enemy on the run. The pursuit was a huge operation, with four armies up: First Canadian in the north with the coast as their left boundary, Second British, of which the regiment, of course, formed part, on their right; to their right came First US Army, then Third US Army farthest south. They totalled more than thirty-seven divisions, the maximum strength that could be mustered, and each army group had its own tactical air force, a force consisting of over half a million fighting men. As they crossed the Seine they covered a front some 200 miles wide but which, by the time they reached the German border, had increased to nearer 300 miles. While the advance was in progress, General Eisenhower, in accordance with his original plan, assumed direct command of all land forces in northern France. Montgomery retained command of 21 Army Group in the north, whilst 12 Army Group remained under Bradley.

Once across the Seine, Eisenhower thrust north-east at the greatest possible speed and to the utmost limit of his supplies. His purpose was to overrun, as quickly as possible, the launch-sites of the flying-bombs, which had been harassing England since mid-June, but especially to take Antwerp. He was driving before him about seventeen German divisions which, he assessed, would have little fight in them for so long as he could deny them the opportunity to re-organize.

Capturing Antwerp quickly, and intact, was key to the plan because of the shorter supply lines it offered. Eisenhower was using 20,000 tons of supplies per day (compared with Allenby's 2,000), all of which had to be carried over his existing rapidly-extending supply lines, stretching all the way back to Cherbourg, and the Mulberry Harbour at Arromanches. In addition, there also had to be carried forward much material now needed for developing the road system and building airfields. He lacked sufficient transport to do all this from Normandy.

Second Army's axis ran broadly north-easterly, the route Amiens-Arras-Douai-Tournai-Brussels-Antwerp-Louvain roughly forming the centre line. Pride of place in the advance had, of course, been given to the armoured divisions, 8 Armoured Brigade's role being sometimes to clear the way for a triumphal entry of one of the divisions into some town, sometimes to act as follow up and sometimes as flank protection. The regiment had a very successful day on 1 September, covering fifty miles, liberating Flesselles, Naours and Doullens in the process. They knocked out four tanks, three anti-tank guns, captured a flying-bomb site and several hundred prisoners but, sadly, lost Sergeant Cribbens, killed at Flesselles.

The capture of Doullens was a particularly fine action. It was preceded by the capture of a V1 site by David Render's troop. He directed the 30 man crew of the site to walk back westward because he was still in action, but when they thought it safe they turned and started to run east and were duly engaged. The advance was resumed on the town itself in which the regiment bumped a position defended by a number of 75mm anti-tank guns and approximately 250 infantry.

A Squadron was leading. After the lead tank had been hit by one of the anti-tank guns, Lieutenant David Render's troop was ordered to work round to a flank and enter the town at right angles to the centre line. The troop had no infantry support but, despite that, entered the town to the rear of the anti-tank defences, advanced through it and killed or took prisoner the complete enemy HQ, including the garrison commander. They then caught the anti-tank positions between the troop and the remainder of the squadron and all the guns were knocked out, despite enemy sniping from windows, and the troop coming under machine-gun fire from behind. The troop also captured intact the bridge carrying the main road through the town. This had very much been David Render's battle, but it was Sergeant Les Jackson, his troop sergeant, a desert veteran who was awarded an immediate MM. Where every tank commander does enough on numerous occasions to be worthy of recognition there was always a dilemma whom to put forward for awards which were so heavily rationed. Here, perhaps, it was all the months in the desert which carried the day over a young troop leader.

By 5 September, the area of Ghent was reached. Here, at St Pierre, Lieutenant Wharton with his troop, found a German garrison over 1,000 strong. He daringly demanded its surrender, and found the commander agreeable if he could do so 'honourably' to one of his own rank. Lieutenant Colonel Christopherson was invited to attend and a formal surrender was contrived without bloodshed.

The regiment moved on again on the 7th, through several more towns, culminating in a slow, triumphal progression through the streets of Brussels itself, which had recently been liberated by Guards Armoured Division. Brussels gave the regiment a wildly enthusiastic welcome, each tank and vehicle swarmed with civilians and festooned with gifts of food and wine. The Rangers laagered at Herschot, on the Louvain road out of Brussels, having covered sixty miles in the day. They spent the next two days on maintenance and re-sampling the enthusiastic welcome reserved in Brussels for anyone in a uniform.

One such party, including in its number no less a personage than the Padre, cadged a lift off the LAD on the regimental wrecker, a Scammell. There were so many in the party that each had to find a perch or handhold wherever he could. The crew of the wrecker, allegedly, had business with a broken-down tank on the far side of the city, and dropped the party off 'on the way through', collecting them much later that night 'on the way back'. The absence of any sign of a tank on tow was explained by a successful repair having been affected. On noticing that the road back to the regiment, although pleasantly straight, seemed more than ordinarily bumpy, they discovered that they had found their way onto a local railway line.

Meanwhile 11th Armoured Division had entered Antwerp on 4 September, finding the harbour almost intact. At first it looked as though Eisenhower's plan had worked. But Antwerp's access to the sea is through the relatively long, narrow and heavily-mined Scheldt estuary, and the eastern bank, from which the whole of the Scheldt could be covered by fire, would remain in German hands until the end of November, no matter how hard the Allies tried to dislodge them.

Eisenhower, having failed to open Antwerp within the necessary timescale, knew this meant a significant reduction in his ability to maintain the offensive due to restricted re-supply. This would lengthen the war unless he secured a dramatic change of fortune. Eisenhower's sole strategic reserve was First Allied Airborne Army. There had been many plans for airborne operations, none of which had been implemented. Montgomery came up with a proposal to use it and Eisenhower was quick to approve. Codenamed Operation MARKET GARDEN the plan was to drop, at the earliest possible opportunity, and whilst the Germans were still unbalanced, First Allied Airborne Army under General Brereton. It comprised 1st and 6th British Airborne Divisions with 52nd (Lowland) Division in air-portable mode, plus three US divisions and a Polish brigade. Their objectives were the bridges and roads running north-east at and between Eindhoven and Arnhem, across the Maas, Meuse, Waal and Lower Rhine and a number of significant canals. The two bridges north-east of Eindhoven at Son and Veghel were assigned to 101st US Airborne while 82nd was to take the next bridges at Grave and Nijmegen; 1st British Airborne and the Polish Brigade were to take the bridge at Arnhem, across the Lower Rhine to be reinforced by 52nd (Lowland) flying in to Deelen. This would secure a corridor, to be held open by XII and VIII Corps, down which Montgomery would drive XXX Corps deep into Germany, thus rendering untenable the Germans' positions in the Low Countries.

It would be futile to hope that the regiment would not be used in some way.

Chapter 35

Battle for Gheel

September 1944

Before Operation MARKET GARDEN could commence it was necessary to secure the start line for it on the Escaut Canal, which lay on 8 Armoured Brigade's axis, some sixty miles north-east of Brussels. To reach that obstacle, a crossing over the Albert Canal, running south-east between Brussels and Maastricht, had to be forced. It was still in enemy hands and formed part of the enemy's new forward line of defence. It was held not by the exhausted divisions that had been pursued relentlessly by the Allies, but by new formations, recently arrived fresh from the Fatherland and manned by young but committed troops, who were often to prove fierce and fanatical fighters. At Gheel it was the German 6th Parachute Division.

On 9 September Guards Armoured Division forced a crossing over the Albert Canal at Beringen and 8 Armoured Brigade, minus the regiment, then in reserve, was passed through with orders to turn north and take Gheel, about two miles east of the Canal, which guarded a better bridge over it. The brigade ran into heavy resistance and, having suffered significant casualties, was unable to break through. Accordingly, on 10 September, 50th Division, supported by the Sherwood Rangers, was ordered to cross opposite Gheel and capture the town. That fine division was now but a shadow of its former self. It had been significantly weakened from losses taken during all the heavy fighting in which it had been engaged since D Day and which had not been made good and was destined to be broken up for reinforcements for other formations in December, reforming as a reserve division in the UK.

By the time the regiment came into action in support of 231 Brigade, 151 Brigade had already established a bridgehead over the Canal. That turned out to be far from secure, the perimeter having been penetrated by enemy infantry and tanks creeping down the sunken lanes criss-crossing it.

Stanley Christopherson recorded:

so the Regiment was immediately ordered into the bridgehead with 151 Brigade. The brigadier had crossed the canal and established his headquarters within the small perimeter, and was even so optimistic as to have brought his caravan. Before bringing the Regiment up I was discussing a plan of action with him when his intelligence officer approached and said 'I think I should tell you sir that there are two enemy tanks in a sunken lane 300 yards to our left flank. If you watch clearly you can see them and it is quite easy to hear them'.

'For God's sake,' exclaimed the brigadier, 'bring your tanks up quickly.'

A certain confusion ensued, as the brigadier's caravan and other elements of his headquarters went hurtling back over the canal, followed by machine-gun bullets from the tanks.

C Squadron, in support of 6th Durham LI, initially restored the situation and, indeed, extended the bridgehead as Stuart Hills, still a troop leader in C Squadron, wrote:

> After we had gone about 100 yards the inevitable Spandaus opened up. The infantry had a rotten time and I could see them falling to the left and right of me.... They then went to ground ... and frantically waved at us to take the lead ... we advanced beyond the infantry cowering in whatever holes they could scrape out of the ground and we put down the heaviest fire we could with both our machine guns and main guns ... at one stage I moved so close to [the enemy's] trenches that I had to reverse my tank in order to depress the gun sufficiently to fire high explosive point-blank. All this had the desired effect. The enemy simply could not cope with the weight of fire we put down and we just ran the trenches over so that the infantry following behind us could poke the Germans out at the point of the bayonet ....
>
> My troop joined the road that ran into Gheel from the west ... I ... put a shell into every house on either side of the street: this would reduce the danger from the Spandau fire that was always such a nightmare for the infantry. As we moved into the town outskirts, we knocked out an 88 millimetre sited near a farmhouse ... our progress was accompanied by the almost constant pinging of Spandau bullets on the armour of the tank.... We then approached a T-junction where another 88mm and ammunition lorry were burning. Germans were now surrendering in ever increasing numbers .... I calculated that in our passage through the town we had fired about 60 shells ... I ... headed straight to the main square of Gheel to cover the northern and eastern approaches. Cpl Burnett just behind me brewed up a German staff car, and three officers who had been in it ran for their lives and we also destroyed four light anti-aircraft guns.... I called up Jack Holman (C Squadron Leader) on the radio to tell him the way was clear. He roared up about ten minutes later in his scout car. The rest of C Squadron had reached Gheel and were either somewhere in the town or on the outskirts.... We assumed the position would soon be consolidated by the arrival of further support....

Little did he know, the whole squadron was fighting for its life.

Another C Squadron troop was in action with A Company 9th Durhams. The company was counter-attacked three times, the troop leader and troop sergeant being wounded in the first action. Corporal Roberts, the senior tank commander remaining, took command, and continued harassing the enemy with fire from his own and the other tank still crewed. He dispersed his tanks, moving from place to place with such good effect as to be largely responsible for breaking up three counter-attacks. In the second counter-attack he killed forty of the enemy, and personally took eleven prisoners, by driving his tank straight at the oncoming Germans and firing continually.

In the northern end of the bridgehead, all three tanks of another C Squadron troop were knocked out when three enemy tanks let the troop go past before shooting them up from the rear, from concealed positions. This triggered a remarkable response from one survivor, Sergeant Jack Robinson, who evacuated the wounded to a place of safety which involved four separate journeys under machine-gun and mortar fire. After making the wounded men as comfortable as possible, he rejoined C Squadron, passing through a part of the village held by the enemy.

On reaching the squadron's leading tank, he discovered that the commander, the troop leader, had been killed. He assumed command of the tank in time to knock out an enemy 88mm SPG and a 75mm SPG which were attempting to break into the village and spent the rest of the day of the 10th and following night in a forward position in the village outskirts guarding the approach. During the night, as there was no infantry available for local protection, he took up a position on the ground with his Bren, and together with the only other remaining tank in the troop he had taken over, broke up an enemy counter-attack.

Elsewhere in Gheel, another C Squadron troop had been cut off from the remainder of the squadron by enemy infiltration within the bridgehead. After the troop leader had become a casualty, SSM William Robson, the Squadron Sergeant Major of C Squadron, but acting as troop sergeant of the troop owing to the shortage of crew commanders due to casualties, took command and fought his way back to the squadron. In spite of inflicting considerable punishment on the enemy, his tank and the remaining tank in his troop were knocked out, and SSM Robson received a bad wound, which included a broken arm. He saw to the wounded and rejoined the squadron in Gheel by foot. On his arrival he took command of another troop which had lost its troop leader and fought for the remainder of the day. He was largely instrumental in breaking up several counter-attacks during the rest of the day, and prevented further enemy infiltration into Gheel.

B Squadron had also been in action. They had, during the afternoon, pushed forward over the canal into the north-western sector of the bridgehead, supporting 9th Durhams in holding the area previously described as being fields criss-crossed with sunken tracks. They were immediately counter-attacked violently but stood their ground. The squadron leader, Major Micky Gold, and Captain Colin

Thomson, the squadron second-in-command, were wounded, and several of the tanks knocked out.

Lieutenant Eric Wharton assumed command and re-organized what was left of the squadron. The position had become serious as enemy infiltration had increased. However, Eric Wharton repositioned the squadron to cover the gaps left in the line, and broke up and frustrated the enemy counter-attack against 9th Durhams' position. He also took command of a troop whose troop leader had been killed, and placed himself where he could best command the position.

He was now helped in a crucial way by Corporal Walter Ewing. In addition to the infiltration by the enemy, there were also signs of a dusk attack. The squadron was asked by the battalion to contact a platoon which was on the extreme left flank but was not in communication. Tanks tried to reach the platoon, but were prevented by a deep ditch, so Corporal Ewing did so on foot, coming under mortar fire in the process and risking being shot in failing light by the platoon he was seeking to reach. He completed his mission and returned with detailed information about both the platoon and the enemy's dispositions, which enabled the infantry and armoured commanders to restore the situation.

Meanwhile, back with Stuart Hills in the centre of Gheel as darkness came, he heard that the road back to the Canal had been cut by the enemy:

> We were effectively surrounded in Gheel.... The enemy were now very close to us in the square. Suddenly a German self-propelled gun appeared down the road I was watching, but I saw him before he saw us and shot him up.... We were now very short of ammunition.

Owing to the intensity of the fighting it was impossible to send up soft-skinned replenishment vehicles into Gheel owing to enemy infiltration. However, Sergeant George Stanton, the mechanical sergeant of C Squadron commanding the fitters' section, whose role was to maintain and repair the tanks, not re-supply them, immediately volunteered to run the gauntlet after dark in his armoured recovery vehicle (ARV) to bring up replenishment. His driver kept his foot down all the way through, which did not spare the ARV from being engaged by enemy machine guns and 6-pounder anti-tank guns, which the enemy had captured from 50th Division. Sergeant Stanton arrived in the centre of Gheel with a complete load of ammunition, sufficient to replenish what remained of the squadron. Without it, C Squadron could not have held the village for the rest of that night and the following day.

He then organized his fitter section into a fighting squad to picket one of the roads leading into the village, and was himself responsible for wiping out an enemy section who had attempted to infiltrate down his street. There is no greater sign that an armoured unit is fighting *in extremis* than when the fitters' section has to reach for its weapons.

Stanley Christopherson recalled that 'The opposing Germans were youthful fanatics and when night fell we plainly heard them shouting in English, 'We are prepared to die for Hitler, we intend to die for Hitler', while Stuart Hills noted that:

The Germans opposing us were very determined. Their infantry kept penetrating within our lines, and then used flares to illuminate our tanks, making them an easy target for their own tanks as they crept up. Our own infantry were so thin on the ground that it was virtually impossible to stop this infiltration....

We remained on the alert throughout the night, which was the worst I have ever spent anywhere.... The Germans kept pushing tanks and SP guns forward. Just before midnight we heard what sounded like a Jagdpanther, but for a long time we could not see where it was. Then Cpl Burnett spotted it creeping down a side street, waited for it around the corner and sent an armour-piercing shell from his 17-pounder into its fighting compartment at just ten yards range. Tank battles at such a short range were not likely to lead to a very long life, I thought to myself, and I am sure everyone else there was thinking exactly the same. Sadly Cpl Burnett was killed by a sniper the next day and my troop lost a very skilled and brave tank commander.

Meanwhile, after dark, SSM Robson, still with his broken arm untreated, collected all the wounded into a monastery in the village until arrangements could be made for their evacuation. Finally, he received a direct order from his squadron leader to take himself and his broken arm to receive medical treatment.

In B Squadron's sector, two enemy tanks managed to infiltrate during the night along a sunken road behind 9th Durhams' position. In the early morning, Eric Wharton, by manoeuvring his tank, forced these tanks to retire towards two of his own tanks which he had positioned; they immediately brewed up both. By morning B Squadron had lost seven tanks.

Stanley Christopherson wrote:

The following day the reserve company of the infantry was attacked by a whole German company, which had been able to infiltrate during the night.... John Mann a Captain in B Squadron was shot dead by a sniper as he was sitting in his tank at a crossroads and his tank was brewed up. The rest of the squadron tanks, supporting the reserve company, caught the attacking infantry in the open and broke up the attack.

Stuart Hills was still in the main square:

At dawn we heard still more German tanks milling around and they began to shell us in earnest. My own tank was covered in bricks, plaster and glass. There was dust everywhere even inside the tank.... When morning came we realized that we had no infantry left in front of us to protect us from Panzerfausts. Just in front of us a Bren Gun Carrier was brewed up, and shells were falling all around.

The Germans must have felt confident that we were finished, because at about midday, when things seemed quieter, their infantry started marching up the road towards us in line. This was a golden opportunity and we made the most of it, firing our machine guns at close range into their formation.... .

Suddenly there was an almighty crash, and Jimmy's [Jimmy McWilliams, C Squadron second-in-command] tank burst into flames. He and all his crew tumbled out except for his driver, Cpl Higgins, whom we presumed (and hoped) had been killed outright. It was a wicked moment: I had no idea from where the shot had come or what kind of weapon had been used, and it was clear that Jimmy's crew were no wiser than us. I moved slightly forward, presuming Jimmy must have been hit by something coming down the street he had been watching, but in truth the shot could have come either from that direction or from one of any number of houses overlooking us.... I sent a message over the air that we were now another tank short.

My mind was full of horrors. I had seen at close as possible range what had happened to Jimmy, and now it was very likely that the same thing was going to happen to me. Here I was sitting in my Sherman with all its firepower, but could not identify any target or even guess in what direction I should be looking.

Sure enough, about two minutes later, there was a terrific sheet of flame and shower of sparks as we were hit. We fired the Browning machine-gun in what we thought was the direction of the shot and backed furiously if rather clumsily into the main square, thankful to be able to move at all. A piece of shrapnel had grazed my forehead and taken my beret with it, but that was the extent of the damage to any of us.... I later found that half a track plate had been shot away on our starboard side, and that a hole had been punched right through the entire sprocket assembly.... .

Sergeant Stan Nesling, commanding a 17-pounder tank, was the troop sergeant of Stuart Hill's troop which was the first to go through the centre of Gheel and which took up a position at the north end of the bridgehead. The other two tanks in his troop had been knocked out by an SP gun firing from some woods about 400 yards away. In spite of being constantly engaged by this SP gun, he remained alone at the north end of the village to prevent enemy infiltration. However, an enemy infantry patrol managed to enter and engage his tank from the cover of a house to his rear. He fired his 17-pounder and Browning into the house but was unable to dislodge them.

He therefore dismounted and stalked the patrol with his Bren gun, giving orders to his gunner to cover him from the tank. Eventually sighting the enemy position, he opened fire with his Bren and wounded and killed several of them. The remainder fled in disorder, leaving behind them two bazookas. Nesling then cleared the rest of the street on foot with his Bren, with his tank giving him covering fire. In that way he held this vital ground.

Stanley Christopherson recalled how:

During the afternoon of the 11th a corporal from the [infantry] machine-gun section which was close to my tank, came across and said 'I should like to confirm, sir, that that there tank is one of yours'. I walked across to where he was standing and saw, somewhat to my consternation, a German Panther very slowly creeping down a lane 300 yards to our immediate front.

Fortunately the gun was pointing over its rear and the commander was looking backwards, anticipating trouble from behind. I couldn't engage from where Robin Hood (my tank) was positioned ... so I rushed across to Dick Holman and Sergeant Charity [A Squadron] whose tank was close at hand and was relieved to find ... they could possibly engage ... I stood on the back of the tank ... Sergeant Charity let fly with his first shot which was high and missed. The Panther immediately halted, and I saw the gun traverse quickly around towards us. Sergeant Charity fired again and once more was high; by this time the gun of the Panther appeared to be pointing directly at me.... I heard Sergeant Charity's repeat order:

'Reload, drop 50.'

'On,' said the gunner

'Fire!' shouted Sergeant Charity.... The tank rocked forward. I gave a shout of delight when I saw the armour-piercing shell had struck and entered the turret of the Panther....

Stuart Hills recalled that:

C Squadron now only consisted of five tanks. There was virtually no infantry support left.... The position was untenable and what was left of the Squadron was withdrawn.

Meanwhile, Sgt Nesling ... still had to come back from his rather exposed forward position. He managed this at top speed with his Browning blazing away.

Next day the regiment retook Gheel, this time in support of 15th (Scottish) Division. The town itself was a shambles, with hundreds of British and German dead lying around, 231 Brigade having suffered 400 casualties. The regiment had suffered two officers and nine ORs killed and four officers and sixteen ORs wounded. Eleven tanks were destroyed and two more damaged, out of a total of thirty-two that started the battle. These were the worst losses suffered by the Sherwood Rangers in Europe in a single action, and the worst since Zem Zem. Major Michael Gold lost an eye and would, as a result, ever after wear a black eye-patch with what can only be described as panache. The fact that the bridgehead was held for as long as it was, and retaken with relative ease, was undoubtedly due to the manner in which the regiment had fought against troops who displayed a degree of fanaticism that the regiment had never witnessed previously.

Stanley Christopherson was awarded an immediate DSO; the citation describing the action added:

> Lt Col Christopherson remained completely undismayed in spite of extremely critical circumstances, and by his courageous example he was successful in restoring the situation. The bold and determined action of this officer was largely instrumental in the maintenance of this all important bridgehead.

Sergeant Nesling won an immediate DCM. When his mother later read the citation, she exclaimed, 'you silly, silly boy you might have been killed', a masterpiece of unintended understatement! 'But I wasn't and they were,' he replied. SSM Robson, Sergeants Robinson and Stanton and Corporal Roberts were all awarded immediate MMs and Lieutenant Wharton an immediate MC, whilst Corporal Ewing was awarded a Belgian Croix de Guerre avec Palme.

Writing citations after an action like Gheel was the pleasant part. The hardest part was the letters home from the CO, the squadron leader, the troop leader and the padre to the families of those killed or wounded and the responses to the many replies. Reading examples, even today, it is impossible to do so without emotion and a realization of just how difficult every word would have been, especially when written, almost inevitably, by someone who was, himself, lucky to still be alive, and for whom the insidiously-dripping tap had dripped for too long.

Luckily, there was a rock at home who fielded all the fall-out, in the form of Myrtle Kellett, Flash Kellett's widow, known to all as Mrs Kellett. She was, informally, the regiment's home headquarters. The reason this was necessary was because the War Office did not provide a TA regiment like the Sherwood Rangers Yeomanry with a formally established and funded home headquarters, as with regular units. This is notwithstanding that the welfare matters that arose for the families of the regiment's casualties continue seventy years on, and are still dealt with by volunteers. For years after Mrs Kellett could no longer carry the burden, for which she was awarded an MBE, the mantle was taken over by Corporal Ken Ewing, who was a member of a tank crew in every single action fought by the regiment during the war without once being knocked out. He truly paid his tribute to his friends and comrades, who were not so lucky.

With Ken Ewing no longer amongst us, the task is continued to this day by a generation who were not even born when these events took place.

Chapter 36

MARKET GARDEN Salient

September–November 1944

The enemy's wholesale retreat was quite definitely at an end, as were hopes for an imminent end to the fighting but, nevertheless, the crossing over the Albert Canal had been forced and therefore the road to the Escaut Canal, XXX Corps' start line for Operation MARKET GARDEN, had been opened.

Operation MARKET GARDEN formed the largest air armada ever seen. It was mounted from airfields throughout the UK and commenced on 17 September, only four days after the Gheel battle had ended. So great was the number of airborne troops involved that, when combined with the RAF's decision on the frequency of lifts, the drop itself took three days to complete.

In this operation the Sherwood Rangers were to be detached from 8 Armoured Brigade to operate in a picketing role in support of 82nd US Airborne Division, which had been dropped between Grave and Nijmegen, to capture the river bridges at Grave and Nijmegen, and the connecting road. For this the regiment had under command an armoured car squadron of the Royals, a light anti-aircraft battery and their usual supporting sub-units. The regiment reached Grave by nightfall on the 20th and duly linked up with the 82nd, shortly after that division had taken Nijmegen bridge. The Rangers found that the 82nd was holding a large area, which even extended across the border into Germany, dominated by the high ground around Dekkenswald and Groesbeek. In addition, within a mile to the south-east lay the vast Reichswald Forest. The regiment was distributed between the various sectors in the 82nd's tactical area of responsibility.

On 21 September, during a reconnaissance under fire in the Nijmegen sector, which produced valuable information concerning enemy strength and dispositions, Recce Troop crossed the Dutch border into Germany between Beek and Wyler, becoming the first British troops to enter Germany. Trooper Cantle of Retford was the driver of the leading vehicle. For his part in the reconnaissance Captain McKay, the troop leader, received an immediate MC. This led to the following announcement by Frank Gillard on the BBC:

> The most cheerful troops I have encountered were those on the Reich border.
> They were men of a County Yeomanry Regiment, the first troops back from

the Middle East to land on D Day, and the first Yeomanry Regiment to land on D Day. And they are now the first British troops to enter Germany.

It speaks volumes for the resilience and morale of the regiment that this was written little more than a week after the desperate affair in Gheel.

By 25 September MARKET GARDEN had failed to achieve its primary objective. However, the operation had secured some important gains: the Allies had secured a fifty-mile-deep salient, which represented a material threat to the enemy, and a crossing over the Waal at Nijmegen was also in Allied hands. The 82nd's main purpose was to keep the salient open against constant enemy pressure. The regiment was heavily engaged in support of that task between 20 September and 6 October when it was relieved. The 82nd and the regiment developed a healthy respect for each other, the divisional commander later writing, 'The Unit on its arrival rendered every possible support to our troops quickly, courageously and without the usual red tape connected with such support' and 'we will always remember the Sherwood Rangers Yeomanry for its splendid fighting qualities'.

The regiment now returned to 43rd (Wessex) Division, taking part in several actions between mid-October and mid-November to hold the salient. As a result of this fighting the Allies were eventually able to stabilize the salient at a width of twenty miles and hold on to the bridge at Nijmegen, gains that would prove extremely valuable later on. During this period, the regiment was reinforced by three complete troops from Lord Leigh's regiment, the Royal Gloucestershire Hussars, and by a number of their officers.

Casualties during MARKET GARDEN and the subsequent period were one officer and five ORs killed and five officers and twenty ORs wounded.

Chapter 37

Battle of Geilenkirchen

November 1944

Operation CLIPPER

The next task faced by Eisenhower's armies was to close up to the Rhine, preparatory to forcing crossings over it. Although the distances were not great, the problems were significant. Supply lines were still over-extended, the Americans having created major congestion in their re-supply chain, including seizing up the railway lines around Paris, forcing the implementation of a road-bound re-supply system, the 'red ball express'. In addition the November rains were the heaviest for many years. There was also the Siegfried Line to be overcome, and an enemy which had now thoroughly recovered its fighting qualities and was holding fast.

A general push was ordered across the entire front. Because of Operation MARKET GARDEN, 21 British Army Group in the north was significantly closer to the Rhine than the US armies in the south, so the main effort was to be concentrated farther south. Another reason for making this the main thrust was to gain control of the dams at the head of the River Roer and thus pre-empt the flooding of the Low Countries.

Geilenkirchen

The sector of front selected for this operation was that immediately west of the Roer and north of the Ardennes, in the area of Geilenkirchen and Duren, on the inter-army boundary between Montgomery's 21 Army Group and the newly-arrived, newly-deployed, and largely-inexperienced Ninth US Army. This formation had been inserted between the British and First US Army. For this operation XXX Corps, including 8 Armoured Brigade, was to be placed under command of Ninth US Army with the Sherwood Rangers detached from 8 Armoured and under command of 84th US Infantry Division, which would become XXX Corps' right-hand formation.

The following illustrates the key elements of the initial order of battle of Ninth US Army for the offensive:

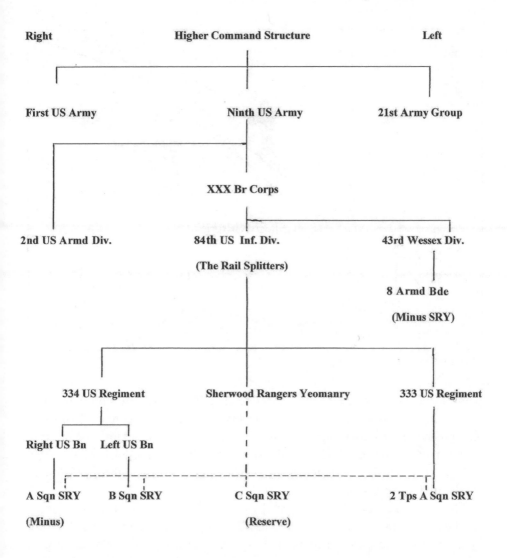

Right — **Higher Command Structure** — **Left**

First US Army | Ninth US Army | 21st Army Group

XXX Br Corps

2nd US Armd Div. | 84th US Inf. Div. *(The Rail Splitters)* | 43rd Wessex Div.

8 Armd Bde (Minus SRY)

334 US Regiment | Sherwood Rangers Yeomanry | 333 US Regiment

Right US Bn | Left US Bn

A Sqn SRY (Minus) | B Sqn SRY | C Sqn SRY (Reserve) | 2 Tps A Sqn SRY

To link up, XXX Corps now moved back down the old MARKET GARDEN centre line to Eindhoven and then south to Geilenkirchen. The regiment, loaded onto tank transporters at very short notice, moved to the coalmining town of Paulenberg; RHQ set up in Schinnen nearby.

Let us look at the ground over which the regiment was to fight. The River Wurm ran broadly in a north-easterly direction passing immediately to the south-east of Geilenkirchen. Immediately to the south-east of the river, and parallel to it, ran a railway line. Just south of Geilenkirchen a branch line left the mainline and ran at right angles in an easterly direction. Both the main line and the branch line sometimes ran through cuttings and sometimes along embankments. When they did either, they formed a tank obstacle and were defended throughout by concrete pillboxes. These two features, the railway line and the pillboxes, together, at this

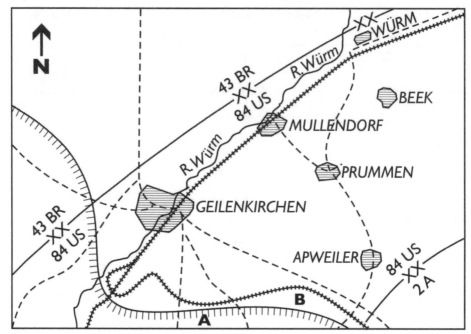

Map 19: Battle of Geilenkirchen.

point, formed the Siegfried Line. The concrete pillboxes had walls up to five-feet thick, were positioned to provide interlocking arcs of fire and mutual support, and impenetrable to anything the regiment possessed. Many had inter-connecting subterranean passages which would also need to be cleared. Each pillbox held about twenty Germans and there were trenches and wire around them which were filled with Germans too.

The low-lying ground was saturated with the heavy rain that had been falling for the past month, and continued to fall. The top surface, described as 'a sea of mud', consisted of a foot or more of sticky clay, and had been thickly sown with mines, making any movement by armour off the roads treacherous at best. The roads themselves were little better than country lanes, not designed to take heavy armour and were also mined. Finally, because the enemy had had ample time to prepare, they had built extra defences opposite the Allies' probable points of attack by heavily mining the railway, which at that point ran through a cutting and the ground immediately either side of it, thereby rendering the whole an anti-tank and anti-personnel obstacle. Not an appealing prospect, but just in case there was anyone left in the regiment with an optimistic view of the next few days, Brigade chose this moment to tell them that all leave was to be cancelled until the end of the winter.

Ninth Army's attack was to be made from the south, with three divisions up: 43rd (Wessex), with 8 Armoured Brigade minus the regiment, to the west/left, was to attack north west of Geilenkirchen, north-easterly up the west bank of the Wurm towards the high ground north-west of Geilenkirchen. In the centre, 84th US Division, supported by the regiment, was to take Geilenkirchen itself and break through the Siegfried Line at the point just described. The plan was to bypass Geilenkirchen to its east, break through the Siegfried Line, and take a northerly axis up the east bank of the Wurm along the line of the railway. By this envelopment of Geilenkirchen, 84th Division hoped that the town would fall without costly street fighting. Their objective was to take the high ground north-east of Geilenkirchen, and then the village of Prummen, a short way to the east of the railway itself, and due east of Geilenkirchen. Under command of Ninth Army was 2nd US Armored Division on the east/right which was to attack the Siegfried Line farther east of Geilenkirchen. In the next phase XXX Corps was to exploit north-west and north-east to more high ground on either side of the Wurm, commanded by the villages of Wurm and Beek.

Like the rest of Ninth Army, 84th Division, known as the 'Rail Splitters', had never been in action before. Notwithstanding, or even because of this, the regiment found them imbued with 'zest and good spirits'. The regiment had been selected by Horrocks to support 84th Division 'because of its previous experience of working with US formations'. The division's plan was to attack two regiments up (the equivalent of brigades): 333rd Regiment, with two troops of A Squadron in support, was to be the left, with Geilenkirchen as its initial objective; 334th Regiment, with the remainder of the regiment, was to be the right regiment on an axis requiring them to break through the Siegfried Line east of Geilenkirchen, and then advance north-east. Stanley Christopherson commented on the initial tie up with 334th Regiment which:

> was commanded by Colonel Rossmond.... After the first conference which had lasted an hour, nothing had been decided. When I remarked on this he said 'I like the Boys to have their say because the Boys have to do the job!' I managed tactfully to persuade him that it would save much time if he and I could decide on a plan, orders for which could be given out ... after which he could ask for comments.... I decided to live at his headquarters and detailed each squadron leader to take up residence at [their] battalion headquarters....

Ninth Army was opposed by 10th SS and 15th PanzerGrenadier Divisions. Both had been patched up, having been in action previously. Tenth SS had been hard fought in Normandy, whilst 15th PanzerGrenadier had fought in Italy, taking heavy casualties, before being withdrawn to North-West Europe, but was probably in better shape than 10th SS.

Ninth Army's detailed plan was for 2nd Armored Division to attack on 17 November on the right, twenty-four hours before the rest. They would be followed by 84th Infantry Division, including the regiment, which would cross its start line at 0700 next day, in the dark, using a searchlight battery to provide 'artificial moonlight'. The Rail Splitters' attack was to be preceded, at 0600, by carefully assembled and rehearsed gapping teams to clear the initial obstacles across the branch line. On the right, 334th Regiment had two such teams, each detailed to gap and bridge the railway feature. One such gap was for use by each of 334th's two leading battalions and their respective supporting arms, including the regiment.

Each gapping team was led by a troop of flails of 1st Lothians and Border Yeomanry, tasked to clear a path through the minefields either side of the railway obstacle. They were followed by Churchill ARK tanks to lay bridges over the railway and Petard AVREs to destroy pillboxes by throwing 'Flying Dustbin' mortar bombs at them, and laying charges against them. Other AVREs carried fascines to bridge smaller anti-tank ditches. Both bridge-layers and AVREs were manned by Royal Engineers. The division was also supported by Churchill Crocodile flame-throwing tanks to help take out the pillboxes. Each gapping team was covered by a troop from the regiment and an infantry platoon.

On the night of 17 November 2nd Armored duly attacked, securing their initial objectives and 84th Division's attack went in at 0600 on the 18th, in the inevitable rain, as the whole area was suddenly lit by the promised 'artificial moonlight'. The attack was on time, notwithstanding the fact that the rehearsal of this complex plan, which had also taken place on the 17th, had become bogged down, leaving much recovery work to re-assemble units. The attack was preceded by a 'terrific' artillery barrage, which had opened up at 0330.

A Squadron, minus the two troops supporting 333rd Regiment, and a third providing close support to 334th's gapping teams, was initially supporting 334th's right front battalion, whose objective was the village of Prummen. B Squadron was initially supporting 334th's left front battalion, whose initial objective was the high ground slightly farther to the north-east of Prummen. This meant that, having crossed the railway and broken through the Siegfried Line, B Squadron would advance north-east, with the railway as its left boundary. It would then roll up the Siegfried Line, between where they had broken through and the high ground just beyond Prummen that was its initial objective. Once A Squadron had crossed, it would, likewise, roll up the Siegfried Line farther to the right, until it was able to attack and take Prummen. C Squadron was in reserve.

The gap on A Squadron's front was cleared as planned but not before the flail breaching the minefield in front of the squadron became bogged two-thirds of the way through. This left John Semken, still in command of the squadron, with no choice but to lead his squadron through the remainder of the uncleared minefield. His luck held till the far edge had been reached when, in what could arguably be some sort of record, his tank detonated four mines simultaneously, an event which irrefutably blew the suspension clean off on both sides, the third tank that John Semken had had knocked out under him during the war. He was awarded the US Silver Star for gallantry, effectively a second MC.

Things did not go as 'smoothly' on B Squadron's front, where there was considerable delay, as the engineers manning the bridge-layers encountered problems establishing the correct pitching of the bridges across the railway. This gave the enemy time to recover from their initial surprise and inflict casualties on the waiting troops. Therefore, B Squadron switched two troops and SHQ to follow A Squadron over their gap where they found the going had become desperate. Nevertheless, they were able to press on towards the pillboxes to the north, leaving their infantry, who were having their own problems crossing the obstacle, to catch up. One by one the pillboxes were reduced. The system used was to force the enemy to close the embrasures in the pillboxes, by firing on them, which permitted the infantry, which had rejoined the armour, to force them to surrender. Intensive use was also made of the Crocodiles which were all too effective.

Back with A Squadron, John Semken was in no condition to continue in command and fight the coming battle, so Captain John Gauntley assumed command of the squadron, consisting, at this stage, of only two troops. Immediately after passing through the gap, the squadron ran into an un-located minefield, and at the same time was engaged by enemy anti-tank guns and pillboxes from its right flank. The squadron suffered tank casualties (including David Render's tank on a mine which had survived since he had joined the regiment before EPSOM), but immediately re-organized and assaulted the pillboxes which were now holding up their infantry, the right battalion of 334th. As a result, the guns in the pillboxes were put out of action and the battalion was able to come up, destroy the pillboxes, capture the German defenders and continue the advance on Prummen.

Before reaching its initial objective, B Squadron bumped another line of pillboxes and put them out of action. Next, the squadron knocked out the anti-tank guns covering the pillboxes, and then killed all the infantry in the slit trenches surrounding the position, enabling the left battalion of 334th to come up and destroy the pillboxes.

One of the key contributors in this action was Sergeant Sidney Collis, who was instrumental in eliminating several pillboxes which dominated the high ground. He was something of a legend, having commanded one of the first tanks to land on D Day and continued to command a tank in every battle in which the regiment had been involved through Normandy, Belgium, Holland and now Germany, fighting his tank with great skill. On four occasions during the fighting in North-West Europe, his tank had been knocked out by anti-tank guns, but this had never deterred him, once recovered, from volunteering to take command of another and continue fighting. For his contribution at Geilenkirchen, and throughout the campaign, he was awarded the DCM. Another key contributor was Sergeant J. Moffett who assumed command when his troop leader was wounded. His troop was one of the first through the gap made by the gapping party and, despite being faced by heavy enemy fire, including rocket launchers, he advanced against enemy-held pillboxes which were delaying the infantry. He was awarded the US Silver Star.

Meanwhile, Sergeant Charles Webb of A Squadron, whose troop had been providing the minefield breaching parties with close support, had been released to rejoin the squadron. Despite being without infantry support, he attacked a nest of pillboxes and accounted for one of them, securing thirty prisoners. He then attacked the pillboxes guarding the approaches to Prummen, accounting for another. John Gauntley then gave him the task of guarding the right flank of the village while A Squadron and its battalion attacked, but Webb attacked right round the right flank of the village and knocked out a 75mm anti-tank gun without loss. Still without infantry assistance, he attacked the village, knowing it concealed German tanks. The crossfire thus produced provided covering fire for 334th's right battalion's assault, which took the village. John Gauntley was awarded an immediate MC and Sergeant Webb an immediate MM.

By the end of the day A and B Squadrons had taken their initial objectives, together with between 200 and 300 prisoners, and the regiment had become the first British unit through the Siegfried Line. However, by nightfall, Prummen had only been partially secured. The state of the ground was bad and 334th's right battalion was suffering extremely heavy shelling and had not been able to bring up its anti-tank guns and consolidate; the enemy still controlled half the village.

C Squadron took over from A Squadron to continue to support 344th's right battalion in Prummen. The squadron had deployed Sergeant Henry Douthwaite's troop to give the battalion close support through the night. He positioned himself in the centre of the village within 200 yards of the enemy infantry and three tanks. With only one other tank left, he had to guard four roads leading into the village centre; the battalion could only muster a handful of infantry at this point. During the night, his tank was twice attacked by German bazooka teams, but each time he drove them off by dismounted action. He next heard an enemy tank approaching, and placed some German mines in the centre of the road; these detonated under the track of the German tank, immobilizing it. Douthwaite then manoeuvred around to the rear of it and set it on fire.

Twice during the night the Germans tried to counter-attack the handful of 344th's men in the village, but on both occasions were frustrated by Sergeant Douthwaite. In the words of the CO of 344th, 'The village would never have been held during that night if it had not been for the initiative and offensive action on the part of Sgt Douthwaite, who in spite of constant enemy shelling and snipers, showed the greatest courage and utter disregard for his own personal safety'. Sergeant Douthwaite was awarded an immediate MM.

However, the Sherwood Rangers had suffered significant casualties, a number of tanks having been destroyed or disabled by mines and John Semken was missing but was found eventually by the Padre, 'bomb happy', late in the afternoon of the 18th, reading poetry in a captured pillbox. Once he had recovered properly, he was back in command of the squadron. The regiment's rule was that commanders who had been knocked out should stand down for twenty-fours because it induced a state of euphoria for a time which affected judgement.

Perhaps the most serious loss was that of Sergeant George Dring who received a bad wound in the hand whilst on one of his famous foot recces. He was stalking a tank, which appeared to be abandoned, when it suddenly opened up. He did not recover from this wound in time to rejoin the regiment before the end of the war, and so became one of the few of its tank commanders to have survived from the beginning. There is an iconic photograph of himself and his crew, taken in Normandy, posed on his tank *Akilla* (his crew youthfully languid, himself all hardened pugnaciousness) and which when he died in his 80s of old age, appeared with his rare obituary in the *Daily Telegraph* (rare in the sense that few military obituaries appear there below officer level).

On the 19th, as it continued to rain, Lieutenant David Alderson's troop, one of the two troops of A Squadron detached under command 333rd US Regiment, supported the American infantry when they took Geilenkirchen, as planned, with relatively little fighting. On the eastern or right bank of the Wurm, B Squadron was still with the left battalion of 334th who had consolidated overnight on the high ground which had been their initial objective. At first light, they commenced the second phase, bypassing Prummen left-flanking to close with their new objective, on the high ground farther to the north-east, south of the village of Wurm. Although constantly under artillery fire, the battle-group reached the north-west corner of Prummen with relatively little trouble. However, they then found the ground they had to cross completely open and covered by anti-tank guns and concealed pillboxes, with inter-connecting arcs of fire. B Squadron debouched into the open from the partial cover of the orchard fringing Prummen and came under withering fire, suffering several casualties, including the squadron leader, Major Peter Seleri, wounded for the second time in the campaign, when his tank was knocked out. They also suffered badly in the going with a number of tanks bogging.

Meanwhile, as mentioned, C Squadron had taken over from A Squadron on the right. It had been assigned to clear the north-eastern end of Prummen and, in doing so, had destroyed four tanks that morning, and by the afternoon was firm in the north-eastern corner of the village, but not without casualties. Major Jack Holman was awarded the US Silver Star for his handling of C Squadron on 19 November.

B Squadron now received orders to join C Squadron, to support C Squadron's battalion in an attack towards Beek later that afternoon. However, it proved impossible to extricate the majority of the squadron from its present position where, if a tank was not already knocked out it was likely to be, since it was both bogged and under fire. As for the remainder, all of four tanks, they found all possible routes to the RV impassable due to saturated ground or roads blocked by knocked-out enemy tanks. The attack, therefore, was postponed until next day.

That day B Squadron had suffered heavy casualties and three brewed tanks, and were down to two officers. This was one of their worst days.

The regiment's casualties on 18 and 19 November were three officers and eight ORs killed, four officers and twenty-four ORs wounded, with twenty of the casualties sustained by B Squadron whose travails were not over; they endured an endless night on the 19th/20th, as Sergeant James Small from the squadron's fitters, supported by others, recovered, one by one, the bogged tanks and their crews. This was done, literally, from under the guns of the enemy's positions all around them.

These night-time recoveries were taking place throughout the regiment and went on until the end of the battle. The ground got so bad that, increasingly, tanks had to be abandoned because they could not be moved. Codes, weapons and maps were removed as part of that process. Every night Sergeant Small was out on foot checking tanks and recovering crews where tanks could not be moved and earned a fine immediate MM in the process. All of this was taking place against the background of continuous rain while, every day, the regiment had to be out of laager long before first light, and did not replenish until long after dark, leaving little time for sleep, let alone to get dry or warm. This was a shattering routine for everyone.

By the 20th Prummen had been cleared fully. A Squadron, now complete, was supporting 333rd. They moved to clear the high ground north-west of Geilenkirchen but encountered huge difficulties from defensive fire from the direction of Beek. C Squadron, still supporting the right battalion of 344th, also sought to cross the open ground and take Beek. However, there were significant numbers of enemy tanks to their front.

B Squadron was still in support of the left battalion of 344th on the north-western side of Prummen. All day both battalion and squadron were pinned down and unable to move forward because the ground was so exposed. Nor could they find a route round on the left flank, due to the railway embankment.

The 21st found rain still falling, and the regiment increasingly paralyzed by the impossible ground, which included sunken roads and the embanked railway. It continued to take steady casualties. An attack on Beek failed.

On the 22nd, as the rain continued, B and C Squadrons were so reduced that they had to form a composite squadron under Major Jack Holman to combine with an American tank battalion. They were to support a fresh battalion of 84th Division, 2nd/405th Regiment, in another attack on Beek, which was still held by tanks and anti-tank guns. This attack, from the direction of Apweiler, was preceded by a barrage and covered by a smokescreen, primarily to protect the infantry's advance. To reach Beek it was necessary to advance over 1,500 yards of open country, completely dominated by high ground, from which the enemy had perfect observation. The tanks led the attack, followed by the infantry and, in spite of intensive fire from pillboxes and anti-tank guns, Captain Geoffrey Coleman's troop was first to reach the orchard in front of Beek, where four Tigers had been reported. Despite the fact that his troop was not supported by infantry, who were held up by two pillboxes in the corner of the orchard, Coleman called for more smoke and, when it came down, led his troop through the smokescreen into the orchard, continuing to advance until he was held up by a ditch which was an anti-tank obstacle. However, as he advanced, he knocked out one Tiger and killed many German infantry.

Corporal Harold Budner, his troop corporal, emerged from the smoke with him, and was heavily engaged by tanks, anti-tank guns and infantry. In reply, he covered the area in front of him with fire. Corporal Budner then made a dash for the road into the centre of the village and, owing to the smoke, his tank was not hit. On reaching the road, his luck ran out; his tank was knocked out by an anti-tank gun covering that approach to the village. Corporal William Pollard was also in the attack and, showing terrific determination, had pushed through Beek and got behind the enemy defensive line defending the village, and there accounted for two more of the Tigers at a range of 200 yards. He was awarded the US Silver Star for this action. The citation adds in respect of the battle generally:

He displayed courage and initiative of a high order throughout the entire period ... always being found where the fighting was fiercest. His aggressive, dauntless spirit and exemplary leadership reflected high credit on himself and the military service of his country.

From Ilkeston, he had been with the regiment since 1941 and had been wounded at Alamein.

Meanwhile Corporal Budner, after his tank had been brewed up, collected some infantry, when they eventually arrived, and led the party, with a view to knocking out the anti-tank gun, but they were pinned down by fire and had to remain concealed until after dark. Unsupported, Captain Coleman also remained in position until dark, engaging any enemy tanks that moved, and German infantry that attempted to use a bazooka against his tank. Eventually his ammunition ran out, but he remained in the same position until after dark. He then collected Corporal Budner and those members of Budner's crew who had been unable to move in daylight, owing to machine-gun fire, bringing them all back to safety, but leaving Beek untaken. Captain Coleman was awarded an immediate MC which had been submitted as a DSO and Corporal Budner an immediate MM.

Meanwhile A Squadron was trying to get on towards Wurm, without much success. The 23rd found the rain continuing and the composite B/C Squadron reduced to five tanks. An American tank squadron attacked Beek, but failed to take it while A Squadron, dealing with pillboxes, was heavily shelled. The regiment was counter-attacked by tanks in both sectors and further casualties were taken. At last, in the evening, the regiment was relieved by American armoured units. It had been a long and weary struggle. Everyone was exhausted and everything was drenched.

Between 20 and 23 November the casualties were four ORs killed, two officers and six ORs wounded. Overall casualties had been heavy – sixty-three, including three officers and twelve ORs killed, while ten tanks had been destroyed, five more damaged and another five bogged beyond recovery. If there is an armoured equivalent to trench warfare, this had surely been it.

However, the American infantry had impressed the regiment. It had been another 'great and proud partnership' which had broken the Siegfried Line and had taken Geilenkirchen and the high ground beyond in the most difficult of situations imaginable.

On the 24th the regiment returned the fifteen miles west from Geilenkirchen to Schinnen, receiving a warm welcome from their newly-made friends there, and a visit from Horrocks, who said that he had chosen the regiment for the task because it was 'one of the most experienced regiments in the western European theatre'; he identified the battle for Geilenkirchen as possibly their finest achievement to date. Stanley Christoperson was awarded the Silver Star by the Americans; this award covers the equivalent of both an MC and a DSO. His citation was such that it would have resulted in a DSO if submitted for one. In effect he had earned two DSOs in three months. Lieutenants R. G. Higgs and R. Longford were each awarded the US Bronze Star for meritorious service. Overall, during the battle, the regiment was awarded one DCM, two MCs, four MMs, six Silver Stars and two Bronze Stars.

Finally, Lieutenant Colonel John Sandars, a Sherwood Ranger, was appointed OBE; he already held the MBE. He was AQMG (M) at HQ Second Army throughout the campaign with one of his key responsibilities being road movement. There had scarcely been a time when this did not present a complicated problem as few major battles had not been preceded by extensive re-grouping, entailing moves of great complexity. Manipulation of the French and Belgian railway system was also key. Sandars was said to have disposed of these problems with conspicuous success, a talent not often associated with an officer in the Yeomanry.

Part VIII

The Second World War
1944–45

The End

Chapter 38

Operation BLACKCOCK

November 1944–January 1945

The Roer Salient

Antwerp was finally opened at the end of November and it became possible for the Allies to build up their resources and reserves in preparation for the Rhine crossing. The Allies, principally the Americans in the south, tried doggedly to fight their way through glutinous mud to close on the Roer. On 16 December the Germans took advantage of this period of consolidation to launch what, for them, amounted to a last throw of the dice. This took the form of a massive four-armies-strong counter-attack through the Ardennes aimed at Antwerp. It became known as the Battle of the Bulge.

Since it was now XXX Corps' mobile reserve, 8 Armoured Brigade was not involved in the Battle of the Bulge. It was covering the area of Schinveld, not far north of Geilenkirchen, a task requiring only one armoured regiment in the line at any time. As a result the regiment enjoyed a prolonged period of badly-needed rest which extended to embrace its sixth and last Christmas of the war, celebrated in the traditional regimental way and shared with the people and children of Schinnen. It included a dinner in the evening for the officers, notable for being the first occasion on which they had all dined together since before D Day.

Tank crews know better than anyone that there are certain key people on whom they rely absolutely to ensure that their tanks remain battleworthy and re-supplied, and that they receive the rations and other supplies that make life possible. Christmas, when there is a great tradition for tank crews to show their appreciation and gratitude to these men, usually in the form of a bottle of something distilled north of the border, was a good time to acknowledge the best of those who served in the regiment in this campaign.

Major Roger Sutton Nelthorpe, HQ Squadron Leader throughout, was the man on whom the entire re-supply chain depended and would receive the MBE. RSM Arthur Barlow was with the regiment throughout the campaign and, with little call for parades, covered every base at some stage in the campaign. During the early days in Normandy he was attached to the echelon, and thanks to his appreciation of the battle and clever handling of the echelon during these difficult days, the regiment was never short of supplies. During the later stages of the deployment, when the regiment had suffered heavy casualties and was short of tank commanders, RSM

Barlow commanded a troop of tanks during several battles. During the final three months of the war, he would organize and command the Tank Collecting Point. He would receive the DCM.

RQMS George Tandy, as RQMS throughout the campaign, was responsible for re-supply, in short the regiment's umbilical cord. During the early days the supply problem was difficult, and he showed the greatest initiative and enterprise to ensure that the regiment never went short. There were difficult times when supporting 82nd Airborne and 84th Infantry Divisions. Such re-deployments tested the umbilical cord because the regiment needed British supplies suitable to an armoured regiment while the division had only American supplies suitable for an infantry battalion. Overcoming that required skilled management. In addition, at Geilenkirchen he displayed great courage when replenishing tanks with fuel and rations in forward positions. He received the American Performance Medal.

Sergeant William Pick was the Regimental Signal Sergeant and controlled the Regimental Wireless Group. Perfect communications is the winning factor of armoured warfare. On many occasions during the heat of a battle, communications between RHQ and squadrons failed, and he restored them every time. During many battles he was the only operator at Tac HQ and controlled the wireless group for many hours on end without a break, often with three squadrons fighting separate battles. His quick grasp of the situation was always quite exceptional. Before taking over this role, Sergeant Pick commanded a tank in a sabre squadron, and during two battles his tank was brewed up. He was later awarded an immediate MM.

In the bleak mid-winter
Frosty wind made moan
Earth stood hard as iron
Water like a stone

Winter had now come in earnest and, at last, a heavy frost was hardening the ground to make it passable for tanks. The cold weather also brought a welcome issue of new, warm tank suits.

The Sherwood Rangers took their turn back in the line on Boxing Day, supporting 52nd (Lowland) Division. There followed a number of actions, notably on the night of 28 December in Vintelen. Lieutenant Cameron's troop had supported infantry against whom some enemy had infiltrated. He had been wounded and Corporal James Redfern, his troop corporal, had taken command, ascertained the house in which the Germans had taken cover, and fired several rounds of 75mm into it. This had compelled the Germans to leave the house and he had immediately killed them with his machine gun. Then he discovered a Spandau, which controlled the main street, and eliminated it, then another, which was covering the HQ of the infantry company he was supporting. During this action his tank had been damaged by enemy fire and he had constantly been engaged by snipers and Germans with hand grenades while handicapped by having trouble with his engine, which constantly refused to start. In the words of the CP attached to the infantry company:

> Cpl Redfern stood in his tank with his head through the cupola, engaging all the enemy he saw. A lot of enemy fire was directed at him as they knew that, as long as he stayed where he was, they could never hold on to the northern part of the village. Never, at any time, did he seem to be the slightest bit worried and I think that the battle for Vintelen would have been far harder for the infantry and would have certainly cost them more men, had it not been for the prompt and successful handling of this situation by Cpl Redfern.

He was awarded the MM.

The situation having been stabilized in Vintelen, Lieutenant David Render counter-attacked and re-took Kievelburg. During these actions twenty Germans were killed and 130 taken prisoner. The enemy still held a salient west of the Roer in the area north of Geilenkirchen.

Operation BLACKCOCK

With the arrival of frost-hardened ground, it became possible to tackle the unfinished business, started at Geilenkirchen, of closing with and seizing crossings over the Roer. As there was snow on the ground the tanks were painted white.

Operation BLACKCOCK, the operation to clear the Roer salient, was assigned to XXX Corps which attacked three-divisions-up on an axis from west to east, 43rd (Wessex) on the right/south in broadly the same position as it had been during the attack on Geilenkirchen, to circle round from the south. Seventh Armoured was on the left/north to circle round from the north, and 52nd (Lowland) Division, supported by 8 Armoured Brigade, in the centre. The Lowland Division's principal objective was Heinsburg.

For the regiment, the operation commenced on 18 January, by which time a thaw had set in and the tanks again suffered some bogging. Notwithstanding this, the regiment, supporting 156 Brigade, captured a series of villages during the course of the next few days. Each squadron was commanded by its second-in-command and each saw some tough fighting.

On 21 January B Squadron supported the attack on Honten, on the Sittard-Heinsberg road which involved an advance of a mile and a half over open country. The leading infantry company had a troop of tanks in close support. Close to the objective, the leading troop came under vicious direct fire from an enemy self-propelled gun (SPG), concealed in the orchards forward of Honten. The leading tank went up on a mine and was set on fire by another SPG from the opposite flank which also knocked out the second tank of the leading troop. As a result, the advance came to a halt, and the infantry were pinned down on the exposed ground in a highly precarious and deteriorating situation. William Pollard, now promoted to Sergeant, who had only recently earned a very fine Silver Star at Geilenkirchen, was commanding the second troop, 500 yards behind, with the supporting companies. At this stage he ignored the known danger from the SPG on the right flank and the reported one on the left, and manoeuvred his tank to a position from where he could see the flash of the SPG on his right. This he destroyed, in spite of being engaged by armour-piercing shot from both SPGs. Having knocked out the first, he turned his attention to the other, which immediately after being heavily engaged, was hit by Pollard. Having eliminated the danger from SPGs, he led the infantry into the village from which eighty German prisoners were captured. He was awarded an immediate MM. Given that the status of the US Silver Star is equivalent to an MM, this made him one of the more highly-decorated tank commanders of the Second World War.

Meanwhile, A Squadron, commanded by Captain Neville Fearn, the second-in-command, had been having a comparatively hard time of it since 18 January, capturing Breberen, Laffelde and Selstan, each against strong opposition. The regiment had worked up to Heinsberg, the final objective, which had, by then, been reduced to rubble. Access was across flat and open country, which was comprehensively covered by enemy SP and anti-tank guns.

The initial attack on 24 January was unsuccessful, the anti-tank screen being too strong, and the regiment suffered significant losses. However, during that attack there was a fine act of courage from one of the tank drivers, Trooper Stanley Knight. His tank had been hit and he was wounded. Although the tank had caught fire, he had driven it to cover before baling out, assisting the co-driver, who was also wounded, out of the tank to a place of safety. On his way back to the RAP, he met another squadron tank attempting to cross the open ground. He had halted and climbed onto the tank, and attempted to guide it into a position from where the enemy SPG, which had knocked out his own tank, could be engaged. In spite of his efforts, this second tank was brewed up. When he eventually reached the RAP, Knight was found to be seriously wounded. He was awarded an immediate MM.

Because of the difficulty of getting across the open ground, the plan switched to a night attack by two companies of 4th King's Own Scottish Borderers (KOSB) with A Squadron in support. The plan was for the attack to be timed to take the town at dawn. It was then A Squadron's task, whilst the ground was still shrouded in early dawn light, and on a pre-arranged signal from the battalion CO, to cross the open ground and support it in clearing up the town.

As is so often the case, 4th KOSB, despite their best efforts, took longer than anticipated to reach the town and, by the time the signal was given, it was daylight. This created a highly precarious situation. If the tanks failed to join the infantry, the infantry would suffer heavy losses and find it hard to hang on. If the tanks crossed the ground, over which the previous daylight attack had failed, the squadron would suffer heavy losses, and still might not be able to join up with the infantry. Neville Fearn decided to use a smoke-screen to obscure the view of the enemy anti-tank gunners, despite which his first three tanks were knocked out by SPGs when halfway across. Sergeant Johnny Lanes, appreciating the importance of the attack, collected the remaining tank of his troop, and made a dash across the same open ground. By using the ground and smoke, and all the speed he could muster, he and his remaining tank reached the town in safety, in spite of being engaged by an SPG from his left flank. Once there he was able to support the infantry. The squadron suffered further tank losses in the attack but the key was that there were now some tanks in the town. Once in the town, Lanes set about shooting up houses, and containing enemy strongpoints. This was made difficult by heavy enemy shelling and sniper activity, which forced the infantry to take cover. Lanes stayed and fought throughout the day.

To quote the CO of 4th KOSB, 'We should never have cleared this town so soon had it not been for the timely arrival of Sgt Lanes and his subsequent aggressive and most effective support.' Sergeant Lanes received an immediate MM, downgraded from the DCM. Great credit went also to Captain Fearn for pulling off an attack which bore a high likelihood of significant failure. The way to the Roer was now open.

The regiment had suffered three ORs killed, and six officers and twenty-three ORs wounded.

Chapter 39

Operations VERITABLE and LEEK

February–March 1945

Ｔhe task in the Geilenkirchen area finally completed, XXX Corps made the eighty-mile move back north to Nijmegen. The uncompleted business awaiting them was the clearing of the Reichswald, held by one enemy division. This initial phase was to be followed by the removal of the enemy from the west bank of the Rhine, preparatory to crossing. It was now that holding the salient open paid dividends. From the Nijmegen area, troops would gain access to the Reichswald and so mount this operation, named VERITABLE, which was to include the Canadians and involve five divisions, the initial task being to break through the Reichswald and form a bridgehead on the far side.

Whilst the forest was being cleared, 43rd (Wessex) Division, supported by 8 Armoured Brigade, would by-pass it to the north, and break out from the bridgehead at Cleve. By so doing they would prepare the way for Guards Armoured Division to strike south for the rear of the forest, cutting off the troops therein, before driving south between the Waal and the Rhine. There they would link up with Ninth US Army, also under Montgomery's command, coming up from the south. The Wyverns' axis, codenamed 'Pope', ran broadly southerly on the route Nijmegen-Kranenburg-Cleve-Louisendorf-Goch.

The regiment was to support 129 Brigade, 43rd Division's leading brigade, for the operation which commenced after dark on 7 February with an air bombardment of Cleve. This was followed by an artillery bombardment, which included the tanks of 8 Armoured Brigade. The total ammunition fired by over 1,000 guns was the largest opening barrage or 'Pepper Pot' of the war. The regiment fired over 10,000 rounds at 4,000 yards.

The regiment, taking advantage of their own barrage, moved on the night of 8 February, crossing the start line near Nijmegen at 1900, with the infantry riding on the tanks. Initially the operation went relatively smoothly and Cleve was entered and therefore 'taken'. Suddenly the place came alive with enemy emerging from cellars and a chaotic fire fight lasted all day. At the same time the water levels began to rise as a result of local sluice-gates being opened, but mostly because the Roer dams many miles upstream had been opened by the Germans as their capture by the Americans appeared imminent. By last light, however, order was restored and 1,100 prisoners taken. The regiment had now played a leading part in the capture of Geilenkirchen, Heinsburg and Cleve, the three largest German towns to have so far fallen to the British.

The only inconvenience was that the water had risen to the point that Cleve was effectively cut off, and the brigade and regiment could only be re-supplied by 150 DUKWs (amphibious six-wheeled 2.5-tonners) which had been made available in anticipation of this eventuality.

This phase of the fighting, which was much stiffer than anticipated, continued until 16 February, which Horrocks described as the turning point. Following this the regiment withdrew to Cleve, of which nothing remained but cellars, albeit luckily well-stocked, for much needed rest and re-organization. Casualties during the week-long operation included one officer and twelve ORs killed and four officers and seventeen ORs wounded, as well as fourteen tanks lost.

Operation LEEK

The regiment was out of the line from 16 February until the night of the 28th, during which time it was, once again, reinforced re-equipped and retrained. Goch, the final objective of Operation VERITABLE, fell to 15th (Scottish) Division. On 24 February 8 Armoured Brigade was placed in support of 53rd (Welsh) Division to begin the final drive for the Rhine. This was Operation LEEK which involved crossing the Niers and the capture of Weeze.

By 28 February the division was threatening Weeze itself and the regiment, detailed to support 128 Brigade's attack on the town, was involved in heavy fighting all day on 1 March, losing six tanks.

One example of the fierceness of those engagements was the action in which Lieutenant Reginald Smith's troop took part in support of A Company, 1st East Lancashires in an attack on a strongly-held position in the area of Hussenoff, due east of Weeze. The enemy resisted fiercely, using bazookas, machine guns and SPGs. The rest of Smith's troop had been knocked out, but he continued advancing in support of the company, firing at every enemy machine-gun post he could see, right to the objective, by which time it was almost dark and the enemy were bringing as much fire as they could to bear on his tank. During the operation, he engaged and knocked out a Panther at 800 yards. After helping the company onto its objective, he assisted in the removal of all its casualties across open country, which was still under enemy fire of all types. In the words of the East Lancashires' CO, 'without the assistance given by this officer's tank, it is very doubtful whether the company would have succeeded in reaching its objective'. Lieutenant Smith was awarded an immediate MC. Weeze fell later that day to 4th/7th Royal Dragoon Guards.

On 4 March the Regiment supported 1st Oxfordshire and Buckinghamshire LI, with whom they shared the same design of a horn and lanyard on their cap badge, in a successful attack on Issum during which they linked up with Ninth US Army coming up from the south.

Two outstanding actions were fought on 6 March, the first involving Lieutenant Richard Hyde's troop in B Squadron, which was supporting a battalion of 71 Brigade. The leading company had taken up a position 2,000 yards east of Issum and, to reach the forward platoon, Hyde had to advance with his troop up a road which was covered by SP gunfire. With the enemy firing armour-piercing shot blind down the road, he used a combination of smoke and speed to reach the platoon in safety. The troop and platoon remained in that position the whole of that day and the following night under continuous shellfire. During the day the enemy parachutists holding the line attempted to counter-attack three times, supported by SPGs. On each occasion the counter-attack was repelled. The enemy also tried infiltration by bazooka teams but failed due to the troop's accurate shooting. During the day Lieutenant Hyde spent much time on foot, endeavouring to locate an SPG which was shelling the position. He succeeded in locating the gun and, as a result of engaging it, forced it to withdraw, earning an immediate MC for the action. The second action was by Lieutenant Frederick Cagney, who was commanding a troop in C Squadron, supporting a battalion of 158 Brigade attacking a wooded area two miles east of Issum. Owing to the boggy nature of the ground, the troop was unable to use the same cross-country axis as the infantry and had to use the main road to the left of and parallel to the infantry. This road was covered by SP fire. Frederick Cagney used smoke and speed and led his troop up the road before swinging into the woods and onto the objective. Due to enemy action, the infantry were delayed for twenty minutes. Meanwhile, the troop found itself on the objective, in the wood, surrounded by enemy infantry and all four tanks were immediately engaged by bazookas and snipers. Cagney immediately called for artillery fire on the objective and gave orders to his troop to engage the enemy with the maximum firepower. As a result, the troop inflicted very severe casualties on the parachutists holding the line and endeavoured to surround them. Because of this, when the infantry arrived on the objective, they suffered very light casualties and captured 100 German parachutists. Lieutenant Cagney was also awarded an immediate MC.

The regiment pressed on to the Rhine which involved two days' fighting, in which they were inhibited by the need to bridge some minor rivers and also encountered more fanatical Germans who sometimes shouted, as they fought, that they would rather die than surrender. The regiment, after all it had been through during five long years, was in no mood to disappoint them. Notwithstanding such resistance, the Rangers gradually closed on the banks of the Rhine. Casualties in this phase were two ORs killed and an officer and ten ORs wounded.

Even though they were in range of Allied guns, the ever resourceful enemy managed to withdraw eighteen divisions across the river, with much of their equipment. However, they left behind 53,000 prisoners. Farther south, First,

Third and Seventh US Armies, supported by First French Army, were still fighting through to the Rhine. On 7 March First US Army had the great good fortune, born out of exceptional opportunism, to capture a rail bridge across the Rhine at Remagen. It was still useable and they quickly put four divisions over to form a ten-mile-deep and twenty-five-mile-wide bridgehead.

Chapter 40

Final Advance

March 1945–May 1946

Operation PLUNDER

Operation PLUNDER was the name for the crossing of the Rhine.

The Rhine crossing had been in planning for many months, which had involved assembling quantities of stores, amphibious vehicles, assault craft, pontoons and bridging material. Crossings were to be made in two sectors, the first, south of the Ruhr, by Bradley; the second, north of the Ruhr, by Montgomery. Under his command Montgomery had First Canadian, Second British and Ninth US Armies. Second British and Ninth US were each to seize one bridgehead north and south of Wesel respectively, attacking with two divisions up. XXX Corps was responsible for the British crossing, the northernmost. The divisions deployed were 51st (Highland), attacking towards Rees on the left/north, and 15th (Scottish), attacking from Xanten on the right/south.

As 8 Armoured Brigade was to support 51st (Highland) Division it was reinforced by the Staffordshire Yeomanry, equipped with DD tanks, in which Lawrence Biddle was now second-in-command. All their recce, command and control, and logistic support elements, were also amphibious and they used Buffaloes and DUKWs, both amphibious load carriers, as support vehicles. Although trained to land on D Day in DDs the Staffords had not been used. They were to lead the crossing, and become the only British armoured regiment ever to have undertaken a fully amphibious operation.

H Hour was 2100 on 23 March and, as usual, was preceded by a day-long barrage, which, as well as targeting enemy positions, provided a permanent smokescreen to disrupt enemy observation of the preparations to cross. PLUNDER went relatively smoothly. The regiment played virtually no part in it, until it became necessary to force the bridgehead on the other side.

On 27 March the regiment crossed with 51st (Highland) Division to liberate northern Holland, the only non-German territory still in German hands. The Allies were anxious to do this as quickly as possible, firstly to free the Dutch living there from the risk of atrocities, and secondly, to capture V–2 rocket sites still operating against the UK, although in the event 27 March was the date of the last such attack. For the next week the regiment fought fiercely northwards towards the Dutch border against strong opposition to enlarge the bridgehead, which was at that stage only four miles deep. Most of the fighting involving the regiment took place around Issleburg, in Germany, and Dinxperloo just to the north, across the border in Holland.

On 27 March Lieutenant Peter Mellowes was ordered to move forward with his troop before dawn to support a battalion of Seaforth Highlanders, who had attacked during the previous night. He had to lead his troop forward on foot owing to the extremely boggy nature of the ground and the presence of many mines. All the while they were under sniper and mortar fire. On arriving at the forward company area he found that, during the night, enemy paratroopers had launched a strong counter-attack, retaken some of the ground, and captured the Seaforth CO and his adjutant. Mellowes led his troop to storm some farmhouses which the company told him was the main enemy strongpoint and centre of their resistance. On moving forward, his tanks were engaged by bazookas and two SPGs, but his attack was successful and the farmhouses were completely destroyed; 100 paratroopers gave themselves up. The Seaforth CO and adjutant were liberated.

Peter Mellowes then made a foot reconnaissance, under fire, to find a place where his tanks could cross the Ijssel, the bridge having been blown. Calling for a smokescreen, and with the help of a bulldozer and scissors bridge, he organized a crossing. As a result, his own troop, supported by another and a company of infantry, formed a firm bridgehead over the river through which another battalion of infantry and squadron of tanks passed to liberate Dinxperloo. He was awarded an immediate MC.

On the night of 27/28 March Lieutenant Dick Holman's A Squadron troop was supporting 1st Gordon Highlanders, with orders to capture some high ground in the area approximately 2,000 yards west of Issleburg. The objective lay behind a raised autobahn under construction which ran from west to east across the axis of advance. Making a night attack, the Gordons almost immediately came under fire from machine guns from their left flank. Holman was ordered forward to support them. To ascertain the exact direction from which the MG-fire was coming, he went forward on foot to contact the forward positions held by the division on his left, but soon discovered that these positions were held by the enemy, who immediately opened fire on him. Returning to his tank, he knocked out two MG teams which were holding up the advance. On returning to the main road, his tank went up on a mine. He dismounted and walked in front of the remainder of his troop, picking up four mines, until he reached the main road and was then called to assist one of the leading platoons of the Gordons on the right of the axis, who were being pinned down by enemy MG-fire coming from the direction of the autobahn. Although under fire, Dick Holman again contacted on foot the leading platoon to ascertain the exact location of the enemy.

On his way back to his tank he found that the road was mined and an obstacle blocked the main road. As no sappers were available, he checked the roadside for mines and removed all that he found and, with the help of his own tank, removed the block. All this was done during periods of enemy mortaring. Holman then led his troop forward to the autobahn and dealt with the enemy MG teams. The infantry were then able to push forward, cross the autobahn and capture their objective by first light. For this he received an immediate MC.

On 28 March during the fighting for Issleburg, Captain Neville Fearn was wounded in the head whilst still serving with A Squadron. He refused to leave until he fell unconscious through loss of blood, a typical example of his endurance and courage, which he had shown throughout numerous battles in North Africa and since he landed on the beaches of Normandy. For his fine performance throughout the North-West European campaign he received a rare immediate DSO.

Both Issleburg and Dinxperloo fell after a fight but the regiment suffered a significant loss when the Squadron Sergeant Major of A Squadron, SSM Henry Hutchinson, who had served as such throughout the period that the regiment had been armoured, was killed. He was a talisman whose death affected deeply a regiment which thought it had become impervious, even to the loss of its own, after seeing so much death. He had earned a fine MM at Alamein recovering wounded tank crews under fire.

The purpose of this fighting had been to punch a hole in the perimeter of the bridgehead through which to pass the Guards Armoured, to exploit the Regiment's success, or to put it less charitably 'swan' through. It was a sore point with the break in brigades that they did the hard work and the armoured divisions got the glory.

A Sherwood Ranger tank commander was heard to call to a very dignified Guards officer sitting in the turret of his tank en route for the swanning part 'mind your paint, Sir, as you go through'.

The regiment was now to enjoy its own 'swanning' as, on 1 April, the pursuit battle started, and the SRY, now back in Holland, moved north as a regimental group, with its battery of guns from the Essex Yeomanry, its company of infantry from 12th KRRC and a squadron of Kangaroo APCs carrying a company of 4th Wiltshires. They moved forward apace to Rurlo, Sergeant Lane knocking out two 88s en route. Beyond Rurlo, A Squadron and 4th Wiltshires took out an enemy rearguard. On 1 April, A Squadron now commanded by Major Enderby, was ordered to take Lochem, which was held by the enemy, from the south. He sent Lt David Renders troop to lead in a right flanking approach from the east. Fourth Troop, commanded by Peter Mellowes was ordered to approach from the south. The troop pushed up the main road and established itself on the viaduct, which crossed the road about 800 yards due south of the town. This operation was to be carried out without the support of infantry, as none were available at the time. The leading 4th Troop tank, commanded by Sergeant O'Pray and driven by Trooper Thomas Potts, received two direct hits from bazookas at very short range, and brewed up. Immediately, Trooper Potts, badly burnt himself, baled out to discover that the remainder of his crew were badly wounded and unable to bale out. He immediately climbed onto the tank to rescue his crew but was shot at by the bazooka team from a slit trench twenty yards away. This team were engaging his troop leader's tank thirty yards to his right rear. Potts jumped off his tank and, armed only with a revolver, attacked the slit trench and shot two of the bazooka team, the remainder fleeing in disorder. He returned to his tank, assisted the wounded to a place of safety, and climbed onto his troop leader's tank to point out further enemy strongpoints which he had located until he was forcibly evacuated, suffering from severe burns. The remaining two tanks of the troop took sixty more prisoners and killed a further sixty. Thomas Potts was awarded an immediate MM. Sergeant O'Pray died from his wounds. On 2 April the regiment took Enschede, supporting three infantry battalions in a fierce battle. Next Henglo fell, the regiment entering the town as it was still occupied by the retreating enemy rearguard, which was nevertheless able to slip away because of huge crowds of joyful citizens preventing the SRY engaging them.

The regiment spent six pleasant days being made welcome in Henglo.

On 9 April the advance continued towards Bremen with the Sherwood Rangers supporting 3rd Division, which meant they had now supported every British infantry division in theatre.

Every day there were skirmishes against fanatical Germans and casualties and near misses.

On 13 April Lieutenant Reginald Reed's B Squadron troop was supporting 4th Dorsets to capture Cloppenburg from the south. The enemy attempted to blow the bridge in the town centre and hold the northern sector. Lieutenant Reed's troop was in the lead, and was first held up by a crater in the centre of the road. He dismounted and reconnoitred a way round on foot; during this recce he was continually sniped at and mortared by the enemy rearguard from south of the river. Having led his troop round the crater, he found that the bridge, although badly damaged, had not been destroyed. Still under fire he organized a party to repair the bridge and then, calling for smoke, led his troop at speed over it into the northern sector of the town. He was immediately engaged by two bazooka teams, which his tank destroyed.

As a result of Reed's arrival on the northern bank of the river, a company of 4th Dorsets, who had been pinned down by fire and in danger of being completely cut off, were released. Lieutenant Reed was then told by members of 4th Dorsets that an SPG was coming towards him. He ordered the rest of his troop to give covering fire, manoeuvred his tank into a fire position and engaged the SPG, which retreated immediately to the woods at the north of the town. The town was captured and he received an immediate MC.

It should be added that the release of the company had its moments since town fighting in tanks is not without risks for friend and foe alike. On this occasion once Lieutenant Reed had located the company he called on the air to Corporal McDonald to tell him that the infantry were in the 'third house from the left' –

but were held up by Germans in the 'fourth house from the left', and he wanted this 'fourth house' knocked down. Could Corporal McDonald from his present position do it with his big gun? Corporal McDonald replied that he could see the 'third house', but the 'fourth house' seemed to be round the corner from him. Should he try a shoot? Next followed some crosstalk as to which was the 'third house' and where you started to count from anyway, and the dozens of listeners on the regimental wireless net began to feel some concern for the immediate future of the infantry in the 'third house'. There were under the regiment's command some Funnies of the type which threw the huge bomb called a 'Flying Dustbin', capable of demolishing several houses at once, and their commander, a most enthusiastic dustbin-hurler, now came on the air to suggest he might try a shoot. A shudder ran through the entire regimental group among listeners far back to the rear echelons, as pained imaginations pictured this enthusiast destroying a score or two of houses on the principle that one would be the 'fourth house from the left'. All this worry was quite unnecessary as Lieutenant Reed had the situation well in hand, the 'fourth house' was duly demolished and the grateful infantry emerged smartly from the 'third house' to continue their advance.

On 19 April, in another such skirmish, the infantry being supported by Sergeant Robert Wheeler's troop were pinned down by intense machine-gun and mortar fire. Having directed the positioning of his other tanks, he advanced his own swiftly into the midst of the enemy position but found he was too close to depress his guns sufficiently to engage. He climbed onto the back of his tank, whereupon the enemy engaged him with rifle and machine-gun fire, and his tank with bazookas. Using the turret for shelter he shot back and threw grenades at the enemy. Such was the ferocity of his attack, that the enemy position, over 200-strong, surrendered, and he took them prisoner. For this he was awarded a richly deserved immediate DCM.

The attack on Bremen began on 21 April. On the 26th A Squadron was supporting 5th Wiltshires of 130 Brigade to capture a portion of the northern sector, bordering on the main part which contained the HQ of the Bremen defences. Owing to numerous streets in the town area, 3rd Troop of A Squadron became detached from their infantry and found themselves sandwiched between two bazooka teams positioned at the ends of a narrow street. As no more infantry were available, 2nd Troop under Corporal Irvine Powell was ordered to go to the relief of 3rd Troop. Powell dismounted at the end of the street and, armed with a Sten gun, stalked the bazooka team, who were attempting to engage 3rd Troop. Attacking them from the rear, he completely surprised them and killed two; the remainder surrendered. He summoned his troop, continued to lead them on foot, and discovered the second team at the far end of the street, against whom he directed his troop's fire. After the first few shots, this second bazooka team surrendered and 3rd Troop was extricated from a position which might have resulted in the loss of all three tanks. The bazooka teams were all either killed or captured, and the infantry were able to occupy the area without opposition or casualties. Corporal Powell received an immediate MM. On 28 April Bremen fell when Lieutenant Talbot's troop captured the German general in his headquarters.

Sergeant Harold Markham was Mechanical Sergeant to A Squadron and whenever a tank fell out of battle, either through enemy action or mechanical trouble, he immediately went right up to it to inspect the damage and, if repairable, commenced work immediately, more often than not under shellfire. On 2 May, after A Squadron had captured the village of Rhada, Sergeant Markham insisted on working on a tank in spite of the fact that the village was under shellfire and continued until he was wounded by a shell which landed close to the tank. Only after receiving a direct order from his squadron leader did he allow himself to be evacuated. He was awarded the MM.

Does it not astonish that, with the war won and manifestly in its last days, so many acts of sacrifice and valour occurred in this extraordinary regiment? That these were but examples of the regiment's culture is evidenced by its casualties during this final phase in which two officers and twenty-one ORs were killed and three officers and fourteen ORs wounded.

The advance continued beyond Bremen with the usual daily battles, until on 4 May, just as the regiment was preparing to attack Bremenhaven, the following order was received by RHQ:

'No advance beyond present positions – stop –
No further harassing fire – stop –
No further tactical move unless ordered – stop -
BBC News Flash confirmed – stop –
German Army on 21 Army Group Front surrenders wef 0800 hours
5th May 1945 – stop –
Details as to procedure later – stop'

That night the champagne was opened and the night sky lit up with a massive *feu de joie*. The Rangers sat around their tanks. The release for the first time of their minds from the all-consuming pre-occupation of staying alive should have brought relief. They had, after all, fought their way over 3,000 miles, in countless engagements of every size, during nearly six years of war. They had, however, seen many close friends and comrades, equal to the regiment's entire strength, fall beside them, killed or wounded. There was, as a result, little sense of joy, relief or deliverance flooding into the vacuum. Instead came grief for all those friends and colleagues lost, who should have shared this moment, and of the guilt that is the burden of the survivor, and which they would carry to their own graves.

How should their war record be evaluated?

No one was better qualified to make that judgement than Lieutenant General Sir Brian Horrocks, who had the regiment under his command from August 1942 to May 1945. On the occasion of its being disembodied he wrote, 'I can hardly imagine a British Army without the Sherwood Rangers, and there is no doubt no armoured regiment can show a finer record of hard fighting'. He later added, 'I still maintain that the Sherwood Rangers Yeomanry took part in more fighting than did any other armoured regiment'.

The regiment's success in the Second World War can also be gauged by its thirty battle honours, its 159 awards, including seventy-eight for gallantry, and above all the 827 casualties killed, wounded or missing

The regiment moved to Hanover and later to Einbeck. On 1 March 1946 the Sherwood Rangers Yeomanry was placed in suspended animation. A memorial service was held in St Mary's Church, Nottingham on 21 September 1946 for the 245 members of the regiment who had given their lives. On that same day the City of Nottingham presented the Freedom of the City to the Sherwood Rangers Yeomanry.

The whole earth is the Sepulchre of Heroes, moments may rise and tablets be set up to them in their own land, but on far-flung shores there is an abiding memorial that no pen or chisel has traced; it is graven not on stone or brass, but on the living heart of humanity. Take these men for your example. Like them remember that prosperity can only be for the free, that freedom is the sure possession of those alone who have the courage to defend it.

Pericles

Author's Comment

To my surprise this account has given rise to three questions which seem pertinent because of their relevance today. It is important that the lessons which those in this account gave their lives learning are not lost, they are spelt out here.

The Role of Volunteers

It goes without saying that if a conventional threat to the home base emerges a significant enlargement of the armed forces to meet that threat will be necessary, this high-tech era of drones, cyberspace and the rest notwithstanding. In the end 'We will fight them on the beaches'. Many will assume this means an enlargement by and of the Regular Army. In fact, historically this is not true as the role of the Regular Army has been to make the initial deployment and hold the line, deliver a trained reseve of past regulars, run the training cadres for the enlargement process and, above all, provide the the senior command structure. It has, on the other hand, had little to do with enlargement as such, since it has been already fully engaged, holding its finger in the dyke until reinforced.

In truth, for a thousand years (during most of which there was no regular 'army') initial enlargement in these circumstances has been triggered by a combination of a pre-existing obligation, as with the feudal system, or a spontaneous response triggered locally by a national call to arms, as in the case of the three wars covered in this account. This was achieved through a network of locations throughout the country where volunteers mustered in peacetime. Originally, once the threat had been addressed or had subsided, the units raised were stood down and melted back into the community. For the last two centuries, starting with the yeomanry, a portion of such units have not been disbanded but have been maintained and, until recently, were recognized as the Territorial Army, based in its training centres, so keeping the conduit for enlargement open in peacetime as the most important, but not its only, role.

Because it has been our way and has worked well, the initial mobilization of volunteers in both world wars was through the structure of the TF/TA and, in both cases, started before war was declared and eventually created a force many times larger than the Regular Army, and was each time one of the war-winning measures. Its strength seems to have been that, by building on an existing structure, well known because of its presence in the neighbourhood, it provided a familiar conduit through which local communities responded to join this existing framework of units, led by former members of the unit concerned, including members already known to them. Response to a call to arms and the unit chosen is a personal thing and is best done eyeball to eyeball.

It appears to have worked better and, crucially, quicker than any of the alternatives: a 'new army' as created by Kitchener, which had no pre-existing structure or culture and took far longer to become useful, or by conscription which was the Regular Army's preferred option and would have been catastrophic if used from the outset, due to its unpopularity. It is true that 'one volunteer is worth ten pressed men'. Conscription is necessary, but has always been best used when all volunteers have joined and more are still needed.

In the last few years this time-honoured system for recruitment of all sorts has been replaced by what must be the most dysfunctional and unsuitable arrangement it is possible to conceive. I refer, of course, to the decision to subcontract recruitment to a civilian contractor. First of all, when it comes to manpower, recruiting and enlargement is the single most important part of defence. If that fails then literally all is lost. There will be no one on the beaches. Secondly, the self evident impossibility of framing a legally-binding obligation for a task the scope of which cannot be defined or priced in advance means the arrangement is either inadequate or unenforceable. Thirdly, to seek to base such a crucial task as recruiting on a commercial organization, the continuing capacity or even existence of which cannot be guaranteed, because that is the very nature of all such organizations, has to be flawed. Fourthly, the moment when it fails catastrophically, will be the very moment of the Nation's greatest need. Fifthly, the remedy is merely to claim for breach of contract when delivery is the only remedy that is of any use. Sixthly, it is hard to conceive of a structure less suited to handle a spontaneous call to arms than this one, because it is not based in the community and the one-to-one engagement, which is the essence, is absent.

The reason enlargement through the Haldane structure of the TA has worked better is because, it seems, only a pre-planned and pre-existing structure of units and formations attracting volunteers responds fast enough and in sufficient numbers, consisting of the best calibre, to achieve critical mass.

For the first time in our history, the truth seems to have been lost in the role assigned to volunteers today, which is solely to bring the partly 'cadreised' Regular Army up to war establishment when necessary, not just when a threat to the home base occurs. The role of forming the units and formations that will generate enlargement is not just absent by accidental omission, but by virtue of the fact that it has been explicitly stated that there are no plans for the TA to generate formed units for deployment. That seems to mean that no plans for enlargement exist at all.

The role of bringing the Army up to war establishment now assigned to the Volunteer Reserve is, of course, a very important one, but one which used to be the role of the Regular Reserve, made up of past members of the Regular Army returning to their own units. This ceased to be the case when it was found, both in the Cold War and the hot ones that have followed it, it failed to deliver sufficiently, due to skill fade and reluctance to be recalled. Not only that but volunteers have been found to be of higher quality and more committed and have performed better.

Volunteers like the new role but they cannot do both because in the event of a major threat they will have already gone with the Regular Army, leaving nothing behind. This, as matters stand, precludes them from providing the strategically vital role as the structure on which the initial enlargement is based and which has hitherto been their primary strategic role and for which they are well suited.

However, this need not be so since, as Haldane and the Cold War showed, the two roles are not mutually exclusive, provided the strategic importance of enlargement is recognized, as it needs to be, and some relatively minor and inexpensive adjustments to the new plans made. In addition, the wasted resource of the regular reservists should be harnessed.

The Role of the Main Battle Tank

The argument goes that the main battle tank (MBT) is not suitable for use in the asymmetric wars of today, even though it has been used successfully and extensively in such wars. Nor, it is said, is it now needed in a fight against an enemy possessing broad parity, the firepower of the MBTs being trumped by the attack helicopter and hand-held fire and forget weapons. Further, any future major war will be fought in built-up areas for which MBTs are not suited. On the other hand, the infantry seem to be consistently overestimating their capability to operate without tanks by using their armoured personnel carriers (APCs) in lieu, albeit fitted with a turret and semi-automatic cannon. It seems that on a modern battlefield, infantry on their feet are thought better able to survive and prevail than crews of MBTs.

Based on the narrative of this book in relation to the fighting in North-West Europe in the Second World War, the last time we fought an enemy of broadly equal value, the foregoing argument seems hard to sustain. The evidence of this account is that no infantry division willingly went into action without the support of MBTs in significant numbers, sixty tanks per infantry brigade. This was not a token issue; the evidence is that the infantry would seldom have prevailed in battle in North-West Europe without the support of MBTs. It must be added that, equally, the tanks would not have survived without the close protection of their own integrated infantry and of the infantry they were supporting. This was a close partnership in which each admired the other and pitied each other's fate, the one to fight without being encased in armour and the other being too large and exposed to fit into a slit trench!

In performing this service for the infantry divisions, in the period between D Day and VE Day, 8 Armoured Brigade suffered such losses that it was resupplied with 1,200 tanks against an establishment of about 200. These would not all be to replace destroyed tanks and included those merely damaged and sent back for repair. Nevertheless, that is a very significant level of attrition. The Sherwood Rangers lost fifty tank commanders in Normandy alone, nearly one for every tank on its establishment. The armour, despite its apparent strength, still paid a huge price to get the infantry onto their objectives, but there was no alternative. Even with the help of the tanks the infantry, on their feet and unprotected, suffered far worse, their casualties outnumbering the tank regiments. Throughout they operated with the benefit of full air superiority, weather permitting (a major caveat even today), so suffered relatively few losses from the air.

In the whole campaign there was almost no occasion when an infantry division was required to fight a mixed force including tanks/heavy weapons without armoured support. The two occasions I am aware of are the Americans at Omaha, because their tanks nearly all sank, and the airborne landings at Arnhem because the tanks could not reach them. Neither went well. There may be examples where an unsupported infantry division fought and won against an enemy which included armour, but I do not know of it.

That tanks cannot routinely fight in towns or close country as a generalization is a myth. For example, much of the campaign in Normandy was fought in the bocage, which had the same characteristics as a built-up area except that vegetation obstructed visibility, and enhanced the chances of the defender, rather than buildings. There were approximately 2,000 tanks on each side in Normandy. That is one of the largest tank versus tank confrontations ever fought. Self evidently they coped in that adverse environment. There were, of course, towns as well. From Belgium onwards, virtually every action fought by the Sherwood Rangers was either for or in a built-up area and they were extremely effective when doing so. Given the foregoing narrative, it is hard to see how infantry could have coped without them when fighting in built-up areas.

On the other hand there were significant numbers of actions when armour without infantry support took ground which conventional wisdom would say only infantry could take, for example, Jig Gold, as described. Two troops of 13th/18th Hussars took Mont Pinçon, a steep entirely forested hill by finding an unguarded track; the Sherwood Rangers at Berjou took a precipitous and heavily-wooded feature as described in this narrative; Gheel fell as described fully in the narrative. None were ideal, but in each case the armour managed to prevail or at least hold its own, albeit with difficulty, with either no or heavily depleted infantry support. Let's be clear this was a partnership and they would, of course, have done better with full infantry support. The point I am making is that tanks, without infantry, could *in extremis* cope with an infantry task, but infantry always needed tanks for an infantry task and could not take on an armoured task. Of course, the indirect fire provided by artillery is vital to both, but it is not a substitute for either.

On the evidence of this account infantry without armour is not an option. Yet it is routinely peddled as such. For clarity, nor is armour without infantry an option, but no one is arguing that infantry are obsolete and that they should be removed from, or demoted in, the order of battle. There are, of course, attack helicopters but, for all their worth, they would not assist the infantry back onto their feet as the tanks were able to do. Also they are extremely vulnerable, even to small-arms fire, and limited in ways that tanks are not.

I understand that instead of tanks the infantry would use turreted APCs to carry the infantry, as well as to provide suppressive fire. If that solution had existed and been used instead of 8 Armoured Brigade in North-West Europe that would have meant up to 1,200 APCs, each containing an AFV crew and pregnant with a rifle section, would have been knocked out so that each kill would have given the enemy not just a tank crew but a rifle section as well – double the attrition. At the very least it would have 'unhorsed' the infantry section and thus degraded the battalion. That begs the question whether we have an APC which can, when fully bombed up and rationed, carry a full AFV crew plus a full rifle section and all the collateral equipment in a manner which would deliver either the AFV crew or the rifle section fit to fight when needed. Warrior cannot; one that could would be huge.

It also begs the question of training priorities. Remember what Stanley Christopherson, who won thirty battle honours in the war, either as the point squadron leader in the desert or as CO in North-West Europe, wrote: 'I am convinced that the most important and essential part of our training [of an armoured regiment] was the original "Individual Training", especially the gunnery and wireless part. The success of any tank v. tank battle depended on accurate and quick fire, and it was quite impossible to fight any kind of battle ... unless wireless communication was good.... ' I suggest that neither of those priorities would make the top three in an infantry battalion, even an armoured one.

This leads to the question as to who provides the suppressive fire when the section dismounts to assault, leaving the APC at best only partially crewed, and how effective it would be compared with an armoured crew, both better trained in the role and with a better gun and protection.

The APC idea also fails to take into account the key point that an armoured regiment has more stamina than an infantry battalion because the physical work of an infantryman is far more arduous. No battalion in Normandy could have taken fifty-five out of seventy-four days in the line as did the Sherwood Rangers. It should be remembered that during the days they were in reserve a high percentage of the time was spent on trade and command skill cadres to prepare casualty replacements for imminent combat. No infantry battalion could have done both that and addressed its needs as a battalion. Further, that stamina question means that, if APCs are to be dual roled as tanks, far more of them would be needed to achieve the same coverage. Surely, given the choice, tanks are a better option.

This is not my view. I have not the experience to comment but it is the view of every Sherwood Ranger who was there and whom I have ever heard discuss the subject. If that is what those who survived to tell us of their experiences say perhaps we should listen.

Shock Action

With the benefit of hindsight it is hard to conclude from this account that one of the the largest strategic errors committed by the high command of the British Army in the last half of the nineteenth century and the early years of the twentieth was to write off cavalry as having been rendered obsolete by the machine gun. That view changed the nature of warfare because it limited the forces capable of shock action and therefore may have played an expensive part in the stalemate in the First World War. That observation is of only historic interest, save for its relevance to the comments which follow.

Despite everything, the British Army does still possess MBTs, 168 to be precise, plus some more in mothballs. This is approximately the same number as 8 Armoured Brigade had. Given the foregoing, there is no doubt how they would be used if we were ever confronted by an enemy of equal value, that is in supporting our infantry who would be overwhelmed by enemy armour without them. There are barely enough even for that task. Better judges than I believe they should have been used that way in Afghanistan, and indeed tanks of the Danish army were.

This brings another matter to the fore. As this account has clearly shown, since the beginning of time the capability to deliver shock action has been one of the essential capabilities of any army. With all our tanks committed to supporting our infantry divisions, what is the plan to deliver that capability? The lack of that capability in the Great War cost both sides obscene numbers of casualties in fighting over a stretch of ground that the armoured elements of our army of the Second World War passed through in a day on their 3,000 mile journey from El Alamein to Berlin, during which dozens of hard-fought battle honours were won by use of shock action delivered by tanks. The contrast between an army with the capability of delivering shock action and one without it could not be starker. If tanks are now deemed obsolete, what has replaced them that has that capability? Nothing, and certainly not attack helicopters. We need to address this. As this account recalls, Horrocks was of the view that the TA produced some of his best armoured regiments, because they were younger and less risk averse. Given the shortage of funding that is an option worth looking at.

Battle Honours

SOUTH AFRICA 1900–1902

THE GREAT WAR

GALLIPOLI 1915 SUVLA SCIMITAR HILL	**MACEDONIA 1916–1917** STRUMA
EGYPT 1915–1916 GAZA EL MUGHAR NEBI SAMWEIL	**PALESTINE 1917–1918** MEGIDDO SHARON DAMASCUS

THE SECOND WORLD WAR

NORTH AFRICA **1940–1943**	**NORTH WEST EUROPE** **1944–1945**	
ALAM EL HALFA	NORMANDY LANDING	GHEEL
EL ALAMEIN	VILLERS BOCAGE	NEDERRIJN
EL AGHEILA	ODON	GEILENKIRCHEN
ADVANCE ON TRIPOLI	FONTENAY LE PESNIL	ROER
TEBAGA GAP	DEFENCE OF RAURAY	RHINELAND
POINT 201 – ROMAN WALL	MONT PINÇON	CLEVE
EL HAMMA	JURQUES	GOCH
CHEBKET EN NOUIGES	NOIREAU CROSSING	WEEZE
ENFIDAVILLE	SEINE, 1944	RHINE
TAKROUNA		

FREEDOMS

NOTTINGHAM   NEWARK   RETFORD   GEDLING

Bibliography

Anon, *Through Palestine with the 20th Machine Gun Squadron* (Privately published)

Anon, *The 8th Armoured Brigade 1939–1945* (Privately published)

Beevor, Antony, *D Day* (Penguin Group, London, 2009)

Biddle, Lt Col Lawrence, MC, *Letters to My Father 1939–1945* (Privately published, 1994)

Birkin, Lt Col R. L., DSO, *The History of the 3rd Imperial Yeomanry* (Privately published)

Churchill, Winston S., *The Second World War* (Cassell & Co Ltd, London, 1948)

Cropper, Andy, *Dad's War – A tank Commander in Europe* (Anmas Publications, Thurlstone, South Yorkshire, 1994)

Delaforce, Patrick, *Monty's Marauders* (Chancellor Press, London, 2000)

Douglas, Keith, *Alamein to Zem Zem* (Editions Poetry, London, 1946)

Falls, Captain Cyril, *History of the Great War – Military Operations Egypt & Palestine from June 1917 to the end of the War* (the copy annotated in ink by Hugh Tallents) (HMSO, London, 1930)

Doyle, Sir Arthur Conan, *The Great Boer War* (Smith, Elder and Co., London, 1900)

Ewing, Ken and Ernie Leppard, *Mareth, March 1943 Breakthrough at Tebaga Gap with the NZ Corps – 8th Armoured Brigade* (Privately published, 1999)

Foster, Philip, *A Trooper's Desert War* (Wilton 65, York, 1994)

Gunn, James, *The Nottinghamshire Yeomanry in World War I* (Privately published)

Hart Dyke, Brigadier T., DSO, *Normandy to Arnhem* (Privately published, 1966)

Hildyard, Captain Myles MBE, MC, TD, *It is Bliss Here* (Bloomsbury Publishing, London, 2005)

Hills, Captain Stuart MC, *By Tank into Normandy* (Cassell & Co., London, 2002)

Holland, James, *An Englishman at War* (Bantam Press, London, 2014)

Jarvis, Robert B., *Chariots of the Lake* (The Heritage Workshop Centre, Lowestoft, 2003)

Keegan, John, *Six Armies in Normandy* (Pimlico, London, 1992)

Lanes, Sergeant J. R. MM, *Diaries* (Privately published)

Lindsay, T.M., *Sherwood Rangers* (Burrup, Mathieson & Co. Ltd, London, 1952)

Pakenham, Thomas, *The Boer War* (Abacus, London, 1992)

Playfair, Major General I. S. O. CB DSO MC et al, *A History of the Second World War, The Mediterranean and Middle East* (HMSO, London, 1966)

Ranfurly, Countess, *To War with Whitaker* (William Heinemann, London, 1994)

Reddish, Arthur, *El Alamein – A Tank Soldier's Story* (Privately published)

Reddish, Arthur, *Normandy 1944 From the Hull of a Sherman* (Privately published)

Reddish, Arthur, *The Final Advance* (Wilton 65, York, 1997)

Richards, Walter, *His Majesty's Territorial Army* (Virtue & Co London 1910)
Scott, Don, *Polar Bears From Sheffield* (Tiger and Rose Sheffield 2001)
Skinner, the Reverend Leslie, RAChD, *The Man Who Worked on Sundays* (Privately published)
Skinner, the Reverend Leslie, RAChD, *The Sherwood Rangers Casualty Book 1944–1945* (Privately published)
Tallents, Major Hugh DSO, *Sherwood Rangers Yeomanry in the Great War* (Philip Allan & Co. Ltd, London, 1926)

Unpublished

National Archives, Kew
War Diaries of the Sherwood Rangers Yeomanry 1914–1919
War Diaries, Sherwood Rangers Yeomanry 1939–1945
War Diaries, 82 Assault Squadron Royal Engineers 1944–45

Other
Anon, *Two Sides of a Battle – War* (Issued by the Army Bureau of Current Affairs)
Archives and records of the Sherwood Rangers Yeomanry, often in the form of cuttings.
Bethell-Fox, Lt John MC, *Green Beach*
Christopherson, Lt Col S. D., DSO MC TD, *Diaries*
Machin family Archives
Newbould, Colonel Christopher CBE, Notes on the D Day Landings
Semken, Major John CB MC, *The War Diary of, 1941 to 1943* (unpublished)
The papers of the 7th Viscount Galway (Department of Manuscripts and Special Collections of the University of Nottingham: Ga C11/92, /93, /216/ 3 to 7,/240, /250, /263, /289/1 and 2, /290/1, /293/2 and 3, /294/1 and 2, /295,1 and 2, /296/1, /299/1 and 2, and /300/1)
The papers, news cuttings and photograph albums of Colonel C. G. C. Money CB (Fusiliers Museum of Northumberland)
Wilson, Mark, Account of the history of 2/1 and 3/1 Notts (Sherwood Rangers) Yeomanry in the First World War

Film/DVD
Assault on Normandy GOLD BEACH Battle for the Beaches, presented by Tim Dormer, Richard Hone, Tim Saunders, Tim Stoneman, Andy Johnson and Andrew Duff. (Pen and Sword Ltd, Barnsley, 2013)

Website
www.sherwood-rangers.org A website established by veterans of the Regiment, illustrating its history, remembering the fallen and including a photo gallery.

Index

Abdy, Maj Jack R. 101, 112–13, 153
Abel Smith, Lt Joscelyn 154, 167
Abu Tulul 130–7
Abyssinia 156, 159, 161, 163
Alam el Halfa 170, 175–8, 311
Albert Canal 226, 274
Alderson, Lt David 283
Aleppo 116–18, 145–6
Alexander, FM H. R. L. G., 1st Earl of Tunis
& Errigal, KG GCB OM GCMG CSI DSO
MC CD PC 172, 179, 187, 211
Allen, Capt R. H. 127–8, 145–6
Allenby, FM E. H. H. Allenby, 1st Viscount,
GCB GCMG GCVO 94, 96, 98–100, 105,
107, 114, 116–19, 121, 123, 127, 130–1,
135–8, 143–6, 156
Amba Giogis 163
Amman 117–23, 126, 137, 143
Anderson, Gen Sir John
D'Arcy, GBE KCB DSO 21, 29, 226, 241
Apweiler 284
Ardagh, Maj Gen Sir John 4
Armies:
　British
　　First 191, 213
　　Second 221, 254–7, 260, 263, 286, 298
　　Eighth 172, 175–6, 179–80, 188–9, 192–3,
　　196, 203, 211, 213, 227
　United States
　　First 221, 254–5, 263, 276, 296–7
　　Third 258, 260, 263, 297
　　Seventh 297
　　Ninth 276–9, 294, 296–8
　French
　　First 297
　Canadian
　　First 255, 260, 263, 298
　Allied
　　First Airborne 265
　Turkish
　　Fourth 118, 137, 143–4

　　Seventh 97, 103, 105–6, 108, 118–19,
　　137–8, 143
　　Eighth 97, 105, 107–8, 118–19, 137–8, 143
　German
　　Panzerarmee Afrika
　　Seventh 221, 255
　　Fifteenth 222, 255, 258
　Other
　　Arab Northern Army 117–20, 137, 143–5
Arnim, Col Gen Jürgen von 213
Arromanches 222, 241, 263
Asnelles sur Mer 232, 241
Auchinleck, FM Sir Claude J. E., GCB GCIE
CSI DSO OBE 171–2

Baden Powell, Lt Gen R. S. S., 1st Baron, OM
GCMG GCVO KCB 37–8
Bailey, Cpl, DCM 87
Barber, Maj 110
Bardia 160
Barlow, RSM Arthur, DCM 289–90
Barnby, Col Francis Vernon Willey, 2nd Baron,
CMG CBE MVO TD 81, 149–59
Barnby, Francis, 1st Baron 150
Bayerlein, Gen Fritz 192, 243
Bayeux xvi, 232, 241–5, 253
Beek (Geilenkirchen) 274, 283–5
Beersheba 98–03, 105, 107
Beirut 117, 143
Beisan 138–40
Benghazi 159–67, 192
Beni Sakr 121–6
Bennett, Maj C. Wilfred 150, 153
Bennett, Lt Col Charles M. T. A. DSO 204
Beringen 266
Berjou 258–60, 308
Bertodano, Capt. 73
Bethell-Fox, Maj John, MC 170, 192, 226, 313
Biddle, Lt Col Lawrence, MC 155, 158, 165,
169, 203, 209, 215, 245, 298, 312
Bietunye 108

Biet ur el Foqa 108
Biet ur el Tahata 108
Bir Abu Khuff 100
Birch, Sgt Edward, MM 252
Birchall, Lt 101, 110
Birkin, Lt Col R. L., DSO 31, 34, 37–40, 45, 53, 59, 312
Bloemfontein 3, 5, 15–18, 20
Bolton, Lord 11
Boshof 20–7, 32, 46–7
Botha, President P. W. 45
Boyle, Lt T 23
Brabazon, Maj Gen J. P. 17
Bracegirdle Sgt William, MM 239
Bradley, Gen Omar 221, 263, 298
Brandwater Basin 36, 39
Breberen 292
Bremen xvii, 301–303
Brereton, Lt Gen L. H. 265
Bricquessard 256
Brigades (Infantry except where otherwise stated)
  British
    Notts and Derby Mtd 67, 72
    2 Armd 186, 204, 206–7
    3 (Notts and Derby) Mtd (see also 7 Mtd and 14 (Imperial Service) Cav) 72, 73, 78, 80, 85, 86, 133, 139, 141–4
    4 Armd 257
    4 London Yeo 80
    5 (Yeo) Mtd (see also 13 (IS) Cav) 120–1, 124–6, 133, 139, 141
    6 Yeo Mtd 105, 124
    7 Mtd (see also 3 (Notts and Derby) Mtd and 14 (IS) Cav) 86, 88–9, 91, 93, 95–100, 105–8, 113, 120, 130–3
    8 Armd (later 8 Ind Armd) 169–70, 176, 179, 182, 184–97, 200, 203, 206–7, 209–11, 215, 219, 227, 243, 245, 249–50, 253–7, 260, 262–3, 266, 274, 276–7, 289, 291, 294–5, 298, 308–10
    9 Armd 180, 182–3, 186
    17 Notts and Derby Yeo 67, 72
    22 Armd 193, 197, 213
    24 Armd 179–80, 182
    9 39, 50
    56 227–8, 233, 242
    69 227, 248
    70 254
    71 296
    128 295
    129 294
    130 256, 302, 257
    146 250
    147 249–50
    151 227–8, 266
    155 110, 113
    156 291
    158 296
    214 257, 259–60
    231 (Malta) 227–8, 232, 237–8, 240–1, 254, 266, 272
    234 106
    11 Cyclist 77
  Imperial
    Imperial Camel Corps 96, 124–5, 130, 132–3
    Imperial Service Cavalry (see also 15 (IS) Cav) 124, 130–1, 133, 139, 141, 143
    13 (IS) Cav (see also 5 (Yeo) Mtd)
    14 (IS) Cav (see also 7 Mtd)
    15 (IS) Cav (see also IS Cav)
  United States
    333rd Regt 278, 280, 283–4
    334th Regt 278, 280–3
  ANZAC
    1 Aus Lt Horse 124–5, 128–9
    2 Aus Lt Horse 124–8
    3 Aus Lt Horse 100, 124–5, 128
    4 Aus Lt Horse 124–7
    NZ Mtd Rifles 127
  Polish
    A/b 256, 266
Briggs, Lt Gen Sir Charles James, KCB KCMG 86, 88
Briggs Maj Gen Raymond, CB DSO 179, 185, 207
British Empire Egyptian Expeditionary Force (EEF) 93–4, 96–7, 105–6, 108–9, 113–4, 116, 118–9, 123–5, 130–1, 133, 136–8, 140, 144
British Expeditionary Force (BEF) 73, 158
Brocklesby Foxhounds 156
Brooks, Capt Geoffrey, GM MC 153, 158
Brownlow, 3rd Earl, GCVO PC VD DL JP 13
Brussels 263, 264, 266
Bu Ngem Road 192, 195,
Budner, Sgt Harold, MM 285
Buffelshoe 41

Buhot 233, 241

Buller, Gen Sir Redvers, VC GCB GCMG 4–9, 15–16, 35, 39

Burnett, C Cpl 267–70

Bush, Maj R. H. 154

Butler, Sgt Joseph, MM 249, 256

Cagney, Lt Frederick, MC 296

Cahagnes 256

Cairo 77–8, 83, 118–19, 136, 172, 186, 189, 192

Calvert, Col A. 110

Cameron, Lt 290

Cantle, Tpr 274

Caumont 255–6, 258

Central Powers 75, 81, 85, 93

Chambois 260

Charity, Sgt 272

Chauvel, Gen Sir Henry G., GCMG KCB 98, 124, 126, 140, 143,

Chaytor's Force 137

Chebket en Nouiges 311

Chesham, Brig Gen Lord (Charles W. C. C., 3rd Baron) 17–18, 21–2, 28, 34–6, 38–41, 46

Chouain 253–254

Christopherson, Lt Col S. D., DSO MC* TD xv, 155, 169, 181–2, 187, 193, 201, 208, 211, 219–20, 241–6, 248, 264, 266, 270, 272

Churchman, Capt Hubert, MC 195

Clark, Sgt George, MM 167

Clarke, Brig Gen Goland V. DSO 130

Cleve 294–5, 311

Clogstoun-Willmott, Lt Cdr N., RN DSO DSC* 234

Cloppenburgh 301

Coke, Lt R. G. 59

Cole, Lt Col 80

Coleman, Capt Geoffrey, MC 284–5

Colenso 7, 15

Collis, Sgt Sidney, DCM 281

Colton, Pte M. H 79

Colvile, Maj Gen Sir Henry KCMG CB 27–8, 33–4

Conde sur Noireau 257–8, 260

Conyers, Maj Lord, MC (see also 5th Earl of Yarborough) 150, 153, 155–60, 170

Cooper, Lt Freddie 170

Corps:
   British
      X Armd 179, 180, 183, 197, 202– 3

Desert Mtd 96–105, 114–17, 120, 124, 127–33, 137– 44

I 4–6, 16

II 8, 15, 18, 26

V 94

VIII 249, 254–255, 265

XII 86, 265

XIII (formerly Western Desert Force) 171, 179, 186

XVI 86, 88

XX 96, 98–100, 103, 105, 107, 113, 117, 119–20, 137

XXI 97–100, 107, 109, 117, 119, 130, 137–8, 143

XXX 171, 179–80, 197, 199, 202, 255, 265, 274, 276–8, 289, 291, 294

United States
   VII 256
   VIII 256

ANZAC
   Aus & NZ 77–8

New Zealand
   New Zealand 199–200, 203, 209

France
   French Corps 77

Greece
   Greek Corps 88

Bulgaria
   Bulgarian Corps 88–9

Turkish
   VIII 123–126

Cotterell, Maj Anthony 246

Cottle, Sgt Maj 32, 58

County Territorial Associations 65–6

Cracroft, Brig 245

Cranley, Lt Col Viscount, MC TD (later Earl of Onslow) 213, 215

Crete 161, 166–8, 171

Cribben, Sgt Leslie, MM 258, 263

Cristot 249

Cronje, Gen Piet 6, 15–17

Custance, Brig E. C. 179

Cyprus 159, 166

Cyrenaica 159–60, 164–5, 188, 191–2

Dalziel, Lt 112, 127

Damascus 117–18, 138, 143–6, 311

Damiye Track 125–6

Dawson, Capt M. S. 13, 17, 21–6, 29, 31–5, 57, 59, 73, 77
de la Rey, Gen Jacobus (Koos) 7, 45–6, 50–1, 54
de Wet, Gen Christiaan 15–16, 33–5, 64, 71, 77, 145
Debarech 63
Dekkenswald 274
Delmar-Morgan, Maj Stephen, MC 175
Dempsey, Gen M E 221
Denison, Col H., CB 67–8
Denison, Capt Max 150, 153
Denman, Sgt J. A., DCM 127
Digby, Sgt Bill 235–6
Dinxperloo 299–300
Divisions (Infantry save where stated otherwise)
  British
    Royal Naval 77
    1st Armd 179, 184–6, 202–4, 207–8
    1st Cav (also see 10th Armd) 155–6, 159–60, 169, 189
    10th Armd (also see 1st Cav) 169–70, 172, 175–6, 179–80, 182–3, 189
    2nd Mtd (see also 5th Cav) xvi, 72, 73, 75, 78, 79, 86, 130, 131, 133
    4th Cav (late Yeo) 116, 117, 138–9, 143–5
    5th Cav (see also 2nd Mtd) 116–17, 133, 135, 138–46
    7th Armd 168, 186, 188–9, 248, 291
    11th Armd 249, 257, 260, 264
    Cavalry 13, 15
    Yeo Mtd 96, 105–10, 113–14, 117
    Gds Armd 249, 264, 266, 294, 300
    1st 6, 18–21, 26–8, 33–4, 36, 38, 45–6, 50
    3rd 138, 221, 257, 301
    6th 15
    7th 15, 138
    8th 36
    9th (Scottish) 15, 27–8, 33
    10th (Irish) 84–5, 90, 96, 108
    11th 81
    12th 36
    15th (Scottish) 249, 272, 298
    20th 36
    21st 36
    22nd 84
    26th 84
    27th 84
    28th 84, 86
    29th 77, 79–80
    43rd (Wessex) 249, 256–9, 262, 275, 294
    49th (W.R.) 221, 249–51, 254
    50th (Northumbrian) xvii, 209, 211, 221, 227–9, 232–3, 237, 242–3, 245, 248–9, 254, 257, 260, 266, 269
    51st (H'ld) 183, 193, 211, 298
    52nd (L'ld) 97, 105, 107–08, 116, 265, 290–1
    53rd (Welsh) 96, 103, 105, 107, 257, 295
    54th (E. Anglian) 97, 107, 138
    59th 257
    60th (2/2nd London) 96, 108, 113, 124–7, 129, 138
    74th (Dismounted Yeo) 96, 105, 108, 116
    75th 97, 106–08
    1st A/b 265
    6th A/b 221, 265
    Cyclist 77
  United States
    2nd Armd 255, 278–9
    1st 221
    4th 221
    82nd A/b xvii, 221, 265, 274–5, 290
    84th (Rail Splitters) xvii, 221, 274–5, 279–80, 284, 290
    101st A/b 221, 265
  ANZAC
    Aus Mtd 96, 99, 105–07, 116, 118, 120–1, 124–7, 133, 138, 140–5
    Aus & NZ Mtd 96, 99–100, 107, 116, 118 124, 131
    1st Aus 77
    9th Aus 165–6, 183
    NZ and Aus 77
    2nd NZ 180, 184–6, 192–3, 197
  Indian
    4th 211
    7th 116
  Canadian
    4th Armd 260
    3rd 221
  Polish
    1st Armd 260
  French
    2nd Armd 260
    Div 89
  Axis Divisions
    Pz Lehr xvi, 192, 243
    10th Pz 200, 279

15th Pz 200, 208, 279
    5th Lt (see also 21st Pz) 164–5
    21st Pz (see also 5th Lt) 200–1, 208
    90th Lt 211
    164th Lt 200
    6th Para 266
    136th *Giovani Fascisti* 200
    12th SS Pz *Hitlerjugend* 251
    Bulgarian
    7th 88
    10th 88
    11th 88
    Turkish
    19th 108–9, 113
Djebel Tebaga 199
Doiran 84–7, 89–90
Douglas, Capt Keith ix, xvi, 170, 184, 187, 189, 193, 196, 201–02, 212, 213, 243
Doullens 263
Douthwaite, Sgt Henry, MM 282
Doxat, Lt A. C., VC 40
Dring, Sgt George, MM* 200, 211, 247, 252, 257, 283
Du Toit, Cmdt 51, 53
Duren 276

East, SSM Tom, DCM MM 110
Eisenhower, Gen Dwight D. 221, 241, 263–265, 276
El Adem 165
El Affule 139–41
El Agheila 164, 172, 188–9, 191, 311
El Alamein 153, 170–5, 179–89, 220, 256, 285, 300, 310, 311
El Ghoraniye 123–4, 127, 129–31
El Gubi 165
El Huweij 124–6
El Jib 108
El Mughar 105–6, 311
Enderby, Maj 300
Enfidaville 212–13, 311
Enschede 301
Entente Cordiale 64, 75
Es Salt 118–19, 123–8, 135, 150
Evers, Tpr 206
Ewing, Cpl Ken 273
Ewing, Cpl Walter 269, 273

Faisal bin Hussein bin Ali al-Hashimi 117–18, 120–3, 137, 143

Fearn, Capt Neville DSO 201, 243, 292–3, 300
Fearon, Maj 73
Fisher, Sgt 58
Flesselles 263
Fontenay le Pesnel 243, 249–151, 253, 311
Foster, Tpr Philip 171, 181–2, 200, 205–6, 208, 235–6, 246, 248
Fox, Sgt 41
Francis, T., DCM 60
French, FM J. D. P., 1st Earl of Ypres, KP GCB OM GCVO KCMG ADC PC 13, 15–16, 26, 56, 59–60, 77, 81
Freyberg, Lt Gen Sir Bernard, 1st Baron, VC GCMG KCB KBE DSO*** 167, 180, 185, 200, 202, 210
Frisby, Cpl 111

Galal Station 188
Gallipoli xvi, 75, 78, 81, 83–6, 90, 95, 98, 130, 311
Galway, Countess of 12, 32
Galway, George E. M. M., 7th Viscount, CB xviii–xix, 9, 11–13, 17, 24–6, 32, 34–35, 43, 45–8, 50, 55, 57, 60, 63, 67, 146
Gamble, Maj A. Massey (Bob) 150
Garratt, Capt Sam, MC 176, 209
Gascoigne, Lt Col R. F. T. 41, 43
Gatehouse, Maj Gen A. H. DSO* MC 175, 179, 183, 187
Gauntley, Capt John, MC 281–2
Gaz 94, 96, 98–100, 103, 105, 107, 114, 121, 145, 311
Gazala 172
Geilenkirchen xvii, 276–9, 281– 6, 289–94, 311
Gheel 202, 266–75, 308, 311
Ghent 264
Goch 294–295, 311
Gola Ridge 87
Gold, Maj Michael (Micky), MC TD 154, 202, 204–6, 219, 253, 259–62, 268, 272
Gondar 163
Graham, Maj Gen 254
Grave 265, 274
Graves, Lt Ken 170, 195
Green, Tpr 54–5
Greenway, Lt Ian, MC 240, 243
Groesbeek 274
Grosvenor, Col Gerald H., 4th Duke of Westminster, DSO PC 153

Haifa 138–44, 157, 159
Haile Selassie, Emperor of Ethiopia 163
Haldane, Rt Hon Richard 65, 67, 71–2, 306, 307
Hales, Chaplain George Frederick, MC 182
Hall, Lt H.C. 59
Hamilton, Gen Sir Ian, GCB GCMG DSO 36, 39, 42–3, 77–81, 83
Hanson-Lawson, Maj John 219, 248, 253
Harbord, Brig Gen C. R., CB CMG DSO 141
Harrison, F. 77
Harter Lt 109–111
Hashemite 117
Hather, A. 77
Heilbron 28–9, 33–4
Hejaz railway 117–23, 131, 137, 143–4
Henglo 301
Herschot 264
Hethershaw, Sgt W. F., DCM 87, 127
Hiensburg 291, 295
Higgins, Cpl 271
Higgs, Lt R. G. 286
Hildyard, Capt Myles, MBE MC TD xv, 154, 167–8
Hills, Capt Stuart, MC x, 233, 235–6, 259–60, 267, 269–70, 272
Hinds, Capt V. G. 153
Holden, Capt Tony 154, 159, 167
Holford, Col 73, 77
Holman, Lt Dick, MC 272, 299–300
Holman Major Jack, MC 235, 259–60, 267, 283
Homs 144
Honten 291
Horley, Lt Monty 235, 240
Horrocks, Lt Gen Sir Brian, KCB KBE DSO MC 170, 179, 202, 255, 278, 286, 295, 304, 310
Hottot 254–6
Hubbard, RSM 73
Hughes, Canon, MC 153
Hunter, Gen *Sir Archibald*, GCB GCVO DSO TD 36, 38–9
Hussein bin Ali, Grand Sharif of Mecca 117
Hussenoff 295
Hutchinson, Henry SSM, MM 181–2, 300
Hutton, Capt Ronald (Ronnie), MC 170, 199, 209
Hyde, Lt Richard, MC 296

illegal wives 157, 160
Illger F. 77

Illger, W. 77
Imperial Yeomanry
  1 IY Bde 17–19, 28, 35–6, 39, 42, 45–6
  3rd Regt 11–12, 14, 16–21, 27–8, 31, 34–5, 40–1, 43, 45–6, 53, 55–6, 59
  5th Regt 40, 45
  10th Regt 17–18, 21, 23, 28, 38, 40,
  13th Regt 27–9, 33
  15th Regt 18
  Belfast Yeo 27
  Dublin Hunt Yeo 27
  Duke of Cambridge's Own IY 27
Ismail Ogu Tepe 78–9
Issleburg 299–300
Issum 296

Jackson, Sgt Leslie, MM 264
Jaffa (Tel Aviv) 105, 107, 118–19, 119, 130, 135, 137, 157
Jenin 138, 140
Jennings Lt J. C. 58–9
Jericho 119, 121, 123–4, 129, 131
Jerusalem 93, 98, 100–1, 105–9, 111, 113–15, 117–19, 121, 123–4
Jis en Damiye 123, 125–6
Johannesburg 10, 15, 26, 37, 45–6
Jones, Capt George 219, 245
Junction Station 105–8
Jurques 257, 311

Karkur 157, 169, 172
Karmelheim 141–2
Kebabe Kh 109, 112
Kellett, Col E. O. (Flash), DSO MP xv, 150, 154, 160, 163–7, 171, 183, 186–8, 193, 196–7, 200–1, 209, 273
Kellett, Mrs Myrtle, MBE 273
Kenna, *Brig Gen* P. A., *VC* DSO 72
Khelevis 167
Khuweilfe 100–1, 103
Kidney 'Ridge' 184–6
Kievelburg 291
Kimberley 6, 15–16, 19–21, 26, 50, 64
King, Sgt J 209
Kirman, Sgt John MM 260
Kitchener, FM, 1st Earl, KG KP GCB OM GCSI GCMG GCIE ADC PC 8, 39, 42, 46, 71, 306
Knight, Maj Bob, MBE 153
Knight, Tpr Stanley MM 292

Knowles, Lt 30
Kopaci 90
Kosturino 85
Kruger, Paul, President xix–xx, 3–5, 45
Krugersdorp 37

la Rivière 232
Ladysmith 4–7, 15–16, 26, 36, 64
Laffelde 292
Lance, Brig Gen 81, 90
Lanes, Sgt James (Johnny), MM 293
Lansdowne, 5th Marquess, KG GCSI GCMG
    GCIE PC 4–5, 9 47–8
Lavarack, Lt Gen Sir John KCMG KCVO KBE
    CB DSO 166
Law, Cpl C. G., DCM 142–3
Lawrence, Capt T. E. (of Arabia), CB DSO 117
Laycock, Capt J. F. (Joe) DSO 13, 26, 60, 72
Laycock, Capt Peter 154, 164, 215
Laycock, Lt Col Michael, MC TD 154, 164,
    169, 176, 181, 191, 202, 219, 226, 241, 245
Laycock, Maj Gen Sir Robert (Bob) KCMG,
    CB, DSO, KStJ 215
Layton, Capt R. C 59, 124, 215
Leakey, Ne 170
Leclerc, Gen P. F. M. 199
le Hamel 232, 235–41
Le Marchant, Lt Dennis 154
Lee, Sgt Kenneth, DCM 185
Leigh, Maj Rupert, 4th Baron 262, 275
Leinster, Capt Terry 248
Lenton, Tpr Derek, MM 176
Ley, Lt Col Gordon 85
Lichtenburg 7, 45–6, 50–1, 53, 55–6, 58, 60, 116
Lindle 27–30, 30, 32–5, 57–8
Lindsay, Capt T. M., MBE 168, 235
Lloyd George, David 93–4
Loades, Cpl James, MM 207, 212
Lochem 300
Longford, Lt R. 286
Lumsden, Lt Gen Herbert, CB DSO*
    MC 179, 187

Machin, Maj E.V. 94
Mafeking 6, 19–20, 26, 43, 45–6, 58, 64
Magersfontein 6, 15–16, 18
Makins Maj 253–4
Maleme 167
Mann, Capt Johnny, MC 235, 251–2, 270
Marble Arch 192

Mareth Line 197 199–200, 202, 208
Markham, Sgt Harold, MM 303
Masefield, Lt John 170
Mason, Maj 111
Matmata Hills 197, 199
McCraith, Col Patrick J. D., MC, TD 154, 178,
    219, 245
McDonald, Cpl Peter, MM 181, 301–2
McGaffy, Capt 112
McGowan, Capt 208
McKay, Capt Ian, MC 248, 274
McWilliam, Capt Jimmy 236, 240, 271
Mediterranean Expeditionary Force 77
Megiddo 139, 311
Mellowes, Lt Peter, MC 299–300
Mersa Matruh 172, 188, 191
Mesopotamian Expeditionary Force 116
Methuen, FM, 3rd Baron GCB GCMG GCVO
    DL 6–7, 15–16, 18, 20–1, 25, 27–8, 31, 33–9,
    40–3, 45, 48, 50, 55, 57–9, 77, 145
Meuvaines 232, 243
Meyrick, Lt Col 18
Milbanke, Lt Col Sir John, VC 72, 80–1
Mills, Tpr 206
Milner, Sir Alfred xix–xx, 3
Mirlees, Maj 81, 85, 90
Misurata 192
Mitchell, Maj Stephen, MC TD 154, 164, 169,
    182, 195–6, 206, 219, 245, 248, 262,
Miteiriya Ridge 180–4, 192
Modder River 6, 15–16, 19, 24–5, 248, 262
Moffett, Sgt J. 281
Moller, Dr C. J. 51, 54
Money, Lt Col C. G. C., CB 46, 50–1, 54, 56
Monkton, Hon Violet 14
Mont Pinçon 256–7, 308, 311
Monte Cristo 16
Montgomery, FM B. L., 1st Viscount of Alamein,
    KG GCB DSO PC 145, 172, 179, 183–4,
    186–8, 197, 199, 202, 209, 219–21, 227, 230,
    235, 249, 257, 263, 265, 276, 294, 298
Moore, Pte, DCM 87
Morse, Lt Sidney 154, 167
Mosque Sheik ab ed Din 109–11
Moss, Capt, MC 101, 135
Murray, Gen Sir Archibald, GCB GCMG CVO
    DSO 93–4

Nabi Samweil 106, 108, 114, 311
Nazareth 138–9, 141, 143

Neame, Lt Gen Sir Philip, VC KBE CB DSO KStJ 165
Nelson, Capt 113
Nelson, Sgt Doug, MM 191, 253
Nesling, Sgt Stan, DCM 271–3
Newhaven 215
New Army 72, 75, 96–7, 306
Ngarimu, 2/Lt Moana-Nui-a-Kiwa, VC 206
Nijmegen xvii, 265, 274–5, 294
Noireau Crossing 258–9, 311
Normandy Landings 311
North, AQMS 170

O'Connor, Gen Sir Richard, KT GCB GBE DSO* MC 145, 165
Odon 252–3, 311
Oglesby, Tpr 58
Oliphant's Nek 37, 39, 42–3, 71, 77,
Ondefontaine 257
O'Pray, Sgt 300–1
Ottoman Empire xvi, 71, 75, 77

Paardeburg 16
Paget, Maj 50–1
Palmer, Sgt Robert MM 239
Parc de Boislonde 249
Parish, Capt Michael, MC 156, 167–8
Patton, Capt 88
Paulenburg 277
Peacock, L/ Cpl Edwin MM 168
Peacock, Lt H. O. ('Hop') 13, 17–18, 20, 22–5, 47, 49, 73
Peakham, Lt Col 50
Pelham-Clinton, Lt 112
Pepper, Farrier 54
Perowne, Capt, MC 109–10, 112–13, 135
Pick, Sgt William, MM 290
Pierce, Capt H.B 111, 113
Pitt, Lt 80
Player, Lt Col J. D. (Donny) 154, 164, 169, 192, 197, 199, 202, 204, 206, 211–13, 243
Point 102 250
Point 103 243
Point 201 199–200, 203, 205, 311
Point 209 205–7
Pollard, Sgt William, MM 285, 291–2
Potts, Tpr Thomas, MM 300–1
Powell, Cpl Irvine, MM 302–3
Pretoria 5, 15, 18, 26, 28, 36, 57
Price, Lt 111, 113
Prummen 277 280–4

Rahman Track 186, 192
Ranfurly, Lt, 6th Earl of, KCMG (Dan) 154, 157–8, 165, 208
Ranfurly, Countess of (Hermione) 156–7, 160
Ransley, Sgt 111–12
Ras Ayal 163
Ras Ghannam 99
Rauray 249–4, 311
Redfern, Cpl James, MM 290–1
Reed, Lt Reginald, MC 301–2
Rees 298
Regiments and Sub-units (See also Yeomanry and Imperial Yeomanry)
  British
    1st R. Horse Arty 186
    R. Scots Greys 169
    4th/7th R. Dgn Gds 219, 227, 232, 295
    7th Hsrs 12, 155
    10th Hsrs 17, 72
    11th Hsrs xv, 196,
    13th Hsrs 95
    18th Hsrs 130
    13th/18th Hsrs 256–7, 308
    23rd Hsrs 262
    5th R. Irish Lcrs 94
    9th Lancers 153
    16th (The Queen's) Lcrs 59
    17th Lcrs 72
    17th/21st Lcrs 220
    24th Lcrs 219, 255–6
    3rd R. Tank Regt 169, 175, 180, 183, 202–3, 215
    4th R. Field Arty (RFA) 21
    Scots Gds 18, 59
    1st Buffs 203–04
    1st Northumberland Fus (Fighting Fifth) 37–8, 50–6, 68
    2nd Devonshires 227–8, 238, 241
    Lancashire Fus 219
    4th King's O. Scottish Brdrs 292
    7th Sc Rifles 112–13
    1st Worcestershires 259
    1st E. Lancs 295
    5th Duke of Cornwall's LI 259
    1st Hampshires 227, 237, 241
    1st Dorsetshires 227, 237, 240
    4th Dorsetshires 301
    1st O. and B. LI 295
    2nd Essex 241–3

7th Notts and Derbys (Robin Hood Rifles) 77
12th King's R. Rifle Corps 220, 255, 300
4th Wiltshires 300
5th Wiltshires 302
6th Durham LI 267
7th Durham LI 243
9th Durham LI 268–70
Seaforth Hldrs 299
10 (Inter-Allied) Commando 215
47 (RM) Commando 228, 238
Layforce II 215
Nottinghamshire Bty RHA 72, 126
Essex Bty RHA 101
82 Asslt Sqn RE 229, 232, 235–9
20 M.G. Sqn 87, 99, 101, 113
ANZAC
  Upper Clarence LH 98
  5 Aus Lt Horse 100
  NZ Bty of Arty 50
  28th (Maori) B 204
  23rd NZ Bn 212
South African
  Kimberley LH 21, 50
  Paget's Horse 50–1
  South African Imperial LH 26
Indian
  20th Deccan Horse 130, 139
  34th Poonah Horse 130, 133
  Jodhpore Lcrs 130–3, 141–2
  Mysore Lcrs 130–3, 141–2
  Hyderabad Lcrs 130, 141
Hong Kong
  Hong Kong Mtn Bty 124
German
  33rd A-Tk Bn 195
Reichswald Forest 274, 294
Render, Capt David x, 256, 263–4, 281, 291, 300
Rhenoster river 34
Rhineland 311
Riggall Sgt 55
Ringrose, Maj Basil, DSO TD 154, 161, 163
Ritchie, Gen 172
River Ijssel 299
River Niers 295
River Rhine 265, 276, 289, 294–8,
River Roer 276, 289, 291, 293–4, 311
River Seine 145, 222, 254–5, 258, 262–3, 311
River Wurm 277, 278, 283, 285
Riviere, Lt Michael 154, 167
Roberts, FM F. S., 1st Earl, VC KG KP GCB OM GCSI GCIE KStJ VD PC 4, 8, 15–16, 18–20, 25–8, 33, 35–6, 38–9, 42, 46, 66

Roberts, Cpl Frederick, MM 268, 273
Robertson, Tpr Robert, MM 176
Robinson, Sgt Jack, MM 268, 273
Robson, SSM William, MM 268, 270, 273
Rolleston, Lt Col Sir Lancelot, KCB, DSO, TD 72
Roman Wall 199–201, 205, 311
Rommel, FM Erwin 164–6, 171–2, 175–6, 180, 186, 191–2
Rossmond, Col 278
Roumana Gap 211
Royal Navy 4, 75, 77, 93, 95, 168, 225–6,
Rudkin, SSM Arthur 57
Rurlo 300
Ryes 232, 241

Salt Lake 79
Sandars Lt Col John OBE 286
Sanders, Sgt Guy, MM 208
Sanders Sgt Robert, MM 250
Sandford, Brig D.A. CBE DSO 161
Sandwith, Lt Col L 18
Saur, Tel 119
Scarbrough, Maj Gen, 10th Earl of, KG GBE KCB GCStJ xviii–xix, 11–12, 21, 23, 27, 31, 35
Schinnen 277, 286, 289
Schinveld 289
Scimitar Hill 78, 81, 311
Scott, Maj William A, MC 182
Scott, MQMS John, MM 195, 209
Seeley, Maj Gen. Jack, DSO 71
Seleri, Maj Peter 248, 258, 283
Selstan 292
Semken, Maj John, CB MC TD x, 161, 170, 175, 214, 220, 248, 251–254, 280–282
Sharon, Plain of 123, 138, 311
Sheria, Tel esh 98, 100–1, 103, 105
Sheriffe, Lt R. T. O. (Bertie) 13, 29, 31–2, 43, 45
Ships
  HMS *Ribble* 95
  HMS *Terror* 164
  HMT *Aragon* 95
  HMT *Cestrian* 91, 94
  SS *Orient* 57
  SS *Tintagel Castle* 56
  SS *Winifredian* 14, 16, 32, 86
  SS *Empress of Britain* 160
Shunet Imrin 121, 123–5, 129
Sidi Barrani 159–60

Siegfried Line 276–80, 282, 286
Simpson, Capt 31–40
Sinclair, Tpr 58
Sirte 192
Skinner, Capt Leslie 230, 233–4, 236, 238, 240, 242, 250
Small, Sgt James, MM 284
Smith, Lt Col Eric 18
Smith, Pte, MM 79
Smith, Lt Reginald, MC 295
Smith-Dorrien, Gen Sir Horace, GCB GCMG DSO ADC 39
Smuts, Lt Gen J. C. (Jan) OM CH DTD ED KC FRS PC 51, 116–18
Sollum 171
Sommervieu 242
South African Republic (Transvaal) xx, 3–6, 15, 26, 37–8, 45, 58–60
Spence, Lt Col Ian 215, 219
Sphakia 168
Spion Kop 15
Spooner, SQMS J. A. 54–5
Spragge, Lt Col Basil 27–8, 33
Spring, Pte, MM 79
Stanton, Sgt George, MM 269, 273
Starkey, Capt Thomas R. 13
Starkey, Capt 29, 31–2
Stephenson, Tpr W. D. 55
Steyn Swift 36–45, 64, 77
St John's Hill 167
St Nicholas's Farm 250–1
St Pierre (Normandy) 243, 245, 249
St Pierre (Flanders) 264
Stockton, Lt Archie 201
Struma River 84, 88–90, 311
Struma Valley 88–90
Suda Bay 166–7
Suffa 109–12
Surtees, Cpl 90
Sutton Nelthorpe, Lt Col Roger, MBE TD 154, 219, 248, 289
Suvla Bay 78, 311
Swift, Tpr 54
Syferbul 42
Symons, Maj Gen Sir William Penn, KCB 5–6

Takrouna 212, 311
Talbot, Lt 303
Tallents, Lt Col Hugh, DSO TD ix, xv, 78–9, 81, 83, 87, 89–90, 99–100, 109, 112–14, 121, 124, 126–8, 131–3, 139–41, 149–50
Tandy, RQMS George 290

Tebaga Gap 197, 199–203, 207, 209, 212, 311
Tel el Aqqaqir 187–8
Territorial Force 12, 64–5, 68, 71, 96–7, 305
Thomas, Gen Sir (Gwilym) Ivor, GCB KBE DSO MC* 256
Thomas, Lt T.G.B. 57–9
Thomson, Capt Colin, MC 206, 239–41, 251, 269
Thorpe, Lt Col H., DSO TD 77, 80–1, 86, 88, 90–1, 95, 103, 107, 114, 149
Thwaites, Sgt Erny, MM 200–1, 209, 211
Timmons, Tpr, MM 140
Titchfield, Col the Marquis of (later 7th Duke of Portland), KG 150
Tobruk 160–7, 172
Tomkins, SSM J. J., DCM 111, 135
Tomlinson 32
Tonge, Capt C. 150
Trans Jordan 118–19, 121–3, 131
Trevor-Roper, Lt A.M. 59
Tripoli (Libya) 160, 164, 189, 191–3, 195–7, 311
Trotter, Capt Henry R. 150, 153, 164
Tunis 212–13
Turner, Lt T. G. 23–4, 32–3, 45, 49–50, 53–4
Tygerfontein 39, 41
Tyrrell, Maj Jack 186

Umm esh Shert 123–7, 129, 131
Union of South Africa 60

Vaalbank 38
Vereeniging, Treaty of 60
Vermaas, Gen 51, 53
Villebois-Mareuil, Maj Gen George Henri Anne-Marie Victor, le Comte de 21, 23–4, 46–9, 56
Villers Bocage 233, 243, 248, 311
Vintelen 290
von Rundstedt, FM K. R. G. 221, 253, 261

Wadi Akarit 209, 211
Wadi Hernel 204
Wadi Mataba 208
Wadi er Rame 132
Wadi Kohle 100
Wadi Zem Zem 192–3, 195–6, 210, 220, 272
Wadi Zigzaou 202
Wallace, Lt Dandy 154, 160
Walster, Sgt 112
Walters, Lt John 155

Warburton, Capt Arthur, DSO TD 220, 238
Warner, Maj D. 149
Warwick, Capt Fredrick (Derrick), MC 154, 164, 182
Wavell, FM A. P., 1st Earl, GCB GCSI GCIE KStJ CMG MC PC 171
Weeze 295, 311
Webb, Sgt Charles, MM 282
Western Desert xv, 171–2, 176, 181, 189, 206
Wharton, Lt Eric, MC 264, 269–70, 273
Wheeler, Sgt Robert, DCM 302
Whitaker, Col A. E. 68, 72, 78
Whitaker, Tpr 155
White, FM Sir George, VC GCB OM GCSI GCMG GCIE GCVO 5, 8
Wigan, Brig Gen J. T., CB CMG DSO 95, 110
Wiggin Lt Col W. H., DSO* 114–15, 142
Willey, Col F V (see 2nd Baron Barnby) 81, 149–50
Willey, Francis, (see also 1st Baron Barnby) 149
William, Capt, MC 182
Williams, Lt Arthur C. ('Job') 13, 22–4, 49
Williams, Lt C. 205
Willoughby, Lt Col 73
Wilson, Maj C. 150
Wilson, FM H. M., 1st Baron, GCB GBE DSO 160
Wilson, Lt Herbert (Bertie) H. DSO 13, 29–31, 45–6, 50, 53–5, 60
Wilson, Lt R. B 37
Wingate Maj Gen Orde, DSO** 163
Wolchefit 163
Wolseley, FM Viscount Garnet, KCB GCMG xvi, xviii–xix, 4–5, 7–10, 46
Wombwell, Lt 37–8
Woodcock, Sgt, DCM 135
Wrangham, Capt 170
Wright, Lt Edward 237
Wurm 278, 285
Wyler 274
Wyndham, George 9–10

Yarborough, 5th Earl of, MC (see also Maj Lord Conyers) 150, 153, 155–60, 170
Yarborough, Countess of 156–7
Yeomanry
  R. Wiltshire (Prince of Wales's Own) 18
  Warwickshire 114

Yorkshire Hsrs (Alexandra, Princess of Wales's Own) 14, 19–20, 28, 37, 39–41, 43, 59, 149, 155
Sherwood Rgrs 1–311
2/1st Nottinghamshire (Sherwood Rgrs) 73
3/1st Nottinghamshire (Sherwood Rgrs) 73
Staffordshire (Queen's Own R. Regt) 106, 117, 169, 175, 180, 183, 203, 207, 298
Shropshire 18
Queen's Own Yorkshire Dgns xviii–xix, 11–12, 14, 20, 28–9, 31, 34, 40,
Duke of Lancaster's Own 117
Northumberland Hsrs 18
S. Nottinghamshire Hsrs 10–14, 20–1, 29, 31–4, 38, 40–1, 46, 57–9, 67, 72, 80, 85–8, 95, 100, 103, 110, 112, 120, 130, 155, 220
R. Buckinghamshire Hsrs 17–18, 23, 105
Derbyshire 67, 72, 80–1, 86, 88, 91
Queen's Own Dorset 105, 117
R. Gloucestershire Hsrs 85, 117, 121, 145, 262, 275,
Hertfordshire 117
Berkshire 18, 23, 95, 105
1st County of London (Middlesex, Duke of Cambridge's Hsrs) 117, 127
Queen's Own Worcestershire Hsrs 18, 114, 117, 121, 124, 126,
Queen's Own Oxfordshire Hsrs 18
1st Lothians and Border Horse 280
Lincolnshire 13, 57, 67, 72, 103, 109–10, 112
City of London (Rough Riders) 130
Inns of Court Regiment 155, 161
B Sqn, Westminster Dgns 228
4th County of London (Sharpshooters) 213
Essex 220, 228, 232, 238, 239, 241, 300
E. Riding 106
York, Lt Col 85
York, Lt 101
Younghusband, Sir George John, KCMG KCIE CB 12, 17, 21, 24, 27–8, 31, 33–4, 37, 40–1, 43

Zahn, Hauptmann Dr 195–6
Zeerust 58